The Princeton Review®

Cracking the

AP®

U.S. GOVERNMENT & POLITICS EXAM

2017 Edition

By the Staff of The Princeton Review

PrincetonReview.com

Penguin
Random
House

The Princeton Review
24 Prime Parkway, Suite 201
Natick, MA 01760
E-mail: editorialsupport@review.com

ISBN: 978-1-101-92002-2
eBook ISBN: 978-1-101-92027-5
ISSN: 1097-2757

Editor: Selena Coppock
Production Editors: Emily Epstein White, Lee Elder
Production Artist: Deborah A. Silvestrini

Printed in the United States of America on partially recycled paper.

10 9 8 7 6 5 4 3 2 1

2017 Edition

Editorial

Rob Franek, Senior VP, Publisher
Casey Cornelius, VP Content Development
Mary Beth Garrick, Director of Production
Selena Coppock, Managing Editor
Meave Shelton, Senior Editor
Colleen Day, Editor
Sarah Litt, Editor
Aaron Riccio, Editor
Orion McBean, Editorial Assistant

Random House Publishing Team

Tom Russell, Publisher
Alison Stoltzfus, Publishing Manager
Ellen Reed, Production Manager
Jake Elred, Associate Managing Editor

Acknowledgments

The Princeton Review would like to thank AP U.S. Government and Politics teacher Deborah Linder and Princeton Review tutor Gina Donegan for their thorough content review and contributions to the 2017 edition of this book.

Contents

Register Your

1 Go to **PrincetonReview.com/cracking**

2 You'll see a welcome page where you can register your book using the following ISBN: 9781101920022.

3 After placing this free order, you'll either be asked to log in or to answer a few simple questions in order to set up a new Princeton Review account.

4 Finally, click on the "Student Tools" tab located at the top of the screen. It may take an hour or two for your registration to go through, but after that, you're good to go.

If you are experiencing book problems (potential content errors), please contact EditorialSupport@review.com with the full title of the book, its ISBN number (located above), and the page number of the error. Experiencing technical issues? Please e-mail TPRStudentTech@review.com with the following information:

- your full name
- e-mail address used to register the book
- full book title and ISBN
- your computer OS (Mac or PC) and Internet browser (Firefox, Safari, Chrome, etc.)
- description of technical issue

Book Online!

Once you've registered, you can...

- Find any late-breaking information released about the AP U.S. Government and Politics Exam

- Take a full-length practice PSAT, SAT, and ACT

- Get valuable advice about the college application process, including tips for writing a great essay and where to apply for financial aid

- Sort colleges by whatever you're looking for (such as Best Theater or Dorm), learn more about your top choices, and see how they all rank according to *The Best 380 Colleges*

- Access a study guide and a variety of printable resources, including bubble sheets for the practice tests in this book, and a glossary of key terms to aid in your review

- Check to see if there have been any corrections or updates to this edition

Look For These Icons Throughout The Book

 Online Articles

 Applied Strategies

 Proven Techniques

The **Princeton** Review®

Part I
Using This
Book to Improve
Your AP Score

- Preview: Your Knowledge, Your Expectations
- Your Guide to Using This Book
- How to Begin

PREVIEW: YOUR KNOWLEDGE, YOUR EXPECTATIONS

Your route to a high score on the AP U.S. Government and Politics Exam depends a lot on how you plan to use this book. Respond to the following:

1. Rate your level of confidence about your knowledge of the content tested by the AP U.S. Government and Politics Exam.

    A. Very confident—I know it all.
    B. I'm pretty confident, but there are topics for which I could use help.
    C. Not confident—I need quite a bit of support.
    D. I'm not sure.

2. If you have a goal score in mind, circle your goal score for the AP U.S. Government and Politics Exam:

    5   4   3   2   1   I'm not sure yet

3. What do you expect to learn from this book? Circle all that apply to you.

    A. A general overview of the test and what to expect
    B. Strategies for how to approach the test
    C. The content tested by this exam
    D. I'm not sure yet

YOUR GUIDE TO USING THIS BOOK

This book is organized to provide as much—or as little—support as you will need, so that you can use this book in whatever way will be most helpful for improving your score on the AP U.S. Government and Politics Exam.

*   The remainder of **Part I** will provide guidance on how to use this book and help you determine your strengths and weaknesses.

*   **Part II** of this book is Practice Test 1. As you'll see in the next section, How To Begin, we recommend you take it now and time yourself so that you have a sense for where you currently stand in the course, and which question types are the trickiest for you. This will help as you work toward creating a study plan and, if time is limited, help you to focus on the sections in which you most need a content review.

*   **Part III** of this book will
    o   provide information about the structure, scoring, and content of the AP U.S. Government and Politics Exam
    o   help you to make a study plan
    o   point you toward additional resources

- **Part IV** of this book will explore various strategies, including
  - o how to attack multiple-choice questions
  - o how to write high-scoring free-response answers
  - o how to manage your time to maximize the number of points available to you

- **Part V** of this book covers the content you need to understand to succeed on the AP U.S. Government and Politics Exam.

- **Part VI** of this book contains Practice Test 2, its answers and explanations, and a scoring guide. If you skipped Practice Test 1, we recommend that you do both (with at least a day or two between them) so that you can compare your progress between the two. Additionally, this will help to identify any external issues: if you get a certain type of question wrong both times, you probably need to review it. If you only got it wrong once, you may have run out of time or been distracted by something. In either case, this will allow you to focus on the factors that caused the discrepancy in scores and to be as prepared as possible on the day of the test.

You may choose to use some parts of this book over others, or you may work through the entire book. This will depend on your needs and how much time you have. Let's now look how to make this determination.

HOW TO BEGIN

1. **Take a Test**
    Before you can decide how to use this book, we recommend that you take a practice test. Doing so will give you an insight into your strengths and weaknesses, and the test will also help you make an effective study plan. If you're feeling test-phobic, remind yourself that a practice test is a tool for diagnosing yourself—it's not how well you do that matters but how you use information gleaned from your performance to guide your preparation.

    So, before you read further, take Practice Test 1 starting at page 9 of this book. Be sure to do so in one sitting, following the instructions that appear before the test.

2. **Check Your Answers**
   Using the answer key on page 29, count how many multiple-choice questions you answered correctly and how many you missed. Don't worry about the explanations for now, and don't worry about why you missed some of the questions. We'll get to that soon.

3. **Reflect on the Test**
   After you take your first test, respond to the following questions:

   • How much time did you spend on the multiple-choice questions?

   • How much time did you spend on each essay?

   • How many multiple-choice questions did you miss?

   • Do you feel you had the knowledge to address the subject matter in the free-response questions?

   • Do you feel that you wrote well-organized, thoughtful free responses?

   • Circle the content areas that were most challenging for you and draw a line through the ones in which you felt confident and/or did well.

4. **Read Part III of this Book and Complete the Self-Evaluation**
   Part III will provide information on how the test is structured and scored. It will also explain the areas of content that are tested.

   As you read Part III, re-evaluate your answers to the questions above. You will then be able to make a study plan, based on your needs and time available, that will allow you to use this book most effectively.

5. **Engage with Parts IV and V as Needed**
   Notice the word *engage*. You'll get more out of this book if you use it intentionally than if you read it passively, hoping for an improved score through osmosis.

   Strategy chapters will help you think about your approach to the types of questions on this exam. Part IV will open with a reminder to think about how you approach questions now and then close with a reflection section asking you to think about how/whether you will change your approach in the future.

Content chapters are designed to provide a review of the content tested on the AP U.S. Government and Politics Exam, including the level of detail you need to know and how your knowledge of the content is tested. You will have the opportunity to assess your mastery of each chapter through test-appropriate questions and a reflection section at the end.

6. **Take Practice Test 2 and Assess Your Performance**
    Once you feel you have developed the strategies you need and gained the knowledge you lacked, you should take Practice Test 2, which starts at page 297 of this book. You should do so in one sitting, following the instructions at the beginning of the test.

    When you are done, check your answers to the multiple-choice section with the correct responses on page 317 of this book. Then, see if a teacher will read your essays and provide feedback for your improvement.

    Once you have taken the test, reflect on which areas you still need to work on, and revisit the chapters in this book that address those deficiencies. Through this type of reflection and engagement, you will continue to improve.

7. **Keep Working**
    As discussed in Part III, there are other resources available to you, including a wealth of information on AP Students. On this site, you can continue to explore areas that you can improve upon and engage in those areas right up until the day of the test.

You can find a course description and overview on the AP Students website, located here: https://apstudent.college board.org/apcourse/ap-united-states-government-and-politics

This site also includes course details straight from the horse's mouth, so to speak, as well as links to .gov resources that provide primary source information on the Constitution, Declaration of Independence, and the various branches of government.

Part II
Practice Test 1

Practice Test 1

Completely darken bubbles with a No. 2 pencil. If you make a mistake, be sure to erase mark completely. Erase all stray marks.

1. YOUR NAME:
(Print)

Last   First   M.I.

SIGNATURE: _____ DATE: _____ / _____ / _____

HOME ADDRESS: _____
(Print)   Number and Street

_____
City   State   Zip Code

PHONE NO. : _____
(Print)

5. YOUR NAME

First 4 letters of last name				FIRST INIT	MID INIT
Ⓐ	Ⓐ	Ⓐ	Ⓐ	Ⓐ	Ⓐ
Ⓑ	Ⓑ	Ⓑ	Ⓑ	Ⓑ	Ⓑ
Ⓒ	Ⓒ	Ⓒ	Ⓒ	Ⓒ	Ⓒ
Ⓓ	Ⓓ	Ⓓ	Ⓓ	Ⓓ	Ⓓ
Ⓔ	Ⓔ	Ⓔ	Ⓔ	Ⓔ	Ⓔ
Ⓕ	Ⓕ	Ⓕ	Ⓕ	Ⓕ	Ⓕ
Ⓖ	Ⓖ	Ⓖ	Ⓖ	Ⓖ	Ⓖ
Ⓗ	Ⓗ	Ⓗ	Ⓗ	Ⓗ	Ⓗ
Ⓘ	Ⓘ	Ⓘ	Ⓘ	Ⓘ	Ⓘ
Ⓙ	Ⓙ	Ⓙ	Ⓙ	Ⓙ	Ⓙ
Ⓚ	Ⓚ	Ⓚ	Ⓚ	Ⓚ	Ⓚ
Ⓛ	Ⓛ	Ⓛ	Ⓛ	Ⓛ	Ⓛ
Ⓜ	Ⓜ	Ⓜ	Ⓜ	Ⓜ	Ⓜ
Ⓝ	Ⓝ	Ⓝ	Ⓝ	Ⓝ	Ⓝ
Ⓞ	Ⓞ	Ⓞ	Ⓞ	Ⓞ	Ⓞ
Ⓟ	Ⓟ	Ⓟ	Ⓟ	Ⓟ	Ⓟ
Ⓠ	Ⓠ	Ⓠ	Ⓠ	Ⓠ	Ⓠ
Ⓡ	Ⓡ	Ⓡ	Ⓡ	Ⓡ	Ⓡ
Ⓢ	Ⓢ	Ⓢ	Ⓢ	Ⓢ	Ⓢ
Ⓣ	Ⓣ	Ⓣ	Ⓣ	Ⓣ	Ⓣ
Ⓤ	Ⓤ	Ⓤ	Ⓤ	Ⓤ	Ⓤ
Ⓥ	Ⓥ	Ⓥ	Ⓥ	Ⓥ	Ⓥ
Ⓦ	Ⓦ	Ⓦ	Ⓦ	Ⓦ	Ⓦ
Ⓧ	Ⓧ	Ⓧ	Ⓧ	Ⓧ	Ⓧ
Ⓨ	Ⓨ	Ⓨ	Ⓨ	Ⓨ	Ⓨ
Ⓩ	Ⓩ	Ⓩ	Ⓩ	Ⓩ	Ⓩ

IMPORTANT: Please fill in these boxes exactly as shown on the back cover of your test book.

2. TEST FORM

_____

3. TEST CODE   **4. REGISTRATION NUMBER**

⓪	Ⓐ	⓪	⓪	⓪	⓪	⓪	⓪	⓪	⓪	⓪
①	Ⓑ	①	①	①	①	①	①	①	①	①
②	Ⓒ	②	②	②	②	②	②	②	②	②
③	Ⓓ	③	③	③	③	③	③	③	③	③
④	Ⓔ	④	④	④	④	④	④	④	④	④
⑤		⑤	⑤	⑤	⑤	⑤	⑤	⑤	⑤	⑤
⑥	Ⓖ	⑥	⑥	⑥	⑥	⑥	⑥	⑥	⑥	⑥
⑦		⑦	⑦	⑦	⑦	⑦	⑦	⑦	⑦	⑦
⑧		⑧	⑧	⑧	⑧	⑧	⑧	⑧	⑧	⑧
⑨		⑨	⑨	⑨	⑨	⑨	⑨	⑨	⑨	⑨

6. DATE OF BIRTH

Month		Day		Year	
◯ JAN					
◯ FEB					
◯ MAR	①	①	①	①
◯ APR	①	①	①	①
◯ MAY	②	②	②	②
◯ JUN	③	③	③	③
◯ JUL		④	④	④
◯ AUG		⑤	⑤	⑤
◯ SEP		⑥	⑥	⑥
◯ OCT		⑦	⑦	⑦
◯ NOV		⑧	⑧	⑧
◯ DEC		⑨	⑨	⑨

7. SEX

◯ MALE
◯ FEMALE

The **Princeton Review**®

© The Princeton Review, Inc.

FORM NO. 00001-PR

Section ① Start with number 1 for each new section.
If a section has fewer questions than answer spaces, leave the extra answer spaces blank.

1. Ⓐ Ⓑ Ⓒ Ⓓ Ⓔ
2. Ⓐ Ⓑ Ⓒ Ⓓ Ⓔ
3. Ⓐ Ⓑ Ⓒ Ⓓ Ⓔ
4. Ⓐ Ⓑ Ⓒ Ⓓ Ⓔ
5. Ⓐ Ⓑ Ⓒ Ⓓ Ⓔ
6. Ⓐ Ⓑ Ⓒ Ⓓ Ⓔ
7. Ⓐ Ⓑ Ⓒ Ⓓ Ⓔ
8. Ⓐ Ⓑ Ⓒ Ⓓ Ⓔ
9. Ⓐ Ⓑ Ⓒ Ⓓ Ⓔ
10. Ⓐ Ⓑ Ⓒ Ⓓ Ⓔ
11. Ⓐ Ⓑ Ⓒ Ⓓ Ⓔ
12. Ⓐ Ⓑ Ⓒ Ⓓ Ⓔ
13. Ⓐ Ⓑ Ⓒ Ⓓ Ⓔ
14. Ⓐ Ⓑ Ⓒ Ⓓ Ⓔ
15. Ⓐ Ⓑ Ⓒ Ⓓ Ⓔ

16. Ⓐ Ⓑ Ⓒ Ⓓ Ⓔ
17. Ⓐ Ⓑ Ⓒ Ⓓ Ⓔ
18. Ⓐ Ⓑ Ⓒ Ⓓ Ⓔ
19. Ⓐ Ⓑ Ⓒ Ⓓ Ⓔ
20. Ⓐ Ⓑ Ⓒ Ⓓ Ⓔ
21. Ⓐ Ⓑ Ⓒ Ⓓ Ⓔ
22. Ⓐ Ⓑ Ⓒ Ⓓ Ⓔ
23. Ⓐ Ⓑ Ⓒ Ⓓ Ⓔ
24. Ⓐ Ⓑ Ⓒ Ⓓ Ⓔ
25. Ⓐ Ⓑ Ⓒ Ⓓ Ⓔ
26. Ⓐ Ⓑ Ⓒ Ⓓ Ⓔ
27. Ⓐ Ⓑ Ⓒ Ⓓ Ⓔ
28. Ⓐ Ⓑ Ⓒ Ⓓ Ⓔ
29. Ⓐ Ⓑ Ⓒ Ⓓ Ⓔ
30. Ⓐ Ⓑ Ⓒ Ⓓ Ⓔ

31. Ⓐ Ⓑ Ⓒ Ⓓ Ⓔ
32. Ⓐ Ⓑ Ⓒ Ⓓ Ⓔ
33. Ⓐ Ⓑ Ⓒ Ⓓ Ⓔ
34. Ⓐ Ⓑ Ⓒ Ⓓ Ⓔ
35. Ⓐ Ⓑ Ⓒ Ⓓ Ⓔ
36. Ⓐ Ⓑ Ⓒ Ⓓ Ⓔ
37. Ⓐ Ⓑ Ⓒ Ⓓ Ⓔ
38. Ⓐ Ⓑ Ⓒ Ⓓ Ⓔ
39. Ⓐ Ⓑ Ⓒ Ⓓ Ⓔ
40. Ⓐ Ⓑ Ⓒ Ⓓ Ⓔ
41. Ⓐ Ⓑ Ⓒ Ⓓ Ⓔ
42. Ⓐ Ⓑ Ⓒ Ⓓ Ⓔ
43. Ⓐ Ⓑ Ⓒ Ⓓ Ⓔ
44. Ⓐ Ⓑ Ⓒ Ⓓ Ⓔ
45. Ⓐ Ⓑ Ⓒ Ⓓ Ⓔ

46. Ⓐ Ⓑ Ⓒ Ⓓ Ⓔ
47. Ⓐ Ⓑ Ⓒ Ⓓ Ⓔ
48. Ⓐ Ⓑ Ⓒ Ⓓ Ⓔ
49. Ⓐ Ⓑ Ⓒ Ⓓ Ⓔ
50. Ⓐ Ⓑ Ⓒ Ⓓ Ⓔ
51. Ⓐ Ⓑ Ⓒ Ⓓ Ⓔ
52. Ⓐ Ⓑ Ⓒ Ⓓ Ⓔ
53. Ⓐ Ⓑ Ⓒ Ⓓ Ⓔ
54. Ⓐ Ⓑ Ⓒ Ⓓ Ⓔ
55. Ⓐ Ⓑ Ⓒ Ⓓ Ⓔ
56. Ⓐ Ⓑ Ⓒ Ⓓ Ⓔ
57. Ⓐ Ⓑ Ⓒ Ⓓ Ⓔ
58. Ⓐ Ⓑ Ⓒ Ⓓ Ⓔ
59. Ⓐ Ⓑ Ⓒ Ⓓ Ⓔ
60. Ⓐ Ⓑ Ⓒ Ⓓ Ⓔ

The Exam

AP® U.S. Government and Politics Exam

SECTION I: Multiple-Choice Questions

DO NOT OPEN THIS BOOKLET UNTIL YOU ARE TOLD TO DO SO.

At a Glance

Total Time
45 minutes
Number of Questions
60
Percent of Total Grade
50%
Writing Instrument
Pencil required

Instructions

Section I of this examination contains 60 multiple-choice questions. Fill in only the ovals for numbers 1 through 60 on your answer sheet.

Indicate all of your answers to the multiple-choice questions on the answer sheet. No credit will be given for anything written in this exam booklet, but you may use the booklet for notes or scratch work. After you have decided which of the suggested answers is best, completely fill in the corresponding oval on the answer sheet. Give only one answer to each question. If you change an answer, be sure that the previous mark is erased completely. Here is a sample question and answer.

Sample Question   Sample Answer

Chicago is a   Ⓐ ● Ⓒ Ⓓ Ⓔ
(A) state
(B) city
(C) country
(D) continent
(E) village

Use your time effectively, working as quickly as you can without losing accuracy. Do not spend too much time on any one question. Go on to other questions and come back to the ones you have not answered if you have time. It is not expected that everyone will know the answers to all the multiple-choice questions.

About Guessing

Many candidates wonder whether or not to guess the answers to questions about which they are not certain. Multiple-choice scores are based on the number of questions answered correctly. Points are not deducted for incorrect answers, and no points are awarded for unanswered questions. Because points are not deducted for incorrect answers, you are encouraged to answer all multiple-choice questions. On any questions you do not know the answer to, you should eliminate as many choices as you can, and then select the best answer among the remaining choices.

GO ON TO THE NEXT PAGE.

UNITED STATES GOVERNMENT AND POLITICS

Section I

Time—45 minutes

60 Questions

Directions: Each of the questions or incomplete statements below is followed by five suggested answers or completions. Select the one that is best in each case and then fill in the corresponding oval on the answer sheet.

1. The Constitution as ratified in 1788 most clearly reflects the Framers' commitment to

   (A) the idea of direct democracy
   (B) the principle of limited government
   (C) the abolition of slavery
   (D) protecting the rights of the accused
   (E) maintaining the primacy of the states

2. Which of the following most accurately describes *The Federalist Papers*?

   (A) The Federalist party platform during the presidency of John Adams, the first Federalist president
   (B) A popular anti-British booklet of the pre-Revolutionary era
   (C) A collection of essays arguing the merits of the Constitution
   (D) A series of congressional acts defining the relationship between the federal and state governments
   (E) The laws under which the South was governed during Reconstruction

3. A Supreme Court that demonstrates a willingness to change public policy and alter judicial precedent is said to be engaging in

   (A) judicial activism
   (B) due process
   (C) judicial restraint
   (D) *ex post facto* lawmaking
   (E) judicial review

4. A writ of *certiorari* from the Supreme Court indicates that the Court

   (A) will review a lower court decision
   (B) has rendered a decision on a case
   (C) has decided not to hear an appeal
   (D) will recess until the end of the calendar year
   (E) plans to overturn one of its previous rulings

5. All of the following statements about Congress are true EXCEPT:

   (A) Only Congress can pass laws.
   (B) A proposed amendment must be approved by two-thirds of the delegates in both houses of Congress.
   (C) Congress can override a presidential veto if two-thirds of the House and Senate agree to do so.
   (D) Congressional power over the bureaucracy is less than that of the president.
   (E) Congress cannot establish an official church of the United States.

6. The Supreme Court issued the opinion quoted below in its ruling on which of the following cases?

   "We conclude that in the field of education the doctrine of 'separate but equal' has no place. Separate educational facilities are inherently unequal."

   (A) *Gideon v. Wainwright*
   (B) *Marbury v. Madison*
   (C) *Engel v. Vitale*
   (D) *Regents of University of California v. Bakke*
   (E) *Brown v. Board of Education of Topeka*

GO ON TO THE NEXT PAGE.

Congressional Job Approval Ratings

7. Which of the following conclusions about congressional job approval ratings since 1975 is supported by the data in the graph above?

(A) The approval rating of Congress was higher in the early 1990s than in the late 1990s.

(B) Congress was more popular in the mid-1990s than in the late 1980s.

(C) Americans are usually displeased with the performance of Congress.

(D) A majority of Americans disapproved of the performance of Congress immediately after September 11, 2001.

(E) The popularity of Congress has been stable since 2000.

8. Which of the following best describes the practice of "ticket splitting"?

(A) A presidential nominee selects a running mate who can appeal to voter groups whose support of the nominee is weak.

(B) A voter chooses the presidential nominee of one major party, but chooses congressional nominees of the other major party.

(C) A mayor orders the local police force to hand out fewer parking violations in the weeks leading up to the general election.

(D) A delegate to a national party convention supports the front-runner but remains uncommitted on the party platform.

(E) A member of Congress votes against legislation proposed by his or her party leader.

9. The House Rules Committee is considered among the most powerful in the House of Representatives because it has great power over the

(A) ethical conduct of House members

(B) selection of federal judges

(C) number of subcommittees that a standing committee may establish at any given time

(D) scheduling of votes and the conditions under which bills are debated and amended

(E) regulations governing federal elections

10. Compared with political parties in countries such as England and Israel, both of which have multiparty systems, American political parties are

(A) less interested in influencing the outcome of elections

(B) less clearly identified with consistent political ideologies

(C) less effective at raising money from political supporters

(D) better able to reflect the goals of their entire constituencies

(E) more likely to organize around a single issue or goal

11. Which of the following people would most likely be accused of influence peddling?

(A) A congressperson who retires to take a position teaching political science at a university

(B) A former president who advises a current president on a particular foreign policy issue

(C) A voter who researches the positions of all candidates in a race before choosing whom to support

(D) A judge who consistently hands down the maximum sentence to convicted felons

(E) An official who leaves the State Department to work as a paid consultant to foreign governments

12. The primary function of political action committees (PACs) is to

(A) contribute money to candidates for election

(B) coordinate local get-out-the-vote campaigns

(C) promote the defeat of incumbents in the federal and state legislatures

(D) organize protest demonstrations and other acts of civil disobedience

(E) contact Congress to suggest legislation

GO ON TO THE NEXT PAGE.

13. Voters who rely exclusively on television network news coverage of national elections are most likely to be aware of

    (A) which special interest groups have endorsed which candidates
    (B) the relative strength of each candidate's support, as indicated by public opinion polls
    (C) candidates' positions on international issues
    (D) candidates' positions on domestic issues
    (E) candidates' congressional voting records

14. While best known for protecting freedom of speech and religion, the First Amendment also protects Americans' right to

    (A) due process of the law in any criminal case
    (B) retain personal property unless justly compensated by the government
    (C) not be subjected to excessive fines or unusual punishment
    (D) petition the government for a redress of grievances
    (E) not be searched without probable cause

15. Two related cases that focused on the right to privacy for all American citizens were

    (A) *Near v. Minnesota* and *New York Times v. Sullivan*
    (B) *Texas v. Johnson* and *Morse v. Frederick*
    (C) *Thornhill v. Alabama* and *Cox v. New Hampshire*
    (D) *Epperson v. Arkansas* and *Lemon v. Kurtzman*
    (E) *Griswold v. Connecticut* and *Roe v. Wade.*

16. Of the following, American federalism is most clearly exemplified by the

    (A) system of checks and balances among the three branches of the national government
    (B) process by which international treaties are completed
    (C) special constitutional status of Washington, D.C.
    (D) Tenth Amendment to the Constitution
    (E) president's power to grant reprieves and pardons

17. All of the following are specifically mentioned in the Constitution EXCEPT

    (A) judicial review
    (B) the national census
    (C) rules of impeachment
    (D) the State of the Union address
    (E) length of term of federal judgeships

18. Which of the following correctly states the relationship between the federal and state judiciaries?

    (A) Federal courts are higher courts than state courts and may overturn state decisions on any grounds.
    (B) The two are entirely autonomous, and neither ever hears cases that originate in the other.
    (C) The two are generally autonomous, although federal courts may rule on the constitutionality of state court decisions.
    (D) State courts are trial courts; federal courts are appeals courts.
    (E) State courts try all cases except those that involve conflicts between two states, which are tried in federal courts.

19. The line-item veto was found unconstitutional because

    (A) it gave executive powers to the legislature
    (B) it gave legislative powers to the bureaucracy
    (C) it gave legislative powers to the president
    (D) it delegated too many powers to the states
    (E) it permitted the Senate to use judicial review to reverse the House of Representatives

20. Among the executive branch's checks on the legislative branch is the president's power to

    (A) call special sessions of Congress
    (B) introduce bills to the floor of Congress
    (C) address Congress during its debate on bills
    (D) vote on acts of Congress
    (E) disband congressional committees

21. The amount of access cabinet secretaries have to the president is most likely to be controlled by the

    (A) vice president
    (B) president's chief of staff
    (C) national security advisor
    (D) chair of the Federal Reserve Board
    (E) president's press secretary

GO ON TO THE NEXT PAGE.

22. Which of the following presidential powers is shared with the Senate?

    (A) Deploying troops
    (B) Drafting appropriations bills
    (C) Negotiating treaties
    (D) Forcing Congress into session
    (E) Nominating vice presidents

23. Republican candidates for president who tend to be more successful in the primaries tend to be more conservative than rank-and-file Republicans because

    (A) moderate Republicans are less likely than conservative Republicans to gain widespread support in the general election
    (B) most moderate Republicans have approved of the Democratic presidential candidate
    (C) most rank-and-file Republicans do not care whether their party's nominee shares their political views
    (D) party activists, whose political participation is disproportionate to their numbers, tend to be very conservative
    (E) the Republican Party does not allow rank-and-file members to participate in the selection of the party's nominee

24. What is the primary reason that the committees in the House of Representatives are more influential than they are in the Senate?

    (A) The difference in size between the two chambers means that more work is done on the floor in the Senate and more work is done in committees in the House.
    (B) The Senate as a whole has confirmation powers that the House does not have.
    (C) Members are appointed to the committee in the House but are elected to committees in the Senate.
    (D) A member of any party can serve a committee in the House, but only major party members can serve on committees in the Senate.
    (E) Committee membership enables members of Congress to work for the special interests of their constituents.

25. Which of the following accounts for the fact that the power and prestige of the presidency have grown since 1932?

    I. America's increased prominence in international affairs
    II. continually improved public confidence in the federal government
    III. the New Deal and other programs that have expanded federal responsibility
    IV. the president's increased visibility, due to the development of mass media

    (A) I only
    (B) I and IV only
    (C) I, III, and IV only
    (D) II and IV only
    (E) II, III, and IV only

26. Which of the following generally results when the Senate and House of Representatives pass different versions of the same bill?

    (A) The president signs the version he prefers.
    (B) The bill goes back to each house's committee and restarts the legislative process.
    (C) All amendments to the bill are invalidated, and the original version of the bill is sent to the president to sign.
    (D) The Senate's version of the bill is sent to the president because the Senate is the higher legislative body.
    (E) The two legislative bodies form a conference committee.

GO ON TO THE NEXT PAGE.

27. All of the following statements concerning the likelihood that a person will vote are true EXCEPT:

    (A) When there is a strong front-runner in a state, people in that state are less likely to vote.
    (B) White-collar workers are more likely to vote than are blue-collar workers, with the exception of blue-collar workers who belong to unions.
    (C) Voters who are registered as independent are less likely to vote than those who are registered Democrats or Republicans.
    (D) Minorities with high incomes are as likely to vote as are whites.
    (E) There is no difference in the likelihood of voting among those with undergraduate degrees and those with postgraduate degrees.

28. A member of which of the following demographic groups is most likely to support a Republican presidential candidate?

    (A) Married white male
    (B) Unmarried white female
    (C) African American, male or female
    (D) Youths under the age of 25, male or female
    (E) Individuals earning below poverty-level wages, male or female

29. The Civil Rights Act of 1964 was passed to reinforce the

    (A) presidential veto
    (B) system of checks and balances
    (C) states' power to challenge federal regulation
    (D) Fourteenth Amendment
    (E) Taft-Hartley Act of 1947

30. Which of the following best illustrates a use of the elastic clause?

    (A) The Supreme Court allows a lower court ruling to stand by refusing to hear an appeal.
    (B) A congressional committee prevents the full chamber from voting on legislation by delaying its report.
    (C) Congress passes legislation establishing a national speed limit.
    (D) A member of the House of Representatives introduces a bill to increase federal income tax rates.
    (E) A governor issues an executive order requiring all state employees to submit to drug testing.

31. According to *The Federalist Papers*, federalism has which of the following effects on political factions?

    (A) It provides a structured environment in which factions may flourish.
    (B) It limits the dangers of factionalism by diluting political power.
    (C) It allows factions to dominate on the national level while limiting their influence on state governments.
    (D) It eliminates any opportunity for factions to form.
    (E) It prevents factions by declaring them illegal.

32. The Constitution, as originally ratified, addressed all of the following weaknesses of the Articles of Confederation EXCEPT the

    (A) lack of a chief executive office
    (B) national government's inability to levy taxes effectively
    (C) absence of a central authority to regulate interstate trade
    (D) insufficiency of the government's power to raise an army
    (E) omission of a universal suffrage clause

33. Congress's power to determine national policy

    (A) usually increases as a president's popularity decreases, and vice versa
    (B) has declined steadily since the ratification of the Constitution
    (C) is severely limited by the "elastic clause" of the Constitution
    (D) increases during times of war
    (E) stems primarily from its control over the judicial branch

34. Which of the following statements about cabinet departments is FALSE?

    (A) They are established by the legislative branch.
    (B) Their members often don't have much influence over presidential decisions.
    (C) They cannot all be run by leaders who belong to the same political party the president does.
    (D) Not every federal agency is a cabinet department.
    (E) Their heads are appointed, and fired, by the president.

GO ON TO THE NEXT PAGE.

35. Which of the following statements about the electoral college is correct?

(A) Each state must split its electoral votes among all the candidates that receive votes.
(B) Each state is equally represented in the electoral college.
(C) The electoral college was created by an amendment to the Constitution.
(D) The results of electoral college voting tend to distort the winner's margin of victory, when compared with the popular vote for president.
(E) Each state's delegation to the electoral college consists of that state's U.S. senators and representatives.

36. Which of the following statements is true of congressional incumbents who run for reelection?

(A) Incumbent senators are more likely to be reelected than are incumbent members of the House of Representatives.
(B) Incumbents are prohibited by law from spending more on their reelection campaigns than their challengers spend.
(C) Incumbents have a great advantage over challengers because they are better known and can raise campaign funds more easily.
(D) Ever since the 1994 election, the majority of congressional incumbents have failed in their reelection attempts.
(E) Most incumbents who run for reelection are unopposed in the general election.

37. Before serving in the House of Representatives or Senate, the greatest number of federal legislators

(A) own and operate small businesses
(B) are professional athletes
(C) teach political science at the college level
(D) work as journalists
(E) earn law degrees

38. A member of the House of Representatives wishing to influence tax policy would most likely try to serve on which of the following committees?

(A) Commerce
(B) Ways and Means
(C) Education and the Workforce
(D) Resources
(E) Judiciary

39. The spoils system of awarding civil service jobs was replaced by the merit system as a result of the

(A) Truman Doctrine
(B) Fair Labor Standards Act of 1961
(C) National Industrial Recovery Act
(D) Civil Rights Act of 1964
(E) Pendleton Act of 1883

40. The boundary lines of congressional districts must be redrawn every 10 years to

(A) reflect population shifts indicated by the national census
(B) guarantee the turnover of the majority of congressional seats
(C) make sure each state's congressional delegation exactly mirrors its residents' party affiliations
(D) determine which party's leader will be named Speaker of the House
(E) increase the number of female and minority members of Congress

GO ON TO THE NEXT PAGE.

	Eligible voters	Registered voters	Votes cast	Turnout, registered voters	Turnout, all eligible voters
1986	178,566,000	118,399,984	64,991,128	54.89%	36.40%
1988	182,778,000	126,379,628	91,594,693	72.48%	50.11%
1990	185,812,000	121,105,630	67,859,189	56.03%	36.52%
1992	189,529,000	133,821,178	104,405,155	78.02%	55.09%
1994	193,650,000	130,292,822	75,105,860	57.64%	38.78%
1996	196,511,000	146,211,960	96,456,345	65.97%	49.08%
1998	200,929,000	141,850,558	73,117,022	70.6%	36.4%

Source: Federal Election Commission

41. The chart above best supports which of the following conclusions?

(A) No more than half of all eligible voters ever participate in federal elections.
(B) The number of registered voters always increases between elections.
(C) Voters have been more dissatisfied with their electoral choices in the 1990s than they were during the 1970s.
(D) Voter turnout for midterm congressional elections is generally lower than it is for presidential elections.
(E) Voter turnout for the 1996 presidential election was the lowest for any presidential election during the twentieth century.

42. Interest groups representing businesspeople and investors are often among the most successful lobbying groups in Washington, D.C., for all of the following reasons EXCEPT

(A) Such groups have the financial resources to mount sustained campaigns on their own behalf.
(B) Many such groups have been in existence for several decades or more, allowing them to master the legislative system and to develop close ties with legislators.
(C) In many districts, these groups' constituents make up the majority of voters.
(D) These groups' constituents contribute heavily to many legislators' campaigns, and in doing so, gain greater access to legislators.
(E) Economic lobbyists often campaign for obscure or minute changes to tax law about which the public knows little, and therefore frequently meet little opposition.

43. Among the following groups that have traditionally supposed the Democratic Party, which has the least liberal constituency?

(A) White Southerners
(B) Labor union members
(C) African Americans
(D) Northern ethnic minorities
(E) Environmentalists

44. Voters in which of the following categories would be LEAST likely to vote?

(A) Blue-collar workers who belong to a union
(B) Professionals
(C) Voters who are active in their political parties
(D) Voters aged 18–29
(E) Voters in swing states

45. People who join a political party other than the one to which their parents belong most often do so because of

(A) peer pressure
(B) economic issues
(C) religious beliefs
(D) pressure from their employers
(E) issues of international politics

46. Which of the following best describes the fate of most popular third-party movements?

(A) They displace one of the two major parties and become major parties themselves.
(B) They are ultimately abandoned by the public because their politics are perceived as too radical.
(C) Their supporters become frustrated and withdraw from the political process.
(D) They remain active participants in the American political system indefinitely.
(E) They disintegrate when one or both of the major parties adopt the third party's goals.

GO ON TO THE NEXT PAGE.

47. A constitutional amendment would be required to ban flag burning because that activity is currently protected by the right to

    (A) due process
    (B) assembly
    (C) free exercise of religion
    (D) protection against confiscation of private property
    (E) free speech

48. The Supreme Court's decision in *Miranda v. Arizona* was based mainly on the

    (A) Constitutional prohibition of *ex post facto* laws
    (B) incorporation of the Fifth Amendment through the due process clause of the Fourteenth Amendment
    (C) Eighth Amendment restriction against cruel and unusual punishment
    (D) abolition of slavery by the Thirteenth Amendment
    (E) "full faith and credit" clause of the Constitution

49. The Supreme Court has used the practice of selective incorporation to

    (A) limit the number of appeals filed by defendants in state courts
    (B) extend voting rights to racial minorities and women
    (C) apply most Bill of Rights protections to state law
    (D) hasten the integration of public schools
    (E) prevent the states from calling a constitutional convention

50. The largest portion of the federal budget covers the costs of

    (A) national defense
    (B) the Department of Energy
    (C) interest on the national debt
    (D) entitlement programs
    (E) tax collection

51. Which of the following accurately describes congressional committees?

    I. The committee chairpersons always belong to the majority party.
    II. Seats on each committee are divided between the two major parties in exact proportion to the parties' representation in Congress.
    III. They recommend whether Congress should pass various pieces of legislation, and those recommendations are always approved by the full congressional body.
    IV. When a committee vote results in a tie, the vice president casts the tie-breaking vote.

    (A) I only
    (B) II only
    (C) I and III only
    (D) II and III only
    (E) I, II, and IV only

52. The primary goal of the Gramm-Rudman Acts of 1985 and 1987 was to

    (A) strengthen the military
    (B) increase funding for social programs
    (C) reduce the federal deficit
    (D) limit the president's ability to conduct foreign policy
    (E) allow citizens easier access to government records

53. The term "iron triangle" refers to the interrelationship of the

    (A) president, Congress, and the Supreme Court
    (B) electorate, Congress, and political action committees
    (C) local, state, and federal governments
    (D) State Department, the Pentagon, and the National Security Council
    (E) federal bureaucracy, congressional committees, and lobbyists

GO ON TO THE NEXT PAGE.

54. A sound bite would most likely be used during a presidential election in order to

    (A) avoid "horse race" politics
    (B) provide the audience with a candidate's view in a limited amount of time
    (C) reduce the amount of negative advertising used
    (D) ensure a candidate is presented in the best light
    (E) emphasize who won and lost presidential debates

55. Which of the following most accurately describes the right of American citizens to privacy?

    (A) The right to privacy is determined entirely by the states on a case-by-case basis.
    (B) The right to privacy is explicitly granted in the Preamble to the Constitution.
    (C) The Supreme Court has ruled that the right to privacy is implied by the Bill of Rights.
    (D) Common law requires the government to respect citizens' right to privacy.
    (E) Americans have no right to privacy, but the government rarely violates individuals' privacy because to do so is not in the government's interest.

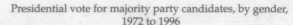

Presidential vote for majority party candidates, by gender, 1972 to 1996

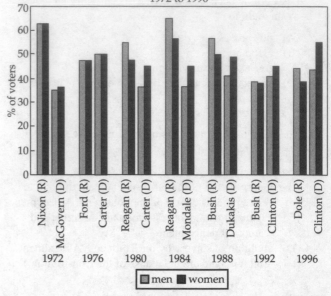

Source: *New York Times*/CBS exit polls

56. The graph above supports which of the following conclusions about presidential elections?

    (A) If only men had voted in the 1980 election, Jimmy Carter would have won.
    (B) There is little difference in the level of support that the Republican Party receives from men and women.
    (C) The gender gap was more prominent in the 1980s and 1990s than it was in the 1970s.
    (D) In order for a Republican candidate to win, he or she must receive more votes from women than from men.
    (E) The 1976 election was the closest in history.

GO ON TO THE NEXT PAGE.

Dissemination of Medicare Benefits by Region (Millions of $)

	2000	2004	2008	2012
North	12.4	13.2	14.0	16.4
Northeast	8.2	9.0	9.6	10.1
Midwest	12.0	13.2	14.2	15.0
West	14.8	16.2	15.8	17.0
East	9.8	10.4	10.4	11.0
South	11.8	13.6	16.2	18.4

57. Which of the following statements can be inferred from the table above?

    (A) The dissemination of Medicare funding has continually increased across all regions between 2000–2012.
    (B) The West received the most Medicare funding in 2012.
    (C) In 2008, the Northeast received approximately one and a half times the amount of Medicare funding as the North.
    (D) The South experienced the greatest increase in Medicare funding from 2000–2012.
    (E) In 2004, the Midwest and the East received the same amount of Medicare funding.

58. The difference between a pardon and a reprieve is

    (A) a pardon lasts 10 years, while a reprieve lasts one year
    (B) a reprieve grants a release from legal punishment, while a pardon postpones it
    (C) a pardon grants a release from legal punishment while a reprieve postpones it
    (D) only state governors can issue pardons
    (E) only state governors can issue reprieves

59. The government promotes preferential treatment for members of groups that have historically suffered from discrimination by means of

    (A) the New Federalism
    (B) affirmative action programs
    (C) Social Security benefits
    (D) bills of attainder
    (E) gerrymandering

60. The exclusionary rule was established to

    (A) create "separate but equal" facilities to facilitate racial segregation
    (B) allow private organizations to restrict their memberships
    (C) limit the government's ability to use illegally obtained evidence
    (D) deny control of interstate commerce to the states
    (E) provide the president with greater independence in negotiating foreign policy

STOP
END OF SECTION I

IF YOU FINISH BEFORE TIME IS CALLED, YOU MAY CHECK YOUR WORK ON THIS SECTION.
DO NOT GO ON TO SECTION II UNTIL YOU ARE TOLD TO DO SO.

UNITED STATES GOVERNMENT AND POLITICS

SECTION II

Time—1 hour and 40 minutes

<u>Directions:</u> You have 100 minutes to answer all four of the following questions. Unless the directions indicate otherwise, respond to all parts of all four questions. It is suggested that you take a few minutes to plan and outline each answer. <u>Spend approximately one-fourth of your time (25 minutes) on each question</u>. Illustrate your essay with substantive examples where appropriate. Make certain to number each of your answers as the question is numbered below.

1. The advent of the Internet has greatly affected politics.

    (a) Identify two ways that candidates are using the Internet in their campaigns.

    (b) For each of the methods identified in part (a), explain the advantages to the candidates of using the Internet in this way.

    (c) Identify and explain one way that the Internet can harm a candidate's campaign.

GO ON TO THE NEXT PAGE.

Markstein © 2001 *Milwaukee Journal Sentinel*. Reprinted with permission. All rights reserved.

2. The debate over soft money has been a common and important feature of American politics.

    (a)   Define "soft money."

    (b)   Describe the opposing points of view expressed about soft money by the congressmen in this cartoon.

    (c)   Explain the arguments for and against soft money.

GO ON TO THE NEXT PAGE.

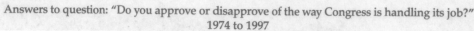

Answers to question: "Do you approve or disapprove of the way Congress is handling its job?"
1974 to 1997

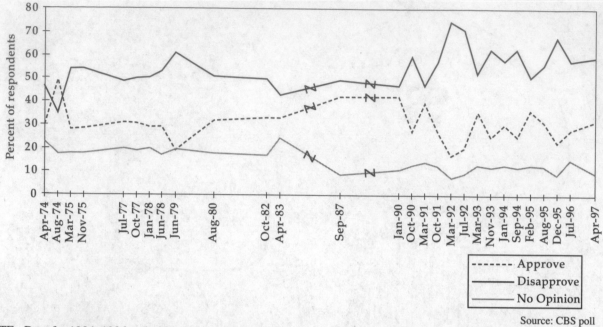

Source: CBS poll

NOTE: Data for 1984–1986 and 1988–1989 not available.

3. Using the above graph and your knowledge of U.S. politics, perform the following tasks:

    (a) Describe the overall trend in citizens' attitudes toward Congress. Assess the degree to which public opinion has changed since 1974.

    (b) Explain the causes and results of ONE dramatic shift in public opinion indicated in the graph.

    (c) Explain why, despite the shifts in public approval, incumbent members of Congress usually win reelection.

4. Since 1789, the United States Constitution has defined the organization and function of the government. Despite this continuity, there have been changes in the way the scope and purpose of the Constitution is interpreted.

    (a) Describe two ways in which formal amendments can be made to the Constitution.

    (b) Explain why formal amendments are rarely made.

    (c) Explain two other ways through which the scope and purpose of the Constitution have been changed. Describe one specific example of each method.

END OF EXAMINATION

Practice Test 1:
Answers and
Explanations

PRACTICE TEST 1 SCORING WORKSHEET

Section I: Multiple-Choice

$$\underline{\hspace{4cm}} \times 1.0000 = \underline{\hspace{4cm}}$$

Number of Correct   Weighted
(out of 60)   Section I Score
                               (Do not round)

Section II: Free Response

Question 1 $\underline{\hspace{3cm}} \times 2.500 = \underline{\hspace{3cm}}$
                 (out of 6)   (Do not round)

Question 2 $\underline{\hspace{3cm}} \times 3.000 = \underline{\hspace{3cm}}$
                 (out of 5)   (Do not round)

Question 3 $\underline{\hspace{3cm}} \times 2.500 = \underline{\hspace{3cm}}$
                 (out of 6)   (Do not round)

Question 4 $\underline{\hspace{3cm}} \times 2.500 = \underline{\hspace{3cm}}$
                 (out of 6)   (Do not round)

AP Score Conversion Chart U.S. Government and Politics	
Composite Score Range	AP Score
93–120	5
82–92	4
66–81	3
48–65	2
0–47	1

Sum   = $\underline{\hspace{4cm}}$
               Weighted Section II
               Score (Do not round)

Composite Score

$$\underline{\hspace{3cm}} + \underline{\hspace{3cm}} = \underline{\hspace{3cm}}$$

Weighted   Weighted   Composite Score
Section I Score   Section II Score   (Round to nearest
                                          whole number)

ANSWER KEY

1.	B	21.	B	41.	D
2.	C	22.	C	42.	C
3.	A	23.	D	43.	A
4.	A	24.	A	44.	D
5.	D	25.	C	45.	B
6.	E	26.	E	46.	E
7.	C	27.	E	47.	E
8.	B	28.	A	48.	B
9.	D	29.	D	49.	C
10.	B	30.	C	50.	D
11.	E	31.	B	51.	A
12.	A	32.	E	52.	C
13.	B	33.	A	53.	E
14.	D	34.	C	54.	B
15.	E	35.	D	55.	C
16.	D	36.	C	56.	C
17.	A	37.	E	57.	D
18.	C	38.	B	58.	C
19.	C	39.	E	59.	B
20.	A	40.	A	60.	C

MULTIPLE-CHOICE SECTION: ANSWERS AND EXPLANATIONS

1. **B** The term *limited government* refers to the concept of defining government powers by means of a constitution. A constitution specifies what the government is allowed to do, and also what it may not do. In setting distinct limits on government power, the Framers of the U.S. Constitution hoped to prevent the government from achieving the same level of power as had the British monarchy.

    Incorrect Answers:

    (A) *Direct democracy* refers to a form of democratic government in which all citizens vote on all issues. The Constitution established a representative democracy, in which citizens vote for representatives who, in turn, act on their behalf and assume the nation's legislative and executive duties.

    (C) The abolition of slavery did not occur until 1865 with the ratification of the Thirteenth Amendment. The Framers of the Constitution did not seriously consider abolition.

    (D) As ratified in 1788, the Constitution did not yet have a Bill of Rights. The Bill of Rights was ratified in 1791; only then did the Constitution reflect a concern for protecting the rights of the accused.

    (E) Compared with the Articles of Confederation (which it replaced), the Constitution weakened the power of the states relative to the power of the federal government. Under the Articles, the states were mostly autonomous and exerted great control over the national government. The Constitution shifted the balance toward the federal government.

2. **C** *The Federalist Papers* is the collective name given to a group of essays written by Alexander Hamilton, James Madison, and John Jay in support of ratification of the Constitution. The essays were published anonymously in newspapers in New York and Virginia, two states in which ratification was both critical and uncertain.

    Incorrect Answers:

    (A) The Federalist Party did not have a platform. Party platforms are the product of political conventions, which did not become a part of American politics until after the demise of the Federalist Party.

    (B) This answer describes *Common Sense* by Thomas Paine and *The Rights of the British Colonies Asserted and Proved* by James Otis, among other documents.

    (D) The relationship described in this answer is defined by the U.S. Constitution.

    (E) The postwar South was governed under the Military Reconstruction Act of 1867.

3.   **A**   *Judicial activism* refers to the actions of a court that frequently strikes down or alters the acts of the executive and/or legislative branches. Activist judiciaries are also willing to overturn previous rulings. Judicial activism expands the court's impact on public policy.

Incorrect Answers:

(B)   *Due process* refers to those rules that protect individuals from unfair treatment by the government. The due process clause of the Fourteenth Amendment prohibits the states from depriving citizens of life, liberty, or property without a fair and impartial hearing. The clause was intended to protect the rights of newly freed slaves in the post-Civil War South.

(C)   *Judicial restraint* is the opposite of judicial activism. The term refers to judicial action that demonstrates an unwillingness to break with precedent or to overturn legislative and executive acts.

(D)   An *ex post facto* law allows governments to prosecute citizens for acts that were legal at the time they occurred, but were later deemed illegal. *Ex post facto* laws are prohibited by the U.S. Constitution.

(E)   *Judicial review* is the Supreme Court's power to overturn a law on the grounds that it is unconstitutional. Judicial review is not mentioned in the Constitution. The practice was established by Chief Justice John Marshall in the 1803 decision *Marbury v. Madison*.

4.   **A**   A writ of *certiorari* is a document issued by the Supreme Court that requests all the records pertaining to a case. When the Court issues a writ of *certiorari*, it indicates that the Court will consider the case. A writ of *certiorari* is issued when four of the nine justices agree to hear a case.

Incorrect Answers:

(B)   The Supreme Court meets on Wednesdays and Fridays to vote on cases they have heard during the week. Afterward, one justice is chosen to write the majority opinion. Justices are given the chance to change their vote and to offer alternate concurring opinions (if they side with the majority but feel the majority opinion is either incomplete or incorrect) or dissenting opinions (if they disagree with the majority vote). Only when this process is complete does the Court hand down its final decision.

(C)   When the Supreme Court decides not to hear a case, it simply rejects the appeal and the lower court decision stands. No writ is necessary.

(D)   The Supreme Court meets 36 weeks a year, from the first week of October until June. It recesses occasionally to discuss cases and write decisions. No writ is necessary for a recess.

(E)   The Supreme Court issues no official warning when it plans to overturn a previous ruling. When the Court agrees to hear a case concerning a subject on which it has already ruled, however, the possibility is great that the Court is considering altering at least part of its previous opinion.

5. **D** Be careful because this is an "EXCEPT" question. All of the statements about congressional powers are true except for choice (D). When it comes to control of the bureaucracy, Congress has more power than the president. For example, Congress has the power to affirm or reject presidential appointments, abolish agencies, determine the funding an agency receives, and change agency jurisdiction if unsatisfied with policy implementation.

6. **E** In 1954, the Supreme Court heard the anti-segregation case *Brown v. Board of Education of Topeka*, a lawsuit brought on behalf of Linda Brown (a black school-age child) by the NAACP. Thurgood Marshall, who would later become a Supreme Court justice, argued the case for Brown. In its ruling, the Court overturned the "separate but equal" standard as it applied to education; "separate but equal" had been the law of the land since the Court had approved it in *Plessy v. Ferguson* (1896). In a 9 to 0 decision, the court ruled that "separate educational facilities are inherently unequal."

    Incorrect Answers:

    (A) *Gideon v. Wainwright* (1963) found that defendants in state criminal trials are entitled to legal representation even if they cannot afford it. *Gideon* thus resulted in the creation of state-sponsored public defenders.

    (B) *Marbury v. Madison* (1803) established the principle of judicial review.

    (C) *Engel v. Vitale* (1962) determined that forced prayer in public schools violated the establishment clause of the First Amendment.

    (D) *Regents of University of California v. Bakke* (1978) found that University of California's racial quota system of admissions violated the Civil Rights Act of 1964. This ruling complicated the implementation of many affirmative action programs by rejecting the use of simple quota systems. However, the Court also ruled that University of California could consider race as *one* of many factors in determining admission policy.

7. **C** Upon quick scan of the graph, a simple deduction is that Congress is usually "flunking" in the eyes of the American people. There's a burst in approval just after the attacks of September 11, 2001, but don't be mislead by that answer choice—it is saying the opposite of what the graph is showing. Choice (C) is supported by the data, as a majority of Americans (that is, more than 50%) approved of Congress's performance only from the late 1990s until about 2004; that's less than 10 years, and the graph shows data for more than 30.

    Incorrect Answers:

    (A) This choice is incorrect because the approval rating of Congress was in the 20–40% range in the early 1990s and in the 30–50% range in the late 1990s.

    (B) This option is incorrect because the approval rating of Congress was in the 25–35% range in the mid–1990s and between 35% and approximately 43% in the late 1980s.

(D) This choice is incorrect because approximately 85% of Americans approved of Congress's performance immediately following September 11, 2001 and that choice says that Americans "disapproved" of Congress during that era.

(E) This is incorrect because the approval rating of Congress was less than 50% in 2000, rose to approximately 85%, then fell to below 30%; in no other period did the popularity of Congress see such dramatic changes.

8. **B** *Ticket splitting* has become a common phenomenon in the past 30 years. While Democrats enjoyed control over both houses of Congress in the decades following World War II, the years since the inauguration of Ronald Reagan have seen Congress split more often, more closely, and more contentiously than ever before due to the increase in ticket splitting.

Incorrect Answers:

(A) This answer choice accurately describes an action typically taken by presidential candidates. However, it does not define *ticket splitting*.

(C) This answer choice describes an action that few politicians would attempt and fewer would admit to trying. Although it mentions *tickets*, it has nothing to do with *ticket splitting*.

(D) This answer captures the basic idea of *ticket splitting*, which occurs when a voter does not adhere to the party line. However, it does not define the term *ticket splitting* as it is conventionally used.

(E) Congresspersons vote along party lines between 60% and 80% of the time (the number varies from Congress to Congress and from issue to issue). The action described in this answer choice, then, is exceptional behavior. However, it does not define the term *ticket splitting* as it is conventionally used.

9. **D** Because the membership of the House of Representatives is so large, the process by which bills are debated and amended must be limited (in the Senate, which is smaller, fewer rules govern this process). The task of setting these limits falls to the House Rules Committee. Because the Rules Committee controls the terms of debate and the scheduling of floor votes, it is considered among the most powerful House committees. The majority party dominates the Rules Committee. During the 105th Congress (in 1997), Republicans held nine seats on the committee, while Democrats held four (the number of Democrats and Republicans on any given committee is negotiated by the parties after each election. Generally, the majority party takes two-thirds of the seats on the most important committees to ensure the party's dominance of those committees).

Incorrect Answers:

(A) The House Ethics Committee investigates ethics charges against House members.

(B) The Senate has the power to provide "advice and consent" to the president on judicial nominees. The House has no power in this area.

(C) There is no single committee that sets a limit for the number of House subcommittees. The number of subcommittees is limited by budget and staffing considerations.

(E) The House Committee on Government Reform and Oversight considers changes to federal election procedures.

10. **B** Parties in multiparty systems tend to be smaller and more closely identified with particular ideologies and political goals. Parties in a two-party system, on the other hand, present more general platforms in order to win a simple majority of the electorate.

Incorrect Answers:

(A) Influencing the outcome of elections is a primary goal of all political parties. American political parties are no exception.

(C) American political parties are extremely effective at raising money, and American elections are the costliest in the world.

(D) In a multiparty system, each party more closely mirrors the ideology and political goals of its members. The United States' two parties reflect only a narrow range of political perspectives, and many Americans' political views fall outside that range.

(E) American political parties rarely focus on a single goal or issue because doing so may alienate potential supporters. American political parties are organized around very general beliefs. The Democrats tend to believe that government intervention can be effective and so have a greater inclination toward regulation of businesses and social issues. Republicans tend to distrust government intervention and, in most instances, oppose government regulation. There are a few hot-button issues (abortion rights, gun rights) that cause some contradictions in these political party belief systems.

11. **E** When government officials resign from office, many remain in Washington to work as consultants. Such individuals can use the contacts they made while in government to influence public policy. Often they work as or with lobbyists. The term *influence peddling* is used to describe their actions when they exploit friendships with current government officials to achieve a political goal.

Incorrect Answers:

(A) *Influence peddling* refers specifically to actions that directly affect government policy.

(B) Although a former president may be trying to influence a current president, the action described does not define the term *influence peddling* as it is conventionally used.

(C) *Influence peddling* refers specifically to the actions of lobbyists. Therefore, this answer is incorrect.

(D) See the explanation for (C).

12. **A**   Political action committees (PACs) are organizations created for the purpose of raising political funds and distributing them to candidates.

Incorrect Answers:

(B)   The primary purpose of PACs is to raise funds for electoral campaigns. The action described in this answer choice is performed both by political parties and by state and local governments.

(C)   The vast majority of PAC contributions go to incumbents. The goal of PACs is to endorse the election of those who represent their points of view. They do not try to defeat all incumbents per se, but rather those who are their political opponents.

(D)   The primary purpose of PACs is to raise funds for electoral campaigns. Although many PACs are affiliated with the types of public interest groups that organize protests, this is not something that PACs themselves generally do.

(E)   See the explanation for (B).

13. **B**   Network news programs tend to favor information that changes regularly and can be communicated quickly. Public opinion poll results fit both of these criteria. In contrast, candidates' positions on issues are often complex and difficult to capture in sound bites or TV-friendly phrases and clips. Furthermore, they rarely change. Therefore, news programs may report such information once during an election, but they will not report it repeatedly as they do poll results. As a result, the network news audience is most likely to be aware of where candidates stand in the current polls.

Incorrect Answers:

(A)   The stances of special interest groups on positions is usually stable, so network news will usually report on the position once, then not again, since "no change" is not usually considered newsworthy. Contrast this with the low stability of public opinion toward candidates.

(C)   Candidates' positions on international issues tend to be stable and considered newsworthy one time only (except when a candidate switches).

(D)   Candidates' positions on domestic issues tend to be stable and considered newsworthy one time only (except when a candidate switches).

(E)   Candidates' voting records are stable and considered newsworthy one time only (except when a new vote is newsworthy or a switch from past votes).

14.   **D**   This is a simple memorization question. As the question stem says, most people think about only freedoms of speech and religion when speaking of the First Amendment, but it will benefit you on the exam to be familiar with the lesser-discussed facets of each Amendment. The First Amendment states that "Congress shall make no law…abridging…the right of the people…to petition the Government for a redress of grievances."

Incorrect Answers:

(A) This choice probably looks familiar because it's in the Fifth Amendment.

(B) Same here—Fifth Amendment.

(C) This choice is the Eighth Amendment.

(E) This one is the Fourth Amendment. Accordingly, they can all be eliminated. Be sure to re-read those Amendments regularly!

15.   **E**   While the right to privacy is not explicitly mentioned in the Constitution, in *Griswold v. Connecticut* the Warren Court ruled that the Bill of Rights contained an implied right to privacy. In the case of *Roe v. Wade*, the Court established national abortion guidelines by extending the inferred right of privacy from *Griswold v. Connecticut*.

Incorrect Answers:

(A) You can eliminate this choice because *Near v. Minnesota* and *New York Times v. Sullivan* focused on freedom of the press, not privacy.

(B) You can cross off this choice because the cases of *Texas v. Johnson* and *Morse v. Frederick* were rulings regarding freedom of speech.

(C) Throw out this choice because cases *Thornhill v. Alabama* and *Cox v. New Hampshire* were related to the freedom of assembly and association.

(D) The cases of *Epperson v. Arkansas* and *Lemon v. Kurtzman* were related to freedom of religion, so you can eliminate (D) also.

16.   **D**   *Federalism* is a system under which the federal government shares power with the states. The Tenth Amendment to the Constitution reserves to the states all powers not granted the national government by the Constitution. Therefore, it is instrumental in defining the relationship between the two levels of government, which is the essence of federalism.

Incorrect Answers:

(A) The system of checks and balances among the three branches of the federal government concerns the national government only. Because federalism involves the relationship between the states and the federal government, this cannot be the correct answer.

(B) International treaties are the sole responsibility of the federal government, and do not relate to the states in any way.

(C) Washington, D.C., does have special constitutional status as the nation's capital. The federal government plays a role in governing the city, and the city is not represented in Congress. However, Washington's constitutional status has little influence on American federalism.

(E) The president's power to grant reprieves and pardons is solely a function of the federal government. Because federalism involves the relationship between the states and the federal government, this cannot be the correct answer.

17. **A** *Judicial review* is the Supreme Court's power to overturn laws on the basis of their constitutionality. Judicial review is not mentioned in the Constitution. The practice was established by Chief Justice John Marshall in the 1803 decision *Marbury v. Madison*.

Incorrect Answers:

(B) The census must be taken every ten years, according to Article I, Section 2 of the Constitution, which states the following:
"The actual Enumeration shall be made within three years after the first meeting of the Congress of the United States, and within every subsequent term of ten years."

(C) The rules governing the impeachment of the president are contained in the body of the Constitution. To bring about an impeachment, the House of Representatives must vote to bring an impeachment trial (thus serving a role equivalent to that of a grand jury). The Senate serves as the trial jury, and the Supreme Court presides.

(D) Article II, Section 3, of the Constitution states that the president "shall from time to time give to the Congress information of the state of the union."

(E) The Constitution states that federal judges "both of the supreme and inferior courts shall hold their offices during good behavior." This means that judges are appointed for life and can be removed only for criminal or disgraceful behavior.

18. **C** Each state has its own set of laws, and violations of those laws are prosecuted in state courts. The federal government also has a set of laws, and violations of these are tried in federal courts. Occasionally, the two legal systems overlap. For example, the defendants in the Oklahoma City bombing trial destroyed a federal building and killed federal employees, all federal crimes. Clearly the bombing also violated state laws prohibiting murder, destruction of property, and reckless endangerment. When this happens, the federal and state governments negotiate to decide who will try the case.

State cases, however, may be appealed to federal courts on constitutional grounds. Thus, although the two court systems are generally autonomous, they are not completely independent of each other.

Incorrect Answers:

(A) Federal courts may overturn state court decisions, but only on the grounds that a defendant's constitutional rights were violated. Federal courts may not rule on whether state courts have correctly applied state law (state Supreme Courts are the final arbiters of such cases).

(B) See the explanation for (C).

(D) This is an incorrect statement. Federal courts are not solely appeals courts.

(E) See the explanation for (C).

19. **C** The Constitution specifically delegates to the president the power to veto laws. It does not mention the power to veto parts of laws. The Supreme Court declared the line-item veto unconstitutional in *Clinton v. New York* on the grounds that the Constitution does not give the president the authority to cancel parts of taxing and spending bills because this would give the president too much legislative influence.

Incorrect Answers:

(A) The line-item veto gave legislative powers to the president, not executive powers to the legislature.

(B) The bureaucracy has no role in the line-item veto. The bureaucracy is responsible for carrying out the laws enacted by Congress and signed by the president. If the president's line-item veto power had been upheld, the bureaucracy would have had to implement the law as passed.

(D) The line-item veto did not involve the states.

(E) Judicial review is performed by the Supreme Court, not the Senate. If the Senate objects to a House bill, it merely votes against the bill.

20. **A** The president may, "on extraordinary occasions, convene both Houses, or either of them, and in case of disagreement between them, with respect to the time of adjournment, he may adjourn them to such time as he shall think proper." Otherwise, the president's powers to influence legislation are primarily political. As the most prominent political figure in the United States, the president can strongly influence public sentiment on legislation.

Incorrect Answers:

(B) The president may not introduce bills to the floor of Congress. He or she may recommend bills to Congress, but Congress is under no obligation to consider those bills.

(C) The president has no power to address Congress, except when he or she delivers his or her State of the Union address. Of course, the president does not need to speak on the floor of Congress to influence congressional votes, because his or her position on most bills is a matter of public record. As the leader of his or her party, the president also exerts some influence over the way congresspersons of his or her party vote.

(D) The president may not vote on congressional acts. He or she has a much greater power, however: the power to reject congressional legislation through a veto. The vice president votes in case of a tied vote in the Senate.

(E) The president has no power to disband congressional committees. Under extraordinary circumstances he or she may adjourn the entirety of Congress, but he or she has no special power to dissolve a committee. If the president did, he or she could stop any congressional investigation of his or her administration by dissolving the committee in charge of the investigation. That, needless to say, would run counter to the system of checks and balances.

21. **B** Access to the president is handled primarily by the chief of staff, who screens requests from other executive officers to meet with the president. The chief of staff is often the president's closest confidant. He or she knows the president's agenda and can help coordinate executive actions to best accomplish those goals. The close relationship between the two allows the chief of staff to filter reports and any requests headed for the president's desk in an effort to keep the president from becoming overwhelmed. The chief of staff also mediates disputes among various cabinet offices.

Incorrect Answers:

(A) Vice presidents have as much or as little power as the president gives them. Former Vice President Al Gore was more active than most who preceded him. Other vice presidents have had very few official duties.

(C) The national security advisor is one of the president's top foreign policy advisors. However, he or she does not control the president's schedule.

(D) The chair of the Federal Reserve Board exerts tremendous influence over the American economy.

(E) The press secretary provides press releases and answers press queries on behalf of the president.

22. **C** Article II, section 2 of the Constitution says that two-thirds of the Senate must concur with a treaty, so choice (C) is correct.

Incorrect Answers:

(A) The president alone is responsible for deploying troops and forcing Congress into session.

(B) Congress is responsible for appropriations bills.

(D) See Choice A reasoning above.

(E) Vice presidents are chosen by delegates at the parties' national conventions.

23. **D** Those most active in both the Republican and Democratic parties tend to be further from the political center than are average or *rank-and-file* party members. Because party activists control much of the nomination process and because they are more likely than others to vote in primary elections, successful presidential nominees tend to reflect the political agendas of these activists. This has been particularly true of the Republican Party in recent years; most candidates for the Republican presidential nomination focus great effort on winning support from the party's small but powerful ultraconservative wing.

Incorrect Answers:

(A) The opposite is true. While conservative Republicans are generally more successful in the primaries, these same candidates have a more difficult time appealing to the moderate general electorate in November.

(B) Party members are expected to support their party's presidential candidate. If (B) were true, no Republican could ever win the presidency, because most Democrats and moderate Republicans would vote Democratic. Such a sizable coalition would win every election.

(C) People join the political party that most closely reflects their political views. Most Republicans do care whether their presidential nominee shares their views, at least on a few issues they consider important.

(E) Rank-and-file members participate in the Republican nominating process by voting in primary elections.

24. **A** The large size of the House of Representatives means that more work can be done in committees than when all representatives are assembled on the floor.

Incorrect Answers:

(B) Confirmation powers are not relevant to committees, so eliminate this choice.

(C) In both the Senate and the House, members to committees are assigned by the majority party, so eliminate this choice.

(D) Committees in both the Senate and the House consist of members from both parties, although the majority party generally has more members.

(E) Finally, although choice (E) is true, it does not account for differences between the two chambers of Congress.

25. **C** America's increased prominence in foreign affairs (I) has increased the power of the president. As chief of state, the president receives and negotiates with foreign leaders. Congress generally allows the president great leeway in handling foreign relations. Therefore, as America's role in world affairs has increased, so too has the power of the presidency. Increased government responsibilities (III) are enforced and partly administered by the executive branch. As leader of the executive branch, the president has gained power as a result of this increased responsibility. Constant media exposure (IV) has given the American public greater awareness of each president since Franklin Roosevelt. The president is now better known and more widely heard than at any time in the past. This allows the president to influence voters in a way that no president before 1932 possibly could.

Incorrect Answers:

(A) This answer is partly correct. However, statements III and IV are also true.

(B) This answer is partly correct. However, statement III is also true.

(D) Statement II is incorrect. Public confidence in the government has been in decline since the 1960s. The Vietnam War, the Watergate scandal, the Iran-Contra affair, and the government shutdown of 1993 are just a few of the events that have resulted in increased public cynicism toward the government.

(E) Statements III and IV are true, but so is statement I, which is not included in this answer choice. Also, statement II is incorrect (see explanation for (D)).

26. **E** The House and the Senate must pass the same version of a bill before the president may consider it. Often, the two houses pass different versions of the same bill. They then meet in a conference committee to draft a compromise bill, which then returns to each house to be voted on again. Bills drafted by conference committees usually bypass the committee stage and are immediately scheduled for a floor vote in each house.

Incorrect Answers:

(A) The president may not sign a bill until an identical version of it has been passed by both the House and the Senate.

(B) Before a bill such as the one described returns to each house, the two houses meet to try to draft a compromise bill. Bills drafted by conference committees usually bypass the committee stage and are immediately scheduled for a floor vote in each house.

(C) See the explanation for (E).

(D) See the explanation for (E).

27. **E** Note that this is another "EXCEPT" question, so don't let the phrasing trick you. Only (E) is false because there is a strong correlation between higher education and a tendency to vote. Therefore, individuals with postgraduate degrees are more likely to vote than individuals with only undergraduate degrees, so (E) is the right answer.

Incorrect Answers:

(A) This choice is incorrect because it's true—people are less likely to vote if they believe one candidate is too far ahead of the others.

(B) This choice is also true, as white-collar workers do vote more often than blue-collar workers, but people who belong to unions are very likely to vote.

(C) A strong party affiliation makes one more likely to vote.

(D) Minorities, except those with high incomes, vote less often than whites, so this option is also true.

28. **A** Married, white males have preferred the Republican candidate for president in every election since 1972.

Incorrect Answers:

(B) While the voting habits of white females overall can vary, unmarried white females have favored the Democratic candidate in every presidential election since 1992 (Clinton, Gore, Kerry, and Obama).

(C) Since Franklin Roosevelt's presidency, African Americans have overwhelmingly identified as Democrats in a trend that continues to the present. Barack Obama won a whopping 96% and 93% of the African American vote in 2008 and 2012, respectively.

(D) The majority of youths voted for candidates Jimmy Carter (1976), Bill Clinton (1996), and Barack Obama (2008 and 2012).

(E) Individuals earning below poverty-level wages tend to favor social programs for low-income individuals (Medicaid and the Affordable Care Act are examples) promoted and supported by Democratic candidates more than Republican candidates.

29. **D** The Fourteenth Amendment states that

"No state shall make or enforce any law which shall abridge the privileges or immunities of citizens of the United States; nor shall any state deprive any person of life, liberty, or property, without due process of law; nor deny to any person within its jurisdiction the equal protection of the laws."

The amendment proved ineffective, however, in preventing racial discrimination and segregation. Civil rights advocates had to struggle for almost 100 more years before the government banned all discrimination based on race, religion, gender, or national origin with the Civil Rights Act of 1964. The Civil Rights Act gave the government the power to enforce desegregation by cutting off federal funding to discriminatory programs. It also allowed the Justice Department to file desegregation suits.

Incorrect Answers:

(A) The presidential veto is a presidential action while the Civil Rights Act of 1964 prevents discrimination against citizens.

(B) The system of checks and balances ensures that none of the three government branches get too powerful. This system was unaffected by the Civil Rights Act of 1964.

(C) This answer choice is the opposite: The Civil Rights Act of 1964 empowered the federal government over state government.

(E) The Taft-Hartley Act of 1947 was designed to restrict some of the rights granted to unions by the Wagner Act of 1935. It prohibited closed shops (which required union membership as a prerequisite to hiring), restricted labor's right to strike, prohibited the use of union funds for political purposes, and gave the government broad power to intervene in strikes.

30. C Among the powers granted Congress by the Constitution is the right to pass laws "necessary and proper" to the performance of its duties. This section of the Constitution is called the *elastic clause* because it allows Congress to stretch its powers beyond those that are specifically granted it (called *enumerated powers*) by the Constitution. When Congress passed a national speed limit law in 1974, it invoked the elastic clause by citing its enumerated power to regulate interstate trade.

Incorrect Answers:

(A) The elastic clause pertains to Congress, not to the Supreme Court.

(B) This answer describes a common event, but it does not illustrate the elastic clause as described in the explanation for (C).

(D) Raising taxes is among Congress's enumerated powers. Therefore, the action described in answer (D) does not illustrate the elastic clause as described above in the explanation for (C).

(E) The elastic clause pertains to Congress, not to state executives such as governors.

31. **B**   In "Federalist No. 10," James Madison warns of the dangers of political factions. He also acknowledges that political factions are inevitable. He concludes that American federalism, as embodied in the U.S. Constitution, checks the dangers of factions through the separation of powers, making it difficult for a faction to control the entire governing process. According to Madison, so many different regional and economic agendas are represented in federal and state government that it would be impossible for any single group to gain undue control or disrupt the entire system.

Incorrect Answers:

(A) *The Federalist Papers* take a negative view of political factions and would not have approved of any political system that encouraged their growth.

(C) According to *The Federalist Papers*, Republican federalism limits the influence of political factions on all levels of the government.

(D) In "Federalist No. 10," Madison acknowledged that political factions form whenever people disagree and whenever individuals put their personal welfare above the best interests of the state. Political factions, he concluded, are inevitable in any system so long as humans remain human.

(E) *The Federalist Papers* were written in defense of the U.S. Constitution, which does not ban political factions.

32. **E**   Each of the answer choices correctly identifies a weakness of the Articles of Confederation. However, neither the Articles nor the original Constitution had a universal suffrage clause. Under both, blacks and women were among those who had no right to vote, and states could add further restrictions on the right to vote. Many states allowed only property owners to vote, for example.

Incorrect Answers:

(A) Under the Articles of Confederation the national government was entirely dependent on the states to enforce national law, as it had no executive powers of its own. The Constitution rectified this problem by establishing the executive branch of government.

(B) Under the Articles of Confederation state governments held the power to impose trade tariffs. The Constitution grants this power to Congress.

(C) Under the Articles of Confederation the national government had no authority to regulate interstate trade. The Constitution grants this power to Congress.

(D) Under the Articles of Confederation the national government was dependent on the states to provide soldiers for national defense. This system proved unreliable at best. The Constitution grants Congress the power to raise an army.

33. **A** The Constitution is not precise in explaining how the president and Congress are to share power. As a result this relationship is dynamic, relying partially on the political popularity of the two institutions. When a president is popular—as Franklin Roosevelt was when he first took office—he can parlay that popularity into political clout and may dominate national policy decision making. When a president is unpopular—as Truman was in the year preceding his reelection—then Congress gains the upper hand and can largely determine national policy on its own.

Incorrect Answers:

(B) Congress's power to determine national policy relies on the relative political strength of Congress and the president. Since the ratification of the Constitution, Congress has seen its powers grow and shrink in conjunction with its political fortunes.

(C) Congress's power is in fact expanded by the elastic clause, which grants Congress the right to pass laws "necessary and proper" to the performance of its duties. Congress regularly uses the elastic clause to broaden its scope of influence.

(D) During times of war, the president grows more powerful relative to Congress. Congress is hesitant to challenge the president in wartime, as most congresspersons believe that the country must remain unified during emergencies.

(E) Congress exerts little control over the judicial branch. It can pass laws, such as sentencing guidelines, that limit judicial action. The Senate confirms federal judicial appointments and so influences the judiciary in that way. By and large, however, the judiciary is independent of congressional influence.

34. **C** The president appoints cabinet leaders and can appoint whomever he or she chooses without regard for their political party membership, so (C) is the correct answer.

Incorrect Answers

(A) Although the leaders are appointed, the departments are established by Congress.

(B) Despite this connection, cabinet departments often have goals that differ from those of the president.

(D) There are 15 cabinet departments and numerous other sub-agencies or independent agencies with cabinet-rank status.

(E) This choice is true—the president appoints cabinet members and controls that.

35. **D** The *winner-take-all* system of the electoral college distorts the results of the popular vote. In 1992, Ross Perot received 19% of the popular vote but 0 electoral votes. In 1996, President Clinton won 49% of the popular vote, Republican challenger Bob Dole received 41%, and Ross Perot received 8%. In the electoral college, however, Clinton won 70%, Dole 30%, and Perot 0%. The discrepancy was also apparent in 2000.

	% of Popular Vote	Electoral Vote	% of Electoral Vote
Gore	48.38	267	49.63
Bush	47.87	271	50.37
Nader	.42	0	0
Buchanan	2.74	0	0

The election of 2000 was one of the closest in American history. It was unusual because the winner of the popular vote lost the election in the electoral college. A difference of 400 to 500 popular votes in Florida would have given the election to Gore because he would have received all of Florida's electoral votes. As it turned out, Bush won the presidency by the minimum number of electoral votes possible, with Gore winning the national popular vote.

Incorrect Answers:

(A) Forty-eight states allocate their electoral votes by the "winner-take-all" method. The two exceptions are Maine and Nebraska, which give two electoral votes to the candidate who wins a plurality of the statewide vote, and one vote to the winner of each of the state's congressional districts. In 1996, Maine had four electoral votes, Nebraska had five.

(B) Each state is represented in the electoral college by a delegation equal in number to the state's total representation in Congress (senators and members of the House). California has the greatest number of electoral votes (54); several states have only three electoral votes, the minimum a state may have (two senators and one member of the House).

(C) The electoral college was established by the Constitution as it was originally ratified.

(E) Senators and representatives are prohibited from the electoral college by the Constitution. Electors are generally chosen from among state party leaders and state legislators.

36. **C** Even in 2010, a reactionary and anti-incumbent election, 85% of Republican incumbents and 70% of Democratic incumbents were still returned to office. In short, incumbents have a huge advantage over challengers, primarily because voters are better acquainted with incumbents.

Incorrect Answers:

(A) Winning reelection to the Senate is considered slightly more difficult than winning reelection to the House. Because the Senate is a smaller legislative body than the House, each seat in the Senate is relatively more powerful than a seat in the House. As a result, Senate races are more hotly contested than House races.

(B) No such spending limits exist in House campaigns. Incumbents usually outspend their challengers by considerable sums during election campaigns.

(D) Even in anti-incumbent election cycles, such as 1994 or 2010, an overwhelming majority of incumbents were returned to office by voters.

(E) Of 362 incumbents who ran for reelection in 1994, only 26 were unopposed. The great majority of incumbents face a challenger in the general election.

37. **E** Of the members of the 111th Congress, 225 (42%) earned a law degree prior to serving in office. This fact should come as no surprise, given that the business of Congress is to pass laws. And as prominent members of the community, lawyers often have the standing to run for and win elected office.

Incorrect Answers:

(A) In the same Congress, 38% of members were former businesspeople, but given the purpose of Congress, lawyers are a safer guess.

(B) Given the percentages of lawyers and business people, 80% in total, a professional athlete could be a legislator, but the majority are not.

(C) See the explanation for answer (B).

(D) See the explanation for answer (B).

38. **B** The House Ways and Means Committee controls tax and trade legislation. It is considered one of the most powerful committees in Congress.

Incorrect Answers:

(A) The Commerce Committee considers legislation on such topics as consumer affairs, medicine and medical research, energy, and national and international trade. It is a powerful committee and as such has some influence on tax policy, but not as much as the Ways and Means Committee, which considers all tax legislation before it reaches the floor of the House.

(C) The Education and the Workforce Committee considers legislation concerning national testing, public schools, and workplace issues.

(D) The Resources Committee considers legislation concerning the United States' natural resources.

(E) The Judiciary Committee considers legislation covering numerous topics such as patents, crime, immigration policy, telecommunications regulations, and Constitutional amendments.

39. **E** The Pendleton Act of 1883 was passed in response to charges of patronage in the awarding of government jobs (the "spoils system"). The Pendleton Act created the Civil Service Commission to oversee examinations for potential government employees.

Incorrect Answers:

(A) The Truman Doctrine was a foreign policy of the United States at the outset of the Cold War. Its goal was to contain Soviet expansion.

(B) The Fair Labor Standards Act of 1961 increased the minimum wage to $1.15 per hour.

(C) The National Industrial Recovery Act was a New Deal program that sought to revitalize U.S. industry during the Depression.

(D) The Civil Rights Act of 1964 banned discrimination in public places and gave the government the power to prosecute discriminatory institutions and businesses. It also allowed the government to cut off funding to segregationist and discriminatory programs.

40. **A** To maintain the "one person, one vote" principle of American government, Congress is required to redraw election districts every 10 years, in conjunction with the national census.

Incorrect Answers:

(B) Regardless of when congressional districts are redrawn, congressional incumbents are reelected at a rate of approximately 90% or more.

(C) Redistricting is a political battle in which the party in power attempts to draw districts in such a way as to increase their representation in Congress. Frequently, redistricting plans are challenged in court by the minority party.

(D) The Speaker of the House is chosen by the majority party in the House of Representatives.

(E) Redistricting can increase the number of female and minority congresspersons. In recent years, the courts have, on occasion, forced Congress to create minority districts and take other measures to increase minority representation. However, this has not historically been the purpose of redistricting. Congressional lines have been redrawn every ten years since the beginning of the republic, yet increased female and minority representation is a relatively recent phenomenon.

41. **D** The chart shows that between 66% and 78% of registered voters participate in presidential elections (1988, 1992, and 1996), but that only slightly more than half participate in midterm congressional elections (1986, 1990, and 1994).

Incorrect Answers:

(A) More than half of all eligible voters participated in the elections of 1988 and 1992. Furthermore, this chart provides information only for elections between the years 1986 and 1996. Therefore, any answer that draws a conclusion about elections in years before 1986, as answer (A) does, must be incorrect.

(B) The number of registered voters actually decreased between 1992 and 1994. Furthermore, this chart provides information only for elections between the years 1986 and 1996. Therefore, any answer that draws a conclusion about elections in years before 1986, as (B) does, must be incorrect.

(C) The chart provides no information about elections during the 1970s. Also, this answer assumes that voter satisfaction can be gauged by turnout rates, which is a disputable conclusion.

(E) Because this chart provides information only for elections between the years 1986 and 1996, answer (E), which requires you to draw a conclusion about all elections during the twentieth century, must be incorrect.

42. **C** Businesspeople and investors constitute a small but powerful segment of U.S. society. They are the majority of voters in only a very few, very wealthy voting districts.

Incorrect Answers:

(A) Lobbyists representing businesses and investors are typically better funded than those representing the interests of people with lower incomes.

(B) Business lobbies, such as the U.S. Chamber of Commerce, are among the most enduring in Washington. Over their many decades in the capitol, these groups have made and maintained relationships with many important policy makers.

(D) Because election campaigns are so expensive, candidates must solicit funds. People who donate generously gain the candidate's friendship in return. Although legislators do not always follow their donors' suggestions—indeed they cannot because they have many different donors with diverse goals and interests—they must pay close attention if they expect to receive contributions to their next campaign.

(E) The most effective lobbies in Washington are those campaigning for obscure changes to regulations and tax codes. Because these issues are not widely followed by the public, lobbyists who pursue such changes encounter less opposition.

43.   **A**   Of the five groups mentioned, white Southerners are easily the most conservative. In recent years this group's traditional support for the Democratic Party has dwindled to the point that many southern congressional seats that had been held by Democrats since the end of Reconstruction are now held by Republicans. Many Southerners joined the Democratic coalition after the Civil War ended (the Republicans, remember, were the party of the abolition movement). This allegiance was strengthened during the New Deal, but has weakened since. A large segment of the white South adheres to conservative fundamentalist Christianity and is uncomfortable with the government activism and social programs associated with the Democratic Party.

Incorrect Answers:

(B)   Labor unions are traditionally perceived as liberal, particularly concerning government regulation of the workplace.

(C)   The majority of African Americans support some form of the liberal social programs that Democrats generally support and most Republicans oppose.

(D)   Northern ethnic minorities are traditionally liberal on economic issues. Some, particularly those that are predominantly Catholic, can be conservative on social issues. However, they are generally more liberal in this regard than are white southern fundamentalists.

(E)   Environmentalism is strongly associated with liberalism, as many of its goals involve government regulation of America's natural resources.

44.   **D**   Younger voters are less likely to vote than older voters. Politically active voters, such as those in unions or those who are active in party politics, are more likely to vote; therefore, you may eliminate (A) and (C). Generally, voters with more education and higher incomes are more likely to vote, so eliminate choice (B), since professionals earn more money than those without professional degrees. Voters in swing states are more likely to vote because they are more likely to feel that their votes matter; therefore, eliminate (E).

45.   **B**   People usually join their parents' political party. When their political beliefs change, they do so as a result of economic issues. Of all political issues, economic issues have the greatest impact on personal politics.

Incorrect Answers:

(A)   As people grow older, the views of their peers more greatly influence their political beliefs. Young people generally have little interest in politics, and as a result peer influence on their political beliefs is minimal. In any case, the economy has a greater influence on individual political outlooks.

(C) Because people generally have the same religious beliefs as their parents, religion is extremely unlikely to cause them to choose a party different from the one their parents have chosen.

(D) Employers rarely pressure employees to alter their party allegiance. They are somewhat more likely to seek their support for individual candidates or referenda. By and large, employers do not attempt to influence their employees' political beliefs.

(E) Most Americans do not follow issues in international politics closely, and these issues have little influence on the political beliefs of most.

46. E Of the many popular third parties in American history, only the Republican Party has progressed to the level of a major party. All others were absorbed by one or both of the major parties. The Populists, for example, campaigned for direct election of senators, a graduated income tax, and shorter workdays. Eventually both major parties took up these issues. As they did, the Populist coalition fell apart.

Incorrect Answers:

(A) There have been at least ten prominent third parties in American history. Of them, only the Republican Party went on to become a major party.

(B) A few third parties have had radical goals, but most radical parties never gain enough support to become "popular third-party movements." Some third parties grow around the popularity of a single individual: Ross Perot, George Wallace, and Theodore Roosevelt are some examples. Others champion progressive goals that are later adopted by one or both of the major parties. Examples of these include the Free Soil Party and the Populist Party. Even some of the Socialist Party's goals (especially those concerning workplace conditions) were later adopted by the Democratic Party.

(C) Some supporters of third parties become disenchanted when their candidates fail, but most rejoin the political mainstream.

(D) See the above explanation for question 45, (E).

47. E Because flag burning is usually done as an act of political protest, it is considered speech and is protected by the First Amendment. Due process, (A), has to do with your rights as a prisoner. Assembly, (B), has to do with the freedom to gather in public. The free exercise of religion, (C), is just that, and the American flag is a part of the separation of church and state. And unless your flag is first being confiscated and then burnt, (E) remains the best answer.

48. **B** In *Miranda v. Arizona*, the main question was whether the Fifth Amendment protection against self-incrimination should be applied to state law. The court sided with Miranda and decided that the due process clause of the Fourteenth Amendment did apply to the Fifth Amendment, and that his confession was inadmissible in court. The Court then ruled that the police must advise a suspect of his rights before questioning begins. These rights have come to be known as *Miranda rights*.

Incorrect Answers:

(A) An *ex post facto* law allows governments to prosecute citizens for acts that were legal at the time they occurred but that later became illegal. *Ex post facto* laws are prohibited by the U.S. Constitution. For more on the issues in the *Miranda* case, see the explanation for answer (B).

(C) *Miranda v. Arizona* did not involve cruel and unusual punishment, so this choice is irrelevant.

(D) This case did not involve slavery in any way, so the Thirteenth Amendment is irrelevant here.

(E) The states are required by the Constitution to accept the court judgments, licenses, contracts, and other civil acts of all the other states. This obligation is contained in the "full faith and credit" clause.

49. **C** In 1833, the Supreme Court ruled that the Bill of Rights applied to the federal government only and not to state governments. Since the early part of the twentieth century, however, the Supreme Court has used the "due process" and "equal protection" clauses of the Fourteenth Amendment to extend *some* of the Bill of Rights protections, but has done so on a case-by-case basis. This process of incorporating *some* of the Bill of Rights protections to state law is called selective incorporation.

Incorrect Answers:

(A) See the explanation for (C).

(B) Voting rights have been extended to minorities and women by amendments to the Constitution and by various congressional civil rights acts.

(D) In the early 1970s, the Supreme Court upheld busing children to schools other than the ones closest to their homes to hasten integration. However, that is not what is meant by "selective incorporation." For a definition of this term, see the explanation for (C).

(E) See the explanation for (C).

50. **D** According to the Congressional Budget Office, Social Security alone made up 24% of federal spending in 2014. Other entitlement programs, including Medicare, Medicaid, and CHIP, added significantly to that percentage, making entitlement programs the "largest slice of the pie," in terms of federal dollars.

Incorrect Answers:

(A) In 2014, the defense department took 17% of all federal spending.

(B) The Department of Energy is just a small slice of the 17% of federal money put toward non-defense discretionary spending.

(C) Interest on the national debt made up 6% of all federal spending in 2014.

(E) The Internal Revenue Service, part of the Department of Treasury, has the responsibility to collect U.S. taxes and is just a small slice of the 17% of federal money put toward non-defense discretionary spending.

51.　**A**　The majority party in each house controls all of that house's committees. The committee chair is always a member of the majority party.

Incorrect Answers:

(B) The number of Republicans and Democrats sitting on each committee is determined by negotiation, but the majority party always dominates the most important committees (usually by a two-to-one majority).

(C) Congress takes committee recommendations into consideration, but it does not follow all (or even most) of those recommendations.

(D) See the explanation for (B). Also, Congress takes committee recommendations into consideration, but it does not follow all (or even most) of those recommendations. Thus, statement III is also incorrect.

(E) Statement I is correct, but statements II and IV are incorrect. When a committee vote results in a tie, the result simply remains a tie vote.

52.　**C**　The Gramm-Rudman Acts were intended to reduce budget deficits. Their best-known provision, in favor of automatic across-the-board budget cuts, was ruled unconstitutional by the Supreme Court. Although the laws failed to substantially reduce the federal deficit, they did heighten public awareness of the deficit issue.

Incorrect Answers:

For this type of detail question, you really need to know what the Gramm-Rudman Acts were; the other choices are wrong because they don't deal with budget deficits.

53.　**E**　Iron triangles are sometimes referred to as *subgovernments*. They are formed by the close working relationship among various interest groups, congressional committees, and executive agencies that enforce federal regulations. Working together, these groups can exert a powerful collective influence over legislation and law enforcement.

Incorrect Answers:

For this detail question, (A), (B), (C), and (D) are all wrong because they do not accurately describe the iron triangle.

54. **B** A sound bite refers to a brief remark, extracted from a longer piece of audio, that summarizes a politician's comments, views, or beliefs. Accordingly, (B) is the correct answer. "Horse race" politics occurs when the press is more concerned about who is up or down in the polls than with reporting information on the candidates' positions and qualifications. Eliminate (A). Sound bites can be negative or positive, so neither (C) nor (D) is necessarily correct. Choice (E) does not reflect a reason that sound bites are used; polling data shows who the public believes won or lost.

55. **C** In the 1965 Supreme Court case of *Griswold v. Connecticut*, the Court ruled that the Bill of Rights contained an implied right to privacy. The Court ruled that the combination of the First, Third, Fourth, Fifth, Ninth, and Fourteenth Amendments added up to a guarantee of privacy. The *Griswold* case concerned a state law banning the use of contraception. The Court decision overturned that law.

    Incorrect Answers:

    (A) The right to privacy is guaranteed by the federal government. States must comply with this protection under the Fourteenth Amendment.

    (B) The right to privacy is implied by the Constitution; it is never directly stated. For more information, see the explanation for (C).

    (D) Common law consists of the entire body of previous judicial decisions. It originated in medieval England and persists to this day, underlying much of American statute law (laws passed by legislatures). Common law does not guarantee the right to privacy.

    (E) See the explanation for (C).

56. **C** The chart shows little difference between the presidential votes of men and women in both the 1972 and the 1976 elections. Starting with the 1980 election, however, a clear gender gap can be seen, with women consistently giving greater support to the Democratic candidate than the men do.

    Incorrect Answers:

    (A) The chart shows that, had only men voted, Ronald Reagan would have won the 1980 election by a greater margin than he actually did.

    (B) The chart shows that from 1980 forward a smaller percentage of women than men voted for the Republican presidential candidate.

    (D) Because the chart illustrates only the percentage of votes from each gender, it is impossible to draw a conclusion about the number of votes that the candidates received from men and women.

    (E) Because the chart depicts election results only from 1972 to 1996, it is impossible to draw a conclusion concerning every presidential election in history.

57. **D** The graph shows that the South experienced the greatest increase in Medicare funding from 2000–2012, having increased by $6.6 million over the 12-year period. Eliminate (A) because the West did not experience a continual increase in funding; funding declined from 2004 to 2008. Choice (B) can be eliminated because the South received the most Medicare funding in 2012. Eliminate (C) because, in 2008, the North received approximately one and a half times the amount of Medicare funding as the Northeast. Finally, eliminate (E) because the Midwest and the East did not receive the same amount of Medicare funding in 2004.

58. **C** The right to pardon is extended to both presidents and governors and is the full release from legal punishment. Presidents and governors can also issue reprieves, but a reprieve is merely a postponement of legal punishment.

Incorrect Answers:

(A) As mentioned in the explanation for (C), pardons last forever.

(B) As mentioned in (C), pardons are permanent whereas reprieves are postponements, which makes this an opposite answer.

(D) Presidents have the ability to issue pardons.

(E) Presidents have the ability to issue reprieves.

59. **B** Programs designed to rectify social inequality based on past racial and gender discrimination are called affirmative action programs. Most such programs create special hiring and educational opportunities for women and racial minorities.

Incorrect Answers:

(A) The New Federalism was the name of Ronald Reagan's attempted reorganization of the federal government. Its goal was to shift governmental power from the national government to the states. The plan failed. States feared that the New Federalism would result in higher state budgets, resulting in unpopular tax increases.

(C) Social Security benefits are payments made to the elderly, disabled, and other entitled beneficiaries from a government trust fund. The source of the fund is a tax (called FICA) collected on payrolls and individual paychecks.

(D) A bill of attainder is a legislative act that applies to an individual or easily identified group in such a way as to constitute punishment. (For example, if the legislature passed a law that prevents John Smith from driving because John Smith is a political agitator.) Bills of attainder are unconstitutional.

(E) Gerrymandering refers to the process of dividing a geographical area into political divisions in such a way as to achieve an unlawful or ulterior goal. (For example, redrawing voting districts so that minority voters are split into different districts and their power consequently diluted.)

60.   C   The exclusionary rule holds that evidence obtained in unwarranted searches must be excluded from trial. It also requires the government to have just cause to search private property and to demonstrate that cause before a judge. The rule was established by the Supreme Court decision *Mapp v. Ohio*. The case involved Dollree Mapp, who had been convicted in Ohio for possession of obscene materials. Her original conviction was based on evidence found by police who were looking for evidence of illegal gambling. The police had not obtained a search warrant to search for either evidence of gambling or pornography, so the search was illegal.

Incorrect Answers:

(A) The Supreme Court decision *Plessy v. Ferguson* established the principle of "separate but equal," which was later overturned in *Brown v. Board of Education*.

(B) Because this involves excluding people, it is a tempting answer choice. However, this is not the meaning of the term *exclusionary rule*.

(D) Interstate commerce is controlled by the federal government under provisions of the Constitution. For an explanation of the exclusionary rule, see the explanation for (C).

(E) See the explanation for (C).

FREE-RESPONSE SECTION: ANSWERS AND EXPLANATIONS

Remember that you need to answer all four free-response questions in 1 hour and 40 minutes, so you do not have time to waste, nor can you skip any questions. Nevertheless, you should take time to brainstorm some ideas and to organize what you come up with before you start to write each response. Otherwise, your responses will probably be incomplete, disorganized, or both.

You should average about 25 minutes per question and that amount of time should be sufficient. Make sure you read each question carefully and respond directly to each of its components in your response. The questions are about broad issues, but they ask for specific information. A general free response that fails to address specific concerns raised by the question will not earn a high score.

Question 1

Let's break this question down into its parts so that you don't feel overwhelmed. First up, part (a), two ways that candidates are using the Internet in their campaigns. One point will be earned for each way that you identify how candidates are using the Internet. Possible answers may include the following:

- Fund-raising through the Internet. In the 2004 primary, Howard Dean raised $27 million online. Online fund-raising has exploded since then, with Barack Obama raising over $500 million from the Internet alone. He broke all fund-raising records by raising $150 million for the month of September 2008, with $100 million coming from online donations.
- Contacting supporters through e-mail. Many candidates send out a weekly e-mail blast to their supporters. John Kerry had more than 3 million names on his campaign e-mail list after his loss in 2004, while Barack Obama was able to gain a staggering 13 million addresses en route to his 2008 victory. President Obama's transformation of this list into his grassroots group "Organizing For America" has been used to help mobilize popular support for his policies.
- Posting videos of speeches to campaign websites or YouTube.
- Posting Internet advertisements. Candidates can purchase ads on websites that are frequented by potential supporters.
- Using social media such as Facebook, Twitter, Instagram, Snapchat, and the like to make policy statements and respond instantly to news and attacks.
- Posting the candidates' positions on issues. In the 2008 campaign, John McCain and Barack Obama both had sophisticated websites where viewers could learn about the candidates' positions on myriad issues, including health care, the economy, energy policy, immigration, veterans' affairs, education, the war in Iraq, and more.
- Linking to favorable stories in the media.

That wasn't so bad. You were probably able to rattle off the majority of reasons with no problem, just by thinking about what you see online in your day-to-day life.

For Each of These Methods, Explain the Advantages to the Candidate

Now let's tackle part (b) of that question—based on these methods, what are the advantages of Internet campaigning? You should go ahead and brainstorm another list for this one. One point will be earned for each explanation of advantages to the candidate. Possible answers may include the following:

- Cost-effectiveness
- Increased contact with supporters
- Help to get candidate's message out
- Speed
- Bypassing the media
- Campaign retaining control of the content and message
- Environmental responsibility

How Can the Internet Harm a Campaign?

Of course, while Internet campaigning has its advantages, there are also some negative aspects. This third part of the question is worth another two points. One point is earned for identifying how the Internet can harm a candidate's campaign, and one point is earned for the explanation. An explanation point will not be earned if the answer does not connect the harm with how it affects the candidate's campaign. So be sure that you don't go off on a tangent with your discussion of potential drawbacks. Always bring it back to the question and give them the information that they are seeking. Possible examples may include the following:

- One-sided blogs
- Attack videos and ads
- Evidence of a candidate's mistakes posted online
- Viral e-mails that spread unsubstantiated rumors
- Instant social media analysis of a candidate's gaffes

Now you have a plethora of items to support your claims in the essay. All you have to do is flesh out each point to include everything you know about the effects of the Internet on politics.

Here's How to Crack It

1. The advent of the Internet has greatly affected politics.

   (a) Identify two ways that candidates are using the Internet in their campaigns.

   (b) For each of the methods identified in part (a), explain the advantages to the candidate of using the Internet this way.

   (c) Identify and explain one way that the Internet can harm a candidate's campaign.

Always start by reading the question carefully. If necessary, reformulate it in your own words so that you are sure exactly what you are being asked. On the exam, the questions are in a green booklet; use some blank space in that green booklet to make lists from your brainstorming, as we just did. Outline your response, incorporating the best points from the list you brainstormed. Don't skip this step: The best responses are well planned. In order for your reader to follow you, you have to know where you are going before you start.

When the question asks you to define or identify a concept, that is all you have to do. You don't need to write a long paragraph or give an example. Simply define and identify.

Often, one of the four free-response questions will involve interpretation of some sort of graphic, whether it be a chart, a graph, data, or a cartoon. You may be asked to identify a trend in the chart or to interpret the cartoon. Usually, it will be quite obvious what the information in the graphic is about, so don't overthink these aspects of such questions.

When the question asks you to explain or analyze a concept, you need to make sure that you have written an adequate response that addresses all parts of the question. This part of your answer should be at least a paragraph long. It is advisable to include an example in your response. Often that example you included can be just the tool you need to demonstrate your mastery of the material. And here's what makes the AP Government and Politics exam so much fun: Your examples don't necessarily have to be factual. Often you can make up your own example. If you can think of an actual example, that's great; but if not, just make up a plausible sounding theoretical example.

So for part (c) you might talk about how Barack Obama had to combat viral e-mails during the 2008 presidential campaign claiming that he was not born in the United States and that he was a Muslim. Another strong example for (c) comes from George Allen's 2006 reelection campaign for the Virginia Senate, when he was harmed by the ramifications of calling an opponent's supporter "macaca." Furthermore, it's worth noting that the Internet can ruin a candidate's chances for election before the campaign even begins. In 2011, New York Congressman Anthony Weiner, an advocate for 9/11 first responders' issues and touted candidate for the 2013 New York City mayoral race, resigned from Congress in disgrace after a highly publicized scandal involving lewd photos and inappropriate messages sent via Twitter. But even if you couldn't think of a real-life example, you could offer a hypothetical example of an imaginary candidate harmed in a similar case of the Internet being used to reveal evidence or spread word of negative incidents, real or alleged.

Note that no part of the rubric gives points for an introductory paragraph, thesis statement, or conclusion. You can include those if you must, but you will get no points at all for doing so. It is more advisable to put that time into writing thorough explanations or analyses for those sections of the question. Time wasted on writing content that will not contribute to your grade is time that you're *not* thinking about and writing what the graders are looking for. Just because you don't have to worry about the usual writing elements such as introductions, thesis statements, transitions, or conclusions, doesn't mean that you won't be expected to write cohesive responses.

One common mistake that students make is not addressing the question fully. For example, if a question asks you to explain how the commerce clause has allowed the federal government to strengthen civil rights, you must give a specific explanation that connects the commerce clause to federal power and civil rights. If you just wrote about the use of the commerce clause and didn't connect it to civil rights, you will not earn the points. Or in the sample question about how the Internet might harm a candidate's campaign, make sure that you clearly connect the harm to a candidate. This might seem obvious, but you'd be surprised how often students get off on a tangent and lose sight of what the question is asking about. So, don't go on a rant about how blogs are coarsening political discourse and then forget to connect your answer to how blogs can harm a candidate.

Sample Excellent Free Response

Currently, candidates use the Internet to
1. Solicit donations from their supporters
2. Send out immediate responses to what their opponents have said

A candidate can save money by contacting his or her supporters through e-mail and asking them for donations. Previously, candidates would spend millions of valuable campaign dollars on mass mailings to potential supporters asking for money. Now, a candidate can just send out a mass e-mail that costs very little. These mass e-mails do not waste paper as a traditional mail pamphlet would, so this technique is more environmentally friendly as well. If you visit a candidate's website, you will often be asked to sign up with your e-mail address. Once you do that, you can expect to receive countless e-mails with information about the candidate and requests for money. Sometimes the candidate will ask your opinion of various issues through polls on their websites. Then they can specifically tailor their requests for donations to the issues in which you've expressed interest. In 2004 Howard Dean jumped into a lead in the Democratic primaries through his ability to excite supporters and raise money through the Internet. Then in 2008, Barack Obama's campaign was able to raise so much money, mostly through the Internet, that he was able to forego public financing for his presidential run.

Before the Internet, there would have been a time delay when a candidate wanted to respond to something that an opponent had said. A candidate might have sent out a fax or issued a press release to the media. Then he had to sit back and hope that the media would air his response. Now, to address immediate issues, a candidate can send out an e-mail blast to his supporters. He can send his press releases not only to the media but also to sympathetic bloggers. He can slip an answer to The Drudge Report. For example, if your opponent gave a speech advocating a federal health insurance program to protect all citizens, you could send out an e-mail detailing how much such a program would cost and how your opponent will have to raise taxes to pay for his program. Blogs and supportive opinion sites would then quote you directly or use your talking points to craft their own criticism of your opponent.

One way that the Internet can harm a candidate's campaign is how it can amplify a candidate's gaffes. With video-sharing websites such as youtube.com, a video of a candidate making a mistake can be posted and then played over and over again. People can post that video on their own blogs and then make fun of the candidate. Networks can use that video to broadcast the blunder. Late-night comics can use the video to ridicule the candidate. We saw this happen to George Allen when he called a supporter of his opponent a "macaca." Once the supporter was able to upload the video of that short interchange onto the Internet, Allen's campaign was irrevocably damaged, as cable TV, political websites, and bloggers began to ridicule George Allen. The word "macaca" is a little-known word that is commonly understood to be a racial slur used in Francophile African nations. Allen's mother grew up in the Francophile African nation of Tunisia, which led people to assume that he used this word as a racial slur. Allen insisted that he didn't know the meaning of "macaca" when he said it, but the damage was already done. His campaign was completely thrown off stride and never fully recovered. No one cared about anything else he had to say; all they wanted to talk about was his "macaca moment." Important issues and policies fell by the wayside, as the media and the constituents focused entirely on this bizarre exchange. All of this because someone posted a short video onto the Internet. Without the video, the interchange might have been described, but it wouldn't have had the same impact that the video provided. In today's video-sharing Internet age, candidates have had to become much more careful of everything they say or do. One misstep or poor word choice can spell the end of their campaigns.

Question 2

What Is Soft Money?

"Soft money" is money donated by corporations and unions directly to political parties. Soft money contributions are supposed to be used for such general purposes as get-out-the-vote campaigns, voter registration drives, expenses involved in the day-to-day running of party headquarters, and campaign propaganda that relates to the party rather than to specific candidates: For example, T-shirts and balloons that say "Vote Democrat" as opposed to "Vote Clinton."

Corporations, unions, and trade groups are all prohibited by law from donating directly to candidates. Up until recently, they had been able to make unlimited soft-money contributions. According to the electoral watchdog organization Common Cause, the top 50 soft-money contributors in 1996 each donated an average of $800,000. Top donors such as Philip Morris, AT&T, and the Trial Lawyers Association each contributed more than $2 million. In 1996, the two parties raised a total of $260 million in soft money.

In 2002, Congress passed the Bipartisan Campaign Reform Act (BCRA), also known as the McCain-Feingold bill. This law made it illegal for the major political parties to raise and spend soft money, though other organizations still can and do. This law was upheld by the Supreme Court in *McConnell v. FEC* (2003), though some provisions were struck down in *Citizens United v. Federal Election Commission* (2010).

In the *Citizens United* case, the Court removed limits on groups that fund political action without explicitly endorsing or coordinating with specific candidates, declaring these to be free speech. The funds subsequently raised by these so-called Super PACs have increased considerably the amount of soft money spent on elections.

Why Do the Congressmen in the Cartoon Want to Defend Soft Money, and Who Doesn't?

Soft money became an important source of campaign financing for several interrelated reasons.

- In the 1976 Supreme Court case *Buckley v. Valeo*, the Court ruled that election spending limits could not be imposed on candidates and parties. The Court ruled that, in politics, spending is equivalent to speech; spending limits, therefore, violate the First Amendment. The Court allowed for spending limits only when they are voluntary. For example, presidential candidates are eligible for federal matching funds, but only if they agree to comply with spending limits. The Court did, however, allow limits on the amount that an individual can contribute to a candidate or party, stating that "to the extent that large contributions are given to secure a political *quid pro quo* from current and potential office holders, the integrity of our system of representative democracy is undermined." As a result of the Court's partial rejection of spending limits, elections quickly grew more expensive. That trend escalated rapidly; in the 2000 election (the last presidential election before BCRA), candidates and parties spent more than $3.4 billion on campaigns.
- As noted above, federal law limits the amount of money an individual may contribute to general federal elections and individual candidates to no more than $2,500 per election to any federal candidate, $30,800 per year to a national party, and $10,000 per year to a state or local party committee. To a PAC (political action committee) endorsing a candidate or candidates by name, individuals can contribute no more than $5,000. The lack of limits on Super PACs—those that do not coordinate with or endorse specific candidates—have, since 2010, made those groups a promising funding option for parties and candidates seeking to circumvent hard money restrictions.

- Federal law also prohibits corporations, labor unions, and trade associations from contributing directly to candidates. Since 1978, however, the Federal Election Commission (FEC) has allowed corporations and unions to make unlimited donations to political parties for those general purposes described above. This money is what is known as "soft money." Every year since 1978, both parties expanded the purposes for which they used soft money. In 1996, for example, both parties used soft money for the first time to finance television ads. These ads did not specifically mention candidates and so may not have technically violated FEC regulations. However, in every other way they were virtually identical to individual campaign ads, and the intent of these ads was certainly the same as those of campaign advertisements. Though the Super PACs created after the 2010 *Citizens United* decision cannot endorse or coordinate with specific candidates, they have followed this same strategy, intensifying the practice.
- The FEC has very little enforcement power. Its rulings rarely come in time to affect election results. Most of its decisions, in fact, come long after elections are over. Furthermore, the commission's staff and funding have recently been cut drastically, leaving it even less capable of performing its function. In 1996, both parties pushed the limits of FEC regulations. Critics charge that the parties flagrantly broke the rules, knowing that punishment would come too late to change the election results.
- In 1996 the Supreme Court loosened restrictions covering party spending on behalf of candidates. While not removing all spending limits, the Court's decision indicated that any such limitations were subject to the Court's rejection on First Amendment grounds. Each party used the Court's decision to expand its use of soft money.

Before the passing of BCRA, soft money was a hot topic on Capitol Hill. The 2010 *Citizens United* decision and subsequent development of Super PACS have triggered further debate. Most congressmen wanted to defend soft money because it was in their interest to do so. Incumbents always receive the vast majority of all campaign contributions, and soft money contributions strengthened their reelection chances.

Congress was not unanimous on the subject, however. The Democratic Party wanted across-the-board limits on donations, while the Republicans did not. Donation limits would have hurt the Republicans, who received more donations from wealthy Americans than the Democrats. Before the McCain-Feingold bill, the Republican Party raised 50% more soft money than the Democratic Party.

The Republicans, conversely, wanted a ban on soft-money contributions from labor unions, and would have also accepted a ban on donations in congressional elections made from outside the candidate's district (House) or state (Senate). Democrats rejected the limit on contributions from labor unions for one obvious reason: Unions are strong supporters of the Democratic Party. They would have accepted such a ban if a similar one was placed on corporate donations. The Republicans, of course, rejected this idea; total corporate donations to the Republican Party far exceed union donations to the Democratic Party.

Democrats also rejected the Republican proposal for regional limitations on donations. This proposal would have particularly stung the Democrats in the House. Because many Republicans represent wealthy districts, a restriction on outside donations would not hurt them too badly; they would still be able to raise the necessary campaign funds from within their districts. Many Democrats, however, represent poor urban districts. A restriction on outside donations would deprive these Democratic candidates of much of their campaign funding. For these reasons, many Americans saw both sides of the debate as self-interested parties trying to gain electoral advantage, not as legitimate reformists trying to develop a fair system.

Despite the obstacles standing in the way of campaign finance reform, the collapse of Enron and other corporations created an atmosphere that allowed the McCain-Feingold/Shays-Meehan Campaign Finance Reform Act to make it through Congress. It is now known as the Bipartisan Campaign Reform Act, and the jury is still out as to whether it has truly curbed spending.

Should There Be Greater Restrictions on Soft Money? Why or Why Not?

Supporters of the ban on soft money argue that it is the only way to end the upward spiral of election costs. They also believe that such massive campaign contributions from corporations and unions make the average voter extremely cynical about the political process. Few voters believe that those who donate $1 million to a campaign expect nothing in return.

There are, however, legitimate arguments against limits on soft money. A recent *Time* magazine editorial pointed out that a limit on donations to political parties would merely increase the political power of issue advocacy groups, such as the Christian Coalition, the Sierra Club, and the National Rifle Association. These groups, like political parties, run televised advertisements and campaign for candidates. Unlike parties, issue advocacy groups are not required to disclose who donates to them or how much they donate. The net result, therefore, would be a system in which the public was less informed about corporate and union political donations.

Here's How to Crack It

2. The debate over soft money has been a common and important feature of American politics.

   (a) Define "soft money."

   (b) Describe the opposing points of view expressed about soft money by the congressmen in this cartoon.

   (c) Explain the arguments for and against soft money.

Any time a free-response question comes with a cartoon, chart, graph, or quotation, graders will be looking to see whether you understand it. Always make sure to convey an understanding of such material, aside from answering whatever questions you are asked about it. In the case of this cartoon by Markstein, if, at some point, you explain his depiction of Congress at large and of Senators McCain and Feingold, it will be clear that you get the point of the cartoon.

As with any response, you must define key terms in the question, whether or not you are explicitly asked to define them. Here you are specifically asked for the meaning of the term *soft money*, but you should have been prepared to define it even if you were not asked to do so.

Another component of the question has to do with the politics of soft money: Why do some in Congress favor it, while others seek to restrict it? You need reasonable explanations for holding each position.

Finally, you need to evaluate the arguments for and against soft money. You should explore both sides, and express your personal opinion on this issue. Whichever side you choose, you will have to justify your decision.

You should resist the tendency to answer each question separately in a series of unconnected paragraphs. Try to craft a response that addresses all the questions that comprise this topic. A logical way to organize your response would be to make each question the focus of one paragraph, with smooth transitions between them. The difference may not seem great, but the presentation is more impressive if you prove that you see the connections among the distinct questions by answering them all in one response.

Sample Excellent Free Response

"Soft money," the funds that flow from unions and corporations to political parties, have been the target of reformers and satirists in recent years. Unlike the hard money that goes directly from individuals to candidates, soft money is not restricted. As such, it is supposed to be used for only general party purposes, such as get-out-the-vote drives and advertisements for the party as a whole, rather than particular candidates. Parties have nevertheless found ways to avoid the regulations and gain individual electoral advantage from soft money. For that reason, among others, political cartoonists may criticize soft-money contributions. Because incumbents in general, and incumbent Republicans in particular, tend to benefit more than challengers, much support for soft money, like much opposition to it, is self-interest masquerading as public spirit. Partisan politics aside, there are reasons to worry about unlimited money being funneled into the political system.

Most members of Congress want to defend soft money because, as incumbents, they benefit from it more than those trying to unseat them. Because of limits on individual contributions, candidates depend on soft money, even if they misuse it. The Federal Election Commission is too understaffed to catch misuse of funds until after the election has been won. The cartoonist points out that the majority of Congress is dismayed to find that the opposition persists in trying to limit such an advantageous technique for reelection.

Some members of Congress, such as Senators McCain and Feingold (pictured in the cartoon), favor limits on soft money. Many Democrats favor governmental oversight on soft money because they fear the greater fund-raising prowess of the Republican Party. A few good-government types on both sides of the aisle honestly worry about the corrupting influence of soft money, although some members win points with voters by speaking out against soft money while continuing to slyly accept such funds.

Those who argue in favor of less restriction on soft money donations can point to the Supreme Court's 1976 ruling in *Buckley v. Valeo*. Here, the Court defined campaign contributions as a form of free speech and shot down many limits that had been put in place by the Congress of the 1970s. Many libertarians and others who believe in expansive definitions of speech are strong supporters of this ruling and are unperturbed by soft money and its role in American politics. Opponents of soft money cheered the passage of the Bipartisan Campaign Finance Reform Act of 2002—the McCain-Feingold plan—for dramatically limiting the amount of soft money funneled to political parties from interest groups, but though the law was upheld by the Supreme Court in 2003 under *McConnell v. FEC*, some of its restrictions were struck down under the 2010 *Citizens United v. FEC* decision. This leads a third group, cynics, to point to the old adage that trying to stop the flow of money in politics is like trying to stop water from flowing downhill. Instead of stopping the flow of soft money to political parties, the McCain-Feingold Act and the *Citizens United* decision now mean soft money flows to "independent" 527 groups and political action committees (Super PACs) that are formally unaffiliated with the candidate they support. As a result, soft money's influence in politics today remains pervasive—perhaps more than ever before.

Question 3

The first part of question 3 requires relatively little outside information. It is designed to test your ability to read a graph and draw conclusions based on your reading. You must then demonstrate a general understanding of the public's perception of Congress. The second part of the question does require outside information, as it asks for a historical cause for the shift in public opinion demonstrated in the graph. You have more than one good option to satisfy the second question; these options are discussed below in more detail than you would need to earn the highest score on this question. The last part of the question asks you to go well beyond the data in the graph and relate public perception of Congress as a whole with voters' perceptions of their own member of Congress. This part of the question demands information about the rate of reelection of incumbents and the recognition of an apparent paradox: People think little of Congress as an institution, but apparently like their own representatives well enough to reelect them quite often.

Describe the Overall Trend in Citizens' Attitudes Toward Congress. Assess the Degree to Which Public Opinion Has Changed Since 1974.

The trends reflected in this chart are ambiguous enough to allow you a couple of options. You could emphasize the upward trend in public disapproval of Congress. Conversely, you could focus on the fact that the public's approval rating of Congress, while fluctuating over the last 20 years, has generally hovered around the 30% mark, and so has not changed dramatically. Let's explore both options.

- Disapproval ratings have increased. In August of 1974, less than 50% of all Americans disapproved of the way Congress handled its job. That percentage dipped below 50 during the Reagan administration, but it rose above 50% during the Bush administration and has stayed there since. The upward trend in Americans' disapproval of Congress roughly corresponds to the drop in the number of Americans with no opinion of Congress. Even though Congress's approval rating has remained about the same over the last 20-plus years (approximately 30%), Americans overall are more dissatisfied with Congress than they were in the past.
- Approval ratings have remained relatively stable. In April of 1974, approximately 30% of all Americans approved of the job Congress was doing. In August 1997, Congress's approval rating was up slightly, to approximately 32%. The fluctuations in approval ratings of Congress throughout the period shown on the chart demonstrate that American opinion of Congress is volatile for the short term but relatively stable over the long term. The chart does show that disapproval ratings have increased during the period shown. However, it could be argued that this is a temporary aberration. Disapproval ratings were also high during the Ford administration (peaking at 55%) and reached 60%, slightly above their April 1997 level, during the Carter administration.

There is also a third option: acknowledge both trends. Any of these three options, if well executed, will get you on your way to a 5 on this essay.

Explain the Causes and Results of ONE Dramatic Shift in Public Opinion Indicated in the Graph.

The graph illustrates several dramatic changes in public opinion about Congress. Let's consider each.

- **August 1974.** Public approval of congressional performance reached its highest level for the period shown in the chart. In August of 1974, Richard Nixon was forced to resign from the presidency because Congress was initiating impeachment proceedings. The unusually high approval rating shows that the public agreed with this action. Public opinion of Congress often, although not always, fluctuates in inverse proportion to the president's popularity. In other words, when a president is popular, Congress tends to be less popular, particularly if its relationship with the president is adversarial. When a president is unpopular, however, Congress's approval ratings may increase, unless the public is generally dissatisfied with government, in which case everybody's approval ratings drop. In August of 1974, Richard Nixon's approval rating was abysmal (26%, the lowest recorded since 1936), and, not surprisingly, public approval of Congress soared.

- **March 1975.** Public disapproval of Congress jumps from 36% to 54% in just six months. The reason: economic woes. The United States entered a period of extended economic inflation during the mid-1970s. Conflicts in the Middle East led to increased oil prices and a gasoline shortage, doubling gas prices and forcing Americans to wait on line to buy gas for the first time since World War II. During this era, public approval of government was low: Both Congress and President Ford were regarded by the public as incompetent.

- **June 1979.** Public disapproval of Congress reaches 60%. Again, economic problems resulted in a loss of confidence in the government, as the inflation rate exceeded 13%. Also, during this period American concern over nuclear weapons and energy peaked. The Three Mile Island nuclear disaster in March 1979 raised fears that the government was not properly regulating the nuclear energy industry. In June, Congress blocked passage of an arms reduction treaty with the Soviet Union.

- **March 1992.** Public approval ratings bottom out below 20%, and disapproval ratings soar above 70%. During this period, the Democratic Congress was continually at odds with Republican President George Bush, Sr. The hot political issue during this period was the federal deficit, for which the public blamed both Congress and the president. Public opinion of the entire government was extremely low, as demonstrated by the fact that Ross Perot, a presidential candidate with no government experience, won 19% of the popular vote in the general election that year.

- **December 1995.** Public disapproval of Congress increases again in the aftermath of the federal government shutdown. In this case, the majority of Americans held Congress responsible for the shutdown. In particular, they blamed the Republican leadership and the many hard-line conservative representatives who had gained office during the "Republican revolution" in 1994.

Why Do Incumbent Members of Congress Usually Win Reelection?

Regardless of the way you described public opinion in answering the first two parts of the question, it's clear that more people have disapproved of Congress than have approved of it, almost without interruption, for at least 25 years. From your study of congressional elections, however, you may recall that politicians that get elected to Congress, especially after they have gotten reelected once, tend to be quite successful at continuing to win reelection every two years after that, and for as long as they continue to run. This question asks you to consider whether disapproval of Congress as a whole translates into disapproval of individual representatives. The short answer is that it does not. Just as you may think little of professional athletes as a group yet still root for the home team, a negative assessment of the group does not translate into a negative assessment of every member. Members of Congress often run successfully for reelection by asking to be sent back to Washington to clean up the mess there, thus distancing themselves from Congress as an institution. Similarly, voters may see public spending elsewhere as a waste of their money while viewing spending in their own district as beneficial and a reason to reelect their representative who brought it home. You need to show in your essay that you are aware of and can account for the high rate of reelection of individual members of Congress in the face of the persistent disapproval of Congress as a whole.

Here's How to Crack It

3. Using the above graph and your knowledge of U.S. politics, perform the following tasks:

   (a) Describe the overall trend in citizens' attitudes toward Congress. Assess the degree to which public opinion has changed since 1974.

   (b) Explain the causes and results of ONE dramatic shift in public opinion indicated in the graph.

   (c) Explain why, despite the shifts in public approval, incumbent members of Congress usually win reelection.

Graders evaluating answers to this question want to see, first of all, that you can read a graph and draw conclusions based on the information it presents. They will be looking at your response to the second part of the question to see if you can recall a single historical event or set of circumstances that you can link to a shift in the public's opinion of Congress. You need to identify the event or circumstances as well as establish a probable connection to the poll data shown. In answering the third part of the question, you need to demonstrate your familiarity with the high reelection rate of members of Congress and explain how it can coexist with the data in the graph. It is possible to address the three parts of the question in a straightforward manner. If you don't complicate your task with an elaborate introduction and conclusion, you could probably answer this question in less that 25 minutes, creating extra time for one of the other questions or for taking a short break between questions.

Sample Excellent Free Response

Generally, negative public opinion of Congress over the last 25 years has fluctuated somewhat as a function of various events, and has failed to translate into electoral difficulties for individual members of Congress running for reelection.

Two major trends are noticeable in the chart. First, public disapproval of Congress has risen since 1974. In 1974, disapproval ratings were below 50 percent. They even dropped below 40 percent in April 1974. Since then, however, disapproval ratings have generally been above 50 percent and at times have been much higher. Approval ratings, on the other hand, have remained near 30 percent. Overall, it seems that public opinion of Congress has changed slightly for the worse since 1974. More people formerly had no opinion of Congress; most of those people seem to have shifted over to the disapproval category. This is probably because media coverage of Congress has grown more extensive and more negative over the past 20 years.

One dramatic shift in public opinion of Congress took place in December 1995, when the graph shows disapproval reaching the second highest peak recorded there, near 70 percent. The failure of both the president and Congress to agree on a budget caused a shutdown of all nonessential activities of the federal government. The Republican majority in Congress wanted to speed up deficit reduction and cut funding of social programs. When the Democratic president would not agree, Congress shut down the government rather than pass stop-gap appropriations bills. The public disapproved of the government shutdown and blamed Congress for it, resulting in much higher levels of disapproval.

Although disapproval of Congress has remained high, the public is not refusing to reelect incumbent representatives who seek to keep their seats. Members have expanded district office staffs, providing helpful, nonpartisan constituent services that keep their name recognition high and their individual popularity well above that of Congress as a whole. High levels of public spending allow representatives to claim credit for new buildings, roads, canals, and the like, and lead voters to appreciate the benefits their district is getting from their congressperson, even if they view Congress as a whole as spendthrift for repeating that spending in each of the other districts.

Thus Congress remains relatively unpopular, occasionally extremely so, but individual representatives are not tainted by that disapproval when they run for reelection.

Question 4

On this Free Response Question, students may earn a total of eight points on this question. Two points are available for part (a), two for part (b), and four for part (c).

Part (a) asks you to explain how formal amendments are made to the Constitution. You'll earn one point for each of the two you explain. Although the question does not state so, one must be about the proposal and one must be about ratification.

Proposal may include

- Two-thirds vote (extraordinary, not simple, majority) in the Senate and the House of Representatives
- National convention called by Congress but initiated by the request of two-thirds of the state legislatures

Ratification may include

- Approval of three-fourths of the state legislatures
- Special conventions in three-fourths of the states

Part (b) asks you to explain why formal amendments are rarely made. You will earn one point for stating a reason and other another point for elaborating on that reason. Some of the possible reasons you may choose to discuss include the difficulty of obtaining the number of votes needed, the cost incurred by having a convention, or time limits imposed for a bill to be approved as an amendment.

Part (c) asks you to describe two additional ways that the interpretation of the Constitution can be changed. You will earn one point each for identifying two possible ways and one point each for giving a specific example of those ways. Some of the ways you might discuss include the following:

- Judicial Review
  Possible Examples: *Dred Scott v. Sanford, Brown v. Board of Education,* or *Miranda v. Arizona*

- Elastic (Necessary and Proper) Clause
  Possible Examples: formation of a national bank or Roosevelt's New Deal

- New Political Norms
  Possible Examples: the presidential cabinet, members of the House of Representatives living in the districts they represent, or the president delivering an annual State of the Union address in front of Congress

Part III
About the AP U.S. Government and Politics Exam

- The Structure of the AP U.S. Government and Politics Exam
- How AP Exams Are Used
- Other Resources
- Designing Your Study Plan

THE STRUCTURE OF THE AP U.S. GOVERNMENT AND POLITICS EXAM

The AP U.S. Government and Politics Exam is a two-part test. The chart below illustrates the test's structure.

Section	Question Type	Number of Questions	Time Allowed	Percent of Final Grade
I	Multiple Choice	60	45 minutes	50
II	Free Response	4	100 minutes	50

The test is designed to test an overview of U.S. government. It doesn't give all subjects equal weight, however. Here's how the test questions break down.

Subject	Percent of Questions
Constitutional underpinnings	5 to 15
Political beliefs and behaviors	10 to 20
Political parties, interest groups, and mass media	10 to 20
Institutions of government: Congress, president, judiciary, and bureaucracy	35 to 45
Public policy	5 to 15
Civil rights and civil liberties	5 to 15

While most of the questions deal with the institutions of government, the questions are nearly evenly divided among the four institutions. There are no definition questions, although you need to know the definitions of words to understand the questions. The questions tend to deal with the dynamics of how government operates within a political environment. For example, you may be asked how interest groups attempt to influence policy making in Congress and the bureaucracy or how the president attempts to influence Congress through public opinion. The test writers want to know whether you understand the general principles that guide U.S. government and the making of public policy.

In addition to the multiple-choice questions, there are four mandatory free-response questions. You'll have a total of 100 minutes to answer all of them. You should spend approximately 25 minutes per question, but be aware that you must manage your own time. Additional time spent on one question will reduce the time that you have left to answer another. Writing more than is necessary to answer the question will not earn you extra points.

The graders assign each of your free-response answers a numerical score. Weighing the average on the free responses and the score on the multiple-choice questions each as 50%, the graders create a final score from a low of 1 to a high of 5. The chart below tells you what that final score means.

Score (Meaning)	Percentage of test takers receiving this score	Equivalent grade in a first-year college course	Credit granted for this score?
5 (extremely qualified)	11.9%	A	Most schools 9.8%
4 (well qualified)	12.4%	A–, B+, B	Most schools 13.6%
3 (qualified)	26.5%	B–, C+, C	Some do, but some don't 24.7%
2 (possibly qualified)	24.6%	C–	Very few do 25%
1 (no recommendation)	24.6%	D	No 26.9%

The data above is from the College Board website and based on the May 2015 test administration.

To score your multiple-choice questions, award yourself one point for every correct answer and credit 0 points to your score for every question you left blank. Remember that there is no longer a guessing penalty on the test. This will give you a raw score.

Here's what that score would translate into on the AP U.S. Government and Politics Exam, assuming you performed as well on the essay questions.

Multiple-Choice Raw Score	AP Score
0 to 26	1
27 to 35	2
36 to 43	3
44 to 52	4
53 to 60	5

Of course, if you follow our advice for how to write a good free-response essay, you could score higher on the free-response section than on the multiple-choice section and thus potentially increase your final score by one point.

How Will I Know?
Your dream college's website may list such information or you can contact the school's admission's department to verify AP exam score acceptance information.

HOW AP EXAMS ARE USED

Different colleges use AP Exams in different ways, so it is important that you visit a particular college's website in order to determine how it accepts AP Exam scores. The three items below represent the main ways in which AP Exam scores can be used.

- **College Credit.** Some colleges will give you college credit if you receive a high score on an AP Exam. These credits count toward your graduation requirements, meaning that you can take fewer courses while in college. Given the cost of college, this could be quite a benefit, indeed.

- **Satisfy Requirements.** Some colleges will allow you to "place out" of certain requirements if you do well on an AP Exam, even if they do not give you actual college credits. For example, you might not need to take an introductory-level course, or perhaps you might not need to take a class in a certain discipline at all.

- **Admissions Plus.** Even if your AP Exam will not result in college credit or even allow you to place out of certain courses, most colleges will respect your decision to push yourself by taking an AP Course or, even, an AP Exam outside of a course. A high score on an AP Exam shows mastery of more difficult content than is typically taught in many high school courses, and colleges may take that into account during the admissions process.

OTHER RESOURCES

There are many resources available to help you improve your score on the AP U.S. Government and Politics Exam, not the least of which are your **teachers**. If you are taking an AP course, you may be able to get extra attention from your teacher, such as feedback on your essays. If you are not in an AP course, you can reach out to a teacher who teaches AP U.S. Government and Politics to ask if he or she will review your essays or otherwise help you master the content.

Another wonderful resource is **AP Central**, the official website of the AP Exams. The scope of the information available on this site is quite broad and includes the following:

- course descriptions, which include further details on what content is covered by the exam
- sample questions from the AP U.S. Government and Politics Exam
- free-response question prompts and multiple-choice questions from previous years

The AP Students home page address is: **http://apcentral.collegeboard.com/home.**

Finally, **The Princeton Review** offers tutoring, small group instruction, and admissions counseling. Our expert instructors can help you refine your strategic approach and enhance your content knowledge. For more information, call 1-800-2REVIEW.

DESIGNING YOUR STUDY PLAN

In Part I, you identified some areas of potential improvement. Let's now delve further into your performance on Practice Test 1, with the goal of developing a study plan appropriate to your needs and time commitment.

Read the answers and explanations associated with the multiple-choice questions (starting at page 30). After you have done so, respond to the following questions:

- Review the topic chart on page 72. Next to each topic, indicate your rank of the topic as follows: "1" means "I need a lot of work on this," "2" means "I need to beef up my knowledge," and "3" means "I know this topic well."

- How many days/weeks/months away is your exam?

- What time of day is your best, most focused study time?

- How much time per day/week/month will you devote to preparing for your exam?

- When will you do this preparation? (Be as specific as possible: Mondays and Wednesdays from 3:00 P.M. to 4:00 P.M., for example)

- Based on the answers above, will you focus on strategy (Part IV) or content (Part V) or both?

- What are your overall goals for using this book?

Part IV
Test-Taking Strategies for the AP U.S. Government and Politics Exam

PREVIEW

Review your Practice Test 1 results and then respond to the following questions:

- How many multiple-choice questions did you miss even though you knew the answer?

- On how many multiple-choice questions did you guess blindly?

- How many multiple-choice questions did you miss after eliminating some answers and guessing based on the remaining answers?

- Did you find any of the free-response questions easier or harder than the others—and, if so, why?

HOW TO USE THE CHAPTERS IN THIS PART

Before reading the following strategy chapters, think about what you are doing now. As you read and engage in the directed practice, be sure to think critically about the ways you can change your approach.

Chapter 1
How to
Approach
Multiple-Choice
Questions

THE BASICS

The directions for the multiple-choice section of the AP U.S. Government and Politics Exam are pretty simple. They read as follows:

Directions: Each of the questions or incomplete statements below is followed by five suggested answers or completions. Select the one that is best in each case and then fill in the corresponding oval on the answer sheet.

In short, you're being asked to do what you've done on many other multiple-choice exams: Pick the best answer and then fill in the corresponding bubble on a separate sheet of paper. You will *not* be given credit for answers you record in your test booklet (by circling them, for example) but do not fill in on your answer sheet. The section consists of 60 questions, and you will be given 45 minutes to complete it.

The College Board also provides a breakdown of the general subject matter covered on the exam. This breakdown will not appear in your test booklet; it comes from the preparatory material the College Board publishes. Here again is the chart we showed you in Part III:

Subject	Percent of questions
Constitutional underpinnings	5 to 15
Political beliefs and behavior	10 to 20
Political parties, interest groups, and mass media	10 to 20
Institutions of government: Congress, president, judiciary, and bureaucracy	35 to 45
Public policy	5 to 15
Civil rights and civil liberties	5 to 15

Constitutional underpinnings	• the political and economic circumstances at the time of the framing of the Constitution • the motivations of the Framers • the weaknesses of the Articles of Confederation • the strengths of the Constitution • separation of powers • the nature and political impact of federalism • principles of democratic government • system of checks and balances
Political beliefs and behavior	• the ideological beliefs people maintain regarding their government • political socialization • public opinion and its impact on policy • how and why citizens vote as they do • the methods of political participation • the reasons citizens disagree over political beliefs and behavior
Political parties, interest groups, and mass media	• what parties do and how they operate • how parties are organized • how parties link citizens to government • how parties help make and use the rules of elections • how electoral laws affect the outcome of elections • what interest groups do and what makes them effective • the role of PACs and their impact on the political process • the types of mass media • the purpose of the media • the impact of the media on the political agenda

The institutions of government: Congress, president, judiciary, and bureaucracy	• the structure and function of the legislature, executive branch, judiciary, and bureaucracy • the structural and political interrelationships of the institutions of government • the connections between the national government, citizens, political parties, public opinion, elections, interest groups, and the states
Public policy	• the process of making public policy • citizen participation in policy making • the interactions between Congress, the courts, and the bureaucracy on policy making • the impact of elections in policy making • the participants in domestic and economic policy making • the limitations of domestic and economic policy making
Civil rights and civil liberties	• substantive and procedural rights and liberties • the impact of the Fourteenth Amendment on rights and liberties • the consequences of judicial interpretation on rights and liberties

As you can see, the primary focus of the test is the nuts and bolts of the federal government. The test also emphasizes political activity—the factors that influence individual political beliefs, the conditions that determine how and why people vote, and the process by which groups form and attempt to influence the government. All these subjects, you should note, are important. As much as 30% (or as little as 10%) of your exam may focus on constitutional issues and civil rights.

TYPES OF QUESTIONS

The majority of questions on the multiple-choice section of the test are pretty direct. Here's an example.

1. A "pocket veto" can occur only when

   (A) Congress amends a bill
   (B) the president is out of the country
   (C) a bill passes Congress with a greater than two-thirds majority in each house
   (D) the Supreme Court has ruled that the proposed legislation is unconstitutional
   (E) a bill reaches the president's desk within 10 days of the end of a congressional session

Sometimes, the College Board makes the questions a little trickier. One way it does this is by phrasing a question in such a way that four answers are correct and one is incorrect. We call these questions "NOT/EXCEPT" questions because they usually contain one of those words (in capital letters, so they're difficult to miss). Here's an example.

2. In the twentieth century, the Democratic Party traditionally received majority support from all of the following groups EXCEPT

   (A) the wealthy
   (B) African Americans
   (C) Jews
   (D) union members
   (E) teachers

Another way the College Board tricks test takers is the Roman Numeral format question. This type of question can have more than one correct answer. Here's an example.

3. The increased use of the presidential primary since the 1960s has had the following effect(s)

   I. Weakened the influence of the political parties
   II. Increased the power of political activists in the parties
   III. Increased the cost of running for political office
   IV. Increased the drama of the party convention
   V. Decreased the number of persons challenging incumbents

   (A) I only
   (B) I, II, and III only
   (C) II and III only
   (D) II and IV only
   (E) III, IV, and V only

Once or twice during the multiple-choice section, you will be asked to interpret an illustration, often a map or a political cartoon. These are usually rather easy. The key is *not* to try to read too much between the lines. Here's an example.

"Sorry, but all my power's been turned back to the states."

Lee Lorenz ©1981 from *The New Yorker Collection*. All Rights Reserved.

4. The principle of government most relevant to the cartoon is

    (A) judicial restraint
    (B) checks and balances
    (C) federalism
    (D) executive privilege
    (F.) representative democracy

Finally, there will be one or two questions on the test asking you to interpret a graph or chart. Again, these are usually very direct, and the most important thing for you to do is *not* to over-interpret the data. The correct answer will be indisputably supported by the information in the chart. Here's an example.

Average, highest, and lowest approval ratings, by percentage of all eligible voters, for U.S. presidents, 1953 to 1974			
	Average	Highest	Lowest
Eisenhower	65	79	48
Kennedy	70	83	56
Johnson	55	79	35
Nixon	49	67	24

Source: Gallup poll

5. Which of the following conclusions can be drawn from the information presented in the chart above?

(A) Eisenhower was the most consistently popular president in the nation's history.
(B) Kennedy received greater congressional support for his programs than did any other president during the period in question.
(C) Nixon's lowest approval rating was the result of the Watergate scandal.
(D) The difference between Johnson's highest and lowest approval ratings was the greatest for any president during the period in question.
(E) Eisenhower and Johnson were equally well liked by all Americans.

Answers to these and other drill questions appear at the end of this chapter.

HOW TO CRACK THE MULTIPLE-CHOICE SECTION

The AP U.S. Government and Politics Exam is, by Educational Testing Service (ETS) standards, a straightforward test. Unlike the SAT, for example, on the AP U.S. Government and Politics Exam the questions and answers are not designed to trick you. The subject matter can be found easily in this workbook, often in the chapter summaries. You should, however, not be lulled into believing the test is easy because it covers material that can be readily obtained from reading the newspaper and watching television. This so-called "street knowledge" is not enough to ensure a passing grade on the exam. The AP U.S. Government and Politics Exam is an academic test that requires knowledge from the textbook. Information acquired from contemporary sources such as newspapers and television will probably not be needed in the multiple-choice sections of the test. It will, however, be needed for the essay sections of the test, particularly if you are asked for examples.

If you've paid attention in class, you should do well on this test. If you haven't paid close attention, you may still be able to master the material if you review intensively. Use the subject review that appears later in this book as your guide. Either way, you will do better if you know what to expect of the test. On the next few pages, we'll discuss some things that all AP U.S. Government and Politics Exam multiple-choice sections have in common.

The Questions Are of Mixed Difficulty

The examination is made up of questions of varying difficulty. It is not unusual to have many questions on the examination that fewer than 50% of the students answer correctly. Some are so difficult that fewer than 25% of students answer them correctly. There are also some very easy questions, which the vast majority of students answer correctly. But watch out for the really difficult questions that may involve very technical issues, such as committee seniority or campaign finance reform.

There Are No Trivial Pursuit Questions on This Exam

Here's some more good news. The AP U.S. Government and Politics Exam doesn't ask about trivial matters. You will probably never see a question on the exam such as this one.

6.   The American equivalent of the British
     Exchequer is the

     (A)   House Finance Committee
     (B)   Internal Revenue Service
     (C)   United States Mint
     (D)   Office of Management and Budget
     (E)   Federal Reserve Board

To answer this question correctly, you would have to be fairly familiar with the British government. The AP U.S. Government and Politics Exam does not require such knowledge. This question is atypical in another way as well: It does not have a varied selection of possible answers. Even if you had known that the British Exchequer has something to do with money and government, you could not have eliminated any of the incorrect answers on this question. On an actual AP test, at least a couple of these answers would have been completely unrelated to finance, and you could have eliminated them to guess from among the remaining answers.

Process of Elimination

It is more important to focus on eliminating incorrect answers than on finding the correct answers because that is the most efficient way to take a multiple-choice exam. Use Process of Elimination (POE) to whittle down the answer choices to one, because incorrect answers are much easier to identify than the correct one. When people look for the correct answer among the answer choices, they have a tendency to try to justify how each answer may be correct. They'll adopt a forgiving attitude, but this is a situation in which a savage brutality is needed. Eliminate incorrect answers. Terminate them with extreme prejudice. If you've done your job well, only the correct answer will be left standing at the end.

All of this probably sounds pretty aggressive to you. It is. Good test takers take multiple-choice tests aggressively. They sift through the answer choices, discard incorrect answers without remorse, guess with impunity, and prowl the test searching for questions they can answer, all with the tenacity and ruthlessness of a shark. All right, maybe that's a bit overdramatic, but you get the point. So, eliminate as many answers as you can to increase your odds of answering difficult questions correctly.

Common Sense Can Help

Sometimes answers on the multiple-choice section contradict common sense. Eliminate those answers because common sense works on the AP U.S. Government and Politics Exam.

Think about which of the answer choices to the question below go against common sense.

7. Which of the following best explains the way in which federal legislation is implemented?

(A) Most laws outline general goals and restrictions, which the federal bureaucracy interprets and translates into specific guidelines.

(B) The manner of implementing federal legislation is negotiated between a joint congressional committee and a presidential advisory committee.

(C) All of the regulations pertaining to a piece of legislation are contained within the legislation itself.

(D) After a bill is signed, all disputes pertaining to its implementation are decided by the congressional committee responsible for the bill.

(E) The details of implementing congressional legislation are worked out in the courts on a case-by-case basis.

Here's How to Crack It

You should have been able to apply common sense to eliminate (D) and (E) pretty quickly. Congressional committees work on bills *before* they reach the floor for a vote, and this work takes up all their time. They would hardly have time to hear all disputes concerning bills that have already passed. Furthermore, such a system would violate the system of checks and balances, because the responsibility for interpreting laws belongs to the judiciary. All the same, the details of congressional legislation could never be worked out in the courts. There would simply be too many cases for the courts to be able to process them all. Similarly, (B) contradicts the principle of separation of powers. It is the executive branch's responsibility to enforce the law; it is not required to confer with Congress on the manner in which it performs this task. Choice (C) is impractical. You have no doubt seen "photo ops" of politicians standing before the mountains of federal regulations on the books. Those regulations are created by the federal bureaucracy as guidelines for implementing legislation. They are not contained within the legislation itself. The correct answer, by POE, is (A).

Answer Key for Sample Questions in This Chapter

1. E
2. A
3. B
4. C
5. D
6. B
7. A

Summary

o Rest assured that the AP U.S. Government and Politics Exam tests a relatively small amount of information. Be confident: You can review this material fairly quickly and still get a good grade on this exam.

o Familiarize yourself with the different types of questions that will appear in the multiple-choice section.

o Remember that most of the questions on this exam are of medium difficulty. The test does not bother with trivial matters or minute exceptions to general trends. The test writers want to know that you understand the general principles underlying U.S. government.

o Tailor your studying to suit the test's most common topics. Don't spend a lot of time studying civil rights and civil liberties until you have completely reviewed the workings of the federal government and the basics of political behavior.

o Use POE on all but the easiest questions. Once you have worked on a question, eliminated some answers, and convinced yourself that you cannot eliminate any other incorrect answers, you should guess and move on to the next question.

o Use common sense.

o Remember not to leave any questions blank. There is no "guessing penalty" on this exam!

Chapter 2
How to
Approach
Free-Response
Questions

OVERVIEW OF THE FREE-RESPONSE SECTION

You may be surprised to see the words "free response" at the start of this chapter. No essay? What is a "free response," anyway? The first thing to be aware of is that this response is hardly free. The College Board wants a very specific type of writing, and it is one that you might not be used to. Forget the idea of crafting a fine piece of writing that convinces the reader of your opinion. Instead, think "just the facts, ma'am." Your basic goal here is to read the questions and answer them to the best of your ability. Don't get too hung up on crafting a perfectly organized essay with transitional phrases—this section of the AP should almost stand for "Answer the Prompt"—just crank out a straightforward, clear answer and show the graders that you know your stuff.

You will have 100 minutes to answer four questions, so be sure to budget your time well. Give as much detail as necessary to answer the question, but no more! Above all, don't worry. So long as you know the basics of American government, this section should be a breeze.

WHAT ARE THE FREE-RESPONSE QUESTIONS LIKE?

The AP U.S. Government and Politics free-response section contains four free-response questions. Each counts equally. The entire free-response section counts as 50% of your examination grade. Even though the free responses are all mandatory, you may have some choices within a free-response question. For example, a question may look like this:

1. Procedural due process rights have been expanded since the early 1960s.

   (a) Define procedural due process and explain why it is important to the American legal system.
   (b) Explain the difference between procedural due process and substantive due process.
   (c) Choose two of the following cases and explain how they expanded procedural due process rights.
      • *Mapp v. Ohio*
      • *Gideon v. Wainwright*
      • *Escobedo v. Illinois*
      • *Miranda v. Arizona*

Choices within questions allow you to showcase what you know best, instead of having to write about many subjects, some of which you might not remember as well. Again, depth-not-breadth is the focus here. Think of this as a "data dump" where you can show off your knowledge and "wow" the grader. Note that you will not get a higher score for writing more than what the question requires. You cannot make up points lost in a previous free-response question, so be sure to focus on only the topic that the question asks about. If there is a choice within a question, make certain you choose the subject you know the most about. Be explicit.

Also remember that if the question deals with a Supreme Court case, you shouldn't worry about the background of the case. It is the ruling and the consequences that are important.

If you are confronted with a free-response question that you feel unprepared to answer, don't panic. Skip it and come back to it later. Writing another free-response essay may get your juices flowing and prompt you to recall your knowledge of the first subject. Just remember to keep track of your time so that you have time to return to the question that you skipped.

You cannot be penalized for just *attempting* to write an answer. Therefore, never leave a free-response question blank. Write something about the subject, even if it is just basic knowledge you picked up from a magazine or a website.

The free-response essays are graded using an answer standard, to which only the graders have access. A certain number of points is given for each piece of information supplied correctly. The numerical grade of the essay is determined by adding the points earned for each part of the response.

Each free-response essay uses a different scoring standard. One essay could be graded using a total of five points, another a total of seven points, and another a total of ten points. While the total score for each question may differ, the value of each question is equal in determining the final score on the free-response section. Each of the four free-response questions is worth one-eighth of the total exam, or 12.5%. The highest possible score on the free-response section is 60 points.

A simple way for you to get an idea of the kinds of questions that might be asked, and the structure of an answer standard, is to visit the College Board website at **www.collegeboard.com**. In the section devoted to Advanced Placement, you will find AP U.S. Government and Politics free-response questions from the last five years, with the grading standard for each question. These are extremely helpful. They allow you to acquaint yourself with how the points break down and what the graders are seeking. Be sure to check them out.

Another way to understand the types of questions that may be asked is to look in the table of contents of an AP U.S. Government and Politics textbook. Test writers essentially take the concepts found in a few individual chapters and combine them into a question. For example, they may ask about the ways in which interest groups attempt to influence policy. Information about such a question will be found in the chapters on interest group politics, elections, and the branches of government. The test writers are trying to force you to synthesize (combine, analyze, and evaluate) many separate pieces of information into a coherent point of view. Therefore, the question may be written like this:

1. Interest groups can have both a positive and negative impact on American politics.

    (a) Describe one positive effect that interest groups have on politics.
    (b) Describe one negative effect that interest groups have on politics.
    (c) Choose one of the groups below and identify two methods it uses to affect public policy.
        • NRA
        • AARP
        • AMA
        • NOW

In the free-response section you will not be required to write a complete essay with a thesis statement, evidence, and conclusion: There simply isn't time. This response is an opportunity to showcase your knowledge of U.S. government and politics, not a time to highlight your understanding of proper syntax and your hatred of dangling modifiers. You won't be graded down if you *do* write a thesis statement, evidence, and conclusion, but this practice will waste precious time that you could have spent writing a more complete answer for what they *do* ask of you. **Do exactly the tasks that the question asks of you.** This may seem obvious, but many students get off track and neglect to address all facets of the questions with clear responses. If the question asks you to analyze data by explaining trends shown in a graph, do so. Make sure your analysis can be backed up by the data in the graph. If the graph question contains a Part B (it often does), it will probably ask for an explanation of the data in the graph. This part of the answer will come from your knowledge of the subject. Because time is a factor, and you will be awarded no more points for extras, do nothing more than what the question asks.

See the next page for an example of a stimulus-type free-response question.

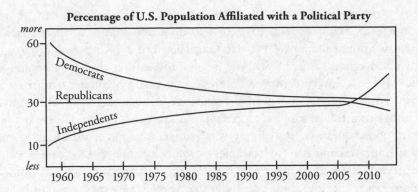

Percentage of U.S. Population Affiliated with a Political Party

2. Using the information in the chart and your knowledge of United States politics, complete the following tasks.

   (a) From the data in the chart, identify two trends that have occurred in the membership of the political parties in the past fifty-five years.

   (b) Based on your knowledge of American politics, explain what impact the two trends that you identified in Part (a) have had on those running for political office.

Part (a): Answer (Keep in mind that this is just an outline.)

- The data shows that the number of Republicans has remained mostly constant.
- The data shows that the number of Democrats has declined.
- The data shows that the number of Independents has increased, especially in the 2000s.
- The data shows that the two political parties are approximately equal in number.
- The data shows that the Independents have mostly come from the Democratic Party.
- The data shows that there are now more self-described Independents than members of the two major parties.

Part (b): Answer

- Independents are people who belong to no party. They vote for the candidate they like best regardless of the party with whom the candidate is affiliated. Independents are usually upset with one of the parties because of the positions they have taken on particular issues. Independents tend to be centrists. Therefore candidates will try to appeal to Independents by taking centrist positions, because Independents will probably decide the outcome of an election. This often makes it difficult to differentiate the policy positions of candidates. Perhaps this is one reason voters say it doesn't matter who they vote for, which in turn can cause depressed voter turnout.

Note that the question in Part (a) does not ask for a thesis statement. It simply asks you to analyze the data. Part (b) also does not require a thesis statement. It contains an explanation of the data and the impact of decreasing party affiliations on elections. You should now be able to see that the free-response essay on the AP U.S. Government and Politics Exam really is different from an essay that you might write in your normal English or History class: It doesn't stress the importance of a thesis, supporting paragraphs, and conclusion. When answering a free-response question, you simply want to share as much information and as many strong, well-constructed examples as you can think of. Don't stress yourself out worrying about the format and flow. Simply get the information from your brain onto the paper and show the grader that you have a strong grasp of U.S. governmental policies and precedents.

Be Optimistic

Both the exam writers and the graders realize that 25 minutes is not very much time to respond to a question. They understand that it will take about five minutes for you to understand the question and begin to organize your answer. Obviously, there is not enough time to give a very in-depth answer. Because of the time constraints, you will have to choose only those parts of your answer that give the strongest response to the question. The graders are not looking for the final word on the subject. Instead, they are checking to see whether you can

- address the question
- clearly explain the issues involved

These should be your goals in writing your AP U.S. Government and Politics Exam free-response essays.

PLANNING AND WRITING YOUR FREE RESPONSE

There are two essential components to writing a successful timed free response. The first is to plan what you are going to write before you start writing. The second is to use a number of tried-and-true writing techniques that will make your essay better organized, better thought out, and better written.

Before You Start Writing

Read the question carefully and figure out what you are being asked. Then, brainstorm for a minute or two. In your test booklet, write down everything that comes to mind about the subject; there is room on the back pages of the booklet and in the blank space at the bottom of the question pages. Look at your notes and consider the results of your brainstorming session as you decide which points you will argue in your response. Tailor your argument to the information, but don't make an argument that you know is wrong or with which you disagree. If you do either of these things, your response will probably be awful. Finally, go through the results of your brainstorming. Some of what you wrote down will be "big picture" conclusions, some will be facts that can be used as evidence to support your conclusions, and some will be interesting material that, nonetheless, will not fit into a well-organized free-response essay and should be discarded.

Next, make an outline. The outline should be brief—just a few words for each paragraph. You should plan to write as many paragraphs as are appropriate for answering the question. For example, some free responses will require two paragraphs on relevant issues; others will need five. Sometimes the question or part of the question can be answered with a couple of paragraphs and a bulleted list. If the question does not require a full essay, you should not write one.

As You Are Writing

Observe the following guidelines:

- **Keep sentences as simple as possible.** Long sentences get convoluted very quickly and will give your graders a headache.
- **Use appropriate political science terminology.** Don't overdo it, however, because it will look as if you're trying to show off. Remember that good writing doesn't have to be complicated; most great ideas can be stated simply. *Never* use a word if you are unsure of its meaning or proper usage. A malapropism may give your graders a good laugh, but it won't earn you any points and will probably cost you a higher score.
- **Write clearly and neatly.** Here's an easy way to put graders in a good mood. Graders look at a lot of chicken scratches; it strains their eyes and makes them grumpy. Also keep in mind that they have as little as two minutes to read each response. Neatly written essays make them happy. When you cross out, do it neatly. Write in blue or black ink. If you're making any major changes—for example, if you want to insert a paragraph in the middle of your response—make sure you indicate them clearly.
- **Define your terms.** Most questions require you to use terms that mean different things to different people. One person's "liberal" is another person's "conservative" and yet another person's "radical." The folks who grade the test want to know what *you* think these terms mean. When you use them, define them. Take particular care to define any such terms that appear in the question. Almost all official College Board materials stress this point, so don't forget: Define any term that you suspect can be defined in more than one way.

- **Use structural indicators to organize your paragraphs.** Another way to clarify your intentions is to organize your response around structural indicators. For example, if you are making a number of related points, number them ("First…Second…Finally…"). If you are attempting to compare and contrast two viewpoints, use the indicators "on the one hand" and "on the other hand" or "whereas."
- **Stick to your outline.** Unless you get an absolutely brilliant idea while you're writing, don't deviate from your outline. If you do, you'll risk winding up with an incoherent response.
- **Back up your ideas with examples.** Yes, we've said it already, but it bears repeating. Don't just throw ideas out there and hope that you're right. You will score big points if you substantiate your claims with facts. If you cannot recall real, specific examples, use hypothetical situations to illustrate your point.
- **Try not to write just one or two paragraphs.** A too-short response will hurt you more than will one that is too long.

HOW TO CRACK THE FREE-RESPONSE QUESTIONS

Answering the free-response questions on the AP U.S. Government and Politics Exam is not very different from answering the essay questions you have been answering all your life. The keys to success are the following:

- **Read the question carefully.** Tailor your answer to the question. When you have written all your notes and your outline, and you are prepared to begin writing your response, reread the question to ensure your answer is right on target.
- **Answer each part of the question directly.** If one part of the question asks how Jefferson's concern about term limitations is relevant today, you should probably have a sentence in your essay—and in a fairly prominent place such as the first paragraph or the first line in a subsequent paragraph—that reads "Jefferson's concern is relevant (or irrelevant) today." Don't be coy.
- **Don't panic.** As you scan the four questions, you may well come to rest on the one that deals with a subject your teacher didn't cover or you didn't get around to studying. Don't worry: Everyone finds some questions harder than others. To build your confidence, answer the question you find easiest before turning to the intimidating one.
- **Watch your time.** You need to average no more than 25 minutes per question. The biggest mistake you can make, with the exception of failing to respond to the question, is failing to leave yourself enough time to answer all four questions. It's okay to spend as much as 30 minutes on a given question, but you'd better make it worthwhile. You also probably don't want to spend that much time on the first essay or you'll feel rushed while writing the remaining three.

- **If you draw a total blank on a question, take a deep breath and ask yourself what you do know about the topic.** You may realize that you know more than you think. Try to figure out what the question is asking and/or how you can approach it.
- **If you are running out of time on your fourth free-response question, abbreviate and write partial sentences.** The graders know that you may have to rush to finish the last question. Although, under ideal circumstances, you would write in complete, well-considered sentences, you may not have time to do so. Don't panic: Do the best you can and know that the graders will give you some leeway at the end of your response—especially if you are clear and coherent at the beginning and throughout the middle.

Summary

o   Read questions carefully. Look for the multiple parts of each question. Make sure you respond to each of these parts of the question—the graders will be looking for your response to each part.

o   Mark up the question. You may bracket the core of the question, underline the operative words such as *identify*, *discuss*, *describe*, and *analyze*, or circle limiters like, "since 1992," "give one example," and "list three."

o   Look out for questions that require a definition of a term. If they ask for a definition, write one.

o   Although you are not writing a history essay, making chronological points can strengthen your writing in certain areas (for example, the development of civil rights law). Do not write a mere list of historical data points in chronological order. Political science relies on analytical writing to substantiate claims, so back up your statements with proof.

o   Don't start writing until you have brainstormed, chosen a thesis if required, and written a brief outline.

o   Follow your outline. Stick to one main idea per paragraph. Support your ideas with facts.

o   Write clearly and neatly. Don't use sentences that are too long. Toss in a couple of political science terms that you know you won't misuse. When in doubt, stick to simple syntax and vocabulary.

o   Take a watch to the exam and spend 25 minutes on each response. Write explicitly and without equivocation.

o   Every piece of data that supports your argument should be linked to it. Do not just list information without relating it to the point you are trying to make.

Chapter 3
Using Time
Effectively to
Maximize Points

Very few students stop to think about how to improve their test-taking skills. Most assume that if they study hard, they will test well, and if they do not study, they will do poorly. Most students continue to believe this even after experience teaches them otherwise. Have you ever studied really hard for an exam, and then blown it on test day? Have you ever aced an exam for which you thought you weren't well prepared? Most students have had one, if not both, of these experiences. The lesson should be clear: Factors other than your level of preparation influence your final test score. This chapter will provide you with some insights that will help you perform better on the AP U.S. Government and Politics Exam, as well as on other exams.

PACING AND TIMING

A big part of scoring well on an exam is working at a consistent pace. The worst mistake that inexperienced or unsavvy test takers make is to come to a question that stumps them, and rather than just skip it, they panic and stall. Time stands still when you're working on a question you cannot answer, and it is not unusual for students to waste five minutes on a single question (especially a question involving a graph or the word EXCEPT) because they are too stubborn to cut their losses. It is important to be aware of how much time you have spent on any given question and on the section on which you are working. There are several ways to improve your pacing and timing for the test.

- **Know your average pace.** While you prepare for your test, try to gauge how long you take on five, ten, or twenty questions. Knowing how long you spend on average per question will help you identify how many questions you can answer effectively and how best to pace yourself for the test.
- **Have a watch or clock nearby.** You are permitted to have a watch or clock nearby to help you keep track of time. It is important to remember, however, that constantly checking the clock is in itself a waste of time and can be distracting. Devise a plan. Try checking the clock after every fifteen or twenty questions to see if you are keeping the correct pace or whether you need to speed up; this will ensure that you're cognizant of the time while not permitting you to fall into the trap of dwelling on it.
- **Know when to move on.** Since all questions are scored equally, investing appreciable amounts of time on a single question is inefficient and can potentially deprive you of the chance to answer easier questions later on. If you are able to eliminate answer choices, do so, but don't worry about picking a random answer and moving on if you cannot find the correct answer. Remember, tests are like marathons; you do best when you work through them at a steady pace. You can always come back to a question you don't know. When you do, very often you will find that your previous mental block is

gone, and you will wonder why the question perplexed you the first time around (as you gleefully move on to the next question). Even if you still don't know the answer, you will not have wasted valuable time that you could have spent on easier questions.

- **Be selective.** You don't have to do any of the questions in a given section in order. If you are stumped by an essay or multiple-choice question, skip it or choose a different one. In the section below, you will see that you may not have to answer every question correctly to achieve your desired score. Select the questions or essays that you can answer and work on them first. This will make you more efficient and give you the greatest chance of answering the most questions correctly.

- **Use process of elimination on multiple-choice questions.** Many times, one or more answer choices can be eliminated. Every answer choice that can be eliminated increases the odds that you will answer the question correctly. The section on multiple-choice questions will go through strategies to find these incorrect answer choices and increase your odds of choosing the correct answer.

Remember, when all the questions on a test are of equal value, no one question is that important. Your overall goal for pacing is to get the most questions correct. Finally, you should set a realistic goal for your final score. In the next section, we will break down how to achieve your desired score and ways of pacing yourself to do so.

GETTING THE SCORE YOU WANT

Depending on the score you need, it may be in your best interest not to try to work through every question. Check with the schools to which you are applying. Do you need a 3 to earn credit for the test? If you get a raw score of 43 (out of 60) on the multiple-choice section and do as well on the essays, you will get a 3.

AP Exams in all subjects no longer include a guessing penalty of a quarter of a point for every incorrect answer. Instead, students are assessed solely on the total number of correct answers. A lot of AP materials, even those you receive in your AP class, may not include this information. It is really important to remember that if you are running out of time, you should fill in all the bubbles before the time for the multiple-choice section is up. Even if you don't plan to spend a lot of time on every question and even if you have no idea what the correct answer is, you need to fill something in.

Based on the most recent information available from the College Board, out of 120 points total for the four free-response and multiple-choice questions, students needed at least 93 points to get a score of 5, 82 points for a 4, 66 points for a 3, and 48 points for a 2.

Below is a table to give you an idea of approximately how many questions you must get right and how well you must do on the essays to get the score you need. Realize that these numbers are approximations and will vary from year to year depending upon test performance. From these data, it becomes readily apparent that you must attempt and perform well on the essays to have a chance to score a 4 or 5. As you take practice tests, you can use this information to evaluate how best to get the score you want and what areas of the exam are hindering your progress. There are multiple ways to achieve your desired score. It is important to remember that guessing is no longer penalized and that you must put in energy and effort on the essays to perform well.

How to Get the Score You Want		
Total AP Score Desired	Multiple Choice Correct (out of 60)	Total Score Needed on Free Response Questions
5	60	33
	50	43
	40	53
	35	58
4	50	32
	40	42
	35	47
	30	52
3	40	26
	35	31
	30	36
	20	46
2	30	18
	25	23
	20	28
	15	33

TEST ANXIETY

Everybody experiences anxiety before and during an exam. To a certain extent, test anxiety can be helpful. Some people find that they perform more quickly and efficiently under stress. If you have ever pulled an all-nighter to write a paper and ended up doing good work, you know the feeling.

However, too much stress is definitely a bad thing. Hyperventilating during the test, for example, almost always leads to a lower score. If you find that you stress out during exams, here are a few preemptive actions you can take.

- **Take a reality check.** Evaluate your situation before the test begins. If you have studied hard, remind yourself that you are well prepared. Remember that many others taking the test are not as well prepared, and (in your classes, at least) you are being graded against them, so you have an advantage. If you didn't study, accept the fact that you will probably not ace the test. Make sure you get to every question that you know something about. Don't stress out or fixate on how much you don't know. Your job is to score as high as you can by maximizing the benefits of what you do know. In either scenario, it is best to think of a test as if it were a game. How can you get the most points in the time allotted to you? Always answer questions you can answer easily and quickly before you answer those that will take more time.

- **Try to relax.** Slow, deep breathing works for almost everyone. Close your eyes, take a few, slow, deep breaths, and concentrate on nothing but your inhalation and exhalation for a few seconds. This is a basic form of meditation, and it should help you to clear your mind of stress and, as a result, concentrate better on the test. If you have ever taken yoga classes, you probably know some other good relaxation techniques. Use them when you can (obviously, anything that requires leaving your seat and, say, assuming a handstand position won't be allowed by any but the most free-spirited proctors).

- **Eliminate as many surprises as you can.** Make sure you know where the test will be given, when it starts, what type of questions are going to be asked, and how long the test will take. You don't want to be worrying about any of these things on test day or, even worse, after the test has already begun.

The best way to avoid stress is to study both the test material and the test itself. Congratulations! By buying or reading this book, you are taking a major step toward a stress-free AP U.S. Government and Politics Exam.

REFLECT

Think about what you learned in Part IV, and respond to the following questions:

- How much time will you spend on multiple-choice questions?

- How will you change your approach to multiple-choice questions?

- What is your multiple-choice guessing strategy?

- How much time will you spend on the free-response questions?

- How will you change your approach to the free-response questions?

- Will you seek further help, outside of this book (such as a teacher, tutor, or AP Students), on how to approach multiple-choice questions, free-response questions, or a pacing strategy?

Part V
Content Review for the AP U.S. Government and Politics Exam

Chapter 4
The
Constitutional
Underpinnings

CONCEPTS

- Why did the Articles of Confederation fail?
- What was the immediate impact of Shays' Rebellion?
- What motivated the Framers of the Constitution? Were they elitists or pragmatists?
- Why did the Framers create a republican form of government?
- Why did the Framers create a federal system of government?
- What is the purpose of checks and balances and the separation of powers?
- Why are plurality systems democratic but unstable?

ENLIGHTENMENT PHILOSOPHIES

The Framers of the Constitution lived in a unique time when new ideas on how government should be organized and run challenged conventional wisdom regarding the roles of people and their governments. The Enlightenment was an eighteenth-century philosophical movement that began in Western Europe with roots in the Scientific Revolution. The focus was on the use of reason rather than tradition to solve social dilemmas.

The following Enlightenment philosophers contributed directly to the formation of thought that led to the creation of the American Constitution and government.

- **Thomas Hobbes:** Hobbes's famous work *Leviathan* (1660) argued that if humans were left to their own devices, chaos and violence would ensue. In a state of nature, life would be "solitary, poor, nasty, brutish, and short." He argued that the best way to protect life was to give total power to an absolute monarch because man cannot be trusted to rule himself.
- **John Locke:** While Hobbes was concerned primarily with the protection of life, Locke went further and argued in his *Second Treatise on Civil Government* (1690) that liberty and property also needed to be respected. According to Locke, life, liberty, and property were natural rights granted by God; it was the duty of all governments to respect and protect these rights. If the government did not, Locke contended, the citizens have the right of revolution.
- **Charles de Montesquieu:** Montesquieu was a French philosopher who greatly influenced the founders. His *De l'Esprit des Lois* (*The Spirit of the Laws*, 1748) advocated for the separation of power into three branches of government.
- **Jean-Jacques Rousseau:** Rousseau argued that the only good government was one that was freely formed with the consent of the people (1762). This consent was shown in a powerful "social contract," which was an agreement among people.

THE WEAKNESS OF THE ARTICLES OF CONFEDERATION

The first government of the newly born United States of America was formed under the **Articles of Confederation**, the predecessor to the Constitution. These Articles were informally followed from 1776 to 1781 when they were ratified and so named. The government under the Articles achieved some notable accomplishments, including the following:

- It negotiated the treaty that ended the Revolutionary War (on favorable terms for the United States' victorious army).
- It established the **Northwest Ordinance**, creating methods by which new states would enter the Union.
- It set the precedent of **federalism**, whereby the states and central government shared governing responsibilities.

However, the Articles of Confederation had insurmountable weaknesses that placed the newly independent states at risk. The year 1783 was the official end of the American Revolution and the post-revolution transitional period was marked by states being wholly unprepared to manage their own affairs. By 1787, trade between the states was in decline, the value of money was dropping, potential threats from foreign enemies were growing, and there was the real threat of social disorder from groups within the country. The inability of the state of Massachusetts to effectively deal with **Shays' Rebellion**, a six-month rebellion in which more than 1,000 armed farmers attacked a federal arsenal to protest the foreclosure of farms in the western part of the state, was a major concern at the Constitutional Convention. The nation's leaders began to see the necessity of a stronger central government, as Shays' Rebellion frightened the statesmen and exposed the weakness of the Articles of Confederation.

The federal government under the Articles

- could not draft soldiers
- was completely dependent on the state legislatures for revenue—the federal government was not permitted to tax citizens
- could not pay off the Revolutionary War debt
- could not control interstate trade
- had no Supreme Court to interpret law
- had no executive branch to enforce national law
- had no national currency
- had no control over import and export taxes imposed between states
- needed unanimity to amend the Articles
- needed approval from 9 out of 13 states to pass legislation (69% majority)

These deficiencies of the Articles of Confederation were the direct causes for calling a convention. But amending the articles became so difficult that James Madison did not have difficulty persuading the other delegates that a complete rewrite was necessary. The result was the **Constitution**, and the convention came to be known as the **Constitutional Convention**.

Review Source Documents
Many students mix up the Constitution with the Declaration of Independence. Be sure to read through the Constitution (found in the back of your book) and the Declaration of Independence a few times before your exam.

The Constitutional Convention

When the Framers of the Constitution met in Philadelphia in 1787, they were divided over their views of the appropriate power and responsibilities of government. Some saw the current government, formed under the Articles of Confederation, as weak and ineffective, while others believed that changes to the Articles would be infringements on the responsibilities of state governments and intrusions into the lives of citizens. Some historians (such as Charles Beard) see the convention as an elitist conspiracy to protect the wealth of the rich, while others see the convention as a meeting of political pragmatists who knew that by protecting everyone's property and rights, they could best protect their own. Today, the generally accepted view is that the Framers were pragmatists.

The delegates agreed that a stronger central government was necessary but were fearful of the corrupting influences of power. How to control the federal legislature was a central theme at the convention. The large states seized the agenda at the beginning of the convention and proposed the **Virginia Plan**, a recipe for a strong government with each state represented proportionately to its population. The small states worried that a government dominated by the large states would be overly strong, so they proposed the **New Jersey Plan**, under which each state would be represented equally. The **Great** (or "**Connecticut**") **Compromise** created the solution: a **bicameral** (two-house) **legislature** with a House of Representatives, based on population, and a Senate, with equal representation for all states.

Another major conflict arose over the representation of slaves. (Remember that slaves could not vote then.) Northerners felt that slaves should not be counted when determining each state's number of electoral votes, while Southerners disagreed. The "solution" was the infamous **Three-Fifths Compromise**, in which the decision was made that slaves would count as three-fifths of a person when apportioning votes.

Under the Articles of Confederation there was no executive authority to enforce laws. The Framers of the Constitution corrected that problem by addressing the issue of a chief executive, or president. Under the Constitution, the executive is the enforcer of law and a second check on the power of the legislature. Before bills become law, they require presidential approval, and the president has the power to veto acts of the legislature. However, presidential power is not absolute. Congress can override a presidential veto if two-thirds of both houses of the legislature vote to do so.

In order to arbitrate disputes between the Congress and the president, between states, and between the states and the central government, the Framers created the Supreme Court.

Despite all of the compromises that were reached at the convention, acceptance of the Constitution was by no means assured. It had to be submitted to the states for ratification. Supporters and opponents of the Constitution broke into two camps, **Federalists** and **Anti-Federalists**. Alexander Hamilton, James Madison, and John Jay wrote a series of newspaper articles supporting the Constitution, collectively known as *The Federalist Papers*. These essays are the primary source for understanding the original intent of the Framers. They were designed to persuade the states of the wisdom of a strong central government coupled with autonomous political power retained by the states.

The Anti-Federalists opposed the creation of a stronger national government, arguing that a Constitution would threaten citizens' personal liberties and effectively make the president a king. Keep in mind that only 12 years prior, these people had declared independence from Britain, and many were fearful that a large government with a Constitution would recreate that same state of tyrannical control from which they had just escaped.

The opposition to the Constitution centered on the lack of a **Bill of Rights** that would protect the rights of individuals from government infringement. Once the Federalists guaranteed that a Bill of Rights would be added to the Constitution immediately after ratification, opposition diminished, and the Constitution became the foundation of American government.

> **"Federalist No. 10"**
> One of the most famous and important articles is "Federalist No. 10," which advocates for a large republic (and warns of the dangers of democracy). Interestingly, the Federalists opposed the creation of a Bill of Rights, as Hamilton feared that once citizens' rights were written down explicitly, they would later be interpreted as a list of the *only* rights that people had. He also felt that the various states' Bills of Rights were sufficient protections of individual rights.

THE CONSTITUTION AS AN INSTRUMENT OF GOVERNMENT

The Constitution is vague and skeletal in form, containing only about 5,000 words. It was intended to be a blueprint for the structure of government and a guide for guaranteeing the rights of citizens. It was written to allow change, anticipating unknown needs of future generations, through amendments that require widespread support. The branches of government have all grown and evolved since the ratification of the Constitution.

- The first three articles of the Constitution set up the threefold separation of powers that are the Legislative, Executive, and Judicial branches. More on that in a few pages.
- The **necessary and proper clause** of the Constitution (Article I, Section 8) allows Congress to "make all laws" that appear "necessary and proper" to implement its delegated powers. This is also called the **elastic clause.** For example, there is nothing in the Constitution that creates the Federal Reserve System, which is the central bank for the United States. Neither is there any mention of a cabinet in the executive branch. The Federal District Courts and the Courts of Appeals were both created by congressional elaboration.

You can find the full text of the Constitution beginning on page 277 of this book.

- "The executive power shall be vested in a President of the United States of America" has given presidents the power to issue **executive orders**, which have the same effect as law, bypass Congress in policy making and are not mentioned in the Constitution. Presidents use them as part of the enforcement duties of the executive branch. **Executive agreements** between heads of countries have many of the same elements as treaties. These agreements bypass the ratification power of the Senate but are not mentioned in the Constitution. An extreme example of an executive order is Executive Order 9066, in which Franklin D. Roosevelt ordered people removed from a military zone. It was no coincidence that these people were Japanese American and German American. This order paved the way for all Japanese Americans on the West Coast to be sent to internment camps for the duration of World War II. Thousands of German Americans and Italian Americans were also sent to internment camps under executive order.

- When the Supreme Court decided the case of *Marbury v. Madison* in 1803, it drastically increased its own power by granting itself the ability to overturn laws passed by the legislature, also known as **judicial review**. To learn more about judicial review, check out page 200.

- Finally, custom and usage have changed the system to meet differing needs. The political party system, with its organization, technology, and fund-raising capabilities, was created from custom and usage. The rules used in Congress were also created from custom and usage.

Federalism

Central to the Constitution is the idea that the United States government is a federal government. The term **federalism** describes a system of government under which the national government and local governments (state governments, in the case of the United States) share powers. Other federal governments include Germany, Switzerland, and Australia. Contrast this with a **confederation**, a system in which many decisions are made by an external member-state legislation; decisions on day-to-day matters are not taken by simple majority but by special majorities, consensus, or unanimity—and changes to the Constitution require unanimity. But let's get back to federalism for now.

The Supreme Court (which we'll discuss in depth later) handed down a few important decisions concerning the relationship between the national government and local governments. Know these two, in particular, for your exam:

- *McCulloch v. Maryland* (1819). The Court ruled that the states did not have the power to tax the national bank (and, by extension, the federal government). This decision reinforced the supremacy clause of the Constitution, which states that the Constitution "and the laws of the United States which shall be made in pursuance thereof…shall be the supreme law of the land; and the judges in every state shall be bound thereby, anything in the Constitution or laws of any State to the contrary notwithstanding."

- *Gibbons v. Ogden* (1824). The Court ruled that the state of New York could not grant a steamship company a monopoly to operate on an interstate waterway, even though that waterway ran through New York. The ruling increased federal power over interstate commerce by implying that anything concerning interstate trade could potentially be regulated by the federal government.

Under federalism, some government powers belong exclusively to the national government, some exclusively to the states, and some are shared by the two. Those powers that belong to the national government only are called **delegated, expressed,** or **enumerated powers.** Among them are

- printing money
- regulating interstate and international trade
- making treaties and conducting foreign policy
- declaring war

Powers that belong exclusively to the states are called **reserved powers.** According to the Tenth Amendment, these powers include any that the Constitution neither specifically grants to the national government nor denies to the state governments. These powers are not listed in the Constitution; in fact, they are made up of all powers *not* mentioned in the Constitution. They include

- the power to issue licenses
- the regulation of intrastate (within the states) businesses
- the responsibility to run and pay for federal elections

Some powers are shared by the federal and state governments. These are called **concurrent powers.** Among them are the powers to

- collect taxes
- build roads
- operate courts of law
- borrow money

The Constitution specifies which powers are denied to the national government and which powers are denied to the states. Those powers are listed on the next page.

The Constitution also obliges the federal government to guarantee the states a republican form of government and protection against foreign invasion and domestic rebellion. The federal government must also prevent the states from subdividing or combining to form new states without congressional consent. The states, in turn, are required by the Constitution to accept the court judgments, licenses, contracts, and other civil acts of all the other states; this obligation is contained in the "**full faith and credit**" clause. The states may not refuse police protection or access to their courts to a U.S. citizen just because that person lives in a different state; this provision appears in the **privileges and immunities clause.** Finally, the states usually must return fugitives to the states from which they have fled; this process is called **extradition.**

The **supremacy clause** of the Constitution requires conflicts between federal law and state law to be resolved in favor of federal law. State laws that violate the Constitution, federal laws, or international treaties can be invalidated through the supremacy clause.

The nature of federalism has changed over time. For the first part of the nation's history, the federal and state governments remained separate and independent. The relationship between the national and state governments during this period is called **dual federalism**. What little contact most Americans had with government occurred on the state level, as the national government concerned itself primarily with international trade; the construction of roads, harbors, and railways; and the distribution of public land in the West.

The Federal Government Does Not Have the Power to	The State Governments Do Not Have the Power to
• suspend the writ of *habeas corpus*, (which protects against illegal imprisonment), except in times of national crisis • pass *ex post facto* (retroactive) laws or issuance of bills of attainder (which declare an individual guilty of a capital offense without a trial) • impose export taxes • use money from the treasury without the passage and approval of an appropriations bill • grant titles of nobility	• enter into treaties with foreign countries • declare war • maintain a standing army • print money • pass *ex post facto* (retroactive) laws or issuance of bills of attainder (which declare an individual guilty of a capital offense without a trial) • grant titles of nobility • impose import or export duties

Categorical Grants
Examples of categorical grants include Head Start, Medicaid, and the Food Stamp Program.

As with all parts of the Constitution, the definition of federalism is in the eye of the beholder. Ideological **States' Righters** define federalism as a relationship in which the states retain most of the political power. **Nationalists** often see the federal government as being supreme in all matters and ultimately in control.

Most federal government programs, such as those to aid the poor, clean the environment, improve education, and protect the handicapped, are administered through the states. The federal government pays for these programs through grants-in-aid, which are outright gifts of money to the states. Nationalists prefer to tie strings to the grants, ensuring that the federal government maintains control over the money. States' Righters want no strings attached, leaving decisions about how the grant money is to be used to state and local governments, who they believe know best how to use it.

Nationalists like **categorical grants**, aid with strict provisions from the federal government on how it may be spent. States' Righters like **block grants**, which permit the state to experiment and use the money as they see fit. In the final analysis, however, the federal government can use a number of techniques, including direct orders and preemption, to force the states to abide by federal law. The federal government can also use a crossover sanction, which requires a state to do something before a grant will be awarded. An example would be to raise the drinking age to 21 before federal highway money to build state roads is released.

Advantages of Federalism
- Mass participation: Constituents of all ages, backgrounds, races, and religions can participate by voting on both local and national issues.
- Regional autonomy: States retain some rights and have choices about public policy issues such as gun control, property rights, abortion, and euthanasia.
- Government at many levels: Politicians are in touch with the concerns of their constituents.
- Innovative methods: States can be laboratories for government experimentation, to see if policies are feasible.

Disadvantages of Federalism
- Lack of consistency: Differing policies on issues like gun control, capital punishment, and local taxes can clog the court system and create inequality in states.
- Inefficiency: Federalism can lead to duplication of government and inefficient, overlapping, or contradictory policies in different parts of the country.
- Bureaucracy: Power can be spread out amongst so many groups; it can result in corruption and a stalemate.

Separation of Powers

The Framers of the Constitution decided that no one faction of the government should be able to acquire too much power. To prevent this, they borrowed the concept of the **separation of powers** from the French political philosopher **Charles de Montesquieu**. The Framers delegated different but equally important tasks to the three branches of government. The **legislative branch** (Congress) makes the laws; the **executive branch**, led by the president, enforces the laws; and the **judicial branch** interprets the laws.

Separation of powers also prevents a person from serving in more than one branch of the government at the same time. A congressperson (legislative branch), for example, may not also be a judge (judicial branch), nor a cabinet member (executive branch). If a congressperson were appointed to one of these positions, he or she would first have to resign his or her seat in Congress.

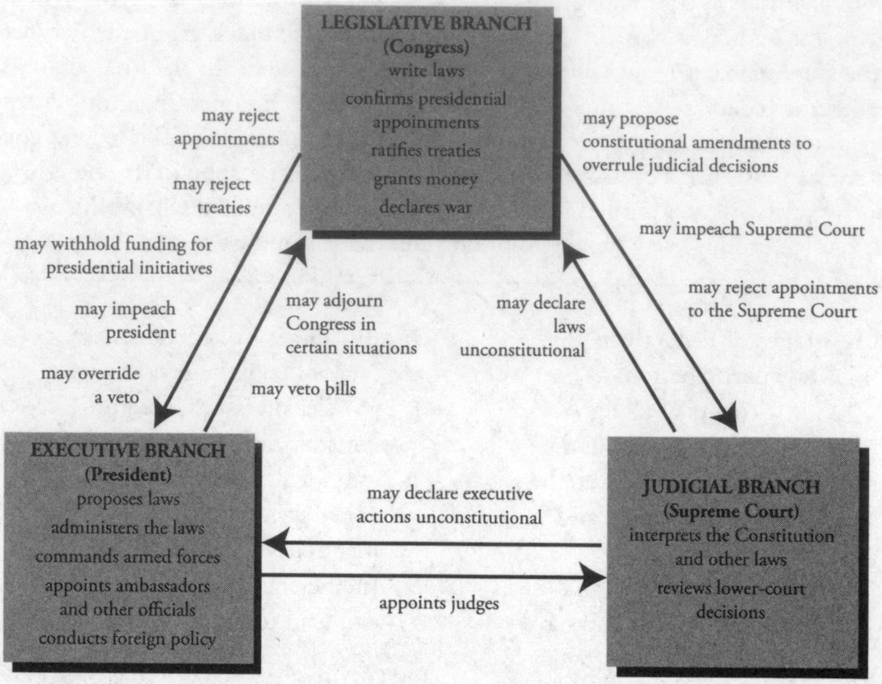
LEGISLATIVE BRANCH
(Congress)
write laws
confirms presidential appointments
ratifies treaties
grants money
declares war
may reject appointments
may reject treaties
may withhold funding for presidential initiatives
may impeach president
may override a veto
may adjourn Congress in certain situations
may veto bills
may declare laws unconstitutional
may propose constitutional amendments to overrule judicial decisions
may impeach Supreme Court
may reject appointments to the Supreme Court
EXECUTIVE BRANCH
(President)
proposes laws
administers the laws
commands armed forces
appoints ambassadors and other officials
conducts foreign policy
may declare executive actions unconstitutional
appoints judges
JUDICIAL BRANCH
(Supreme Court)
interprets the Constitution and other laws
reviews lower-court decisions

The System of Checks and Balances

The system of **checks and balances** is another constitutional safeguard designed to prevent any one branch of government from becoming dominant. The system of checks and balances requires the different branches of government to share power and cooperate with one another to accomplish anything of importance.

- **Nomination of federal judges, cabinet officials, and ambassadors.** The president chooses nominees for these positions. However, the president's nominees must be approved by the Senate.
- **Negotiation of treaties.** The president is empowered to negotiate treaties. No treaty can go into effect, however, until it is approved by two-thirds of the Senate.
- **Enactment of legislation.** Only Congress may pass laws. However, the president has the power to **veto**, or reject, legislation. The president's veto power encourages the legislature to consider the president's position on a law, and to negotiate with the president to prevent a veto. Congress can also check the president's veto by **overriding** the veto, but to do so it must pass the same law with a two-thirds majority in both houses (a congressional override is difficult, but not impossible). If Congress succeeds in overriding the president's veto, the legislation becomes law regardless of the president's position. Finally, the courts may determine the constitutionality of the law. Thus, the courts have the power to overturn laws passed by Congress and approved by the president (only on constitutional grounds, however; judges may not overturn laws simply because they don't like them).

Note the use of the word "encourages." As can be seen with regards to President Obama's support of the Affordable Care Act, the legislative bodies still have the freedom to choose their own approach to a law.

AMENDMENT PROCESS

One reason that the Constitution has lasted more than 200 years is that it is flexible. (Think of the elastic clause!) Many of its provisions require interpretation, allowing the document to become more conservative or progressive as the times warrant. Furthermore, the Constitution can be changed through **amendments** (the addition of provisions to the document).

To amend the Constitution, a proposed amendment must be introduced to both houses of Congress and approved by a two-thirds majority in each. The amendment is then passed on to each of the fifty state legislatures. Three-fourths of the state legislatures must **ratify** (approve) the amendment for it to become part of the Constitution. The states themselves are allowed to determine how many votes are required to ratify an amendment. Most states require a simple majority of their legislatures, but seven states require either three-fifths or two-thirds majorities. Also, rather than use the state legislatures, Congress can mandate that each state use a **ratifying convention**, with delegates expressly elected to vote on the proposed amendment. This method was once used to ratify the Twenty-First Amendment, which ended Prohibition in 1933.

The Constitution allows for a second means of amendment. Two-thirds of the state legislatures could petition Congress to call a **constitutional convention**. Because no constitutional convention has ever taken place, nobody knows for certain how extensively conventioneers would be allowed to alter the Constitution. Could they rewrite it entirely, or would they be restricted to amendments mentioned specifically in their petitions for a convention? Fear that a constitutional convention could attempt drastic alterations has persuaded many state legislators to oppose any call for a convention. There are ongoing movements in many states to call a constitutional convention to add a balanced budget amendment to the Constitution. While about 30 state legislatures have approved a convention, the movement has not yet met the bar of 34 states required to call the convention.

Proposal Methods	Ratification Methods
• Proposed amendment wins $\frac{2}{3}$ majority in the House and Senate • Used for all 27 amendments	• $\frac{3}{4}$ of all state legislatures approve of the amendment • Used 26 times (not for Twenty-First Amendment)
• A constitutional convention is called by $\frac{2}{3}$ of state legislatures. Any amendment can now be proposed at the convention • This method has never been used	• $\frac{3}{4}$ of special state-ratifying conventions approve the amendment • Used only once, for the Twenty-First Amendment

AMENDMENTS

The Bill of Rights (December 15, 1791)

The first ten amendments were added to the Constitution within three years of its ratification. These amendments are known collectively as the Bill of Rights. Originally written by James Madison, many provisions of the Bill of Rights have been expanded and clarified over the years.

The First Amendment

Supreme Court Justice (1932–1937) Benjamin Cardozo said that the First Amendment of the Bill of Rights contains "the fundamental principles of liberty and justice which lie at the base of all of our civil and political institutions."

- **Freedom of religion.** The government may not interfere with an individual's right to practice his or her faith as described in the **free exercise clause**. Furthermore, as stated in the **establishment clause**, Congress may not establish an official church of the United States nor give a particular faith or sect preferential treatment over others. This constitutional provision is usually referred to as the separation of church and state.
- **Freedom of speech and freedom of the press.** Congress may not pass a law that prevents citizens from expressing their opinions, either in speech or in writing. Nevertheless, the Supreme Court has placed some limits on these freedoms. Speech or writing intended to incite violence or used to intentionally slander or libel is not protected. Justice Oliver Wendell Holmes articulated the **clear and present danger test**, in which the government has the right to interfere in free speech if it poses a threat to others, in the case of *Schenck v. United States* (1917). Nevertheless, criticism of the government and its politics is protected. When it comes to censoring the press, there are few instances in which the government can use **prior restraint**—crossing out sections of an article before publication. These strong protections for the press were established in the case of *Near v. Minnesota* (1973).
- **Freedom of assembly and freedom to petition the government.** The Constitution protects the people's rights to assemble peacefully, to hold demonstrations, and to ask the government for changes in policy. Rallies and demonstrations that encourage or incite violence and those that do not seek official sanction to trespass on public property are not protected.

The Second Amendment

The Second Amendment to the Constitution, which protects the citizens' right to bear arms, has led to a debate over whether the Constitution protects citizens' rights to bear arms under all circumstances, or only when those citizens serve in "well-regulated militias."

The Third Amendment

The most antiquated of all the amendments, though not at the time of its creation, the Third Amendment forbids the quartering of soldiers and the direct public support of armed forces. It was a direct reaction to the British practice of using civilian support to conduct military operations.

The Fourth Amendment

The Fourth Amendment places restrictions on government agencies regarding criminal or civil procedural investigations and does much to protect an individual's "person, house, papers, and effects against unreasonable searches and seizures." This amendment was most dramatically reviewed in the twentieth century, as evidenced in *Mapp v. Ohio* (1961). Questions regarding the use of probable cause, traffic-stop and stop-and-frisk searches, and the use of search warrants have led to challenges regarding the interpretation of the **exclusionary rule** regarding evidence seized without proper procedures. In its original form, the exclusionary rule holds that all evidence unlawfully gathered must be excluded from judicial proceedings.

The Fifth Amendment

The Fifth Amendment does the most to protect an individual from the broad powers of the federal government. It provides a guarantee of a **grand jury** when a suspect is held for a capital or other "infamous" crime. It eliminates the possibility of a person being maliciously prosecuted for the same crime again and again by prohibiting **double jeopardy**. It establishes the right of the government to seize property for public use under the auspices of **eminent domain** but only if such seizure can be "justly compensated." Nor may defendants be forced to testify against themselves if on trial, thus prohibiting **self-incrimination** (commonly known as "pleading the fifth"). The most significant attribute of the Fifth Amendment is its mandate that the federal government not deprive an individual of "life, liberty, or property by any level unless **due process of law** is applied."

The Sixth Amendment

This amendment allows persons accused of a crime to be prosecuted by an impartial jury in a "speedy" public trial. Individuals have the right to be informed of their charges, to confront witnesses, to subpoena witnesses for their defense, and to have a lawyer for their defense. The sixth amendment forms the basis for **habeas corpus**, which protects against unlawful imprisonment and ensures that a person cannot be held indefinitely without being formally charged before a judge or in a court, or without a legal reason to extend his or her detention.

The Seventh Amendment

Although statutory, or written, law has come to replace or supersede common law, which is law based on past court decisions, the Seventh Amendment allows for trial by jury in common-law cases.

The Miranda rights, which you may be familiar with ("You have the right to remain silent..."), help to maintain both the Fifth and Sixth Amendments. They remind the accused that they do not have to incriminate themselves (Fifth) and that they are guaranteed the right to representation (Sixth). These rights were cemented as a result of the landmark Supreme Court decision in *Miranda v. Arizona* (1966).

The Eighth Amendment

The Eighth Amendment prohibits excessive bail in federal cases. Yet its most significant challenges have arisen from the clause that prohibits "cruel and unusual punishment." **Capital punishment** is one of the most contentious issues of the modern day. At issue is whether it constitutes "cruel and unusual punishment." Federal and state Supreme Courts have taken different positions on this debate.

The Ninth Amendment

The Ninth Amendment reaffirms the principles of a limited federal government. "The enumeration in the Constitution, of certain rights, shall not be construed to deny or disparage others retained by the people" means that rights not specifically mentioned in the Constitution are still protected—everyone has the right to brush their hair, for example—even though that right is mentioned nowhere in the Bill of Rights. Although somewhat vague in its premise, the Ninth Amendment has led to the implied right to privacy and other questions regarding individual rights not identified or even understood at the time of the creation of the Constitution.

The Tenth Amendment

The Tenth Amendment defines the relationship between the states and the national government under the concept of federalism. It states that when powers are not defined or delegated by the Constitution, the states have **reserved power** to make their own individual judgments—so long as they do not infringe with the explicit rules of the Constitution and the federal government. State issues such as the death penalty, speed limit, and drinking age are within the jurisdiction of the states to decide so long as they do not contradict the Constitution.

Early Amendments (1795–1804)

The Eleventh Amendment (1795)

This amendment was passed as a response to the Supreme Court ruling of *Chisholm v. Georgia* (1793), which held that states did not enjoy sovereign immunity from lawsuits brought by residents of other states. In order to overrule *Chisholm*, the Eleventh Amendment provides that states may not be sued in federal court by citizens of another state or country without the consent of the states being sued.

In *Hans v. Louisiana* (1890), the Supreme Court held that the Eleventh Amendment establishes that states possess sovereign immunity and are therefore generally immune from being sued in federal court without their consent. This issue has been revisited and states sovereign immunity has been strengthened by cases including *Blatchford v. Native Village of Noatak* (1991) and *Alden v. Maine* (1999).

The Twelfth Amendment (1804)

Originally, under Article II of the Constitution, those selected as electors for choosing the president got to cast *two* votes. The candidate who got the highest number of votes won the presidency, while the runner-up got the vice presidency as a consolation prize. The Twelfth Amendment was created following the debacle of the election of 1800—a tie between Thomas Jefferson and Aaron Burr, who split the Republican vote. This amendment ensured that electors would now have to cast separate votes for the president and the vice president.

The Civil War, Civil Rights, Civil Liberties Amendments (1865–1870)

The Thirteenth Amendment (1865)

This amendment prohibited the institution of slavery except as punishment for a convicted crime, and was a direct result of the Union victory in the Civil War.

The Fourteenth Amendment (1868)

Remember, the Bill of Rights did not originally apply to state law. After the Civil War, Northerners pushed for a constitutional amendment that would prevent the South from denying equal rights to the newly freed slaves. The Fourteenth Amendment was designed to accomplish this purpose, stating that

> *No state shall make or enforce any law which shall abridge the privileges or immunities of citizens of the United States; nor shall any state deprive any person of life, liberty, or property, without due process of law; nor deny to any person within its jurisdiction the equal protection of the laws.*

The Fourteenth Amendment expanded the right to due process to all Americans; however, it did not immediately apply the protections of the Bill of Rights to all state laws. Instead, the Supreme Court has used the "due process" and "equal protection" clauses to extend most of the Bill of Rights protections but has done so on a case-by-case basis. This process of incorporating some of the Bill of Rights protections to state law is called **selective incorporation**.

The Fifteenth Amendment (1870)

The Fifteenth Amendment granted voting rights to males of all races, and was originally designed to extend voting rights to newly freed male slaves. Ultimately, the Supreme Court and southern states later narrowed, and in some cases eliminated, the provisions of this amendment during the late nineteenth and early twentieth century. Voter rights were only later made secure by the passage of the Twenty-Fourth Amendment and the Voting Rights Act of 1965.

Progressive Era Amendments (1913–1920)

The Sixteenth Amendment (1913)

Before the passage of this amendment, most revenue was gathered through tariffs that placed a large burden on the poor. The Sixteenth Amendment gave Congress the power to collect taxes on income, which allowed for the creation of a **progressive income tax** that fell more on the rich.

The Seventeenth Amendment (1913)

This amendment provided for the direct election of United States senators. Previously, senators had been selected by the state legislatures. The Seventeenth Amendment shifted the responsibility for choosing senators from the legislatures to the general voting public.

The Eighteenth Amendment (1920)

Known as the Prohibition amendment, this amendment prohibited the manufacture, sale, and transportation of alcohol in or out of the United States.

The Nineteenth Amendment (1920)

This amendment granted voting rights to all American women.

Later Amendments (1933–1992)

The Twentieth Amendment (1933)

Before the passage of the Twentieth Amendment, there was a long gap in between when the new president was elected (early November) and when he took office (March 4). This gap proved especially damaging to the nation first in 1860–1861, when southern states seceded as Lincoln waited to take office, and again in 1932–1933 when the nation was in the grip of the Great Depression and anxiously waiting for Franklin Delano Roosevelt (FDR) to take the reins. As a result, this amendment clearly defined the procedures regarding the specifics of presidential and legislative terms and shortened the amount of time between presidential election and inauguration (now January 20).

The Twenty-First Amendment (1933)

Prohibition had largely led to the rise of organized crime and widespread lawbreaking. The Twenty-First Amendment recognized the failure of this government experiment and repealed prohibition, allowing for the legalization of the sale of alcohol.

The Twenty-Second Amendment (1951)

In response to FDR's unprecedented four presidential election victories, this amendment limited the president to two terms.

The Twenty-Third Amendment (1961)

This amendment allowed the residents of Washington, D.C., to vote in presidential elections, bringing the total national electoral count to 538.

The Twenty-Fourth Amendment (1964)

The Twenty-Fourth Amendment eliminated the racially discriminatory practice of forcing African Americans to pay poll taxes when attempting to vote in Southern state elections.

The Twenty-Fifth Amendment (1967)

Following the assassination of John Kennedy and given the age of his successor, Lyndon Johnson, this amendment provided clarity regarding the selection of a new vice president should the position become vacant. The Twenty-Fifth Amendment also formally permitted the vice president to assume the presidency temporarily in the event of a presidential disability.

The Twenty-Sixth Amendment (1971)

In response to the number of young people fighting in the Vietnam War, the Twenty-Sixth Amendment lowered the voting age from 21 to 18.

The Twenty-Seventh Amendment (1992)

This is a sleeper amendment that was passed more than 200 years after it was first proposed. If Congress votes itself a pay increase, that increase cannot take effect until after the next election.

Informal Changes to the Constitution

Some changes to the Constitution have been initiated either by changes in custom or interpretation of the document. Sometimes, these informal changes gradually give way to more formal changes. For example, when George Washington became president, he served two terms and elected not to serve a third term. Every president after Washington continued this custom until Franklin Roosevelt was elected president four times. Because of Franklin Roosevelt's four terms in office, the Twenty-Second Amendment to the Constitution was proposed and ratified. In this case, an informal custom became a formal change.

STATE AND LOCAL GOVERNMENTS

The Constitution does not stipulate the form state governments must take. The states are instead free to form whatever governments they choose, provided that the government is defined by a state constitution and that the constitution is approved by Congress. However, most state governments are structured after the federal government.

All states have an executive branch led by a **governor**, whose duties to the state are similar to the president's duties to the nation. Governors direct state executive agencies, which oversee areas such as education, roads, and policing.

They command the state National Guard and may grant **pardons** and **reprieves**. Most have the power to appoint state judges, with the "advice and consent" of one of the state's legislative bodies. Governors have veto power over acts of the state legislature.

An Exception
Nebraska has a unicameral legislature, meaning that they have one legislative chamber or house.

All states but one have bicameral legislatures modeled after the House of Representatives and the Senate. In the same way that Congress enacts federal law, the state legislatures enact state law. The legislatures have the power to **override** the **gubernatorial veto** (the word *gubernatorial* means *relating to the governor*). Governors have many of the same executive powers as presidents. However, many governors may use a **line-item veto** to reject only parts of bills. Presidents were denied this power by the Supreme Court under the ruling that a federal line-item veto would take too much power away from the legislative branch. We'll discuss line-item vetoes in greater detail in Chapter 8.

All states also have state judiciaries to interpret state law. These judicial systems consist of trial courts and appeals courts, as does the federal judiciary. They hear both criminal cases (in which an individual is accused of a crime) and civil cases (in which disputing parties can sue to receive compensation).

KEY TERMS

- Articles of Confederation
- Northwest Ordinance
- federalism
- Shays' Rebellion
- Constitution
- Constitutional Convention (of 1787)
- Virginia Plan
- New Jersey Plan
- Great Compromise
- bicameral legislature
- Three-Fifths Compromise
- Federalists
- Anti-Federalists
- *The Federalist Papers*
- Bill of Rights
- necessary and proper clause (elastic clause)
- presidential practice
- executive order
- executive agreement
- judicial review
- confederation
- delegated powers
- reserved powers
- concurrent powers
- full faith and credit clause
- privileges and immunities clause
- extradition
- supremacy clause
- dual federalism
- States' Righters
- Nationalists
- categorical grants
- block grants
- separation of powers
- Charles de Montesquieu
- legislative branch
- executive branch
- judicial branch
- checks and balances
- veto
- override
- amendment
- ratify
- ratifying convention
- constitutional convention
- First Amendment
- free exercise clause
- establishment clause
- clear and present danger test
- exclusionary rule
- grand jury
- double jeopardy
- eminent domain
- self-incrimination
- due process of law
- habeas corpus
- capital punishment
- selective incorporation
- Sixteenth Amendment
- progressive income tax
- Twenty-Second Amendment
- governor
- pardons
- reprieves
- gubernatorial veto
- line-item veto

Summary

o   Remember that the Articles of Confederation were ultimately too weak to serve as a viable governing constitution for the new nation.

o   Know the important philosophers that influenced the Framers: Hobbes, Locke, Montesquieu, and Rousseau.

o   The Constitutional Convention in Philadelphia resulted in a new governing document that sought to balance the autonomy of the states with a stronger federal government.

o   The vagueness of some sections of the Constitution along with elements like the elastic clause make the document adaptable to changing times.

o   The United States, through the Constitution, was the first nation to practice federalism: a balance of power between the states and the federal government.

o   In keeping with the principles of Montesquieu, the Founders created a government split into three branches and gave each branch the power to check the other two.

o   Try to remember all twenty-seven Amendments by era: the Bill of Rights, the early amendments, the Civil War Amendments, the Progressive Era Amendments, and the later amendments.

o   Many powers that are not formally declared in the Constitution have been taken on by the president and Congress—you should be aware of this "unwritten Constitution."

o   Know a bit about how state and local governments function and how they interact with the federal government.

Chapter 4 Drill

See Chapter 11 for answers and explanations.

1. Shays' Rebellion is significant because it

   (A) led to the overthrow of British rule
   (B) scared American elites, leading to the adoption of the Constitution
   (C) caused the American colonies to join together in the face of a threat from the French
   (D) led to the enactment of slavery in the South
   (E) narrowly avoided overthrowing the government of Vermont

2. Which of the following was NOT a problem with the Articles of Confederation?

   (A) There was no strong federal army to prevent revolutions.
   (B) The Articles were almost impossible to amend.
   (C) Each state was taxing trade with other states.
   (D) States were establishing ties with foreign powers.
   (E) The Articles did not adequately protect the freedom of the states.

3. The issue of the representation of slaves was decided by the

   (A) Three-Fifths Compromise
   (B) Connecticut Compromise
   (C) Commerce and Slave-Trade Compromise
   (D) Bill of Rights
   (E) Articles of Confederation

4. The principle of American government that establishes concurrent state and national governments is known as

   (A) separation of powers
   (B) limited government
   (C) federalism
   (D) checks and balances
   (E) judicial review

5. The Virginia Plan would have created a

   (A) legislature dominated by the small states
   (B) legislature dominated by the big states
   (C) legislature controlled by the slave states
   (D) legislature that balanced control between the large and small states
   (E) constitutional monarchy

6. Which of the following acts of the Confederation, later affirmed by the first American Congress, established a method of admitting new states into the United States?

   (A) The Pendleton Act
   (B) The Three-Fifths Compromise
   (C) The New Jersey Plan
   (D) The Bill of Rights
   (E) The Northwest Ordinance

7. The Fifth Amendment to the Bill of Rights protects American citizens' right

   (A) to free speech
   (B) to bear arms
   (C) against unreasonable searches and seizures
   (D) against double jeopardy
   (E) against cruel and unusual punishment

REFLECT

Respond to the following questions:

- For which content topics discussed in this chapter do you feel you have achieved sufficient mastery to answer multiple-choice questions correctly?

- For which content topics discussed in this chapter do you feel you have achieved sufficient mastery to discuss effectively in an essay?

- For which content topics discussed in this chapter do you feel you need more work before you can answer multiple-choice questions correctly?

- For which content topics discussed in this chapter do you feel you need more work before you can discuss effectively in an essay?

- What parts of this chapter are you going to re-review?

- Will you seek further help, outside of this book (such as a teacher, tutor, or AP Students), on any of the content in this chapter—and, if so, on what content?

Chapter 5
Public Opinion
and the Media

CONCEPTS

- What is public opinion?
- What is the public agenda, and how is the agenda shaped?
- How is public opinion measured?
- What role does the media play in shaping public opinion?
- What effect does the media have on individual political beliefs and voting behavior?

Public opinion, simply put, is how people feel about things. Pollsters measure the public's opinion of everything from television programs to commercial products to political issues. Networks, companies, and politicians commission these polls because they seek the approval of the public.

Obviously, public opinion is not uniform: Even the most popular television shows attract a minority of all Americans. Furthermore, many programs are designed to receive favorable ratings from a specific subgroup of society rather than from the public at large. Networks, for example, seek high ratings from young, middle-class audiences, as these are the audiences most sought after by advertisers. Because advertisers are less interested in senior citizens, networks seek their approval less aggressively.

The same holds true for political issues. Most Americans—the **general public**—care more about the political issues that affect their day-to-day lives directly. A political issue does not have to interest the majority of Americans, then, to be considered important by politicians. If an issue is of enough importance to a smaller group—the **issue public**—to cause those voters to become more politically active, that issue may well become an important political issue. Furthermore, very few politicians seek the approval of the general public as a whole. With the exception of the president, all politicians have much smaller constituencies, and they measure the public opinion of these constituencies in order to appeal to them. Members of the House of Representatives, for example, are interested primarily in the concerns of their home districts, which are often quite different from the concerns of the general public.

CHARACTERISTICS OF PUBLIC OPINION

Those who measure public opinion are not just interested in the direction of public opinion—that is, how the public is feeling at a given moment. They also want to know how strongly the public feels and how likely people are to change their minds. That is why they try to gauge the following characteristics of public opinion:

- **Saliency.** The saliency of an issue is the degree to which it is important to a particular individual or group. For example, Social Security is an issue with high salience for senior citizens. Among young voters, Social Security has a much lower salience.

- **Intensity.** How strongly do people feel about a particular issue? When the intensity of a group's opinion is high, that group can wield political influence far beyond their numbers.
- **Stability.** Public opinion on issues changes over time. Some dimensions of public opinion, such as support for democracy and a controlled free-market economy, remain relatively stable. Others, like presidential approval ratings, can change quickly, as was the case during the last two years of George H. W. Bush's administration. During the Gulf War (January 1991), President Bush recorded the highest approval ratings of any president since 1945. Less than two years later, the majority of Americans showed their disapproval of his performance as president by voting against him.

In the United States, public opinion is measured regularly through elections. Elections measure public opinion indirectly, however, because votes for—or against—candidates can rarely be translated into clear and specific opinions. Referenda measure the public's opinion on specific issues (a **referendum** submits to popular vote to accept or reject a measure passed by a legislative body). Public opinion is measured most frequently and directly by **public opinion polls.**

POLLS MEASURE PUBLIC OPINION

Public opinion polls are designed to determine public opinion by asking questions of a much smaller group. Pollsters achieve this through **random sampling**, a method that allows them to poll a representative cross section of the public. When polling by phone, pollsters use a computer that dials numbers randomly. When conducting **exit polls** at polling places on election day, they target voting districts that collectively represent the voting public and randomly poll voters who are leaving the voting place. This method discourages bias, which may occur if pollsters were to approach only those voters who seemed most friendly or anxious to participate.

> Polling Accuracy
> When performed correctly, polls can measure the opinions of 300 million Americans by polling a mere 1,500 of them within about a 5% margin of error.

For a poll to accurately reflect public opinion, its questions must be carefully worded. A poll that asks, "Do you approve or disapprove of the death penalty?" would likely yield a very different response from one that asks, "Would you want the death penalty imposed on someone who killed your parents?" Most pollsters try to phrase questions objectively. Polls generally ask multiple-choice questions, which are closed-ended, as opposed to open-ended questions (such as, "Explain why you approve or disapprove of the death penalty"). Closed-ended questions yield results that are more easily quantifiable, providing a more accurate read of the direction and intensity of public opinion.

Even with those controls, polls cannot be 100% accurate. Polling organizations know how accurate their polls are and include this information with the poll results. The accuracy is measured as a sampling error and appears as a percentage with a plus and minus sign to the left (for example, ±4%). The **sampling error** tells how far off the poll results may be. Suppose a poll indicated that 60% of Americans favored the death penalty. If that poll had a sampling error of ±4%, the actual percentage of Americans favoring the death penalty could be anywhere between 56 and 64%. Generally, the more respondents a poll surveys, the lower the sampling error.

The best-known poll is the Gallup poll. Many major newspapers and television networks conduct public opinion polls, as do academic and public interest institutions.

WHERE DOES PUBLIC OPINION COME FROM?

Public opinion is made up of the views of individuals. Individuals develop their political attitudes through a process called **political socialization**. Why, and when, do they change? What factors influence a person's political beliefs?

The first factor that influences individual political beliefs is **family**. Most people eventually affiliate with the same political party as their parents. Children's political beliefs are also greatly affected by the moral and ethical values they learn from their parents. Political values learned in childhood stay with many Americans throughout their entire lives. Also important is their **location**—people born in rural states may develop political views that are more socially conservative than those of city dwellers.

As children grow, other factors influence their political socialization. In **school** they learn about history and government and are exposed to the political perspectives of teachers and peers. **Religious institutions** have a similar influence on many Americans. **Mass media** such as television, radio, magazines, and the Web further inform political attitudes. In general, however, youth is a time when many Americans pay relatively little attention to and have little interest in political issues. This is because most political issues have little direct impact on their day-to-day lives.

Those who progress to **higher education** often find themselves questioning their social and political assumptions for the first time. As a result, college can be a time of radical change in an individual's political beliefs. Studies have shown that students retain many of the political attitudes they acquire in college throughout their lives.

As individuals reach adulthood, **real-life experiences** become the primary influence on their political beliefs. Family responsibilities and property ownership tend to make people more conservative. Conversely, individuals who experience bias based on their socioeconomic status, race, or gender may grow more liberal or more cynical about government. Adults continue to be influenced by participation in religious organizations, by the attitudes of their peers, and by what they learn through the news media.

POLITICAL IDEOLOGIES

The terms *liberal* and *conservative* in the previous paragraph refer to the predominant ideologies in the United States. An **ideology** is a coherent set of thoughts and beliefs about politics and government.

The three most common political ideologies in the United States are the following:

- **Conservative.** Conservatives stress that individuals should be responsible for their own well-being and should not rely on government assistance. As a result, they tend to oppose government interference in the private sector. They also oppose most federal regulations, preferring that the market determine costs and acceptable business practices (laissez-faire economics). Social conservatives, who make up a powerful wing of the conservative population, do support government action on social issues. In a 2011 Gallup poll, 40% of Americans considered themselves to be conservatives.

- **Liberal.** Liberals believe that the government should be used in a limited way to remedy the social and economic injustices of the marketplace. They tend to support government regulation of the economy. They also support government efforts to redress past social injustices through programs such as affirmative action. Most liberals believe the government should strictly enforce the separation of church and state, and therefore oppose school-sponsored prayer and proposed bans on abortions, which they perceive as motivated by religious beliefs.

- **Moderate (or Independent).** The beliefs of moderates do not constitute a coherent ideology. Instead, moderates view themselves as pragmatists who apply common sense rather than philosophical principles to political problems. Moderates once made up the largest part of the American public, but with the financial crisis of 2008–2009, polls have shown a small decline in this number.

Compared with citizens of other Western democracies, Americans have fewer main ideological groups. The many extreme political parties that exist in Europe, ranging from right-wing nationalists to left-leaning communists, are practically nonexistent in the United States. Furthermore, perhaps because of the paucity of viable groups, Americans readily vote outside of their self-professed political beliefs. In 2008, for example, 20% of self-identified conservative voters chose the more liberal Barack Obama over conservative Republican candidate John McCain.

Americans who are strongly ideological tend to be the most politically active citizens. They are more likely than other Americans to join political organizations and participate in political activities, such as rallies and boycotts. One result of this phenomenon is that candidates in the presidential primaries must perform a balancing act. To win the primaries, they must first appeal to the more ideological party members. Then in the general elections, candidates must move back to the political center or risk alienating the general voting public.

See the next chapter for a more detailed explanation of political beliefs by party.

Determining Factors in Ideological and Political Behavior

Although there is no one-to-one correlation between people's backgrounds and their political beliefs, people who share certain traits tend to share political beliefs. Here are some of the factors that influence people's ideological and political attitudes.

- **Race/ethnicity.** Racial and ethnic groups who disproportionately populate the lower income levels tend to be more liberal than other Americans. Blacks and Hispanics have been more likely than other Americans to support liberal social programs, for example. There are exceptions to these rules, however: Cuban Americans, for one, have tended to be conservative.
- **Religion.** Among the various religious groups in the United States, Jews and African-American Protestants are generally the most liberal. Catholics also lean toward the political left, although many are conservative on social issues. Devout white Protestants tend to be more conservative. This is particularly true in the South, where white Protestants who attend church regularly are among the nation's strongest supporters of the Republican Party.
- **Gender.** Women tend to be more liberal than men. They are more likely to vote Democratic, more likely to support government social welfare programs, and less likely to support increases in military spending.
- **Income level.** Americans in higher income brackets tend to be more supportive of liberal goals such as racial and sexual equality. They also support greater international cooperation. However, they tend to be more fiscally conservative. Poorer Americans, conversely, are generally more conservative on all issues except those concerning social welfare.
- **Region.** Regional differences arise from different economic and social interests. The ethnic and racial mix of the East Coast has made it the most liberal region of the country (making these "blue states"). In the more religious South, conservatism is predominant (making these "red states"). The West Coast, toward which many Americans continue to migrate, is the most polarized, with strong liberal and conservative contingencies scattered up and down the coast; though, this region has leaned more to the left in recent years. Liberals tend to congregate in cities; elsewhere, small town and more rural voters are generally conservative.

PUBLIC OPINION AND THE MASS MEDIA

The **news media** play an important role in the development of public opinion. News media include all of the following:

- news broadcasts on television (particularly 24-hour cable news networks), radio, and the Internet
- newspapers
- news magazines, such as *Time*
- magazine broadcast programs, such as *60 Minutes* and *20/20*
- newsmaker interview programs, such as *Meet the Press* and *The Daily Show* (which may be a comedy show, but has hosted many political guests and approached interviewing those guests seriously)
- political talk radio and podcasts
- websites, blogs, news aggregators, and online forums, such as *The Huffington Post, Drudge Report,* and *Politico*
- social media such as Facebook, Twitter, Tumblr, and Reddit

These media provide most Americans with their most extensive exposure to politicians and the government. In many ways, they act as an intermediary between the people and the government, constantly questioning the motives and purposes of government actions and then reporting their findings to the public.

Throughout American history, public exposure to news media has consistently increased, both through higher literacy rates and through the expansion of news sources available in print, broadcast, and online. As a result, the media have played an increasingly significant role over the years in shaping public opinion.

Less clear is whether the media have the power to alter public opinion. It is generally believed that the media affect public opinion only when news coverage is extensive and is either predominantly negative or positive. For example, a constant barrage of negative images broadcast from Vietnam in the 1960s is credited with having turned many Americans against the war.

The news media can also alter public opinion when it is volatile: Studies have demonstrated, for example, that public approval of the president is quite volatile and changes depending on whether news coverage of the president is positive or negative. In most other instances, however, the media do not

The Media and the Public Agenda

The most important role the media play is in setting the **public agenda**. By deciding which news stories to cover and which to ignore, and by returning to some stories night after night while allowing others to die after a few reports, the news media play an important part in determining the relative importance of political issues. This power of the media is limited by the public's inherent interest in a story, however. Prior to American involvement in Bosnia, constant coverage of the crisis there did little to raise public awareness of or interest in the story, because many Americans perceived the crisis as too remote to be of interest. In general, the process of setting the national agenda is a dynamic one. The media generally try to report stories that they believe will interest the public, and often there is a domino effect: as interest grows, coverage increases, and the story becomes more important.

greatly impact public opinion. This is in part because the news media cover many stories simultaneously, thus diluting their ability to influence public opinion on any single issue. It is also due in part to the fact that most Americans choose those news media that reinforce their political beliefs. For example, conservative magazines such as the *National Review* are read almost exclusively by conservatives; liberal magazines, such as *The Nation*, are read primarily by liberals and progressives.

In addition to the news media, social media have become crucial tools for major grassroots political movements, both within the United States and abroad. Facebook, Twitter, Tumblr, Reddit, and other such social media sites can act as both a shaper and an indicator of public opinion, mostly with younger demographics (ages 18–25).

Are the News Media Biased?

Critics from both ends of the political spectrum claim that the news media interject their political beliefs into their reports. It seems that not a day goes by without political pundits accusing FOX of being wildly conservative, and MSNBC of pushing a liberal agenda. Conservatives cite polls that have consistently shown that news reporters are more likely to hold liberal views and vote Democratic than are average Americans. Liberals point out that the major news media are owned by large, conservative companies, such as General Electric (NBC) and Disney (ABC). They argue that these companies exert pressure on the networks to downplay or ignore stories that reflect badly on the companies or the economic and political forces that support them.

Many studies have shown that there is less ideological bias in news reporting than is claimed by critics, either in the stories news organizations choose to report or in the way they report them. Over the course of American history, the news media have in fact grown markedly less biased. Most newspapers in the eighteenth and nineteenth centuries were openly partisan; today, many news organizations attempt to maintain journalistic integrity by remaining as objective as possible.

Commercial concerns reinforce this trend toward objectivity. Biased reporting may appeal strongly to one segment of the population, but it would just as surely alienate another segment. Seeking to offend the fewest possible audience members, most news organizations attempt to weed out bias and represent both sides of every story in their reports.

The Audience Factor
A primary source of media bias is the media's need for an immediate audience appeal.

This does not mean, however, that the news media achieve complete objectivity, which is impossible. News organizations must make hundreds of decisions each day about what to report and how prominently to report it. Many local newspapers, for example, ignore all but the most major international stories, and not because they are not newsworthy but rather because their readers are generally uninterested in such stories. Network news broadcasts shy away from more complex stories, both because of time constraints and out of fear that they may bore viewers and listeners.

Time and space constraints also result in bias in news reporting. Time and space concerns affect all news organizations, but they are most acutely felt by television news programs, which report up to 20 stories during their 18 minutes of broadcast time (some half-hour programs feature as many as 12 minutes of advertising!). News broadcasts increasingly use short sound bites to summarize information, with presidential candidates' sound bites decreasing in length from about 40 seconds (in 1968) to about 7.3 seconds today.

Finally, news reports can be biased by the sources that reporters use for their information. Reporters in Washington, D.C., must rely heavily on politicians and government sources for information, for example. The effect of this reliance is complicated. On one hand, reporters try to not offend their government sources with uncomplimentary reports, because they will need to return to those sources for future stories. Furthermore, there is the danger that reporters in Washington will become too close to the people and events they cover, resulting in bias. On the other hand, reporters must maintain their credibility and so must demonstrate their independence. They cannot consistently file favorable reports on the subjects they cover and expect to remain credible to the viewer. Furthermore, surveys have demonstrated that reporters are more skeptical about the motives of politicians than average Americans are. This skepticism is reflected in their reporting. This may in part explain why public confidence in the government has decreased as the news media have grown more prominent.

Most modern politicians understand the power of the media and, accordingly, attempt to influence coverage. They stage events that yield appealing photographs (photo ops) and provide voluminous documented information in support of their positions (press releases). They plan appearances on shows with specific audience demographics that they are seeking, such as *The Daily Show* if they are seeking the youth vote. One famous photo op was President George W. Bush's speech aboard the USS Abraham Lincoln on May 1, 2003. A banner reading "Mission Accomplished" hung behind the president as he spoke, and it caused much controversy, as that was the final day of combat operations in Iraq. Many politicians felt that the banner was irresponsible and misleading, because casualties have continued for many years afterwards. Attempts to manipulate media reports have grown more frequent and more sophisticated in recent years. Many politicians have studied the masterful way in which Ronald Reagan handled press coverage and have attempted to copy his successes.

KEY TERMS

- public opinion
- general public
- issue public
- saliency
- intensity
- stability
- referendum
- public opinion polls
- random sampling
- exit polls
- sampling error
- political socialization
- ideology
- conservative
- liberal
- moderate (Independent)
- news media
- public agenda

Summary

o Public opinion is measured by looking at saliency, intensity, and stability.

o Data about what people think come from polls, and many politicians base their decisions on polling data.

o Political socialization is the term used to describe how people learn about politics as they grow and mature.

o There are three basic political ideologies in America: conservative, liberal, and moderate.

o Know which factors tend to lead to which ideologies. A black woman in Chicago is more likely to be liberal than a white man from the rural South.

o The media plays a major role in the perception of government by placing certain policies and news events in the spotlight. This is also known as creating a public agenda.

Chapter 5 Drill

See Chapter 11 for answers and explanations.

1. The strength of the public's feelings about an issue is known as

   (A) intensity
   (B) saliency
   (C) stability
   (D) intransigence
   (E) zealotry

2. Which of the following is generally NOT a source of political socialization?

   (A) Family
   (B) School
   (C) Life experiences
   (D) Indoctrination by the two major political parties
   (E) Religion

3. A liberal would probably support

   (A) lower taxes
   (B) deregulation of industry
   (C) government subsidized health care for the poor
   (D) restrictions on the right to abortions
   (E) a ban on gay marriage

4. A conservative would probably support

   (A) higher taxes
   (B) scaling back laws that regulate industry
   (C) affirmative action
   (D) increasing access to abortions
   (E) increasing the power of bureaucracies like the Environmental Protection Agency

5. Which of the following is generally NOT a factor in determining ideological behavior?

   (A) Race/Ethnicity
   (B) Religion
   (C) Gender
   (D) Region
   (E) Birth order

6. Politicians would most likely attempt to generate positive media stories in all of the following ways EXCEPT

   (A) volunteering at a soup kitchen
   (B) championing a popular cause
   (C) changing positions on controversial issues
   (D) appearing in photographs with military veterans
   (E) granting interviews to reporters with similar ideologies

7. Which of the following is considered to have low stability in U.S. public opinion?

   (A) Presidential approval ratings
   (B) Support for an incumbent U.S. House Representative running unopposed
   (C) Voters' party identification
   (D) U.S. Supreme Court approval ratings
   (E) Support for Social Security benefits

REFLECT

Respond to the following questions:

- For which content topics discussed in this chapter do you feel you have achieved sufficient mastery to answer multiple-choice questions correctly?

- For which content topics discussed in this chapter do you feel you have achieved sufficient mastery to discuss effectively in an essay?

- For which content topics discussed in this chapter do you feel you need more work before you can answer multiple-choice questions correctly?

- For which content topics discussed in this chapter do you feel you need more work before you can discuss effectively in an essay?

- What parts of this chapter are you going to re-review?

- Will you seek further help, outside of this book (such as a teacher, tutor, or AP Students), on any of the content in this chapter—and, if so, on what content?

Chapter 6
Political Parties, Interest Groups, PACs, 527 Groups, and Linkage Institutions

CONCEPTS

- What coalitions make up the two main political parties in the United States?
- Why do third parties so often fail in U.S. politics?
- What effect has dealignment had on political parties?
- Are there serious policy differences between Democrats and Republicans?
- Who supports the two parties and why?
- How does the Constitution control special interests?
- How have interest groups helped to democratize the U.S. political system?
- Why are interest groups a threat to democracy?
- What role do interest groups play in setting the political agenda?
- What techniques do PACs use to get their messages across?
- How do interest groups achieve and exert their influence?

In the previous chapter we reviewed how individuals develop their political beliefs. Few political acts, however, are the work of a single person. Rather, most politically active people work within groups to achieve common political goals. The AP U.S. Government and Politics Exam expects you to know about four types of political groups. They are **political parties, interest groups, political action committees (PACs)**, and **527 groups**. This chapter reviews everything you need to know about the organization and activities of these groups.

POLITICAL PARTIES

As we've mentioned, few successful political accomplishments are the work of one person. More often, such a person joins with other like-minded individuals to form organizations that try to influence the outcomes of elections and legislative struggles. **Political parties** are unique among these groups in that they play a formal role in both of these processes. Although they are not mentioned in the Constitution, political parties became a mainstay of U.S. elections by the year 1800. Parties arose in the United States as a means of uniting those who shared political ideals, enabling them to elect like-minded representatives and pursue similar legislative goals. To those ends, parties endorse candidates for office and assist in their election efforts. In return for this support, parties expect candidates to remain loyal to goals defined by the party leadership.

The United States has two major political parties: Democrats and Republicans. This **two-party** or **bipartisan system** is reinforced by the nation's electoral system. U.S. election rules, which have been agreed upon by members of the two parties, also make it difficult for all but the two major parties to win a place on the ballot, further strengthening the two-party system.

No Partying
The Framers of the Constitution disliked political parties and hoped to prevent them.

Party Characteristics

Don't forget these facts about political parties.

- Parties serve as intermediaries between the people and the government.
- Parties are made up of grassroots members, activist members, and leadership.
- Parties are organized to raise money, present positions on policy, and get their candidates elected to office.
- Parties were created outside of the Constitution—they are not even mentioned in the document but were developed in the 1790s.

The major purpose of political parties is to get candidates elected to office. In the past, candidates were chosen by the party hierarchy, with little or no public input. However, since 1960, more states have passed laws requiring parties to select candidates through state-run **primary elections**. These primaries have reduced the power of political parties. Candidates must raise their own money for primaries, campaigning for their party's nomination with little to no support from the party itself. If the parties don't control the money, they can't control the candidates. This levels the playing field, but multiple candidates for the nomination can splinter the party membership.

FUNCTIONS OF MODERN POLITICAL PARTIES

Political scientists identify three major subdivisions of political parties.

- **The party among the electorate.** Voters enroll in and identify with political parties. They generally vote for candidates who represent their party.
- **The party in government.** Government officials belong to political parties. They act together to pursue common goals, although regional and ideological differences sometimes subvert their efforts.
- **The party organization.** A group of people who are neither elected officials nor average voters, the party organization is made up of political professionals who recruit candidates and voters, organize campaign events, and raise money to promote the party.

Political parties perform all of the following functions:

- **Recruit and nominate candidates.** The parties are the major players in electoral politics. They seek out candidates to run in their primary elections. They also create the rules by which candidates seek their nominations. In nearly all elections, nomination by one of the major parties is a prerequisite to victory. For example, in the 2008 Democratic primary, Barack Obama and Hillary Clinton continued to campaign until Obama had enough delegates to secure the nomination, at which point the Democratic party formally announced him as their candidate.

- **Educate and mobilize voters.** Political parties fund propaganda campaigns to persuade voters to choose their candidates. They send mailings, hold rallies, and run advertisements. They target regions in which their support is strong and campaign to persuade voters in those regions to vote on election day.
- **Provide campaign funds and support.** The national parties have committees dedicated to raising funds for House and Senate campaigns. State parties also raise funds for candidates for both state and national office. Although most candidates rely primarily on their own personal campaign support staff, they also need the help of the state or national party organizations.
- **Organize government activity.** Parties act as an organizing force in government. The House and Senate organize their leadership and committee systems strictly along party lines, as do state legislatures.
- **Provide balance through opposition of two parties.** Each party serves as a check on the other by constantly watching for and exposing weakness and hypocrisy. The minority party (provided a single party controls both the White House and the Congress) performs the role of the *loyal opposition*, constantly critiquing the performance of the party in power.
- **Reduce conflict and tension in society.** The two-party system promotes compromise and negotiation in two ways: by encouraging parties to accommodate voters and encouraging voters to accept compromises in policy. The Republican Party, for example, includes both religious social-conservatives and libertarians. To assemble winning coalitions, the party must somehow appease both groups. The groups, in turn, must be willing to compromise if they wish to prevent the Democrats from prevailing.

U.S. political parties are not hierarchical. The national party organization and each of the state and local organizations are largely autonomous and serve different functions; one does not necessarily take orders from the other.

Party committees are organized by geographic subdivisions. Locally, committees at the precinct, town, ward, and electoral district levels coordinate get-out-the-vote drives, door-to-door canvassing, and leaflet distribution. These party committees are staffed mostly by volunteers, and their work is largely concentrated around election time. The next largest geographic grouping is the county. County committees coordinate efforts in local elections and organize the efforts of committees on the precinct level. They also send representatives to each polling place to monitor voting procedures.

State committees raise money and provide volunteers to staff campaign events. They provide support to candidates for both state and national offices. National legislative elections, however, are also the responsibility of the powerful congressional district and senatorial committees. These committees, chaired by incumbents and staffed by professionals, are part of the national party organization. They are most likely to become involved in these legislative elections when the possibility exists of gaining or losing a seat. Because incumbents usually run for reelection and are often reelected easily, the congressional and senatorial committees are active in a minority of election efforts during each electoral cycle.

The national party plans the **national conventions** held every four years to nominate a presidential candidate. It sponsors polls to keep party members informed of public opinion and manages issue-oriented advertising and propaganda.

Are Parties in Decline?

Some political scientists believe that the parties are no longer as powerful or as significant as they once were. Prior to 1968, one party typically controlled both the executive and legislative branches of government. Since that year, however, there have been only a few years of one-party control of these branches (1977 to 1980, 1992 to 1994, 2002 to 2005, and from 2008 to 2010). Americans are voting a split ticket (see page 173) more frequently than ever before. They are more likely to consider the merits and positions of a particular candidate than to merely consider his or her party affiliation. As a result, no one party dominates government, and officials with different political agendas are elected to work together.

Increasingly, modern candidates have taken control of their own election campaigns, relying less on party support than did past candidates. They are now able to appeal directly to the public through television and the Internet. This has left the parties—which once wielded great power over the electoral process—with less power. In their place, media consultants have become the chief movers and shakers in political campaigns.

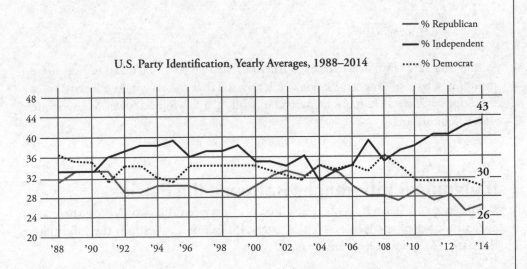

U.S. Party Identification, Yearly Averages, 1988–2014

— % Republican
— % Independent
····· % Democrat

Party Coalitions

Political parties consist of combinations of groups, which consist of combinations of individuals. The larger the coalition, the more likely the candidate will win. Party candidates and party positions on policy are designed to attract more groups of voters, putting together a winning **coalition**.

In the presidential elections of 2008 and 2012, the Republican coalition included the following:

- veterans' groups and military supporters
- religious conservatives
- Libertarians
- opponents of gay marriage
- opponents of affirmative action
- supporters of the development of natural resources on public lands
- rural dwellers

In the same elections, the Democratic coalition included the following:

- disaffected moderate Republicans
- pro-choicers
- African and Hispanic Americans
- members and supporters of labor unions
- gay rights supporters
- people with lower incomes
- city dwellers
- feminists
- environmentalists

While there are always exceptions to the rule, the two parties tend to rely on these groups as a base of support. Regionally, it appears that the east and west coasts and the upper Midwest are more Democratic, while the South and lower Midwest are more Republican.

Ideological Differences Between the Parties

While there are general ideological differences between the two parties, there are also a number of similarities. Neither party, for example, questions the validity of the nation's capitalist economic system.

Although both parties tend to be centrist, there are nevertheless differences in the ways the two parties view the role of government. The greatest ideological differences are between the liberals in the Democratic Party and the conservatives in the Republican Party, the so-called **party bases.** While appealing to the independent centrist voter during election campaigns, each party counts on its base to get out and vote. Party leaders must use great care in choosing policy positions so they do not lose their party base. They must also avoid alienating the moderates of the party by taking extreme left or right positions.

Democrats tend to be	Republicans tend to be
Less disposed to spend on defense	More disposed to spend on defense
Less disposed to use vouchers, or other public funds, to enable certain students to attend private/charter schools	More disposed to use vouchers for private or charter schools and to give governmental aid to parochial schools
More disposed to spend money to advance social-welfare programs	Less disposed to spend money on social-welfare programs
More disposed to use government money for public education	Less disposed to use government money for public education
More disposed to grand tax relief to targeted programs such as the lower and middle classes	More disposed to grand tax relief to everyone, especially the wealthy and corporations
Against private ownership of assault weapons and supportive of broader regulations on the ownership of firearms	Less disposed to regulate firearms

Party Realignment

Party **realignment** occurs when the coalitions making up the two parties fall apart, such as when many of the groups that make up the majority party defect to the minority party. Realignments are very rare and usually occur as a result of some major traumatic event, such as an economic depression or a war. They are signaled by what is called a **critical election,** when a new party comes to dominate politics. Realignments occur over a period of time and show permanence. The New Deal coalition of the 1930s lasted for decades. There have been no realignments since the 1930s.

Depression Politics
The last realignment took place in 1932 as a result of the Great Depression, when the Republican Party became the minority party and the Democratic party became the majority party, with overwhelming numbers of Democrats being elected to every branch of government at every level.

The trend today seems to be toward dealignment. **Dealignment** is usually a result of party members becoming disaffected as a result of some policy position taken by the party. These disaffected party members join no political party and vote for the candidate rather than the party he or she belongs to. Since the 1960s, membership in the Democratic Party has declined significantly, while the number of Republicans has declined modestly. During the same time period, the number of voters self-identifying as independents has increased dramatically.

Third Parties

New parties are occasionally formed in the United States. Unless and until these parties reach the level of a major party, they are called third parties. Third parties form to represent constituencies that feel disenfranchised from both of the major parties. These so-called **splinter** or **bolter parties** usually unite around a feeling that the major parties are not responding to the demands of some segment of the electorate. The Reform Party, under whose banner Ross Perot ran for president in 1996, was an example of a splinter party whose constituency was fed up with "politics as usual."

Sometimes third parties form to represent an ideology considered too radical by the mainstream parties. These **doctrinal parties** reject the prevailing attitudes and policies of the political system. The Socialist Party, the Libertarian Party, and most recently the Tea Party are examples. **Single-issue parties** are formed to promote one principle. The American Independent Party, which sponsored the segregationist candidacy of George C. Wallace in 1968, is an example. Third parties can have a major impact on elections, especially in tight races. The Green Party, which favors strict environmental policies, more government social programs, and controls over big business, ran Ralph Nader for president in 2000. Some analysts have predicted, based on voter patterns and polls, that if Nader had not run, Al Gore would have received a greater number of votes, which would have allowed him to win the election against George W. Bush.

Third-party candidates should not be confused with **Independent candidates**. Independent candidates run without party affiliation. It is very difficult for Independent candidates to overcome the money and organization of the two major parties. Eugene McCarthy, an anti-Vietnam War candidate in 1968, and John Anderson, a fiscal conservative and social liberal in 1980, are two examples.

Why Third Parties Fail

The failure of third parties to elect presidential and other candidates to office is a direct result of an American political system designed to support only two major parties. National campaigns in countries using equal, single-member, plurality voting-district systems (like the United States) require huge sums of money and vast organizations. Also, in American presidential elections, almost all states have a winner-take-all system for electoral votes; the candidate who receives the most votes, even if it is only by one, wins all of the votes in that state. Because the losers get no electoral votes, the electoral count does not always accurately reflect the popular vote. During the 2000 presidential election (which featured the Florida voting controversy), Al Gore won the popular vote by about 500,000 votes nationwide, but George W. Bush was found to have won the Florida electorate, giving him all of Florida's twenty-five electoral votes and, ultimately, the presidency.

All For Many, But All For One

If you're curious, the two states that do not have this winner-take-all system are Maine and Nebraska, and both proportionately distribute their votes by congressional district. If you're even more curious, with the exception of 2008's race between Barack Obama and John McCain, each state has still ended up assigning all of its votes to a single candidate.

INTEREST GROUPS AND LOBBYISTS

Interest groups are organizations dedicated to a particular political goal or to a set of unified goals. Group members often share a common bond, either religious (Christian Coalition), racial (National Association for the Advancement of Colored People), or professional (American Medical Association). In other cases, they simply share a common interest, such as the environment (Sierra Club) or political reform (Common Cause). In any case, they are similar to political parties in that they try to influence the outcome of elections and legislation. Unlike political parties, however, they do not nominate candidates, nor do they normally try to address a wide range of issues.

When interest groups try to influence legislators, we say they are **lobbying** for a bill or issue. The term originated with the historical practice of early lobbyists; they waited in the lobby of the capitol so they could catch legislators coming in and out of session. Today, most lobbyists are highly paid professionals. A number are former legislators, whose experience and friendships in the Capitol make them particularly effective.

There are literally thousands of interest groups in the United States. Most groups fall under one of the following categories:

- **Economic groups.** Economic groups are formed to promote and protect members' economic interests. They include peak business groups such as the U.S. Chamber of Commerce, which represents the interests of all businesspeople. Other groups represent specific trades and industries; among these are the American Farm Bureau Federation and the American Nuclear Energy Council. Labor groups such as the AFL-CIO and the United Auto Workers represent union members. Professional groups include the American Medical Association and the American Bar Association. Most economic groups have existed a long time and have developed strong ties with legislators and bureaucrats. They are also very large, highly influential, and extremely well funded, and either represent or employ large constituencies. As a result, they are usually the most powerful interest groups in Washington, D.C.
- **Public interest groups.** Public interest groups are nonprofit organizations that are generally organized around a well-defined set of public policy issues. Consumer groups usually work to promote safer products and more informative labeling; the most prominent of these groups is Public Citizen, led by **Ralph Nader**. Environmental groups, such as the Sierra Club, advocate preservation of wildlife and wilderness areas. Religious groups such as the Christian Coalition attempt to influence public policy in such a way as to promote or protect their beliefs. Other groups promote causes such as women's rights, minority rights, and political reform. Single-issue groups like the National Rifle Association and Mothers Against Drunk Driving are often among the most powerful public interest groups because of the intensity of their supporters. Single-issue constituents are more

likely than other voters to use a single issue as a litmus test for candidates. Thus, a candidate who advocates gun control runs the risk of losing the votes of all three million NRA members.

- **Government interest groups.** Most states and many cities and other localities maintain lobbying organizations in the nation's capital. A separate group represents the nation's governors, and yet another represents mayors. Most foreign governments and businesses lobby the government as well.

How Interest Groups Influence Government

Interest groups use a number of tactics to disseminate information and persuade Congress, the president, the judiciary, and federal bureaucrats. Those tactics include the following:

- **Direct lobbying.** Representatives of the interest group meet privately with government officials to suggest legislation and to present arguments supporting their positions. Lobbyists are often the source for a great deal of information to young congressmen who are trying to learn about new bills. Some would argue that the lobbyists need to give relatively good information to those congressmen in order to maintain a good relationship with them so that they can lobby them later on their issues.
- **Testifying before Congress.** Interest groups provide expert witnesses at committee hearings.
- **Socializing.** Social events in Washington, D.C., are often political events as well. Interest groups hold social functions and members attend other functions to meet and forge relationships with government officials.
- **Political donations.** Interest groups provide financial support to candidates and parties that champion their causes. Corporations, trade groups, and often unions do so by forming political action committees (PACs) and super PACs for that purpose.
- **Endorsements.** Many groups announce their support for specific candidates. Some groups rate legislators on the basis of their voting records; a high rating constitutes an implicit endorsement of that candidate.
- **Court action.** Interest groups file lawsuits or **class action suits** to protect and advance their interests. They will also submit *amicus curiae* (friend of the court) **briefs** in lawsuits to which they are not a party so that judges may consider their advice in respect to matters of law that directly affect the case in question.
- **Rallying their membership.** Public interest groups often engage in grassroots campaigning by contacting members and asking them to write, phone, or e-mail their legislators in support of a particular program or piece of legislation. In addition, members may engage in demonstrations and rallies promoting their cause.
- **Propaganda.** Interest groups send out press releases and run advertisements promoting their views.

Limits on Lobbying

Several laws limit the scope of lobbyists' activities. Most are ineffective, but stronger efforts to regulate lobbying run the risk of violating the First Amendment right to free speech. The 1946 Federal Regulation of Lobbying Act was intended to allow the government to monitor lobbying activities by requiring lobbyists to register with the government and publicly disclose their salaries, expenses, and the nature of their activities in Washington, D.C.

Other laws prohibit, for limited amounts of time, certain lobbying activities by former government officials. These laws are meant to counteract the appearance of **influence peddling**, the practice of using personal friendships and inside information to get political advantage. Former legislators must wait one year before lobbying Congress directly, for example. However, they may lobby the executive branch immediately after leaving office. Some groups complain of a "revolving door" that pushes former federal employees into jobs as lobbyists and consultants. A limit similar to that of the former legislators also applies to former executive officials. It prevents them from lobbying for five years after they leave the agency that employed them. These limits were determined in *Buckley v. Valeo* (1976), the case that equated donations with free speech. In this ruling, the Supreme Court upheld federal limits on campaign contributions and ruled that donating money to influence elections is a form of constitutionally protected free speech.

Finally, federal laws prohibiting campaign contributions from corporations, unions, and trade associations can be sidestepped through the formation of a political action committee or PAC.

> ### Changes to Campaign Financing
> In January of 2010, the Supreme Court changed many of the campaign finance rules in the case of *Citizens United v. Federal Election Commission*. The court ruled that corporations have a First Amendment right to expressly support political candidates for Congress and the White House. The ruling struck down restrictions that had prevented corporations from spending company money directly on campaign advertising right before an election. In the near future, this groundbreaking case will surely cause many changes in the financing of election campaigns. It is still important to learn how and why these groups function by reading the following sections.

POLITICAL ACTION COMMITTEES (PACS) AND SUPER PACS

The 1974 **Federal Election Campaign Act (FECA)** allowed corporations, unions, and trade associations to form political action committees as a means of raising campaign funds. FECA set restrictions on contributors and contributions, and stipulated that corporate, union, and trade PACs must raise money from employees and members and may not simply draw it from their treasuries. Corporations, unions, and trade associations are not the only groups that form PACs. Many other interest groups form PACs to collect and distribute contributions, as do legislators (these are referred to as leadership PACs). After that change, the **Bipartisan Campaign Reform Act (BCRA) of 2002** (also known as the **McCain-Feingold Act**) further regulated campaign finance and PAC regulated campaign finance and PAC donations by prohibiting unregulated contributions (soft money) to national political parties and limited the use of corporate and union money for ads discussing political issues within 60 days of a general election and 30 days of a primary. Then in 2010, in *Citizens United v. Federal Election Commission*, the Supreme Court overturned BCRA's limits on PAC fundraising for "corporate independent expenditures." Under the terms of the *Citizens United* decision, PACs that donate to specific candidates must operate under limits on their contributors and their donations, but PACs that do not donate to specific candidates—as long as they do not directly coordinate with specific candidates—are not limited in their fundraising. In this context, political donations are considered free speech. These unlimited PACs have come to be known as **Super PACs** and are generally financed by the ultra-rich; however, because of disclosure laws affecting such Super PACs, it can be difficult to identify donors.

Hard vs. Soft: We're Not Talking About Water

For the exam, you should be familiar with the terms "hard money" and "soft money." "Hard money" refers to tightly regulated contributions to candidates, while "soft money" refers to unregulated, unlimited contributions to political parties for general party-building activities such as get-out-the vote drives, voter registration efforts, and ads that say "Vote for Democrats" or "Vote for Republicans." Potential uses of soft money, were limited by Congress with the passage of the McCain-Feingold Act.

For regular PACs, donations from single-candidate PACs to individual candidates cannot exceed $2,500 ($5,000 for a multi-candidate PAC). Such PACs' donations to national political committees cannot exceed $15,000 from multi-candidate PACs and $30,800 from single-candidate PACs. Though Super PACs avoid limits by not directly or officially coordinating with specific candidates, the *Citizens United* decision is vague on what constitutes coordination.

527 GROUPS

A 527 group (named after the section of the tax code that allows them) is a tax-exempt organization that promotes a political agenda, although they cannot expressly advocate for or against a specific candidate. The term is generally used to refer to political organizations that are not regulated by the **FEC (Federal Election Commission)** and are not subject to the same contribution limits as PACs. They avoid regulation by the FEC because 527s are "political organizations" but are not registered as "political committees" subject to campaign finance law contribution limits. Sounds confusing, huh? The line between issue advocacy and candidate advocacy is a huge source of contention and disagreement. Examples of 527s include Swift Boat Veterans for Truth, College Republican National Committee, and The Media Fund. The BCRA changed **soft money** rules to make establishing new 527s a more attractive option than traditional PACs and allowing outside organizations to circumvent the hard money limits of the BCRA (for more on soft money, see pages 190, 274). The *Citizens United* decision, however, makes Super PACs another viable alternative for avoiding such limits.

KEY TERMS

- political parties
- interest groups
- political action committees (PACs)
- Super PACs
- 527 groups
- two-party (bipartisan) system
- primary elections
- splinter (bolter) parties
- doctrinal parties
- single-issue parties
- Independent candidates
- national convention
- split-ticket voting
- divided government
- dealignment

- coalition
- realignment
- critical election
- lobbying
- class action suits
- *amicus curiae* briefs
- influence peddling
- Federal Action Campaign Act
- Bipartisan Campaign Reform Act (McCain-Feingold Act)
- *Citizens United v. Federal Election Commission*
- Federal Election Commission (FEC)
- soft money

Summary

○ Though they are not mentioned in the Constitution, political parties have become an integral part of American government. They may embrace a wide variety of ideologies, but ultimately both parties share the same goal: to be elected by any means necessary.

○ American history has been marked by numerous third parties that have challenged the prevailing duopoly. All have faded away, but if it is popular enough, a third party may influence the two major parties to adopt its ideas.

○ Parties serve many functions in American democracy: They recruit and fund candidates, educate voters, provide a loyal opposition, and run the government—all while mitigating societal tension.

○ When we look at parties, they often turn out to be broad coalitions of disparate ideologies and groups. The Republican Party, for example, blends Libertarians who are hostile to government regulation with religious conservatives who want government to play a greater role in enforcing public morality.

○ Generally speaking, Democrats tend to be in favor of government regulation of industry, redistribution of government money to the poor, and social freedom. Republicans tend to want to empower business to free itself from government rules, encourage people to earn money with assistance from the state, and want more social and moral controls on society.

○ Interest groups are large organizations with strong policy goals, but they are different from political parties in that they do not change their ideologies. These groups try to control the political process by hiring lobbyists to influence legislators and by giving them money as well.

o When labor unions or corporations want to fund candidates, they do so by forming Political Action Committees, or PACs. PACs and Super PACs provide a means to funnel money to a candidate of choice and are regulated by the Federal Election Commission (FEC).

o 527 groups are not regulated by the FEC, and the nature of these groups is a source of great contention. They have become a way for organizations to avoid hard money limits, and their spending has ballooned in recent years, despite efforts to limit and regulate outside money in elections.

Chapter 6 Drill

See Chapter 11 for answers and explanations.

1. Which of the following could be defined as a "splinter" party?

   (A) The Libertarian Party
   (B) The Socialist Labor Party
   (C) The Communist Party
   (D) The Reform Party
   (E) The Green Party

2. Which of the following is NOT a function of American political parties?

   (A) Serving as the loyal opposition
   (B) Fomenting armed rebellion
   (C) Selecting and funding candidates
   (D) Educating the public on issues
   (E) Governing the nation

3. Who of the following people would be most likely to be a Democrat?

   (A) A Cuban American
   (B) An evangelical Christian
   (C) A white Southerner
   (D) A Mexican American
   (E) A pro-life advocate

4. Which of the following is NOT generally a method that interest groups use to influence the government?

   (A) Bribery
   (B) Direct lobbying
   (C) Testifying before Congress
   (D) Political donations
   (E) Endorsements

5. Political Action Committees (PACs) were formed to allow unions and corporations to

   (A) run their own members for political office
   (B) funnel limited amounts of money to candidates of their choice
   (C) funnel unlimited amounts of money to candidates of their choice
   (D) have a voice in government policy meetings
   (E) sit down together to work out their differences

6. During the past three decades, all of the following groups have made up a part of the Republican party's coalition EXCEPT

   (A) religious conservatives
   (B) environmentalists
   (C) Libertarians
   (D) supporters of supply side economics
   (E) supporters of government vouchers to fund private schools

7. Which of the following describes the electorate's change toward the era of Democratic governance that followed the Great Depression in the 1930s?

   (A) Split-ticket voting
   (B) Post-convention bump
   (C) Party dealignment
   (D) Party realignment
   (E) Plurality

REFLECT

Respond to the following questions:

- For which content topics discussed in this chapter do you feel you have achieved sufficient mastery to answer multiple-choice questions correctly?

- For which content topics discussed in this chapter do you feel you have achieved sufficient mastery to discuss effectively in an essay?

- For which content topics discussed in this chapter do you feel you need more work before you can answer multiple-choice questions correctly?

- For which content topics discussed in this chapter do you feel you need more work before you can discuss effectively in an essay?

- What parts of this chapter are you going to re-review?

- Will you seek further help, outside of this book (such as a teacher, tutor, or AP Students), on any of the content in this chapter—and, if so, on what content?

Chapter 7
Elections

CONCEPTS

- Does the media place too much emphasis on irrelevant issues in presidential campaigns?
- Why do incumbents win at such high rates?
- Why is voter turnout so low in the United States?
- What is the impact of primary elections, and who votes in them?
- Why do political parties have such a difficult time holding their coalitions together?
- Why are soft money contributions considered a threat to the election process?
- Why did the Supreme Court have a problem with the imposition of spending limits on PACs?
- Has the Federal Election Campaign Reform Act succeeded in fulfilling the intent of the legislation?
- What accounts for the so-called gender gap?

The federal government holds elections every two years. Each election gives voters the chance to select a new representative in the House of Representatives. Every other election allows them to vote for president. Each of a state's two seats in the Senate is contested every six years; as a result, state voters select a senator in two out of every three federal elections.

To cut expenses and to encourage voter turnout, states often hold their elections at the same time as federal elections. Thus, voters choose not only federal officials at election time, but also state legislators, judges, the governor, and local officials. They may also be asked to vote on referenda and state bond issues.

Thus, many officeholders are chosen and many issues are decided during each election. When the AP U.S. Government and Politics Exam asks about elections, however, it nearly always focuses on the presidential election. This chapter will do the same.

There is one exception to this rule. The AP U.S. Government and Politics Exam always asks at least one question about the **incumbent advantage.** Be sure you know the following two facts, as they will almost certainly be tested on the AP Exam: (1) representatives who run for reelection win approximately 90% of the time; and (2) while incumbent senators have a tremendous electoral advantage, House incumbents have an even greater advantage. Senators must run statewide, and they almost always face a serious challenger. On the other hand, House members run in their home districts, where constituents are often overwhelmingly of one party due to **gerrymandering** (partisan redrawing of congressional district borders). In such races, victory in the primary election virtually guarantees victory in the general election. In fact, each year a number of House incumbents run for reelection unopposed.

THE ELECTION CYCLE

Elections consist of two phases: **nominations**, during which the parties choose their candidates for the general elections, and **general elections**, during which voters decide who will hold elective office.

The majority of states (39) use primary elections to select presidential nominees. All states use some form of primary election to select legislative and state nominees. These elections are usually held between early February and late spring of an election year, with the Iowa caucus and New Hampshire primary enjoying the coveted "first-in-the-nation" position. Each state sets its own rules for these elections, and there is considerable variation in primary procedures from state to state. There are several types of primaries.

- **Closed primary.** This is the most common type. In a closed primary, voting is restricted to registered members of a political party. Voters may vote only for candidates running for the nomination of their declared party. Democrats choose among the candidates for the Democratic nomination, while Republicans choose among Republican hopefuls.
- **Open primary.** In open primaries, voters may vote only in one party's primary, but they may vote in whichever party primary they choose. Voters select the party primary in which they wish to participate in the privacy of the voting booth. Critics argue that open primaries allow voters to sabotage their opponents' primaries by crossing party lines to vote for the candidate *least* likely to win the general election. This is likely to happen only when there are no close contests in one party, however.
- **Blanket primary.** Blanket primaries use the same procedure as the general elections. In blanket primaries, voters may vote for one candidate per office of either party. Only Alaska and Washington state use this primary system.

In primary voting for legislators and state officials, the candidate who receives a **plurality** (greatest number of votes, but not more than half the total votes cast) or majority (more than half) in each primary is declared the winner. Some states require the winner to receive a minimum percentage of the vote, however. If no candidate receives the required share of votes, a **runoff primary** is held between the top two. Runoffs occur most often when many challengers vie for an open office, especially when none of them are well known.

In primary elections for the presidency, voters also choose **delegates** pledged to a particular presidential candidate. Winning delegates attend their party's national convention. Some states select presidential convention delegates at **state caucuses** and **conventions**. This process begins with local meetings of party members, who select representatives to send to statewide party meetings. Compared with primaries, the state caucus and convention process usually attracts fewer participants. Those who participate tend to be more politically active and better informed than typical voters.

The Democratic Party uses a third method to choose some delegates to its national convention. It grants automatic delegate status to many elected party leaders, including congresspersons and important state leaders. These **superdelegates** generally support the front-runner. Critics complain that the superdelegates dilute the importance of the primary elections by making it easier for the party elite to control the nominating process. The Republican Party does not have superdelegates. To promote diversity within the delegate pool, the **McGovern-Fraser Commission** was created in 1968. It recommended that delegates be represented by the proportion of their population in each state.

General elections for federal office are held on the Tuesday after the first Monday of November. Elections in which the president is being chosen are called **presidential elections**. Those that occur between presidential elections are called **midterm elections**.

First Steps Toward Nomination

Nearly all elected officials first receive the endorsement, or nomination, of one of the two major parties. Nominees usually have extensive backgrounds in government. Some presidential candidates are current or former members of the Senate. Many have served as governors. Gubernatorial experience allows candidates to claim executive abilities, because governors serve many of the same government functions in their states as the president does in the federal government. Governors also have the advantage of being able to run as Washington outsiders, as opposed to senators, who usually have extensive federal experience (and whose voting records are often used against them). At a time when public distrust of Washington is high, outsider status can be a significant benefit. Bill Clinton and George W. Bush successfully exploited this factor in their presidential campaigns. Because Barack Obama had only been a senator for four years (as opposed to other candidates like Joe Biden, who had a 36-year tenure in 2008, or Rick Santorum, who had 16 years in 2012), he was also able to successfully campaign as an outsider in 2008.

On occasion, the major parties will pursue a candidate with little or no government experience. Such candidates are invariably popular and well-respected figures, often from the military. World War II General Dwight Eisenhower was such a candidate in his successful 1952 campaign.

A presidential run is an all-consuming endeavor that must begin up to two years before the first primary. As a result, most candidates devote themselves to the effort full time. Jimmy Carter and Ronald Reagan both left their governorships before running for the presidency; Bob Dole retired from the Senate in 1996 to commit himself more fully to his campaign. Others have remained in office and ran successful campaigns. Bill Clinton and George W. Bush are two candidates who remained governors while successfully seeking their party's nomination. Chris Christie's recent White House run was made while he remained governor of New Jersey, and numerous New Jersey newspapers called for his resignation, claiming that he had neglected his gubernatorial duties while campaigning.

Presidents running for reelection and vice presidents seeking the presidency benefit from the prestige of their offices.

Those considering a run for the presidency must first seek support among the party organizations. They must especially seek the aid of influential donors to the party because elections are extremely expensive. Candidates spend much of the early stages of the nomination process meeting with potential donors, establishing PACs to raise funds (more about fundraising below), and campaigning for the endorsements of important political groups and leaders. This entire process is often referred to as testing the waters.

In the year before the first primaries, potential candidates attempt to increase their public profile. They schedule public appearances and attempt to attract media coverage by taking stands on current issues and discussing the goals of their projected presidencies. Candidates are particularly vulnerable to the media during this period. Since the public knows little about most potential candidates, negative reports or media spin can quickly scuttle a campaign (see Newt Gingrich in 2012). As primary season begins, candidates try to raise as much money as possible and to garner as many votes in the primaries as possible, in an effort to win the nomination. Candidates who can't raise their own money and don't get enough votes are quickly forced out of the race. The candidates also begin to assemble campaign personnel—advisors, political consultants, public relations experts, speechwriters, fund-raisers, lawyers, and office administrators—who will help manage the campaign.

On occasion, wealthy candidates have attempted to run for the presidency without needing, or using, federal matching funds. Ross Perot in 1992 and Steve Forbes in 1996 used their own money to campaign, but both campaigns failed. Ross Perot's 1992 campaign spent more money than the Democratic and Republican candidates combined.

Financing Campaigns

A successful presidential campaign requires much more than an appealing candidate. It needs a huge supporting staff, jets and buses, and the resources to hire consultants, pollsters, and advertising agencies. It should come as no surprise, then, that one of the most important skills a candidate can possess is the ability to raise money.

Presidential candidates who meet certain prerequisites may receive federal funding. Primary candidates who receive more than 10% of the vote in an election may apply for **federal matching funds.** These funds essentially double all campaign contributions of $250 and less by matching them. To receive matching funds, candidates must agree to obey federal spending limits: Any candidate who receives less than 10% of the vote in two consecutive primaries loses his or her eligibility for matching funds until he or she wins more than 10% of the vote in another primary.

The federal government funds the general election campaigns of the two major presidential candidates, provided those candidates agree not to accept and spend

Elections and the Elite
Many campaigns fail when testing the waters, long before the public is ever aware of them, due to lack of interest among the political elite.

Setting Limits
In 2012, the federal spending limit was $45.6 million for the primary elections and $91.2 million for the general election.

other donations (an exception is made for up to $50,000 of the candidate's own money). The year 2004 was the first election in which both major party nominees declined public matching funds during the primaries. Independents do not receive federal funding for their campaigns. (In 2008, John McCain accepted matching funds while Barack Obama did not. In the subsequent 2012 race, neither Obama nor Mitt Romney accepted matching funds.) In the 2016 election, at the time of this book's publication, only one presidential contender sought and qualified for public financing (Martin O'Malley).

Despite attempts at campaign finance reform, the trend toward high levels of election spending has continued through the 1990s and into the first decade of the twenty-first century. In the 2004 election, George W. Bush raised $272.5 million and John Kerry raised $250.3 million. Both candidates refused matching funds to avoid all spending limits. This precedent-setting high, however, was swiftly broken in light of the ability for corporations and unions to now donate directly and without limits. The combined expenditures for the 2012 campaign that set Mitt Romney against Obama totaled over $7 billion dollars—just about 14 times as much in only eight years. Without any sort of cap, future candidates may raise even more.

There is currently no public financing of congressional campaigns, and there are no spending limits for congressional candidates. There are, however, limits on the amounts that individuals and political committees may donate to candidates, but these limits have been revised in the twenty-first century, first by the Bipartisan Campaign Reform Act (BCRA) in 2002, and then by *Citizens United v. Federal Election Commission* in 2010. These limits are as follows:

	To a Candidate	To a National Party	To a Political Committee	Total per 2 Calendar Years
Individual may give	$2,600	$32,400	$5,000	no limit
PAC may give	$5,000	$15,000	$5,000	no limit
Non-PAC committee may give[1]	$2,600	$32,400	$5,000	no limit

Many Americans believe that the current campaign finance system has a corrupting effect on government and a talking point among many of the candidates within the 2016 election has been that the public financing system is broken. Efforts to change the system, however, run into several obstacles. The Supreme Court ruled in *Buckley v. Valeo* (1976) that mandatory spending limits on campaigns violate candidates' First Amendment rights to free expression. Furthermore, the system currently benefits incumbents, in that the incumbent's job description is basically the stuff of reelections: meetings, events, talking to voters, photo ops, and so on. Accordingly, legislators are reluctant to make changes because changes would make their reelection more difficult. The permissible donations listed in the above table will change if campaign finance reform is enacted.

---

[1] Political committees that do not meet legal requirements of a PAC (for example, donations from at least 50 contributors).

Primary Season

By January 1 of election year, candidates are campaigning widely among the public. From this point on, candidates participate in debates, campaign from state to state delivering their "stump speeches" (so called because campaigning is often referred to as "stumping"), and choreograph media events—in an effort to draw positive media coverage of their campaigns.

The earliest primaries (New Hampshire's is a prime example) provide a great boost to the campaigns of whoever wins, increasing the candidate's media exposure and making all-important fundraising chores easier. Major financial contributors usually desert the campaigns of the losers in early primaries. Furthermore, candidates who receive less than 10% of the vote in two successive primaries lose their eligibility for crucial federal matching funds. As a result, those who fare poorly in early primaries usually have to drop out of the race long before the majority of delegates have been selected.

Because early primaries are perceived to have grown increasingly important in recent years, many states have pushed forward the date of their primary elections. Many states even hold their primaries all on the same day in early March (called **Super Tuesday**). Large states such as New York and California have moved their primaries forward in hopes of having a greater influence on which candidates win the nominations. Political analysts refer to this strategy as **front-loading**, and the result has been to place increased pressure on candidates to succeed early. Critics argue that it unnecessarily forces voters to choose early in the election process, before they have gotten a chance to know the candidates well.

Primary elections and state caucuses continue into late spring. In many recent elections, however, the party nominee has been decided long before the last elections. Mitt Romney's nomination in 2012 is an example of that very phenomenon.

National Conventions

After the primary season has ended, both parties hold national conventions to confirm their nominee. When no candidate has received the pledge of a majority of convention delegates, conventions decide who the nominee will be; such conventions are called **brokered conventions**. The parties have designed their primary systems to prevent brokered conventions, which can divide the party and cost it the election. The most recent brokered conventions are 1952 for Democrats (Adlai Stevenson) and 1948 for Republicans (Thomas Dewey) making them seem, at least for now, like historical relics.

One of the main purposes of a national convention, in fact, is to unify the party. Primary elections can damage each party, as candidates attack one another and thereby expose rifts within the party membership. Another main purpose of conventions is to make a show of party unity for political gain. Both parties' conventions are nationally televised and are widely covered by the news media. Not surprisingly, most of what occurs on the convention stage is choreographed to appeal to the party faithful and undecided voters watching at home.

That does not mean that conventions are placid affairs, however. Conventions are the site of many political negotiations, as different factions of the party attempt to win concessions in return for their full support during the general election. There are often intense battles over the party **platform**, a statement of purpose and party goals, which, ironically, has little concrete significance. The conventions also offer some political drama, as nominees sometimes wait until the convention to announce their choice of running mates.

The greatest impact conventions can have on general election results is negative. In 1968, for example, rioting outside the Democratic convention in Chicago created a bad impression among voters, especially when contrasted with the unified display at the Republican convention in Miami weeks later. In 1992, ultraconservatives were able to control key elements of the Republican convention. The image the convention created was one of an angry and activist party, which frightened voters and hurt President Bush's reelection campaign. Under normal circumstances, however, conventions usually help their candidates considerably. Polls taken immediately after conventions show the candidates' approval ratings up significantly. This rise in public approval is called a **post-convention bump**.

Nonetheless, it is important to note that national conventions have been altered dramatically in the last century. Until about mid-century, conventions and convention delegates actually selected and nominated the candidate. With the adoption of primary elections, conventions have been transformed into mere coronations with the nominees generally being determined before the convention begins (as with Obama and Romney in 2012).

The General Election and the Electoral College

The remaining candidates continue to campaign for the general election in much the same way as they campaigned during the primaries: holding rallies, participating in debates, running campaign advertisements, and pursuing positive media coverage. There are several key differences between the primaries and the general election. First, during the primaries, candidates run against members of their own party. Because primary candidates are often in general agreement about big-picture issues, their campaigns focus instead on the subtler differences between them. During the general elections, candidates often emphasize the general policy and philosophical differences between the two parties. Put simply, a candidate courts his or her political base during the primary season and then usually attempts to move toward the center in the general election to win undecided votes in hopes of securing the majority.

Candidates planning their campaign strategies must consider the nature of the **electoral college.** This institution was created by the Framers of the Constitution as a means of insulating the government from the whims of a less-educated public. Critics feel the electoral college system is antiquated, but no one has yet successfully proposed an amendment to change it. Presidential elections therefore continue to be determined not by the final popular vote but rather by this institution. Each state is given a number of electors equal to the sum of its federal legislators (senators plus representatives). The winner of the presidential election in each state wins all of that state's electors[2] (which is why it is often referred to as a **winner-take-all system**).

The electoral college system places greater emphasis on election results in large states. Victory by a single vote in California wins a candidate all of that state's 54 electoral votes; a similar margin of victory in Vermont yields only three electoral votes. Despite the number of votes at stake in the large states, candidates will often devote the bulk of their time to "swing" states—areas in which polling indicates a close race. This is the reason that during the 2012 presidential election, states like Ohio, Colorado, and New Hampshire were inundated with political ads while large states whose voters generally go with one party, such as New York, California, and Texas, were relatively quiet. Finally, candidates consider each other's electoral strategies in planning their campaigns. In 1968, the Democratic Party relied on the support of its Southern base. Republican Richard Nixon realized that this support was weakening and campaigned aggressively in the region. Nixon's "Southern strategy" worked in enough Southern states to swing the election to the Republicans.

MEDIA INFLUENCE ON ELECTIONS

With nearly 240 million Americans of voting age, it is clear that candidates cannot come into direct contact with even a small portion of the electorate. Instead, they must rely on the media to get their political message across.

- **News media** provide many voters with daily campaign information. While most news programs occasionally report on the candidates' positions on the issues, they concentrate on the candidates' standing in the polls, or the horse race aspect of the election. This is because news directors prefer information that can be communicated quickly and that changes regularly, such as public opinion poll results. In contrast, candidates' positions on issues are often complex.

---

[2] The two exceptions are Maine and Nebraska, which give two electoral votes to the candidate who wins a plurality of the statewide vote, and one vote to the winner of each of the state's congressional districts. Maine has four electoral votes, Nebraska has five.

Furthermore, they rarely change. Therefore, news programs may report such information once during an election, but they do not report it repeatedly as they do with poll results. As a result, the attention of the network news audience is focused on the campaign game rather than on the candidates' political agendas.

- **Campaign advertisements** provide another, more controlled look at the candidates. Through advertising, candidates attempt to build a positive image with the public. In many cases, they also try to belittle their opponents through negative advertising. Negative advertising works best when the public knows little about a candidate. In 1988, for example, Democratic candidate Michael Dukakis was the subject of several effective negative advertisements. Although he led in the polls prior to the ads, Dukakis's support was weak, as most voters knew little about him. The negative advertisements were effective in destroying Dukakis's lead by portraying him as weak, incompetent, and soft on crime.

ELECTION DAY

There are nearly 219 million Americans of voting age. Of them, around 146 million are registered to vote. In the 2012 election, though, around 126 million actually turned out to vote (57.5% of the country). **Voter turnout** is even lower for midterm elections: Typically less than 40 percent of all eligible voters participated in 2012. American voter turnout rates are among the lowest of all Western democracies.

Certain patterns are detectable in American voters' behavior. The likelihood that an individual will vote corresponds closely to his or her level of education: The more educated a person is, the more likely he or she is to vote. Age is also a factor: Turnout rates are highest among Americans over the age of 40, and lowest among those under the age of 20.

Voter turnout is also influenced in part by how close a race is. Voters are less likely to vote when they believe they know who will win the election. Such was the case in 1996, when many Americans were certain that Bill Clinton would be re-elected. Remember, however, that many federal and state offices are up for grabs on election day. A closely contested race in any of those elections can be enough to motivate voters to participate. Voter turnout can also be affected by various legislation. The National Voter Registration Act (1993), also known as The Motor Voter Act, made voting easier by allowing voter registration at the time someone applies for a driver's license. Conversely, the photo ID laws enacted in some areas at the state level depress voter turnout by requiring voters to show a photo ID before voting. These photo ID laws are controversial, with those who are for them saying it reduces voter fraud and those who are against them saying it decreases voting by impoverished Americans.

On election day, the media report not only election results but also the results of exit polls that break down the vote by age, gender, race, income level, region, and nearly every other demographic imaginable. They do so in an effort to determine the meaning of the results. Why did voters choose one candidate over another? How satisfied were voters with the choices presented them? Were the voters sending a clear message—a **mandate**—or not? Winners search the results for evidence of a mandate. In 1992, Bill Clinton interpreted his victory as a mandate for a more active and progressive federal government. Several historic failures—on efforts to integrate homosexuals in the military and to establish nationalized health care—demonstrated that voter mandates are not always so clear. The voters' message has become more difficult to discern as **split-ticket voting**—voting for a presidential candidate of one party and legislators of the other—has grown more common.

Split-ticket voting leads to **divided government**, when one party controls the Senate or House or both and the other controls the White House. An example of this comes from the composition of the government as of 2015: following the 2014 elections, Republicans have House and Senate majorities, while Democrats control the White House. This can create policy gridlock because these two branches are often at odds with each other. Conversely, it can cause them to work together in the creation of moderate public policy. Lastly, it encourages party **dealignment** because voters do not align with their parties as uniformly as they once did.

KEY TERMS

- incumbent advantage
- gerrymandering
- nominations
- general elections
- closed primary
- open primary
- blanket primary
- plurality
- runoff primary
- caucus
- delegates
- superdelegates
- McGovern-Fraser Commission
- federal matching funds
- Super Tuesday
- front-loading
- platform
- post-convention bump
- electoral college
- winner-take-all system
- voter turnout
- mandate

Summary

o Elections consist of two phases: nominations and the general election. Most nominations are made through party primaries. These can be open, closed, or blanket.

o Candidates need the backing of the major parties along with a compelling back story before they can hope to make a strong campaign for national office.

o Campaign finance was restricted by a complicated web of regulations defined by the election laws of the 1970s along with the 2002 Bipartisan Campaign Reform Act, but new laws were passed in 2010.

o Before the general elections, the candidates need to win their party primaries, which often involves energizing the base. Later, candidates may have to repudiate some of the more radical statements they made to court primary voters in order to win more moderate voters in the general election.

o Nominating conventions used to be where the party nominees were selected, but now they are symbolic coronations of the candidate who has already been selected through the primary process. Still, delegates assemble, cheer, and argue over the drafting of the party platform.

o Presidential candidates must win each state's electors, which is done by getting a plurality of all the voters in that state. This method causes candidates to spend most of their time in "swing" or "battleground" states and can also result in the winner of the popular vote losing the election (as was the case with Al Gore in the election of 2000).

o After all the voting is done, pollsters, the parties, and the media try their best to determine why the people voted the way they did. Exit polls and surveys are the tools used to decipher these factors.

Chapter 7 Drill

See Chapter 11 for answers and explanations.

1. In an *open* Republican primary

   (A) only Republicans can vote
   (B) only Democrats can vote
   (C) only Republicans and Democrats can vote
   (D) only Independents can vote
   (E) every registered voter can vote

2. In a given election cycle, a political action committee (PAC) may contribute to a candidate no more than

   (A) $2,000
   (B) $3,000
   (C) $4,000
   (D) $5,000
   (E) $6,000

3. At a nominating convention, the position that the political party will take is decided by the

   (A) Platform Committee
   (B) Committee on Permanent Organization
   (C) Credentials Committee
   (D) Rules Committee
   (E) Ideology Committee

4. In order to win the election for the presidency, a candidate must

   (A) receive a majority of the votes in the electoral college
   (B) receive a majority of the popular vote
   (C) receive a plurality of votes in the electoral college
   (D) receive a plurality of the popular vote
   (E) receive a unanimous vote from the electoral college

5. Which of the following people is *most* likely to vote in a general election?

   (A) a 25-year-old high school dropout
   (B) a 65-year-old professor
   (C) a 19-year-old college student
   (D) a 16-year-old high school student
   (E) a 30-year-old college graduate

6. In a presidential election, state caucuses differ from state primaries in which of the following ways?

   (A) Only primary winners send delegates to the convention.
   (B) Caucuses usually have lower turnout.
   (C) More states use caucuses than primaries.
   (D) Winners of caucuses must get a majority of votes.
   (E) Voters in primaries choose representatives to vote for them.

7. Results of the 1992 presidential election:

Presidential Candidate	Popular Vote	Percentage of Vote	Electoral Votes
George H. W. Bush	39,104,550	37.5%	168
William J. Clinton	44,909,806	43.0%	370
Ross Perot	19,743,821	18.9%	0

Based on the data in the table above, William J. Clinton won the election because

   (A) he won a majority of the popular vote
   (B) he won a plurality of the popular vote
   (C) he won a majority of electoral votes
   (D) he won a plurality of electoral votes
   (E) he won the highest percentage of the vote

REFLECT

Respond to the following questions:

- For which content topics discussed in this chapter do you feel you have achieved sufficient mastery to answer multiple-choice questions correctly?

- For which content topics discussed in this chapter do you feel you have achieved sufficient mastery to discuss effectively in an essay?

- For which content topics discussed in this chapter do you feel you need more work before you can answer multiple-choice questions correctly?

- For which content topics discussed in this chapter do you feel you need more work before you can discuss effectively in an essay?

- What parts of this chapter are you going to re-review?

- Will you seek further help, outside of this book (such as a teacher, tutor, or AP Students), on any of the content in this chapter—and, if so, on what content?

Chapter 8
Institutions of
Government

CONGRESS

Concepts

- Why do congressional incumbents have an advantage over challengers?
- Why did the Supreme Court strike down majority-minority voting districts?
- Why does Congress continue to maintain the seniority system?
- What is it about the way Congress operates that promotes factionalism?
- Why has it been argued that Congress contributes to the fragmentation of policy making?
- Why do we hate Congress but love our congressperson?
- Why would members of Congress vote against campaign finance reform?
- Why would members of the Senate engage in a filibuster?
- Why is the House Rules Committee so important?
- How does politics enter into the nomination process for independent agencies and the judiciary?
- What impact has the high cost of campaigning had on the legislative process?
- What are the powers of the leaders in the House and Senate?

Congressional Structure

Congress is the bicameral (two-house) legislature responsible for writing the laws of the nation. Congress also serves other functions, such as overseeing the bureaucracy, consensus building, clarifying policy, legitimizing, and expressing diversity. It is made up of a **House of Representatives** of 435 members and a **Senate** of 100 members.

Every 10 years, a **census** is taken by the federal government to count the population to determine the number of each state's **congressional districts**. Each state must then redraw its congressional boundaries to ensure that each district is equal in population. Congressional **redistricting** is done by each state legislature. Therefore, the political party in control of the state legislature controls how the districts are drawn. As much as is legally possible, the legislature will **gerrymander** the district boundaries to give the majority party an advantage in future elections. This is true in every state with the exception of Iowa, which uses an independent commission to form districts. In some states, such as Alaska and Wyoming, the populations are so small that the entire state becomes a congressional district; all states are guaranteed at least one seat in the House.

Congressional Elections

Elections for all the 435 seats of the House of Representatives occur every two years. House members must reside in the district they represent, be a citizen of the state, and be at least 25 years old. Election to the House takes place within each congressional district. The constituencies of representatives are relatively small compared with those of senators, and the House incumbent election rates are very high, averaging more than 90%. Many House members have safe seats and are not seriously challenged for reelection.

Elections for one-third of the Senate occur every two years, with a senator's term lasting six years. Every state is guaranteed two senators, elected on a staggered basis in statewide elections. Senate elections are generally more competitive, expensive, high profile, and draw candidates from other elected offices.

Important Voting Rights Court Cases

Smith v. Allwright (1944). The denying of African Americans the right to vote in a primary election was found to be a violation of the Fifteenth Amendment.

Wesberry v. Sanders (1963). Ordered House districts to be as equal as possible—enshrined the principle of "one man, one vote."

Buckley v. Valeo (1976). The court ruled that giving money to a political campaign was a form of free speech and threw out some stringent federal regulations on fund-raising and election spending.

Shaw v. Reno (1993) and *Miller v. Johnson* (1995). Race cannot be the sole or predominant factor in redrawing legislative district boundaries.

U.S. Term Limits v. Thornton (1995). States cannot set term limits on members of Congress.

Bush v. Gore (2000). Florida's recount in the election of 2000 was ruled to be a violation of the Fourteenth Amendment's equal protection clause.

Shelby County v. Holder (2013). Invalidated part of the Voting Rights Act of 1965, clearing the way for the expansion of photo ID laws.

Congressional Districts and Representation

Descriptive representation means that the elected legislature should reflect the demographic characteristics of the constituency. Minorities and women have always been underrepresented in Congress and state legislatures, which is the reason that the **Voting Rights Act of 1965** encouraged states to take measures to increase minority representation in Congress. Into the early 1980s, little progress had been made. Women, Latinos, and African Americans continued to be underrepresented. In 1982, Congress amended the Voting Rights Act to encourage states to create majority-minority districts, concentrating African American and Hispanic populations into distinct congressional districts. These districts were created to make it more feasible for minority candidates to get elected.

Following the 1990 census, many states redrew their congressional districts, which resulted in an increase of African American representation by 50% and

Hispanic membership by 70 percent. Various districts were drawn to conform to the Voting Rights Act. However, the shape of these districts was sometimes quite bizarre. North Carolina District 12, for example, stretched in a narrow band 160 miles down Interstate Highway 85. A Duke University professor joined with four other white plaintiffs to challenge the constitutionality of District 12. In *Shaw v. Reno* (1993), the Supreme Court surprised many with a split decision. The court invalidated the district in question because its boundaries were neither contiguous nor compact and were drawn with the intent to discriminate through the use of racial gerrymandering. The court ruled that any racial gerrymandering by the state required a compelling state interest, and it did not see such a compelling interest in this district. On the other hand, the Supreme Court has heard other redistricting cases like this one, and has upheld the redistricting or simply declined to take the challenge.

Legislators in North Carolina, Georgia, Texas, and many other states have been accused of playing dirty politics with redistricting. African American and (to a lesser degree) Hispanic voters are overwhelmingly Democrat. (Cuban Americans in Florida tend to vote Republican.) Critics claim that Republican-controlled state legislatures were not motivated by any sense of duty. Instead, they stand accused of trying to remove racial-minority Democrats from other districts to ensure that more Republicans get elected. The political trade-off was to create a guaranteed Democratic district and at the same time gain more Republican seats from the surrounding districts.

> **Packing and Cracking**
> To isolate minorities in the district is known as "packing." To divide them across many districts is "cracking."

To add to the representation controversy, population shifts in the last 20 years have given additional seats in the House to southern states while reducing the number from other regions. In addition, suburban representation has increased, at the expense of both rural and urban areas.

Finally, Congress draws its members primarily from the legal and business worlds. Almost half of the House and more than half of the Senate have a legal background. The reason seems to be that lawyers have many of the prerequisites needed for a successful run for Congress: interest and experience in the law, prominence within the community, and the personal wealth to at least partially fund an election campaign.

Congressional Powers

The Framers had a fear of the power inherent in legislatures. Because of that fear, the Constitution spells out the responsibilities of the legislature in more detail than those of the executive and judicial branches. To further guard against legislative usurpation (control of one house over the other), both houses have unique but complementary powers. The delegated powers, which require both houses to work in concert with each other, include taxing, borrowing money, regulating commerce, raising an army, creating and making rules for the federal courts, establishing naturalization laws, establishing post offices, providing for a militia, and making any law that is deemed necessary and proper for carrying out these powers.

Each house also has unique powers. Only the House of Representatives may initiate tax laws and spending bills. It is the **House Ways and Means Committee** that oversees taxing and spending legislation. The Senate has only amending powers on revenue bills.

The Senate's unique powers include confirmation of presidential nominations to the federal courts and ambassadorships to foreign countries. The Senate must also ratify all treaties signed by the president.

There are also restrictions on congressional actions. Congress may not pass **bills of attainder** (laws that find people guilty of a crime and sentence them to prison without a trial) or *ex post facto* **laws** (that punish people for actions that occurred before the behavior was made criminal) and may not levy export taxes or grant titles of nobility. These same prohibitions apply to states.

The Non-legislative Tasks of Congress

Congress's primary responsibility is to fulfill the legal needs of the nation by writing laws. However, Congress also performs other equally important functions. These include the following:

- **Oversight.** Through its committees and subcommittees, Congress reviews the work of the federal agencies. This helps check the executive branch. It investigates charges of corruption and waste, and it holds hearings where experts and citizens discuss the government's problems and suggest solutions. All committee chairs have the power to subpoena (legally compel) witnesses to appear and testify. It is also the role of the Senate to confirm the members of the president's cabinet as well as to approve nominees for all positions in the federal court system.
- **Public education.** Committee hearings and floor debates increase public awareness of government and societal problems. Floor debates over issues such as gun control, tax cuts, Social Security reform, health care reform, and sending armed troops abroad all help to focus national attention.
- **Representing constituents within the government.** As representatives of their electorates, members of Congress not only vote on laws but also help constituents in their dealings with the government. They receive and can act on complaints about federal services, sponsor voters who seek scholarships or federal contracts, and solicit constituents' suggestions on how to improve the government. In performing this last task, some members of Congress consider themselves delegates whose job it is to mirror the views of their home districts. This is known as the Delegate Model or representational view. Others see themselves as trustees who should consider their constituents' views but should ultimately use their best judgment as experts when deciding how to vote. This is known as the Trustee Model, or attitudinal view.

The Legislative Process

The legislative process is, by design, slow and complicated. This is to prevent Congress from acting hastily. The Framers intended for the process to foster compromise. The result has been that the final versions of bills are often radically different from the initial versions. Without compromise there would be no legislative process.

As many as 10,000 bills are introduced on the floor of Congress each year. Some are written by members of Congress and their staffs; others are drafted by the executive branch and are introduced by a sympathetic member of Congress. Many are suggested or written by interest groups and their lawyers. Regardless of who authors a bill, a bill can be proposed only by a member of Congress. Whoever introduces a bill is called the **sponsor** of the bill.

The legislative process requires the two houses to work cooperatively with each other. All bills must pass both houses in exactly the same form. While the bills must be the same, the debate and voting processes in the two houses differ. Because there are 435 members of the House of Representatives, the process by which bills are debated is limited. The Senate, which is smaller, has fewer rules governing the legislative process.

Unlike the Senate, the House has a **Rules Committee,** which is responsible for determining how long a bill will be debated and, whether to allow an open or closed rule for amending the bill. Open rules allow amendments; closed rules prohibit amendments. When Republicans gained control of the House of Representatives in 1994, they promised most bills would be debated under open rules. Allowing 435 members an opportunity to add amendments to bills became so cumbersome, however, that the House leadership returned to the closed rule process. Because the House Rules Committee controls crucial aspects of the legislative process, it is considered the most powerful committee in the House. The Rules Committee can kill a bill by delaying a vote or by making it easy for opponents to add **poison-pill** (or **"killer"**) **amendments**. The House Rules Committee can also bring bills up for an immediate floor vote.

While the House strictly controls debate, the Senate does not. There are no time restraints placed on senators. A **filibuster** is a tactic used to delay a vote on a bill and tie up the work of the Senate, usually by a senator making a speech that continues for hours on the Senate floor. A filibuster can also happen without actual continuous speeches, although the senate majority leader may require an actual traditional filibuster if he or she so chooses. The only way to end a filibuster is to vote for **cloture,** but this requires the votes of sixty members, which is difficult to achieve when the two parties are evenly represented.

The Senate has no closed rules for amending legislation. Amendments, called riders, do not have to be relevant to a bill. This allows individual senators an opportunity to add amendments, such as "pet" issues or projects for their home state, or to prohibit the actions of executive agencies. "Pet project" riders designed to bring federal money to a home state are called **pork barrels.**

Meat Lovers
"Bringing home the bacon" is one of the reasons incumbent reelection rates are so high. The members of both houses love pork-barrel legislation.

Earmarks—provisions within legislation that appropriate money to a specific project—appear in appropriation bills and authorization bills. There are a few groups that monitor earmarking in the U.S. Congress, but earmarks are no longer allowed by the House.

After debates, bills usually end up passing the House and Senate in different forms, so both versions are sent to a **conference committee**. The members of these conference committees come from the respective committees of the two houses that wrote the bill. The conference committee tries to negotiate a compromise bill, acceptable to both houses of Congress. Once a compromise version has been written, the bill is returned to the two houses for a vote. Failure to pass a bill from a conference committee will kill a bill. If the bill is passed in both houses, it is sent to the White House for the president's signature.

The president has options. If he does nothing for 10 days, the bill becomes law without his signature. If a congressional session ends during those 10 days, the president must sign every bill into law. If he doesn't, the bill will be **pocket vetoed**, requiring the bill go through the entire legislative process again. If there are more than 10 days left in a congressional session, and a president wants to prevent a bill from becoming law, he may veto the entire bill. The president must then give his reasons in writing and return the bill to the house of origination.

At that point, Congress has choices. The two houses may make the required changes, or they may attempt to override the president's veto by a two-thirds vote. If the bill passes both houses by the required two-thirds vote, the bill becomes law without the president's signature. If the house of origination (where the bill was originally introduced) does nothing with the presidential veto, the bill is dead.

In 1996, Congress gave the president the **line-item veto,** empowering the president to veto individual parts of a bill. The constitutionality of the line-item veto was immediately challenged in the Supreme Court (*Clinton v. New York City*). The court struck down the line-item veto as an unconstitutional delegation of legislative authority to the president.

Congress has also attempted to give itself veto power over the actions of the president. In specific instances, Congress would write legislation giving the president broad powers to act but reserve to itself the right to void presidential actions by a vote of one or both houses. This legislative veto was declared unconstitutional by the Supreme Court in *INS v. Chadha* (1983). The only form of veto mentioned in the Constitution is that used by the president.

Legislation by Committee

Most of the legislative business of Congress occurs in committees. Who serves on which committee and what position they hold is determined by a number of factors. The majority party of each house holds all the committee chairs. The majority party will also hold a majority of the seats on each committee, effectively controlling all the business of the committee. On the important committees, the majority usually holds two-thirds of the committee seats.

Generally, the committee member of the majority party with the most seniority becomes the chair and the senior member from the minority party becomes the ranking member. The ranking member becomes chair if the minority party becomes the majority party. This happened in 2001 when a member of the Republican-controlled Senate left the Republican Party to become an Independent. All Democrat ranking members of Senate committees became the chairs, while the Republican chairs became the ranking members. The same principle applies in the House of Representatives.

Committee assignments in the House and Senate are determined by the House and Senate leadership and a caucus of the two political parties. Members of Congress attempt to get on the committees that will allow them to do the most constituent service and help them get reelected. For example, representatives and senators from farm states try to get assigned to agriculture committees.

Committees serve as mini-legislatures, performing the tasks of investigating and debating bills that, due to time constraints, could never otherwise receive the consideration of Congress. Often, the congressional committee assigns the bill to an even smaller group, called a **subcommittee,** for initial consideration. Recently, there has been a proliferation of subcommittees. Subcommittees often determine how money is spent and have therefore become very powerful.

The fate of a new bill depends on much more than its content. The membership of the committee and subcommittee that first considers the bill is crucial. Bill sponsors attempt to draft bills in such a way as to steer them toward sympathetic committees. Supporters of a bill must also decide which house of Congress should consider their bill first, because with the exception of revenue bills, federal bills may originate in either house. To build political momentum, supporters attempt to have the bill introduced in the house most sympathetic to their cause.

The House has more committees than the Senate. House members, however, tend to become more specialized because they serve on fewer committees. As a result, they are considered to have more expertise than senators.

There are four types of committees in Congress.

- **Standing committees** are permanent, specialized committees. Examples include the House Ways and Means Committee, the Senate Judiciary Committee, and the Senate Armed Services Committee. There are twenty standing committees in the House and seventeen in the Senate.
- **Joint committees** are made up of members of both the House and the Senate. These committees are normally used for communicating to the public or for investigations but generally do not send bills to the floor for votes.
- **Select committees** are temporary committees organized in each house for some special purpose. These committees usually carry out investigations for the purpose of writing special legislation. The House Watergate Committee and the Senate Select Committee on Unfair Campaign Practices are examples from the Nixon era. The work of these committees eventually led to campaign reform.
- **Conference committees** are temporary and include members from the committees of the two houses who were responsible for writing a bill. These committees try to negotiate compromise bills, which are then submitted to the two houses for an up or down vote without amendments. Once a compromise bill has been negotiated, the conference committee disbands.

Most bills die almost immediately in a subcommittee due to lack of interest from committee members; unless a committee member takes a special interest in a bill, the bill will either be quickly rejected or ignored until it dies a natural death at the end of the congressional session.

Committees and subcommittees function by calling interested parties and expert witnesses who have some information to give. Lobbyists often testify as expert witnesses. Congress can subpoena reluctant witnesses, forcing them to appear in hearings and can grant immunity to compel them to testify. Once their investigations have concluded, committees begin amending and rewriting sections of bills in meetings called markup sessions.

Committees will sometimes refuse to vote a bill out, hoping to keep it from being considered by the House. A bill stuck in a House or Senate committee is said to be **pigeonholed.** The parliamentary mechanism to force a bill out of committee for a floor vote is called a **discharge petition.**

Committees have responsibilities in addition to writing laws. For example, they are responsible for the oversight of many bureaucratic agencies and departments. Heads of regulatory agencies, which are responsible for enforcing the laws, often appear to give testimony before congressional committees with oversight jurisdiction. If the agency has not followed the intent of the law, the agency head will be in for a rough time. A recent example comes from a congressional investigation of the Secret Service and subsequent resignation by Director Julia Pierson after multiple security lapses involving President Obama and the White House.

Committees also hear testimony from agency heads pleading for money and personnel. Congressional budget cutting and agency reorganization can have a profound impact on an agency's ability to carry out its responsibilities. This is one way that Congress can use the budget to shape policy.

Congressional Leadership

The House

The leader of the House of Representatives is the **Speaker,** who is chosen by the majority party in a special election. The Speaker is powerful because he or she can direct floor debate and has influence over committee assignments and over the Rules Committee. The Speaker can also control which bills go to which committees. The **majority leader** of the House keeps party members in line and helps determine party policy and the party's legislative agenda. The **minority leader** keeps the minority party members in line and helps determine the minority party's legislative agenda. The House majority and minority whips also help their respective party leaders keep the members loyal to the party's legislative agenda. They coordinate members of each party and help garner support for proposed legislation.

The Senate

The vice president is the president of the Senate, and this is his only constitutionally delegated responsibility. However, the vice president is rarely on the floor of the Senate and only votes to break a tie. When the vice president is absent during Senate sessions, the **president *pro tempore*** is the presiding officer. The president *pro tempore* is largely an honorary position and is usually given to the most senior member of the majority party of the Senate. The majority leader has the real power in the Senate because he or she controls the legislative agenda and acts as a power broker and policy initiator. The minority leader can act as a power broker but usually cannot initiate policy or control the agenda.

Why Do They Vote That Way?

Congresspersons are always cross-pressured to influence their vote. These pressures come from their own party and from the opposition. It also comes from the president through jawboning (trying to influence) and from their colleagues by logrolling ("you help me on this bill, and I'll help you on yours"). PACs try to influence votes through contributions, as do constituents and interest groups. Personal ideology and religious beliefs can also impact their judgment. The most important factor in determining the vote of a congressperson is party affiliation. Members of Congress usually—but not always—vote with their parties.

NOTABLE LEGISLATION

National Growth, Expansion, and Institution Building
- **Northwest Ordinance (1787, 1789).** One of the few successes of the Articles of Confederation, providing clear guidelines for the settlement of new territories and a path to statehood. Reaffirmed by Congress under the Constitution in 1789.

Regulation of Government and Industry
- **Pendleton Act (1883).** Eliminated the spoils system of patronage in selection for government jobs and set up an exam-based merit system for qualified candidates.
- **Sherman Anti-Trust Act (1890).** Provided Congress with authority to regulate and break up monopolies—or trusts—in the United States. Abused, however, to break up labor unions.
- **Hatch Act (1939).** Permitted government employees to vote in government elections but forbade them from participating in partisan politics.
- **Freedom of Information Act (1966).** Declassified government documents for public use.
- **Air Quality Act (1967).** The beginning of a series of acts to regulate impacts on the environment.
- **Federal Election Campaign Acts (1971, 1974).** Established the Federal Election Commission and required disclosures of contributions and expenditures, as well as limitations on contributions and presidential election expenditures.
- **War Powers Act (1973).** Limited president's power to use troops overseas in hostilities, put a time limit on use, and gave Congress final power to withdraw troops. Since 1973, all presidents have declared this act unconstitutional and it has been repeatedly ignored.
- **Budget and Impoundment Control Act (1974).** Established congressional budget committees and the Congressional Budget Office, as well as gave Congress the power to prevent the president from refusing to fund congressional initiatives (known as "impoundment").
- **Gramm-Rudman-Hollings Bill (1985).** Set budget reduction targets to balance the budget. Failed to eliminate loopholes.

Rights and Freedoms
- **Espionage Act (1917), Sedition Act (1918).** Severely curtailed the civil liberties of Americans during wartime and greatly increased the power of the federal government in controlling public activity. The Sedition Act was repealed by Congress in 1921.

- **Immigration Act (1924).** This law stringently limited the number of immigrants admitted into the United States and set strict quotas for entry.
- **Voting Rights Act (1965).** Suspended literacy tests, empowered federal officials to register voters, and prohibited states from changing voting procedures without federal permission.
- **Age Discrimination in Employment Act (1967).** Banned age discrimination in jobs unless age is related to job performance.
- **Civil Rights Act** or **Fair Housing Act (1968).** Title II banned discrimination in public places on the basis of race, color, national origin, or religion. Title VII prohibited employment discrimination based on gender.
- **Title IX Education Act (1972).** Prohibited gender discrimination in federally funded education programs.
- **Americans with Disabilities Act (1990).** Protected civil liberties of disabled Americans and mandated "reasonable accommodations" to public facility use.
- **National Voter Registration Act (1993).** Also known as **The Motor Voter Act**, this law allowed people to register to vote when applying for driver's licenses.
- **Patriot Act (2001).** In response to the terrorist attacks of September 11, 2001, Congress granted broad police authority to the federal, state, and local government to interdict, prosecute, and convict suspected terrorists. This law is formally known as the USA-PATRIOT Act, an acronym for "Uniting and Strengthening America by Providing Appropriate Tools Required to Intercept and Obstruct Terrorism."

Government Aid to the People

- **New Deal Legislation (1933–1939).** Legislation that expanded the role of government in the economy and society. Created entities like Social Security, the Securities and Exchange Commission, and the Tennessee Valley Authority. These laws also dramatically expanded the role and size of the federal government.
- **Personal Responsibility and Work Opportunity Reconciliation Act (1996).** The Welfare Reform Act signaled a change in the role of the federal government in the relationship with the states. This law sought to increase the role of personal responsibility in welfare recipients and shifted many responsibilities for welfare provision to state governments.
- **Bipartisan Campaign Reform Act (2002).** Often known as the **McCain-Feingold Bill**, this law banned soft money contributions to national political parties and raised hard money limits to $2,000. In a controversial decision in the case of *Citizens United v. Federal Election Commission* (2010), the Supreme Court struck down several provisions in this law, especially those related to contributions made by corporations to political campaigns.

THE PRESIDENT

Concepts

- How do presidents use their formal and informal powers to get their legislative agenda passed?
- How can Congress curb the foreign policy-making powers of the president?
- How does the president use the appointment power to ensure that policies are carried out?
- What techniques can presidents use to promote their legislative agenda in the face of divided government?
- What impact does the White House staff have on policy making?
- Why would Congress give the president a line-item veto?
- Do executive agreements go against the intent of the Framers of the Constitution?

The Formal Powers of the Presidency

The powers delegated by the Constitution to the executive branch are in Article II, Section 2, but they are less specific than the formal powers of Congress. The broadly defined powers were intended to give flexibility but have instead resulted in greatly expanded power.

The president is responsible for enforcing the laws, handling foreign policy, and serving as the ceremonial head of state. He or she is also the administrative head of the government. He or she can force Congress into session, must brief Congress on the "state of the nation," and can veto legislation, as well as grant reprieves and pardons. But regardless of these expansive powers, he or she must cooperate with Congress because the powers of the presidency are intermingled with the powers of the legislature. The president's appointments of federal judges, Supreme Court justices, ambassadors, and department secretaries all require Senate approval. The president negotiates treaties, but they must be ratified by two-thirds of the Senate. Because Senate ratification is sometimes difficult to achieve—a good example is the defeat of the Treaty of Versailles in 1919—the broad powers of the president to initiate foreign policy came to include **executive agreements** (which do not require Senate approval). These are agreements between heads of countries; under international and U.S. law, they are as binding as a treaty. However, executive agreements usually deal with more routine, administrative matters.

The President as Commander in Chief

The president also serves as **commander in chief** of the armed forces. But the Framers created a complex institutional situation regarding armed conflict. Only Congress has the power to declare war, but only the president can make war. In the nuclear age, the power of Congress to declare war could very well be obsolete. Because missiles can destroy cities within minutes of launch, congressional debate of the pros and cons of declaring war seems impractical, if not silly. While the United States has been in numerous wars since that time, no declarations of war have been made.

While the president is the chief strategist and director of the military forces of the United States, he or she is at the mercy of Congress for the money to wage war. However, once the president has committed troops in conflict, it is unlikely that Congress would refuse to fund the weapons needed for the military. For members of Congress such an action would mean political suicide and probably lead to a constitutional crisis within the U.S. government.

Presidential Powers in Wartime

In the post–Vietnam War era, Congress has attempted to place controls on the war-making powers of the president. Congress passed the **War Powers Act** in 1973 in an attempt to force the president to seek congressional approval before making war. The act specifically limits the president to 10,000 troops for 60 days, with 30 additional days to withdraw the troops, unless Congress grants an extension or declares war. The Supreme Court has never ruled on the War Powers Act, and Congress has never invoked it, although whenever the president commits troops overseas, members of Congress have threatened the president with imposition of the War Powers Act.

In a national crisis, the other branches of government and the American people look to the president for leadership. Initially, presidents will have strong support for their policies. This helps explain why Congress, in 1964, passed the **Gulf of Tonkin Resolution,** giving the president the broad powers to commit unlimited numbers of troops for an unlimited length of time in the Vietnam conflict. President Johnson was unable to bring that war to a conclusion. Strong criticism of his handling of the war led to a general lack of support for his policies, undermining his ability to govern. The same thing happened to President Carter when he was unable to successfully end the Iranian hostage crisis. As president during the Gulf War, George H. W. Bush's ability to quickly bring the war to a conclusion while suffering relatively few casualties resulted in the second-highest approval rating of any president, at 89%.

The Informal Powers

The presidential powers that are not enumerated in the Constitution are referred to as the informal powers, and they are sometimes more important than the formal ones. How well presidents use the informal powers can determine the success of their presidencies.

Presidents are supposed to be morale builders. President Carter's failure to improve the morale of the country contributed to his reelection defeat. President Reagan was a master at morale building, and this characteristic helps explain why he remained popular with the American people.

Presidents serve as legislative leaders and coalition builders. Failure to set and lead the legislative agenda and build coalitions in Congress can doom presidents, particularly when there is divided government (when one or both houses of the legislature are controlled by the opposition party). George H. W. Bush became the "foreign policy president" when he was unable to get his domestic policy agenda passed in a Democrat-controlled Congress. Ronald Reagan and his advisers were experts in building coalitions with Republicans and southern conservative Democrats. This coalition of Republicans and southern Democrats gave Reagan his legislative agenda.

Perhaps the president's most important informal powers are as a policy persuader and communicator to Congress and the American people. Clinton and Reagan were superior communicators. The ability of a president to communicate well with the American people is a very powerful tool for pressuring Congress. Communicating with Congress is also important. Having the congressional leadership down to the White House for lunch and a photo op is another way that presidents try to persuade members of Congress to pass their legislative agenda.

Executive Office of the President

The Executive Office of the President helps carry out the president's administrative responsibilities. It is made up of more than half a dozen agencies involved in the day-to-day operations of the White House and is basically divided into three areas: domestic, foreign, and military affairs. It is staffed by hundreds of personnel located in the White House and the Executive Office Building. All are directly responsible to the president or his designees.

- **The chief of staff** is the top aide to the president. He or she is a person in whom the president has complete trust and is probably a longtime associate and friend. Considered one of the most powerful persons in Washington, the chief of staff is responsible for managing the Executive Office and can control access to the president, thus potentially controlling the information that the president receives. Some presidents, such as Bill Clinton, permitted easy access; others, such as **Richard Nixon**, tended to insulate themselves. Whoever the president chooses as chief of staff can have a tremendous impact on presidential effectiveness. Clinton's first chief of staff, **Thomas McClarty**, a Washington outsider and Clinton friend, ran an undisciplined White House, prone to many errors. He was replaced by a Washington insider, former Congressman **Leon Panetta**, who established order and discipline, emerging as a key policy player in the Clinton administration. In 2009, Panetta became Director of the Central Intelligence Agency. He later resigned from that post to become Secretary of Defense. In 2010, Barack Obama's first chief of staff, former Congressman Rahm Emanuel, left the position to become mayor of Chicago.

- **The National Security Council (NSC)** is headed by the national security advisor, who has direct access to the president in matters relating to military and foreign policy. The NSC has been involved since the late 1940s in the decision-making process during national emergencies. President Kennedy used the NSC during the Cuban missile crisis, President Reagan during the Iran-Contra affair, and President George H. W. Bush during the Gulf War. Unlike the State Department, the NSC is largely free from congressional oversight. For this reason, it has become one of the most favored institutions for many presidents.
- **The Domestic Policy Council** assists the president in formulating policies relating to energy, education, agriculture, natural resources, economic affairs, health and human resources, welfare reform, drug abuse, and crime.
- **The Office of Management and Budget (OMB)** is responsible for preparing the budget of the United States and can be used to control and manage the executive agencies for the president. The OMB has enormous power because of its ability to allocate money to the cabinet departments through the budget process of the executive branch. Increasing or decreasing a department's budget affects how it carries out its responsibilities.
- **The Council of Economic Advisors** is responsible for helping the president make national economic policy. The Council is usually made up of the economists and advises the president on policies that are designed to increase prosperity.
- **The U.S. Trade Representative** is responsible for negotiating complex trade and tariff agreements for the president. Trade agreements such as GATT and NAFTA are negotiated by the Trade Representative on behalf of the president, with the guidance of the White House.

The Cabinet

The **cabinet** is not mentioned in the Constitution but was created through custom and usage. Each cabinet department was instituted by an act of Congress to help administrate the responsibilities of the executive branch.

Each cabinet secretary is appointed by the president and confirmed by the Senate. **Secretaries** can be dismissed at the president's will. Cabinet secretaries are supposed to run their departments and carry out the president's policies. Those who disagree with presidential policy are expected to resign. Secretaries tend to be lightning rods to be used for deflecting criticism and are responsible for explaining and promoting presidential policies. Over time, secretaries tend to represent their own departments more than the president's policies. They are expected to fight for their department's budget, jurisdiction, and personnel. This creates competition and friction between departments and accounts for why presidents usually do not hold full cabinet meetings. Presidents just don't have the time or inclination to listen to the bickering and arguing between department heads.

Still, despite these institutional shortcomings, cabinet secretaries do rule over vast departmental bureaucracies—each containing numerous powerful government agencies. With the recent addition of the **Department of Homeland Security,** there are now fifteen cabinet departments. After the September 11 attacks, it was felt that a cabinet-level department was necessary to counter possible threats to the United States, and more than twenty-two agencies were consolidated into the new department, making it the third-largest executive branch department. Agencies as disparate as the Bureau of Citizenship and Immigration Services (formerly the INS), the Coast Guard, and the Secret Service were consolidated to shape a coherent agenda to protect the United States against potential attacks. The Department of Homeland Security has four functions: to protect the borders; to support local agencies like police and fire departments; to detect chemical, biological, and nuclear weapons; and to analyze intelligence.

A New Addition
Homeland Security is the first top-level government position created since the Energy Department was formed in 1977 and the first large-scale government reorganization since Harry Truman created the Department of Defense in 1947.

Impeachment

The Constitution gives Congress the power to remove the president from office for "treason, bribery, or other high crimes and misdemeanors." The Constitution does not define high crimes and misdemeanors, leaving those definitions to politicians. The only direction in the Constitution is that the House of Representatives impeaches the president (or brings the charges) by a simple majority vote, and if the impeachment passes, the Senate holds a trial with the Chief Justice of the Supreme Court presiding. Removal of the president requires a two-thirds vote of the Senate. The entire process in Congress has been developed as a result of guesswork, custom, and usage.

Because the definition of an impeachable offense is left to the House, **impeachment** is a highly charged political process. Most constitutional scholars place the standard for impeachment as an act against the government or the Constitution, but there seems to be political disagreement over what standard should be used. Conservatives seem to have one standard, while liberals seem to have another. Every impeachment, or near-impeachment, has divided the Congress along party lines, and some scholars have accused members of Congress of using the process to try to undo the result of an election.

No president of the United States has been removed from office. While the House successfully impeached Andrew Johnson for his violation of the Tenure in Office Act, the Senate fell just one vote short of removing him from office. This act was later invalidated by the Supreme Court. The **Watergate** scandal caused Richard Nixon to resign before imminent impeachment proceedings could begin. He knew that the Senate would convict if given the opportunity to vote. The impeachment of President Clinton for lying under oath was very political. All parties knew before the trial began that there was little chance of a Senate conviction. Clinton's defenders claimed that while Clinton's behavior had been improper and had brought dishonor to the Office of the President, his conduct had not risen to the level of an impeachable offense.

Federal judges are appointed for life and can be removed only by the impeachment process. Only eight federal judges have ever been removed by the Senate. One of them is **Alcee Hastings**, who was impeached for bribery and perjury, and is now a member of the same House of Representatives who voted for his impeachment.

THE JUDICIARY AND THE LAW

Concepts

- What circumstances are required for a case to be brought before the Supreme Court?
- How do politics enter into Supreme Court decisions?
- Why can it be said that all judicial decisions are activist?
- Why can it be said that a president's strongest legacy is found in the judiciary?
- What control does Congress have over the judiciary?

American Legal Principles

Although the United States plays host to the interlocking systems of state and federal law, a few underlying principles make up the foundation of our legal system. They are **equal justice under the law**, **due process of law**, the **adversarial system,** and **presumption of innocence**.

All who appear in court in the United States must be treated as equals. The founders were very concerned that the new nation avoid the hierarchical legal systems that plagued many other nations and, as a result, enshrined many amendments in the Constitution that establish **equal justice under the law**. For example, whenever jurors hear a criminal case, they are instructed not to privilege the testimony of a police officer over that of a defendant.

Due process can be divided into two types: **substantive due process** and **procedural due process.** Substantive due process law deals with the question of *whether laws are fair.* Fairness is determined by looking at the Constitution, specifically the Bill of Rights and the Fourteenth Amendment. A law that made it illegal for people with blue eyes to ride motorcycles would constitute a violation of substantive due process. Procedural due process law is concerned with the question of *whether laws are fairly applied.* This might seem less important than substantive due process, but procedural issues are actually at the heart of our legal system. If suspects in certain types of crimes were held for ten years before they ever had a trial, this would be a violation of procedural due process, because the law guarantees everyone a speedy trial. Even if a nation has laws that are fair and just, if they are not applied fairly, they are meaningless.

Strange as it may seem to those of us raised in the United States, many nations do not require both sides of legal cases to be represented by advocates. This inquisitorial system, as it is known, is alien to the United States, where we use the **adversarial system**. As you can probably guess from the name, this principle is based on the premise that the best way to work out questions of fact is to have two sides—or adversaries—debate the burden of guilt or liability in a situation. Some critics say that this system creates too many conflicts—particularly in areas such as family law and divorce, and recommend an increased role for mediators who seek rapprochement and can make legally binding decisions.

In his *Commentaries on the Laws of England*, English jurist and professor William Blackstone said, "Better that ten guilty persons escape than that one innocent suffer," and this number became known as the Blackstone ratio. Benjamin Franklin expanded this, writing "that it is better [one hundred] guilty Persons should escape than that one innocent Person should suffer." In both England and America, the idea that the accused are innocent until proven guilty—the **presumption of innocence**—is one of the bedrock principles of the legal system. As a result, the burden of proof is on the prosecutor in criminal cases, and if there is any reasonable doubt as to a person's innocence, juries are instructed to acquit.

Types of Law

In the United States, most legal cases involve either **civil law** or **criminal law**. The distinction between these two types of law is very important, and knowing the differences and similarities can help a great deal when taking the AP Exam.

Anyone who watches television police or law dramas has at least some familiarity with the trappings of criminal law. This type of law deals with serious crimes that harm individuals or society. If physical violence is involved, then the action will probably end up in the criminal justice system, but fraud and extortion are also crimes. In criminal law, a suspect is arrested and must be indicted. This is done (in most states and at the federal level) by a **grand jury**: a group of 24 to 48 jurors who decide only one thing—whether a trial should commence. Since the grand jury is not deciding guilt or innocence, an accused person does not have many protections at the grand jury level. The prosecution usually has to meet a certain standard of evidence. In fact, defense attorneys are not even allowed to address grand juries. Once the accused is indicted, that person then has the option of **plea bargaining** with the prosecution to agree to a less serious crime and sentence. Still, many cases go to trial. Here it is important to note that in criminal trials, the state (at the state level) or the United States (at the federal level) is the party opposing the accused person. Even if your loved one has been killed, it is not you versus the accused killer, but the government against the accused killer—the government acts as the prosecution. This reflects the basic Lockean premise that when we enter into a society or community, we cede our fundamental right to vengeance and punishment to the state in exchange for protection. Since the presumption of innocence is so important to our legal system, the burden of proof is on the prosecution to prove guilt beyond a **reasonable doubt**. Criminal trials are held before

Yes, Pleas
Something like 95% of all criminal cases end in plea bargains.

petit juries as opposed to grand juries, (these are what most of us think of as simply "juries" that are composed of twelve people). The decision of the jury is known as the verdict, and a guilty verdict can be returned only if all twelve jurors vote to convict. A split jury is known as a "hung jury" and results in a mistrial.

Chances are that you haven't seen a thrilling television drama about civil law (unless you watch *Judge Judy*), but that shouldn't detract from its importance. The civil law system is what determines the results of disputes over things like contracts, property, custody of the children, or an issue of liability. Unlike in criminal law cases, the government is involved in a civil case only if it happens to be the party being sued. There is no prosecution; instead, a plaintiff squares off against a defendant. If a person thinks that they have been wronged, they issue a complaint in civil court. If that complaint is answered—that is, if a judge or jury thinks the complaint has merit—then the case moves forward. As with plea bargaining in criminal law, civil law also has a mechanism to avoid trial—the settlement. In a settlement, the parties negotiate and the issue becomes how much each party is willing to give up to end the lawsuit. If no settlement can be reached, the case goes to trial. Since the stakes in civil law are not nearly as high as in criminal law—a defendant cannot be jailed or executed—the burden of proof is lighter. In order to win a case, a plaintiff need not prove that he is right beyond reasonable doubt. Instead, he merely needs to show that a preponderance of evidence favors his side of the case. This is the equivalent of proving that 51 percent of the evidence points his way. Juries are also used in civil cases, but many states do not require twelve members; some allow as few as five or six. Winning can mean either the payment of monetary damages or equity, in which the loser may be forced to stop doing something that was annoying or harmful to the winner.

Structure and Jurisdiction

The federal courts are responsible for interpreting and settling disputes arising out of federal law; state courts are responsible for interpreting and settling disputes arising out of state law. It is possible for a citizen to commit a single act that violates both state and federal law—trading in drugs and tax evasion are two examples.

There are three levels of federal courts: the Federal District Courts, which have original jurisdiction; the Federal Circuit Courts of Appeals, which hear cases on appeal from the District Courts; and the Supreme Court, which hears appeals of cases dealing with constitutional questions from the Circuit Courts and, in rare instances, original suits between states. The Supreme Court also has original jurisdiction in cases involving foreign ministers, which is intended to prevent states from deciding such cases.

The Supreme Court does not have a jury. It is considered a collegial court because its decisions are made by the nine justices. When the Court acts in **appellate jurisdiction,** it can only decide issues of law and never the facts of a case.

There are 94 **Federal District Courts**, created by Congress to fulfill its delegated responsibility of creating courts inferior to the Supreme Court. Federal District Courts decide both civil and criminal cases in original jurisdiction. The trial court that determines guilt or innocence is the court of original jurisdiction. These courts hear evidence and can use juries to decide the verdict. Federal District Courts can also decide liability in civil cases where monetary losses have occurred. Civil cases can also have juries. It is always possible for a defendant to ask a judge to decide a case, but a judge can refuse the request and force the defendant to have a jury trial. (The Constitution guarantees a jury trial but not a trial decided by a judge.)

There are thirteen **Circuit Courts of Appeals**, which hear cases on appeal from the Federal District Courts or from a state Supreme Court. In these cases someone has to claim that a federal constitutional right has been violated. The Circuit Courts decide issues of law and never issues of fact. Circuit courts have no juries. The decisions of these courts are made by panels of appointed judges. In almost every case, the Circuit Court of Appeals is the court of last resort because the Supreme Court rarely agrees to hear cases appealed from the Circuit Courts. Additionally, most Supreme Court judges rise from the Circuit Courts.

The Politics of the Judiciary

All judges in the federal judiciary (only those on the Supreme Court are called justices) are appointed by the president for lifetime terms. Appointees must go through a confirmation process in the Senate. To maintain judicial neutrality and integrity, impeachment is the only method of removal.

The appointment process has become very political. Some presidents have required potential appointees to fill out a judicial questionnaire to determine their political and judicial ideology. Nominees are almost always of the same party as the president. In nomination hearings before the Senate Judiciary Committee, members of both parties try to determine how potential judges would rule in cases dealing with issues such as abortion rights, affirmative action, or school prayer. The American Bar Association is asked to evaluate a nominee's qualifications and interest groups often present their opinions. Senators in a state where an appointee will sit have traditionally exercised **senatorial courtesy**—they submit a list of acceptable names of nominees to the president. Presidents usually choose a nominee from the list submitted. Senatorial courtesy is expected only when the president and senators are of the same party.

Liberals and conservatives often argue over a nominee's judicial philosophy or level of judicial activism. The central point of the argument is whether the nominee is more or less inclined to second-guess a legislative enactment. As the conservatives see it, the courts are the least democratic branch of government (because judges are appointed, not elected), and when they overturn an act of a legislature, they are overruling the will of the people, as expressed in the most democratic branch of government (the legislature). Judges who are reluctant to overturn the acts of a legislature are said to practice **judicial restraint**. Liberals often see judges as constitutional interpreters who should reflect current values. A judge who has no qualms about overturning a legislative action is considered a **judicial activist**. Compromise over these two positions is sometimes very difficult to achieve. The nomination of **Robert Bork** to be a Justice of the Supreme Court was defeated by liberals because of his judicial philosophy. **Clarence Thomas** was confirmed by the closest Senate vote in U.S. history, over concerns related to his conservative judicial philosophy, lack of experience, and the allegation that he sexually harassed an aide.

Process by Which Cases Reach the Supreme Court

The process that the Supreme Court uses to hear cases is not part of the Constitution. The process is a result of custom and usage, time and tradition.

The Supreme Court will not grant an appeal until all opportunities have been exhausted in the lower appellate courts. In the vast majority of cases, the court refuses to hear the appeal because it agrees with the lower court decision. However, the court may choose to review the decisions of lower courts. If four justices agree to this review, the court issues a **writ of** *certiorari*, a legal document used to request the lower court transcripts of a case.

The Supreme Court will rule only in cases that are real and adverse, which means that the case must involve an actual legal dispute. Such cases are said to be **justiciable**. Disputes over political issues cannot be decided by courts—political disputes are not justiciable. The Supreme Court cannot give advisory opinions. It can rule only in an actual legal case involving litigants. In other words, the court will not rule on hypothetical cases.

The Court also places limits on who may bring cases before it. Simply disliking or disagreeing with a law is not sufficient to bring a case. The petitioner (the person who brings the case) must have some vested interest in the outcome of the case. Such petitioners are said to have **standing**.

Judicial Review

The Constitution does not specifically grant the Supreme Court the right to judge the constitutionality of laws. That power was established by the case of *Marbury v. Madison* (1803). This extremely important power is called **judicial review** and was established by John Marshall, the fourth Chief Justice of the Supreme Court (he served from 1800 to 1835). Marshall was a Federalist who worked to increase the powers of the federal government over the states.

Under Marshall, the court made several other rulings concerning the role of the court and the relationship of the federal government to the states. They include the following:

- *Fletcher v. Peck* (1810). The first case in which the court overturned a state law on constitutional grounds. *Fletcher* established the court's right to apply judicial review to state laws. Previously, judicial review had been applied only to federal law.
- *McCulloch v. Maryland* (1819). The court ruled that the states did not have the power to tax the national bank (and, by extension, the federal government). This decision reinforced the supremacy clause of the Constitution, which states that the Constitution "and the laws of the United States which shall be made in pursuance thereof…shall be the supreme law of the land; and the judges in every state shall be bound thereby, anything in the Constitution or laws of any State to the contrary notwithstanding."
- *Gibbons v. Ogden* (1824). The court ruled that the state of New York could not grant a steamship company a monopoly to operate on an interstate waterway, even though that waterway ran through New York. The ruling increased federal power over interstate commerce by implying that anything concerning interstate trade could potentially be regulated by the federal government.

How the Court Hears Cases

Once the Supreme Court decides to take a case, a complicated legal dance swings into motion. Both sides of the case submit summaries of their arguments and legal foundations for them. These summaries are known as **briefs**. At the same time, interest groups affiliated with both sides of the case submit their own briefs to the Supreme Court. These *amicus curiae* ("friend of the court") **briefs** constitute an effort to sway the justices to one side or the other and can be quite influential in determining the outcome of the case.

Every year from October to April, the court hears **oral arguments** for the cases it has chosen to take. Usually in oral arguments, lawyers for each party have a half hour each to stand before the nine justices and present their arguments. Often, the federal government will take one side or the other, and in these cases the **solicitor general** gets a portion of that half hour to argue on the government's behalf. The solicitor general is the second-ranking member of the justice department (after the attorney general) and typically makes many appearances before the high court—so much so that the solicitor general is sometimes called the "tenth justice." After the oral arguments, the justices meet for a highly secretive conference. At this point, all the justices cast votes, and opinion-writing duties are handed out.

Deja Vu?
There's a lot of overlap between units in AP U.S. Government and Politics course and your teacher can decide how he or she wants to split up the content and cases. So *McCulloch v. Maryland* and *Gibbons v. Ogden* may sound familiar, as we mentioned them earlier in this book in the Federalism unit. Here we mention them as examples of federal v. states rights issues. No court case is about one, single issue, so be sure to think about all of the layers and subtleties.

There are four different types of **opinions**: unanimous, majority, concurring, and dissenting. A **unanimous opinion**, as was the case in *Brown v. Board of Education*, occurs when all of the justices agree—this opinion carries the most force in future legal cases and when legislatures draft new laws. When the justices split, the opinion with the most votes is the **majority opinion**, and it is the opinion that decides the result of the case. Sometimes justices may vote with the majority but take issue with its legal reasoning; these are called **concurring opinions**. Those justices in the minority on an opinion can write a **dissenting opinion**, questioning the reasoning of the winning side. Though these dissents have no immediate significance, if the ideological composition of the court changes, they can sometimes become the legal foundation for future majority opinions.

THE BUREAUCRACY

Concepts

- To what degree is the bureaucracy able to maintain political neutrality?
- How do iron triangles and issue networks foster democratic principles?
- How does Congress control the bureaucracy?
- How does the bureaucracy act to implement the intent of Congress?
- How do regulatory agencies work to protect society?
- How do presidents control their policy preferences through the bureaucracy?

The **bureaucracy** is responsible for ensuring that the policies and programs enacted by Congress and the executive departments are carried out. Because the bureaucracy is responsible for executing the laws, providing for defense, and administering social programs, it is considered part of the executive branch of government. To ensure impartiality, bureaucratic agencies are supposed to function above partisan politics and also ensure that the laws are administered without prejudice.

There are approximately 4 million bureaucrats who are salaried employees of the federal government, with about 2.7 million civilians and 1.4 million in the military. About 30% of the civilian employees work for the Defense Department, while about 15% work for various social agencies, including Social Security and Welfare. No bureaucrat is elected. The fifteen cabinet secretaries and the heads of independent agencies are appointed by the president with the consent of the Senate. Most of the hundreds of thousands of civilian employees who work for the government work for one of the fifteen executive departments or one of the other "cabinet level" agencies considered by the White House to be part of the cabinet (such as the Director of Management and Budget or the Director of the Drug Control Office). These other cabinet level offices are not actual cabinet departments.

The largest department, the Department of Defense, is administered by the **Secretary of Defense**, who must be a civilian and reports directly to the president. Each of the five military services is headed by a uniformed chief of staff, and the five chiefs work together as the **Joint Chiefs of Staff**, headed by a chairman. The Joint Chiefs and their chairman are responsible for carrying out defense policy and report directly to both the Secretary of Defense and the president. The military is therefore subject to civilian control.

Bureaucratic Structure

The bureaucracy is organized as a hierarchy of fifteen pyramids, representing the fifteen executive branch departments:

- Department of State
- Department of the Treasury
- Department of Defense
- Department of Justice
- Department of the Interior
- Department of Agriculture
- Department of Commerce
- Department of Labor
- Department of Health and Human Services
- Department of Housing and Urban Development
- Department of Transportation
- Department of Energy
- Department of Education
- Department of Veterans' Affairs
- Department of Homeland Security

At the top of each pyramid is the secretary of the department, who is appointed by the president and confirmed by the Senate. Directly subordinate to the secretary is the undersecretary, who is appointed by the president without Senate confirmation. Because secretaries and undersecretaries are presidential appointments, they are replaced at the end of a president's term. The position of undersecretary attracts young professionals. Because the pay is low compared with private industry, and the position is temporary, undersecretaries often use the appointment to step up to better positions in the private sector.

Departmental Breakdown

Each of the fifteen departments is broken down into smaller units. These smaller units are called bureaus, offices, or services and are responsible for dealing with either a particular clientele or a specific subject. Examples are

- The Bureau of Land Management (Department of the Interior)
- The Federal Bureau of Investigation (Department of Justice)
- The Internal Revenue Service (Department of the Treasury)
- The Federal Aviation Administration (Department of Transportation)

Below the secretaries are the personnel of the **Senior Executive Service**, including both appointees and non-appointees. Senior Executive Service appointees do not need Senate confirmation. These career officials are supposed to be responsive to the policy goals of the White House and help bureaucrats implement the policy preferences of the chief executive.

Government Corporations

Government corporations are hybrid organizations. They are a cross between a private business corporation and a government agency. Corporations are supposed to have freedom of action and flexibility and produce at least enough revenue to support themselves. Amtrak, the government corporation created to provide railroad passenger service, is an example. Unfortunately, Amtrak has never made a profit and must ask Congress for subsidies to keep itself from declaring bankruptcy and ending passenger rail service in the United States.

Originally created as a cabinet position, the United States Postal Service has become a government corporation. The intent of Congress was to create a mail delivery system that pays its own way without government assistance. Because of electronic messaging systems and competition from package delivery companies, the post office has had to increase its fees, but it is no longer solvent.

More successful, but at times controversial, is the Corporation for Public Broadcasting, which produces and airs both television and radio programs. Funding for the Public Broadcasting System (PBS) comes from both private and government subsidies. Most of its programming is related to public affairs, news, and culture. The controversy often occurs when groups object to the content of programs. Still others object to the government being involved in any service that could be provided by private sector corporations.

Regulatory Agencies and Commissions

Government entities that are not within the fifteen cabinet departments fall into two categories: the independent agencies and the **regulatory agencies,** sometimes called **independent regulatory commissions.** While independent agencies are generally run-of-the-mill bureaucracies with broad presidential oversight, regulatory commissions are given an extraordinary degree of independence to act as watchdogs over the federal government. Congress and the president are not supposed to become enmeshed in the workings of regulatory commissions. The safety regulations for nuclear power plants or securities exchange should not be regulated by politics.

In contemporary societies, the difficulties and complexities of writing legislation are often beyond the abilities and expertise of lawmakers. The result is that legislation is often written in general terms with many gaps that need to be filled in by the agency with jurisdiction. Independent agencies who have the responsibility for filling in these gaps and writing rules are referred to as **quasi-legislative agencies.** Those responsible for rule enforcement and punishing violators are **quasi-judicial agencies.**

Members of Congress do not have the education to deal with the scientific details that are often required to implement legislation. For example, House and Senate members who sit on committees that deal with environmental issues do not generally have advanced degrees in chemistry. It is the experts who work in the enforcing agencies who have that knowledge. Compounding the problems for Congress are the many competing interests that surround every major issue. Environmentalists have their agenda, while the petroleum industry, electric utilities, and lumber interests have theirs. Even the regulating agency with jurisdiction has its own agenda. These competing interests often delay or prevent legislation. This is the clash of the special interests.

In an age of science and technology, it is the faceless bureaucrat the public knows nothing about who often has the answers for Congress. These bureaucrats, on the one hand, are asked for advice and expertise, and on the other hand, are often ignored because of the pressures from interest groups. Working within the regulatory commissions, they are the people responsible for writing and enforcing rules that regulate the environment, the economy, or industry. If they fail to implement the intent of Congress, they are criticized by Congress and the parties regulated, usually for being too restrictive with their rules and too strict in their enforcement policies.

Examples of regulatory agencies include the following:

- **The Federal Trade Commission** is responsible for preventing fraud in the marketplace by preventing price fixing and deceptive advertising.
- **The Securities and Exchange Commission** protects investors by regulating stock markets and policing corporations to prevent false and misleading claims of profits in an effort to increase stock prices.
- **The Nuclear Regulatory Commission** controls how electric power companies design, build, and operate nuclear reactors.
- **The Federal Communications Commission** is responsible for assigning broadcast frequencies, for licensing radio and television stations, and for regulating the use of wireless communication devices.
- **The Food and Drug Administration** is responsible for ensuring the health of the American people by inspecting the food supply for contaminants and spoilage. The agency is also responsible for regulating the sale of over-the-counter drugs and patent medicines.
- **The Federal Energy Regulatory Commission** is responsible for preventing price fixing and price manipulation in electric utilities, interstate oil and gas pipelines, and natural gas suppliers.
- **The Occupational Safety and Health Administration** is responsible for ensuring workers are employed in a safe work environment. For example, OSHA can regulate the type of ventilation in a factory, as well as the type of clothing worn and tools used.

Case Studies

Considered to be one of the most controversial government bureaucracies, the **Environmental Protection Agency (EPA)** was created in 1970 as an independent body. Its mission is the enforcement of the environmental laws passed by Congress. One of the agency's first responsibilities was to enforce the **1970 Clean Air Act.** The intent of the law was to reduce automobile pollution and increase automobile gasoline mileage. The automobile industry lobbied hard to defeat the bill and claimed that they could not meet the requirements of the law by the time specified. They were granted extensions and eventually complied, although trucks and SUVs are still exempt from the law.

The Clean Air Act was amended in 1990 as a result of scientific evidence indicating that the refrigerants used in air conditioners were instrumental in depleting the ozone layer. The EPA successfully pressured chemical companies and air-conditioning manufacturers to find alternatives to the ozone-destroying chemicals. The EPA has also been successful in reducing the pollutants that cause acid rain.

Congress and the EPA
The EPA can sometimes become a foe of Congress, which originally gave the EPA its mandate to act.

Clean air is not the EPA's only problem. It is responsible for enforcement of the **Endangered Species Act.** This highly controversial law is intended to protect endangered wildlife habitats from human encroachment. To implement this goal, environmental impact statements are required whenever construction projects are planned. If there is any possibility that an endangered species could be adversely affected, the EPA has the power to prohibit construction. The EPA's ban on lumbering in areas of the Pacific Northwest—the habitat for the spotted owl—and its decision to block the construction of a dam in Tennessee because of the endangered snail darter fish are two examples. In the Tennessee dam case, Congress overruled the decision of the EPA, even though the Supreme Court had sided with the EPA to stop construction. In addition, Congress further weakened the EPA's enforcement powers by amending the Endangered Species Act to permit exemptions in the future.

Another agency that provokes political contention is the **Equal Employment Opportunities Commission (EEOC).** Created by the 1964 Civil Rights Act, the EEOC is responsible for enforcing the antidiscrimination laws of the United States. This commission has been susceptible to political pressure from both Congress and the White House. It is the EEOC's responsibility to implement affirmative action programs for minorities, to bring suits in cases of racial or sexual discrimination, and to enforce the **Americans with Disabilities Act.** The head of the EEOC is a presidential appointment and is supposed to carry out the policies of the president. If the law conflicts with presidential policy, the EEOC has a problem.

The critics of affirmative action claim the policy is a form of reverse discrimination. Feeling pressure from voters, Congress, and the president, the EEOC first promoted affirmative action and then discouraged the policy. The attempts by this agency to implement the will of Congress have been complicated because both Congress and the White House seem to change their mind at will.

The Americans with Disabilities Act requires the EEOC to enforce laws against employers who discriminate against disabled employees or job seekers. In addition, part of the Disabilities Act requires that public buildings and large businesses be accessible to the disabled. Critics claim that this attempt at helping the disabled live normal lives has cost taxpayers hundreds of millions of dollars and the cost is too high in relation to the number of persons benefited.

Who Runs Regulatory Agencies?

Independent regulatory agencies are run by panels of administrators called Boards of Commissioners. These commissioners are appointed by the president with the consent of the Senate. The terms of these commissioners usually overlap the term of the appointing president. The staggered term is intended to minimize political pressure from the White House. Depending on the commission, terms can range from 3 to 14 years.

Perhaps the best-known regulatory board is the **Federal Reserve Board** (the Fed) because its policies directly affect the buying power of the public. The Fed accomplishes this by regulating banks, the value and supply of money, and interest rates. Its members serve 14-year terms. Its chairman serves a four-year term. One previous head, Alan Greenspan, has served both Democrat and Republican presidents. Today the Fed is run by Janet Yellen, who is the first woman to hold the position.

Because the Fed is an independent agency, its policies can sometimes conflict with the policies of the president. In 1993, in the first weeks of the Clinton administration, Fed Chairman Alan Greenspan told the president that the condition of the economy was worse than the previous Bush administration had told the American people. In addition, the national debt, as bad as it was perceived to be, was actually even greater than anyone realized. Clinton wanted an economic stimulus tax cut to get the economy out of recession. Greenspan told the president a tax cut should not be pursued, and if the White House went forward with the plan, the Fed would raise interest rates. Clinton was forced to break his campaign pledge to lower taxes. Even though the chairman and the president disagreed over economic policy, the president was powerless to do anything about it. In time, the Greenspan policy helped to get the economy out of the recession and into the longest economic boom in American history. Things went so well that Clinton reappointed Greenspan as chairman. Greenspan's legacy would later come into question as a result of the economic collapse of 2008–2009.

Who Controls the Bureaucracy?

Because most boards of commissions and regulatory agencies are appointed by the president with Senate consent, political considerations always play a part in the appointment process. However, presidents come and go with great regularity, as do the appointed governing boards and commissions. It is the rank and file bureaucrats who are permanent, and they do not like political meddling.

While in office, presidents do have the power to promote their supporters and to use the budget to increase or decrease the influence of an agency. Reducing an agency's budget reduces its staff, which reduces its effectiveness. Increasing the agency's budget can have the opposite effect. Presidents can also reorganize an agency.

Congressional power over the bureaucracy is greater than that of the president. The Senate can affirm or reject presidential appointments. Congress can also abolish an agency or change its jurisdiction if it is unhappy with policy implementation. Finally, it is the Congress, through the appropriations process, that has the final say over how much money agencies will receive.

Rule Setting, Alliance Building, and Iron Triangles

The regulatory agencies carry out their responsibilities by setting rules and regulations that industry must follow. Setting regulations is a participatory process in which industry becomes actively involved in determining the rules. Agencies welcome public participation by holding public hearings for testimony and advice. In most instances, the law requires agencies to consult with industry before rules and regulations can go into effect.

Iron Triangles

The rule-making process has fostered the creation of **iron triangles**. Typically iron triangles are informal alliances made up of three groups: (1) a particular industry and its lobbyists (for example, weapons manufacturers), (2) the congressional committee dealing with that industry (the Armed Services Committees of the Senate and House), and (3) the agency that actually is affected (in this case, the Pentagon).

The groups that make up an iron triangle work together to formulate and implement policy in their area of interest. Lobbyists representing industry promote their special-interest agenda by claiming it is in the best interest of the American people. For example, drug companies may lobby the Food and Drug Administration to speed up the certification process for a medication because it will benefit the sick faster. Patients and drug companies will pressure Congress, which then pressures the FDA. These are powerful arguments, but speeding up the process can cause the FDA to overlook something dangerous about the medication.

Special interests also contribute money to congressional campaigns, and large contributors are never shy about asking for help from congressional representatives, who are asked to help put pressure on regulators, or at a minimum, to listen to the arguments that the special interests put forward for their cause.

Political scientists have recently seen a more complex political process at work. When issues affect many groups, pro and con coalitions of interest groups, members of Congress, and bureaucrats form a close working relationship. This political process is called either an **alliance network** or an **issue network** and is far more complicated than a simple three-part iron triangle.

For example, if a large factory was a polluter but had marginal profits, it would probably fight expensive environmental regulations. Compliance might drive the company into bankruptcy. But more is at stake than just the company. There are jobs involved and secondary industries that supply the raw materials for production at the company. A local government, which relies on the tax revenues from the company, also has something at stake. Environmental groups are going to be involved. This complicated situation would certainly result in the creation of issue networks for the purpose of influencing the regulatory agency's decisions.

After all the opportunities for input and debate have been exhausted, the regulatory agency writes and publishes the rules (this is its **quasi-legislative function**). If the industry still objects to the regulation, it can seek remedies in the courts by suing the regulatory agency. In the above example, if the company is forced to comply with the environmental laws, it could appeal the decision to the courts.

Because regulatory agencies invite so much controversy, there has been a recent trend toward deregulating the marketplace (removing government restrictions and regulations). Those in favor of **deregulation** claim that the competition of the marketplace is all the regulation that is needed. The deregulators say that regulation is too expensive and time-consuming and involves too much unnecessary red tape. They note that over the past 25 years, the **Civil Aeronautics Board**, which was responsible for regulating the airline industry, and the **Interstate Commerce Commission**, which regulated railroads and the trucking industry, were successfully phased out with little negative impact on consumers.

The Civil Service and Maintaining Neutrality

Today, the majority of government jobs are filled through the competitive **civil service system**. This system was established in 1883 with the passage of the Pendleton Act, a law that ended the "**spoils system**," or the practice of handing out government jobs in exchange for political support. The Office of Personnel Management (OPM) acts as the bureaucracy's employment agency. OPM administers the civil service examination, publishes lists of job openings, and hires on the basis of merit. The intent is to create a competent, professional bureaucracy instead of one based on the "spoils system." A Merit Systems Protection Board investigates charges of agency corruption and incompetence and is supposed to protect "whistle blowers."

To ensure bureaucratic neutrality, Congress passed the **Hatch Act** in 1939. This law permitted bureaucrats the right to vote but not the right to actively campaign for political candidates, work for parties, or run for office. The act's revision of 1993 is less restrictive, allowing bureaucrats to join political parties, make campaign contributions, and display political advertising in the form of buttons and bumper stickers. Bureaucrats still cannot run for public office at any level, solicit campaign funds from subordinates, or make political speeches.

KEY TERMS

- Congress
- House of Representatives
- Senate
- census
- congressional district
- redistricting
- House Ways and Means Committee
- bills of attainder
- *ex post facto* laws
- oversight
- sponsor
- House Rules Committee
- poison-pill (or killer) amendment
- filibuster
- cloture
- pork barrels
- earmarks
- conference committee
- standing committee
- joint committee
- select committee
- pocket veto
- line-item veto
- subcommittee
- pigeonhole
- discharge petition
- Speaker of the House
- majority leader
- minority leader
- president *pro tempore*
- Hatch Act
- Freedom of Information Act
- Gramm-Rudman-Hollings Bill
- War Powers Act
- Patriot Act
- executive agreement
- commander in chief
- Gulf of Tonkin Resolution
- chief of staff
- National Security Council
- Office of Management and Budget (OMB)
- cabinet
- secretaries
- impeachment
- Watergate
- Supreme Court
- equal justice under the law
- due process of law (substantive and procedural)
- adversarial system
- presumption of innocence
- civil law
- criminal law
- grand jury
- plea bargaining
- reasonable doubt
- settlement
- civil court
- preponderance of evidence
- original jurisdiction
- appellate jurisdiction
- Federal District Courts
- Circuit Court of Appeals
- senatorial courtesy
- judicial restraint
- judicial activism
- writ of *certiorari*
- justiciable
- standing
- *Marbury v. Madison*
- briefs
- *amicus curiae* briefs
- oral arguments
- unanimous opinion
- majority opinion
- concurring opinion
- dissenting opinion
- bureaucracy
- Joint Chiefs of Staff
- regulatory agency (independent regulatory commission)
- Federal Reserve Board
- iron triangle
- alliance (issue) network
- deregulation
- civil service system
- spoils system

Summary

o Remember that Congress is a bicameral (two-house) legislature, split into the Senate (in which all states receive equal representation) and the House of Representatives (in which representation is proportionate to population).

o The number of House seats a state gets is based on its population as determined by a census. Once the number of seats is determined, the state legislature draws the districts—often using partisan gerrymandering to ensure a majority for one party or the other.

o Congress has numerous powers that range from creation of all law, to funding all executive agencies, to declaring war. It is the first institution defined in the Constitution, and most scholars think that the Founders intended it to be the most powerful of the branches.

o How does a bill become a law? It is introduced to the House or Senate, referred to a committee, amended and debated, reintroduced to the general House and Senate, debated and amended once more, harmonized with its counterpart that has traveled through the other legislative body, voted on again, and signed by the president.

o Given the large size of both houses of Congress, committees do most of the work of legislating. Committees can be standing, select, or joint, and are often further divided into subcommittees.

o The House is led by the speaker, while the Senate has two ceremonial leaders (the vice president and the president *pro tempore*) and one actual power broker— the majority leader.

- This chapter has a ton of laws. Try to remember them by using the four categories: (1) National Growth, Expansion, and Institution Building; (2) Regulation of Government and Industry; (3) Rights and Freedoms; and (4) Government Aid to the People.

- The president is the chief executive of the nation and is responsible for enforcing all laws. Over the years, the power of the presidency has grown dramatically—often at the expense of Congress.

- Even though the Constitution gives Congress the power to declare war, the nature of modern warfare has given the president control of this area. Though Congress does have tools to stop a wartime president, using them would generally be tantamount to political suicide.

- Being a good president often means going beyond the powers explicitly listed in the Constitution. Mastery of these "informal powers"—like consensus building or boosting the morale of the nation—often determines presidential greatness.

- The president relies a great deal on the Executive Office of the President (EOP)—his personal staff, which is ensconced within the West Wing of the White House. The EOP is also home to a number of agencies that serve the president and are largely free from congressional oversight.

- America has fifteen cabinet departments, and each contains a huge array of agencies and bureaucracies designed to help enforce the law of the land. The cabinet secretaries are supposed to advise the president, but due to conflicting loyalties most presidents have kept them out of the loop and relied on the EOP and other informal advisors when making policy decisions.

o   If a president has committed "treason, bribery, or other high crimes and misdemeanors," he can be impeached by a majority vote in the House and then removed from office with a two-thirds vote in the Senate.

o   Remember that America has two legal systems—state and federal—and all people are under the jurisdiction of both. The federal system was created by the Constitution—all federal judges are appointed by the president and approved by the Senate, and the nation is divided into 91 federal districts.

o   The Supreme Court rules on some very divisive social issues, and the battle to appoint new members has gotten more intense. Increasingly, presidents are looking to appoint younger and more ideological candidates who share their political philosophies.

o   The Supreme Court is America's court of last resort and gets most of its cases through appeals from lower courts or by granting writs of *certiorari* which cause cases to jump straight to their chambers.

o   Though it is not mentioned in the Constitution, the Supreme Court's most important power is judicial review: the ability to strike down any state or federal law that is unconstitutional. This power was established in the case of *Marbury v. Madison* in 1803.

o   Often called "the fourth branch of government," bureaucrats staff the large executive agencies that run the federal government. To get these jobs, applicants must take competitive exams. Bureaucrats play a huge role in creating public policy by making rules that flesh out vague laws passed by Congress.

o   We see four different types of bureaucracy in Washington: cabinet departments, independent agencies, regulatory commissions, and government corporations. Regulatory commissions are largely free of political control and have broad oversight responsibilities, while government corporations like the Postal Service are expected to turn a profit in the free market.

o   Because the issues dealt with by bureaucrats are so technical and often pertain to a small interest group, we see the formation of iron triangles—cooperation between a bureaucracy (like the Department of Defense), a congressional committee (like the Senate Armed Services Committee), and a special interest group (like weapons and aircraft manufacturers).

o   Bureaucrats are supposed to be politically neutral and stable while their political overlords shift due to election results. Still, many suspect that they may take sides, and laws like the Hatch Act were designed to prevent this from happening.

Chapter 8 Drill

See Chapter 11 for answers and explanations.

1. The official head of the Senate is the

   (A) president of the United States
   (B) vice president of the United States
   (C) president *pro tempore*
   (D) majority leader
   (E) chief whip

2. One of the most important <u>legislative</u> powers of Congress is

   (A) the power to choose a president
   (B) the ability to propose amendments to the Constitution
   (C) the power to ratify treaties (in the Senate)
   (D) the power to confirm presidential appointments (in the Senate)
   (E) the ability to tax and spend

3. Congressional districts for the House are determined in the majority of states by

   (A) a vote held in the Senate by the majority party
   (B) an executive order of the president
   (C) the Supreme Court
   (D) a census and the various state legislatures
   (E) a nonpartisan commission

4. How are cabinet members chosen?

   (A) By the president and are confirmed by the Senate
   (B) By the president and confirmed by both houses of Congress
   (C) By the House and confirmed by the Senate
   (D) By the Supreme Court
   (E) By the president alone—they need no confirmation

5. The Executive Office of the President (EOP) is

   (A) often a favored tool of the president due to the lack of congressional oversight
   (B) relatively powerless since it is mentioned nowhere in the Constitution
   (C) located within the Department of Defense
   (D) a dumping ground for ex-cabinet secretaries who have done a poor job
   (E) always run by the vice president

6. What is the National Security Council (NSC) in charge of?

   (A) Matters relating to immigration
   (B) All matters relating to space exploration
   (C) Advising the president and helping to coordinate American foreign policy
   (D) The construction of nuclear weapons
   (E) Protecting the environment

7. "Senatorial courtesy" is

   (A) the process of getting judicial appointments approved by the House
   (B) when the Senate approves of the president's choice of Supreme Court justice
   (C) when a senator appoints a judge
   (D) when the president gets the approval of the two senators from a state where he is about to name a federal judge
   (E) the law that makes senators immune to prosecution

8. *Marbury v. Madison* (1803) established

   (A) the use of *certiorari* by the Supreme Court
   (B) the power of the court to use judicial review
   (C) the right to always have counsel present in court cases
   (D) the need for government officials to have a warrant in order to tap someone's phone
   (E) a quota system to promote affirmative action

9. The Pendleton Act

   (A) made it illegal for government employees to give money to political campaigns
   (B) was passed in the 1950s
   (C) was ruled unconstitutional
   (D) gave the Supreme Court the power to overturn executive privilege
   (E) limited the spoils system and created a system of civil service exams

10. An iron triangle is

    (A) a name for an agreement between the secretaries of state, defense, and treasury
    (B) the union of the army, navy, and air force
    (C) a phenomenon that never occurs in American government
    (D) another name for the three branches of government
    (E) a policy-making group made of a committee of Congress, an interest group, and a bureaucratic agency

REFLECT

Respond to the following questions:

- For which content topics discussed in this chapter do you feel you have achieved sufficient mastery to answer multiple-choice questions correctly?

- For which content topics discussed in this chapter do you feel you have achieved sufficient mastery to discuss effectively in an essay?

- For which content topics discussed in this chapter do you feel you need more work before you can answer multiple-choice questions correctly?

- For which content topics discussed in this chapter do you feel you need more work before you can discuss effectively in an essay?

- What parts of this chapter are you going to re-review?

- Will you seek further help, outside of this book (such as a teacher, tutor, or AP Students), on any of the content in this chapter—and, if so, on what content?

Chapter 9
Public Policy

CONCEPTS

- Why do the poorest people in the United States have the least political power?
- What role does federalism play in the implementation of social welfare policy?
- Why is it so difficult to pass social welfare policy?
- Why are entitlement programs always a threat to the budget-making process?
- Why can it be said that the president is a secondary player when it comes to the economy?
- Why is it so difficult to write a budget for the United States?
- How can the president use the budget-making process to control his policy initiatives?

The process of public policy making consists of first deciding what the problem is and then deciding how to solve it. Policy making can have the following three purposes:

- **solving a social problem,** such as high crime rates, high unemployment, poverty among the aged, or teenage drinking
- **countering threats,** such as terrorism or war
- **pursuing an objective,** such as building a highway, exploring outer space, or finding a cure for cancer or AIDS

Policy can be achieved by prohibiting certain kinds of behavior, such as polygamy, murder, rape, and robbery. It can also be achieved by protecting certain activities. Granting patents and copyrights to individuals for their intellectual property, protecting the environment, and setting rules for workplace safety are all examples. Policy can promote some social activity; giving tax deductions for donations to charities is an example. Policy can be achieved by providing direct benefits to citizens. These benefits may include building roads, libraries, or hospitals. Benefits can also take the form of individual government subsidies, student loans, and pensions for the elderly.

Policy making can be frustrating because it often depends on public opinion, which can be fickle and unpredictable. The **issue-attention cycle** requires policy makers to act quickly, before the public becomes bored and loses interest. Public complaints over high energy prices can cause a flurry of policy making. But when prices go down, the public forgets about it until the next time.

Policy making often involves trade-offs between competing goods. To find additional energy resources may require access to pristine wildlife reserves. The risks to wildlife and the environment may be too high of a price to pay for the additional energy. Conservation, smaller cars, and alternative energy sources may be better solutions, but each will have its supporters and opponents.

Because policy making can have unforeseen results and can touch off bitter disputes, legislators often use **incrementalism**—the slow, step-by-step approach to making policy—or legislators may decide to use the policy of inaction, because taking no action is one way of making policy. Conflicts over health care reform and Social Security entitlements can result in simply maintaining the status quo (or, not changing a policy).

MAKING POLICY

Policy making has a number of steps, and each is influenced by politics.

- The first involves defining the role of government in solving social and economic problems. The political left sees a greater responsibility for government than the right, with the result that governments on the left are larger, more active, and more expensive than on the right.
- **Agenda setting** identifies the social and economic problems, redefines them into political issues, and ranks them in order of importance. A citizen's socioeconomic status can determine which problems seem important and which don't. Poor people may rank job training high on the agenda, while the rich may rank tax cuts higher. When large numbers of people are affected, the concern will be ranked high. However, there are times when it is those with the most money who will have their issues placed high on the agenda. For example, large energy-producing corporations have a great deal of access to policy makers.

Policy can try to address the concerns of opposing sides. Establishing environmental standards for oil exploration and refining tries to address the concerns of two constituencies: the environmentalists and the petroleum producers.

A momentous event, such as a war, an oil embargo, or a collapsing stock market, may set the agenda. Issues such as universal health care, the war on drugs, or environmental concerns can resurface. Scholars can force issues into the agenda through research studies.

- **Policy formulation and adoption** can be accomplished in a number of ways. Sometimes the most difficult method is the legislative process in Congress, while the easiest may be through the executive branch by the use of executive orders from the president. Rules enacted by regulatory agencies or precedent-setting decisions by the Supreme Court are also sources of policy formulation and adoption. *Brown v. Board of Education* was certainly a policy-making decision.

- **Policy implementation** puts the policy into effect by enforcement through the appropriate government agency. Timetables and rules for carrying out policies as well as anticipating problems are all part of policy implementation. One of the major concerns of policy making is the unforeseen consequences. The "three-strike rule," intended to get career criminals off the streets, has ended most plea-bargaining arrangements, causing more trials and overloaded courts, judges, and jails. The three-strike rule has turned out to be a much more expensive public policy than anticipated.
- **Policy evaluation** is the final step. Does a policy work? Have unforeseen consequences caused other policy problems? Evaluation provides feedback to the policy makers, so that modifications can be made to better solve the problems. Evaluation may determine that the problem has been solved and that the policy can be terminated.

Obstacles to Policy Making

The United States is a pluralist democracy, with multiple centers of power for making policy. Those interested in affecting policy making concentrate their efforts at these many centers. Because the United States has a federal system of government, policy can be made at the local, state, and national levels. Separation of powers creates three policy making centers: the executive, the legislative, and the judiciary. There is also the general bureaucracy, with its multiple policy-making centers. Trying to influence legislation, thousands of interest-group lobbyists, like jellyfish in the sea, descend upon these policy-making centers at all levels of government.

In their efforts to prevent tyranny and corruption, the Framers created a policy-making nightmare by dispersing the power centers. Getting things done is cumbersome and frustrating. Multiple access points cause **policy fragmentation,** where many pieces of legislation deal with parts of policy problems but never deal with the entire problem. The War on Drugs has at least seventy-five congressional committees with some type of jurisdiction or oversight; local and state law enforcement agencies are involved, as well as the Army, Navy, Air Force, Coast Guard, Border Patrol, Immigration and Naturalization Service, customs service, DEA, and the FBI.

Because so many agencies of government are involved, the drug war requires policy coordination. Interagency task forces try to iron out policy problems and conflicts between competing agencies, and Congress uses its oversight powers to change agency jurisdiction and give coherence to policy.

ECONOMIC POLICY

Of all the issues that face politicians, the economy is often the most important. Success or failure usually rests with the person the public perceives as responsible for the condition of the economy; and whether it is true, the electorate usually holds the president responsible. In 1992, the economy was in recession and George H. W. Bush was blamed. In 1996, the economy was booming, and Clinton was given credit and reelected.

Because of the importance of the economy in the eyes of the voters, it is in a politician's self-interest to make policies that will increase people's standard of living. The electorate looks to Washington to achieve this objective. For the policy maker, the vexing question is how to achieve it.

Sound economic policy that achieves prosperity is probably the most elusive of all policies. There are many elements to the problem: inflation, deflation, interest rates, the supply of money in circulation, the profitability of corporations, foreign competition, international agreements, and consumer confidence, just to name a few. Complicating the problem are the various economic theories that drive policy decisions, and the various government agencies and institutions that make decisions affecting economic conditions.

Economic Theory

Capitalist free-market systems in which both government and private industry play a role are called **mixed economies**. Mixed free-market systems are characterized by both private and public (government) ownership of the means of production and distribution of goods and services. The price of goods and services is determined by the free-market interplay of supply and demand. The profits after taxes are kept by the owners.

Free-market economic systems are plagued by periods of prosperity followed by periods of economic contraction (decreased activity, economic downturn). Because the United States has a mixed free-market system, the major problem for policy makers is how to maintain prosperity and economic growth while reducing the impact of the inevitable economic contraction. In capitalist systems, the basic question is to what extent the government should intervene.

Laissez-faire economists believe that the government should never become involved in economic issues. They believe that the narrow pursuit of individual profit serves the broader interest of society. Central to laissez-faire economics is the belief that free markets are governed by the laws of nature and government should not interfere with those laws. In vogue with rugged individualists in the nineteenth century, laissez-faire economics disappeared as a viable government policy option during the Great Depression of the 1930s.

Clinton's Economy
In 1992, Bill Clinton's informal campaign slogan was "It's the economy, stupid!"

Perhaps the most influential economist of the twentieth century was John Maynard Keynes, an interventionist. **Keynesian economics**, on which FDR's New Deal was based, holds that the government can smooth out business cycles by influencing the amount of income individuals and businesses can spend on goods and services.

Fiscal Policy

Fiscal policy refers to the government action of either lowering or raising taxes, which results in more or less consumer spending or enacting of government spending programs, such as building highways or hospitals. Keynesians believe that during economic downturns the government should spend money on projects to inject money into the economy. They are less worried about government deficit spending than about keeping the economy prosperous. A prosperous economy means a larger tax base, which will eventually correct deficit spending. In effect, the Keynesian school believes that when the economy is good, surplus taxes (money left over from tax revenues) should be saved to pay for the government spending that must take place during an economic downturn. Using this school of thought, the policy alternatives are obvious, but questions still remain: Should there be tax cuts? If so, how much, and who should get them? How much spending should the government engage in? How much **deficit spending** (funds raised by borrowing rather than taxation) should be allowed? The answers to these questions are extremely difficult, with major political consequences.

In the 1980s, the Reagan-Bush administration became the champion of the **supply-side** school of economic thought. The supply-siders take issue with supporters of Keynesian economics. Inflation is caused by too many dollars chasing too few goods. If the supply of goods is raised, the cost of the goods will decline. According to this theory, supply-siders argue that the government should cut taxes and spending on domestic programs to stimulate greater production.

Going along with supply-side theory, Congress in the 1980s enacted extensive tax cuts and reductions to social welfare programs, a policy later dubbed "Reaganomics." Inflation was brought under control, but huge yearly **budget deficits**, caused in part by a defense buildup, created a four-trillion-dollar debt. In the 1990s, budget surpluses began to shrink the deficit but these gains were reversed as a result of policies enacted during the Bush and Obama administrations, particularly during the Great Recession. Tax cuts followed by rising costs associated with the War on Terrorism, the invasion and occupation of Afghanistan and Iraq, and government stimulus programs have resulted in record budget deficits. The most recent estimates of the Congressional Budget Office (CBO) have warned against increasingly large budget deficits. In 2010, a $1.5 trillion deficit in the federal budget stoked political controversy and contributed to historic Republican gains in both houses of Congress in the 2010 mid-term elections. The next year, congressional Republicans forced a showdown over plans to increase the federal debt ceiling, generating concern over the United States' international credit rating.

Monetary Policy

Monetary policy refers to the process by which the government controls the supply of money in circulation and the supply of credit through the actions of the **Federal Reserve Board** (the Fed). The Fed can increase the amount of money in circulation by lowering interest rates. Rate reductions make borrowing money less expensive because interest on the money is low. This action usually inflates (expands) the economy, resulting in higher prices and wages. If the Fed raises interest rates, the impact on the economy will be deflationary, resulting in either more stable or lower prices or wages.

Monetary policy can be implemented by the Federal Reserve Board in three ways.

- By manipulating the **reserve requirement,** which raises or lowers the amount of money banks are required to keep on hand. Raising the reserve shrinks the amount of money available for borrowing, which raises interest rates. Lowering the reserve will have the opposite effect, lowering interest rates.
- By manipulating the **discount rate,** which raises or lowers the interest banks pay to the Federal Reserve Banks for borrowing money. Lowering the discount rate will lower the interest rates for consumer loans. Raising the discount rate will raise the interest rates for consumer loans. The higher the rate, the less consumers purchase.
- By manipulating **open market operations,** the Federal Reserve buys and sells United States government bonds. People buy bonds because they have a better interest rate than savings accounts. When the Fed sells bonds, people withdraw money from banks to take advantage of the bond's higher interest rate. Because the bank has less to loan, consumer interest rates go up, which slows consumer spending and economic growth. When the Fed buys bonds, money flows back into the banks, which increases the money available for loans. With more money in the bank for consumers to borrow, interest rates are driven down. Lower interest rates means more consumer spending, which increases economic growth.

Some economists believe that government should intervene only to manipulate the money supply, an idea championed by Milton Friedman. These monetarists believe that the money supply should be increased at a constant rate to accommodate economic growth. Monetarists do not believe that interest rate changes and manipulation of tax rates have much of an impact on economic conditions.

In the 1990s, the U.S. economy expanded without tax cuts, creating record employment levels with little inflation. Many gave the credit to the monetary policy of Alan Greenspan and the Federal Reserve.

The Tools of Economic Policy Making

The president receives advice on the state of the economy from the following departments and agencies:

- the Council of Economic Advisors
- the National Economic Council
- the Office of Management and Budget
- the Secretary of the Treasury

The president can influence the fiscal and monetary policies of these departments and agencies through his appointment power and policy **initiatives**. Remember that fiscal policy involves the budget, and monetary policy involves the money supply.

Fiscal Policy Making

The Director of the **Office of Management and Budget (OMB)** is responsible for initiating the budget process. The director meets with the president to discuss his policy initiatives. The state of the economy is discussed, centering on government revenue projections, which is the predicted income from taxes. Based on the president's priorities, some executive departments will receive more money than others. The OMB then writes the president's budget and submits it to Congress. Upon its arrival the budget is sent to three committees. The **House Ways and Means Committee** deals with the taxing aspects of the budget. **Authorization committees** in both houses decide what programs Congress wants to fund. **Appropriations committees** in both houses then decide how much money to spend for those programs that have been authorized.

Shut It Down

Bill Clinton's conflict with congressional Republicans led to government shutdowns over budget issues in 1995 and 1996. A similar impasse occurred in 2013, leading to a shutdown for 16 days in October of that year.

The budget process is complicated, politically divisive, and, in recent years, nearly impossible to conclude. The president's projected revenues and expenditures often conflict with those of Congress. Congress often simply does not trust the president's numbers, and conversely, the president does not trust Congress's. These yearly budget problems forced passage of the **Budget Reform Act of 1974**, which created the **Congressional Budget Office,** with budget committees in both the House and Senate. The congressional committees set their own revenue and spending levels. Negotiations then take place among the White House and the two houses of Congress in an effort to get one budget acceptable to everyone. Failure to achieve a budget by the beginning of the **fiscal year** could mean shutting down the government and sending employees home. When this occurs, budget stop-gap bills are passed to temporarily appropriate money to keep the government operating.

The **Budget Enforcement Act of 1990** was an effort to streamline the budget process and make it easier to arrive at a compromise budget. The law categorizes government expenditures as either mandatory or discretionary spending. **Mandatory spending** is required by law, to fund programs such as the **entitlement programs,**

Social Security, Medicare, veterans' pensions, and payment on the national debt. **Discretionary spending** programs are not required by law and include defense, education, highways, research grants, and all government operations. Discretionary programs are the primary targets for making cuts to balance the budget.

TRADE POLICY

The United States is by far the richest nation in the world. The output of the economy of the state of California alone ranks among the top ten nations in the world. The economic outputs of each of the three cities of Los Angeles, Chicago, and New York rank among the output of the top twenty nations. For better or for worse, the United States is the largest producer and consumer of products.

Foreign nations depend on the United States as a market for their products, as we depend on them for ours. The ratio of imported products to exported products is called the **balance of trade. Trade deficits** occur when imports exceed exports. Trade deficits cause wealth to flow from a nation. When nations face trade deficits, they often place restrictions on imported goods. The nation facing the restrictions can take retaliation by imposing high import taxes or unfair regulations on products, effectively keeping out foreign goods. Trade wars can result, stopping trade between countries. Trade surpluses are the result of more money flowing into a country than out. The oil-producing nations have huge amounts of money flowing into their treasuries and therefore have large trade surpluses when prices are high.

In an effort to promote trade, the United States signed the **General Agreement on Tariffs and Trade (GATT),** which evolved into the World Trade Organization (WTO). The 125 members of the WTO account for 97% of the world's trade. The organization works to lower tariffs and quotas and reduce unfair trade practices.

In an effort to promote free trade between the United States, Canada, and Mexico, the three nations signed the **North American Free Trade Agreement (NAFTA)** in 1994, effectively removing import tariffs from one another's products. As an economic policy, NAFTA is controversial. It is opposed by U.S. industrial labor unions who fear that jobs will be lost to cheap Mexican labor. Others fear that the industrial capacity of the United States will be damaged because factories will move to Mexico where environmental laws are not strictly enforced. NAFTA supporters claim it will improve the U.S. economy and will also create jobs in Mexico, resulting in less illegal immigration. Supporters also claim that a richer Mexico will purchase more American products. NAFTA has proven to be something of a mixed blessing. Its passage has led to cheaper labor (in Mexico) for many U.S. companies and an increase in trade between the two countries. Nevertheless, many American jobs have undeniably been sent south of the border, and many Mexican farmers are losing their land in a futile attempt to compete with American agribusinesses.

DOMESTIC POLICY

While economic policy is contentious, domestic policy is sometimes even more so because it gets to the very essence of the purposes of government. Liberals believe government has an obligation to provide for social welfare, to help the needy. Conservatives believe **social-welfare programs** are encroachments on individual liberties and responsibilities. They think these programs turn the government into an instrument used to create a permanent class of the underprivileged, dependent upon government handouts. Somewhere in between are the moderates who believe government should provide opportunities and limited help during difficult times.

The twentieth century has seen a dramatic change in the way society perceives the role of government in providing for the basic needs of people. Before the Great Depression, there were no government programs to help people who suffered from the hardships of old age, disabilities, unemployment, and poverty. So many people needed help in the 1930s that the government enacted programs to create jobs, provide housing, and feed the hungry. Later on, the **Great Society** programs of the Johnson administration expanded government welfare programs, but because of the expense and questions about their effectiveness, many of the Great Society programs were eliminated or scaled back during and after the Reagan administration.

Today there are two kinds of social-welfare programs.

- **Social insurance programs** are in reality national insurance programs into which employers and employees pay taxes. Because individuals pay into these programs, the benefits derived are considered by the public to have been earned. There seems to be little public debate over a citizen's "right" to Social Security.
- **Public assistance programs,** on the other hand, are not perceived as earned. These programs are a result of condition and a government responsibility to help the needy. Recipients are not required to pay into the system to get something out. Public assistance is considered by some to be a "handout" to the lazy. Because politicians understand this public perception, public policy initiatives from both parties have concentrated on forcing people on public assistance to either seek work or enter work-training programs.

Social Security

Social Security is an entitlement program mandated by law. The government must pay benefits to all people who meet the requirements of the program. Changing the law would require congressional action. Because the largest voting block of the electorate is made up of those nearing or at retirement age, there is little chance of major changes to the system, even though some experts warn that the Social Security trust fund will go bankrupt in the near future. Currently, entitlement programs account for the largest expense in the federal budget.

In its original form Social Security provided benefits only to retired persons beginning at age 65.

The program has now been expanded to include four categories of persons.

- Retired workers and their survivors who are presently age 65 and older receive monthly payments from the Social Security trust fund. To help maintain a recipient's standard of living, recipients are entitled to a **COLA** (cost of living adjustment) if the inflation rate exceeds 3%. COLAs put a strain on the ability of the trust fund to meet its obligations. Changes in the demographic composition of society are also putting a strain on the system. Society is aging, and the ratio of workers to retirees is declining. Because Social Security is a pay-as-you-go system, the money that is now paid into the system pays the present beneficiaries. As the ratio of workers to retirees continues to decline, workers will be faced with higher taxes to maintain the income of those who are retired.
- Insurance for the disabled provides monthly payments to those citizens who are permanently and totally disabled. This category includes the learning disabled and those dependent on drugs and alcohol.
- **Medicare** provides government assistance to people older than 65 for health care. For those retirees who pay an additional tax on their social security benefit, Medicare Part B will pay approximately 80% of their doctor's bills. The high and rising cost of health care has led some to question the solvency of this program, but recent reports note that it is more than able to cover 100% of its costs through at least 2030.
- **Medicaid** provides medical and health-related services for low-income parents, children, seniors, and people with disabilities. It is jointly funded by the states and federal government and is managed and run by the individual states.
- Temporary unemployment insurance for those out of work provides a weekly benefit, for a limited time. Each state government administers its own unemployment insurance program. Both the federal and state governments pay into a trust fund to provide the benefit. While states have traditionally set their own rules on the amount and duration of benefits, Congress has responded at the federal level to the recession that began in 2009 by helping states offer up to 99 weeks of benefits to the unemployed, significantly more than the previous standard of 26 weeks. In 2012, however, Congress imposed additional restrictions on those extended federal benefits, including a measure to gradually decrease the limit to 73 weeks. With the unemployment rate below 6% at the beginning of 2015, the extension of benefits continues to decrease.

Social Welfare

No matter how well intentioned the government has been, and no matter how much money has been spent, poverty has remained a perpetual problem for policy makers at both the state and federal levels. The first federal welfare programs were established by the Social Security Act in the 1930s. The largest and most controversial became known as Aid to Families with Dependent Children (AFDC).

All social welfare programs are designed to help targeted groups. Public assistance programs, known as welfare, target families whose total income falls below the federally determined minimum amount required to provide for the basic needs of a family. The present amount is approximately $17,000 for a family of four. The larger the family, the more income is required and the more money is paid out. Critics claimed that welfare was an incentive for families to have more children. Further complicating matters were complaints from recipients about a system that was degrading because investigators, looking for welfare cheaters, were invading their privacy.

In addition to AFDC, the federal government has established **supplemental public assistance programs** (known as SSI) to help the disabled and the aged who are living at or near the poverty level. To improve the diet and increase the buying power of the poor, the federal government also provides **food stamps**. Recipients use government-provided debit cards to help pay for food. Both SSI and the food-stamp program are federal programs administered through local and state agencies.

In an effort to reduce the number of people living on public assistance, the **Welfare Reform Act** was passed in 1996. Under the new law, social welfare programs are funded by both the state and federal governments, with the federal government contributing the greatest share in the form of block grants. Block grants are important because they allow states to experiment with new types of programs designed to get people off welfare and into work programs. The administration of programs (the distribution of cash payments) and the incentives for finding work and providing job training are left to the states. The intent of the law is to reduce the welfare rolls and force people to find work. This is accomplished by

- abolishing Aid to Families with Dependent Children (AFDC), which has affected 22% of the families in the United States with children and replacing it with Temporary Assistance for Needy Families (TANF)
- requiring adults to find work within two years or be cut off
- placing a lifetime limit of five years for welfare eligibility, although it is possible to get a waiver if a recipient is actively seeking work
- prohibiting illegal immigrants from receiving assistance

The political debate over public assistance centers on two issues: Who pays how much, and what is the fair standard to be used for the recipient? Both Democrats and Republicans have tried to reduce these programs. Cutting them, however, places more people at risk, reducing food stamp programs and school lunch programs, causing increased hunger. To make matters more complicated, the Welfare Reform Act moved millions off the welfare rolls of the states as it coincided with a boom in unemployment.

Health Care

One of the most vexing problems for policy makers is what to do about the high cost of health care. Americans spend more than 17% of the nation's **gross domestic product**, or **GDP** (the total of goods and services produced in a year), on health care. The United States has the most expensive health care system in the world and is the only fully industrialized nation without a national health care program. High costs have not guaranteed any longer life expectancy, nor better treatment than that found in other industrialized nations. Instead of a national program run by the government, most Americans have relied on various types of insurance programs to pay for health care costs. The premiums for these health care programs are paid by workers and employers. For many reasons, but primarily because of cost, 15.4% of the population was without health insurance in 2010.

As with other government programs, the electorate is divided on how to solve the two issues of universal health care and the burden of health care costs. Voters seem to want increased coverage but there is little evidence to indicate they are willing to pay for it. The only taxes the American electorate seems willing to pay are the so-called "sin taxes"—still fairly unpopular in some circles—on alcohol and tobacco products, which will not generate enough revenues to provide increased coverage. Proposals for "anti-obesity" taxes on sugary drinks and sodas have been met with mixed reactions from the public. Another basic issue for which there is no consensus is whether health benefits should be a government or privately administered program. With little public consensus, over the past two decades, reform has been extremely contentious.

An ill-fated attempt at health care reform was made in the first Clinton administration. The proposed policy called for universal coverage and strict cost controls. The policy would have required increased taxes coupled with cost-cutting limits on the types of medical procedures allowable. The lack of public consensus killed the proposal within a year.

The debate over health care continued during the 2000 presidential election. Both candidates agreed that something had to be done about both escalating costs and the increasing numbers of uninsured. The Democrats promoted a policy of a government-paid prescription drug program for senior citizens. The Republicans promoted a prescription-drug program run by insurance providers, but again there was no consensus.

High Costs
The average cost for these insurance programs is at least $5,000 per year and is rising faster than the cost of living.

The most significant health-care legislation in American history was signed into law by President Obama on March 23, 2010. The **Patient Protection and Affordable Health Care Act**, popularly known as Obamacare, was passed over the course of several months and it generated significant political debate and controversy. The law was celebrated by most Democrats, who touted it as the much-needed solution to the long-term flaws in the American health-care system. Republicans and some independent voters criticized the law, claiming it was an expensive intrusion of the federal government into the public sector. The debate lasted until the midterm elections in November of 2010, when Republicans gained a large number of congressional seats partly as a result of voter discontent with the law.

The most important of the law's provisions allows the federal government, beginning in 2014, to fine individuals who do not participate in an insurance program. This policy, known as the "individual mandate," has been the basis of many Republican criticisms of the law. The attorneys general of twenty-eight states challenged this provision in the law in federal court, claiming that the Constitution prohibits Congress from taxing individuals for not purchasing a product (say, health insurance). However, the Supreme Court ruled that the individual mandate is constitutional in the 2012 case *National Federation of Independent Business v. Sebelius*.

KEY TERMS

- issue-attention cycle
- incrementalism
- agenda setting
- policy implementation
- policy fragmentation
- mixed economy
- laissez-faire
- Keynesian economics
- fiscal policy
- deficit spending
- supply-side economics
- budget deficit
- monetary policy
- Federal Reserve Board
- reserve requirement
- discount rate
- open market operations
- initiative
- Office of Management and Budget (OMB)
- House Ways and Means Committee
- authorization committees
- appropriation committees
- Budget Reform Act of 1974
- Congressional Budget Office
- fiscal year
- Budget Enforcement Act of 1990
- mandatory spending
- entitlement programs
- discretionary spending
- balance of trade
- trade deficit
- General Agreement on Tariffs and Trade (GATT)
- North American Free Trade Agreement (NAFTA)
- social-welfare programs
- Great Society
- Social Security
- COLA
- Medicare
- Medicaid
- supplemental public assistance programs
- food stamps
- Welfare Reform Act
- gross domestic product (GDP)
- Patient Protection and Affordable Health Care Act

Summary

o   Public policy is made when the government decides to take action to solve a societal problem, and consists of five steps

    (1) defining the role of government
    (2) agenda setting
    (3) policy formulation
    (4) policy implementation
    (5) policy evaluation

o   Economic policy has been one of the most important areas of public policy in American history. Policy makers have oscillated between supporting laissez-faire free market principles and redistributionist, interventionist policies.

o   The United States has joined international trade organizations like the World Trade Organization (WTO) and the North American Free Trade Agreement (NAFTA) in order to boost our commerce with the rest of the world. Nevertheless, we still use tariffs and subsidies to protect large swathes of our industry and agriculture.

o   Before FDR, the federal government did not engage in much domestic policy making, but since that era we have seen the rise of programs like Social Security, Welfare (through the Aid to Families with Dependant Children and new state-based systems), and Medicaid.

Chapter 9 Drill

See Chapter 11 for answers and explanations.

1. The Office of Management and Budget (OMB) is in charge of

   (A) assessing the nation's economic health
   (B) writing the national budget to reflect the interests of Congress
   (C) planning out the national budget for the president
   (D) providing long-term and highly theoretical economic advice
   (E) protecting the environment

2. Which of the following is NOT generally a step in the policy-making process?

   (A) Policy formulation
   (B) Abandoning governmental solutions for societal problems
   (C) Policy implementation
   (D) Policy evaluation
   (E) Agenda setting

3. Which of the following is an example of a policy that a believer in laissez-faire economics might support?

   (A) Giving the EPA greater power to fine factories that contribute to global warming
   (B) Increasing taxes across higher income groups to aid the poor
   (C) Creation of a law that protects unions and grants them collective bargaining rights
   (D) The implementation of a flat tax
   (E) Spending more money on farmers to support America's agricultural output

4. Which of the following people would NOT receive money from Social Security?

   (A) Retired workers
   (B) The widow of a retired worker
   (C) A quadriplegic
   (D) A worker who has just lost her job
   (E) A family that is chronically poor

5. When a nation's imports exceed its exports, the country is

   (A) running a trade deficit
   (B) running a trade surplus
   (C) in default
   (D) bankrupt
   (E) automatically expelled from the WTO

6. Which action would a lawmaker who follows the Keynesian school of economics be most likely to take during an economic recession?

   (A) Increase domestic government spending
   (B) Keep domestic government spending the same
   (C) Cut domestic government spending
   (D) Raise the discount rate
   (E) Cut taxes

7. Which of the following programs is categorized as discretionary spending under the Budget Enforcement Act of 1990?

   (A) national debt payments
   (B) Social Security
   (C) veterans' pensions
   (D) Medicare
   (E) education

REFLECT

Respond to the following questions:

- For which content topics discussed in this chapter do you feel you have achieved sufficient mastery to answer multiple-choice questions correctly?

- For which content topics discussed in this chapter do you feel you have achieved sufficient mastery to discuss effectively in an essay?

- For which content topics discussed in this chapter do you feel you need more work before you can answer multiple-choice questions correctly?

- For which content topics discussed in this chapter do you feel you need more work before you can discuss effectively in an essay?

- What parts of this chapter are you going to re-review?

- Will you seek further help, outside of this book (such as a teacher, tutor, or AP Students), on any of the content in this chapter—and, if so, on what content?

Chapter 10
Civil Rights and
Civil Liberties

CONCEPTS

- Why would Justice Thurgood Marshall blame the Supreme Court for the racial policies practiced in the United States before the *Brown* decision?
- Why did the Supreme Court allow the use of affirmative-action programs?
- Why is it said that the Warren Court took the handcuffs off the criminals and put them on the police?
- What mechanism did the Supreme Court use to ensure the rights of defendants in state criminal prosecutions?
- What impact has the interpretation of speech as a preferred right had on the government's power to censure?
- How does the Supreme Court interpret the right to privacy on matters dealing with human reproduction?
- How has the Supreme Court changed its reasoning in dealing with religious activities in schools financed by the public?

How to Discuss a Court Case

First, an important tip: In responding to an essay question involving Supreme Court decisions, do not take more than one sentence per case to explain the relevant background. Explain the essential questions and answers of cases, as well as the reasoning the court used in the decision. The most important aspect of a case, for political science purposes, is its impact on government or society. When asked about a case, make sure the consequences of the decision are discussed. For example, the most important consequence of *Marbury v. Madison* is the establishment of judicial review, which is arguably the most important principle ever enshrined by the court. The consequence of *Heart of Atlanta Motel v. United States* is the affirmation of the power of Congress, through the use of the commerce clause, to end segregation by law in the United States.

The term **civil liberties** generally applies to those protections (enjoyed by all Americans) from the abuse of government power. The term **civil rights** is used specifically to describe protections from discrimination based on race, gender, or other minority status. Often, the term is used to refer specifically to the struggles of African Americans for equal status (for example, the Civil Rights Movement).

The Extension of Civil Liberties
Through American History

In *Barron v. Baltimore* (1833), the Supreme Court determined that the Bill of Rights restricted the national government but not the state governments. It was not until 1925 that the court overturned this ruling, citing Fourteenth Amendment restrictions on the states ("no state shall…deprive any person of life, liberty, or property, without due process of law; nor deny to any person within its jurisdiction the equal protection of the laws"). That case, *Gitlow v. New York*, concerned freedom of speech and freedom of the press. The court ruled that state limits on speech and the press could not exceed the limits allowed the national government.

Since then, the court has applied the Bill of Rights to state law on a case-by-case basis. This process is called **selective incorporation.** Currently, the following rights have NOT been incorporated and may thus be restricted by the states:

- the Third Amendment protection against forced quartering of troops in private homes
- the Fifth Amendment right to **indictment** by a grand jury
- the Seventh Amendment right to a jury trial in civil cases
- the Eighth Amendment protection against excessive bail and fines

All other provisions of the Bill of Rights, however, apply equally to the states and the national government. In defining individual rights, the court has consistently weighed the rights of individuals against the needs of society at large. Therefore, none of the rights guaranteed in the Bill of Rights is absolute.

FIRST AMENDMENT RIGHTS AND RESTRICTIONS

The **First Amendment** guarantees **freedom of speech, freedom of the press, freedom of petitioning the government, freedom of assembly,** and **freedom of religion.** None of these important rights, however, is absolute. Throughout the nation's history, the Supreme Court has ruled that these rights may be limited in the interest of the greater public good. It has also ruled, however, that such restrictions must be well justified, well defined, and limited only to those few instances in which the public welfare is genuinely threatened.

Freedom of Speech

The most famous limit on free speech is the **clear and present danger test.** In the case of *Schenck v. United States* (1919), Justice Oliver Wendell Holmes argued that a person may not falsely scream "fire!" in a crowded theater, because doing so would likely result in panic. The court has also ruled that there is no constitutional protection for false defamatory speech (called **slander** when it is spoken and **libel** when it is in a more permanent form, such as print), **obscenity,** or speech intended to incite violence.

Since the 1940s, the court has followed the **preferred position doctrine** in determining the limits of free speech. The doctrine reflects the court's belief that freedom of speech is fundamental to liberty; therefore, any limits on free speech must address severe, imminent threats to the nation. They must also be limited to constraining those threats; any restriction that fails to meet this test would probably be overturned by the Supreme Court. The court continues to protect offensive but nonthreatening speech such as flag burning (usually undertaken by protesters, who burn the flag as a symbolic indication that the country has failed to protect American values such as democracy and freedom for all).

Important Cases

Schenck v. United States (1919). This case, decided by Chief Justice Oliver Wendell Holmes, established that speech which evokes "a clear and present danger" is not permissible. He famously used the example of someone falsely yelling "fire!" in a crowded theater as an example of prohibited speech.

Gitlow v. New York (1925). This case created the "Bad Tendency Doctrine," which held that speech could be restricted even if it only has a tendency to lead to illegal action. Though this element of the decision was quite restrictive, Gitlow also selectively incorporated freedom of speech to state governments.

Tinker v. Des Moines (1969). Students in an Iowa school were suspended for wearing black armbands to protest the Vietnam war. The court ruled that this suspension was unconstitutional, and that public school students do not "shed their constitutional rights at the schoolhouse door."

Bethel School District v. Fraser (1986). This case gave public school officials the authority to suspend students for speech considered to be lewd or indecent.

Hustler Magazine v. Falwell (1988). In this much-publicized case, the court held that intentional infliction of emotional distress was permissible First Amendment speech—so long as such speech was about a public figure and could not reasonably be construed to state actual facts about its subject. In other words, parody is not an actionable offense.

Texas v. Johnson (1989). *Johnson* established that burning the American flag is an example of permissible free speech, and struck down numerous anti-flag burning laws.

Morse v. Frederick (2007). This case was known as the "Bong Hits 4 Jesus" case, in which the Supreme Court limited students' free speech rights. The justices ruled that Frederick's free speech rights were not violated by his suspension over what the majority's written opinion called a "sophomoric" banner.

Citizens United v. Federal Election Commission (2010). The case established that corporations have a First Amendment right to expressly support political candidates for Congress and the White House.

Freedom of the Press

On occasion the government has tried to control the press, usually claiming national security interests. This occurred during the 1990 Persian Gulf War, when the Pentagon limited media access to the war zone and censored outgoing news reports. The media objected to these limitations. Such conflicts usually end up in the courts, where judges are forced to weigh conflicting national interests: the need to be informed versus security concerns.

An even more contentious issue involves the media's responsibility to reveal the sources of their information. The Supreme Court has ruled that reporters are not exempt from testifying in court cases and that they can be asked to name their sources. Reporters who refuse to do so, as many have, can be jailed. A number of states have enacted **shield laws** to protect reporters in state cases, but in other states and in federal cases reporters have no such protection.

The Pentagon Papers

A previous similar case involved the Pentagon Papers (1971), a secret report on American involvement in Vietnam. The report was leaked to *The New York Times*, which published excerpts from the report. The government tried to halt further publication, claiming that national security was at stake. In that case, the court rejected the government's efforts to prevent publication (called **prior restraint**), ruling that the public's need to be well informed outweighed the national security issues raised. The Pentagon Papers case demonstrates the preferred position doctrine.

As mentioned above, libel and obscenity are not protected by the First Amendment. In the case of *Miller v. California* (1973), the court established a **three-part obscenity test**.

- Would the average person, applying community standards, judge the work as appealing primarily to people's baser sexual instincts?
- Does the work lack other value, or is it also of literary, artistic, political, or scientific interest?
- Does the work depict sexual behavior in an offensive manner?

Important Cases

Near v. Minnesota (1931). *Near* established that state injunctions to prevent publication violate the free press provision of the First Amendment and are unconstitutional. This case is important in that it selectively incorporates freedom of the press and prevents prior restraint.

New York Times v. Sullivan (1964). If a newspaper prints an article that turns out to be false but that the newspaper thought was true at the time of publication, has the newspaper committed libel? This case said no.

New York Times v. U.S. (1971). When Defense Department employee Daniel Ellsburg leaked some confidential files indicating that the war in Vietnam was going poorly, the government sought to prevent the publication of these "Pentagon Papers" by *The New York Times*. In this case, the court held that executive efforts to prevent the publication violated the First Amendment.

Hazelwood School v. Kuhlmeier (1988). In *Hazelwood*, the court held that school officials have sweeping authority to regulate free speech in student-run newspapers.

Freedom of Assembly and Association

The First Amendment protects the right of people to assemble peacefully. That right does not extend to violent groups or to demonstrations that would incite violence. Furthermore, the government may place reasonable restrictions on crowd gatherings, provided such restrictions are applied equally to all groups. Demonstrators have no constitutional right, for example, to march on and thereby close down a highway. They may not block the doorways of buildings. In short, crowd gatherings must not unnecessarily disrupt day-to-day life. That is why groups must apply for licenses to hold a parade or street fair.

The court has also ruled that the combined rights of freedom of speech and freedom of assembly imply a **freedom of association**. This means that the government may not restrict the number or type of groups or organizations people belong to, provided those groups do not threaten national security.

Important Cases

Thornhill v. Alabama (1940). Labor unions have been controversial since the dawn of the industrial revolution—did their strikes constitute a form of unlawful assembly? In *Thornhill*, the court held that strikes by unions were not unlawful.

Cox v. New Hampshire (1941). When a group of Jehovah's Witnesses were arrested for marching in New Hampshire without a permit, they claimed that permits themselves were an unconstitutional abridgment of their First Amendment freedoms. In *Cox*, the court held that cities and towns could legitimately require parade permits in the interest of public order.

Lloyd Corporation v. Tanner (1972). This case allowed the owners of a shopping mall to throw out people protesting the Vietnam War. The key element here is that malls are private spaces, not public. As a result, protesters have substantially fewer assembly rights in malls and other private establishments.

Boy Scouts of America v. Dale (2000). Private organizations' First Amendment right of expressive association allows them to choose their own membership and expel members based on their sexual orientation even if such discrimination would otherwise be prohibited by anti-discrimination legislation designed to protect minorities in public accommodations. As a result of this case, the Boy Scouts of America were allowed to expel any member who was discovered to be homosexual.

Freedom of Religion

The Constitution guarantees the right to the free exercise of religion, meaning that the government may not prevent individuals from practicing their faiths. This right is not absolute, however. Human sacrifice, to give an extreme example, is not allowed. The courts have ruled that polygamy is not protected by the Constitution, nor is the denial of medical treatment to a child, regardless of individual religious beliefs. However, the court has ruled that Jehovah's Witnesses cannot be required to salute the American flag and that Amish children may stop attending school after the eighth grade. In all cases, the court weighs individual rights to free religious exercise against society's needs.

The Constitution also prevents the government from establishing a state religion (the establishment clause). The establishment clause has been used to prevent school prayer, government-sponsored displays of the Christmas nativity, and state bans on the teaching of evolution (because such bans were religiously motivated). However, the wall between church and state is not rock solid. The court has allowed government subsidies to provide some aspects of parochial education (such as lunches, textbooks, and buses). It has also allowed for tax credits for non-public school costs. In deciding whether a law violates the establishment clause, the court uses a three-part test, called the **Lemon test** after the case *Lemon v. Kurtzman* (1971).

- Does the law have a secular, rather than a religious, purpose?
- Does the law neither promote nor discourage religion?
- Does the law avoid "excessive entanglement" of the government and religious institutions?

Important Cases

Engel v. Vitale (1962). This landmark case prohibited state-sponsored recitation of prayer in public schools.

Abington School Dist. v. Schempp (1963). Given the court's ruling in *Engel*, it's not surprising that in *Abington* they decided that the establishment clause of the First Amendment forbids state-mandated reading of the Bible, or recitation of the Lord's Prayer in public schools.

Epperson v. Arkansas (1968). In line with the establishment clause, *Epperson* prohibited states from banning the teaching of evolution in public schools.

Lemon v. Kurtzman (1971). This case dealt with state laws intending to give money to religious schools or causes. The court held that in order to be consistent with the establishment clause, the money had to meet three qualifications: (1) it must have a legitimate secular purpose, (2) it must not have the primary effect of either advancing or inhibiting religion, and (3) it must not result in an excessive entanglement of government and religion. These qualifications are known as the "Lemon test."

Wisconsin v. Yoder (1972). This case dealt with the Amish community's desire to pull their children from public school before the age of 16 so that they could help with farm and domestic work. The court sided with the Amish and held that parents may remove children from public school for religious reasons.

Employment Division v. Smith (1990). This case determined that the state could deny unemployment benefits to a person fired for violating a state prohibition on the use of peyote, even though the use of the drug was part of a religious ritual. In short, states may accommodate otherwise illegal acts done in pursuit of religious beliefs, but they are not required to do so.

THE RIGHTS OF THE ACCUSED

Rights granted to the accused are a fundamental protection against governmental abuse of power. Many of the these rights are found in the Fifth Amendment. Without them, the government could imprison its political opponents without trial or could guarantee conviction through numerous unfair prosecutorial tactics. However, these rights are also controversial. Anti-crime organizations and politicians frequently decry these protections when arguing that it is too difficult to capture, try, and imprison criminals. These accusations have grown louder and more frequent since the 1960s, when the **Warren Court** (the Supreme Court under Chief Justice Earl Warren) greatly expanded those protections that are granted to criminal defendants.

Important Cases

Weeks v. United States (1914). Though the Constitution is unequivocal when it forbids unlawful search and seizure, such ill-gotten evidence was still commonly used to prosecute defendants. Weeks established the exclusionary rule, which held that illegally obtained evidence could not be used in federal court.

Powell v. Alabama (1932). The Constitution is clear in the Sixth Amendment when it guarantees all those accused of a federal crime the right to have a lawyer. But what about those accused of state crimes? Should they get a lawyer if they can't afford one? In *Powell*, the court ruled that state governments must provide counsel in cases involving the death penalty to those who can't afford it.

Betts v. Brady (1942). The Betts case established that state governments did not have to provide lawyers to indigent defendants in capital cases.

Mapp v. Ohio (1961). By 1961, the exclusionary rule meant that any unlawfully gathered evidence could not be introduced in federal court, but such evidence was introduced all the time in state courts. The Mapp case extended the exclusionary rule to the states, increasing the protections for defendants.

Gideon v. Wainwright (1963). This was a powerful repudiation of *Betts v. Brady*. Here, the Warren court strongly holds that all state governments must provide an attorney in all cases for those who can't afford one.

Escobedo v. Illinois (1964). *Escobedo* is another important Warren Court decision. Here, the court held that any defendant who asked for a lawyer had to have one granted to him—or any confession garnered after that point would be inadmissible in court.

Miranda v. Arizona (1966). *Miranda* is the most dramatic and well-known of the Warren Court decisions. The court found that all defendants must be informed of all their legal rights before they are arrested. It is thanks to *Miranda* that we all know the phrase "You have the right to remain silent…" and you can't get through an episode of *Law & Order* without hearing it at least once.

Protection from Self-Incrimination

The Constitution protects individuals from **self-incrimination**. A defendant cannot be forced to testify at trial, and the jury is not supposed to infer guilt when a defendant chooses to not testify. Furthermore, a defendant must be notified of his or her right to remain silent, his or her right to a lawyer, and his or her protection against self-incrimination at the time of his arrest.

For years, the courts rarely admitted into evidence confessions from arrestees who had not been properly "Mirandized." In recent years, however, the Supreme Court has defined some situations in which such confessions are admissible. In 1991, the court ruled that a coerced confession does not automatically invalidate a conviction. Rather, an appeals court may consider all evidence entered at trial. If the court decides that a conviction was probable even without the confession, it may let the guilty verdict stand.

Miranda Rights

This precedent was established in the 1966 Supreme Court case *Miranda v. Arizona*. Ernesto Miranda had been arrested for kidnapping and rape, and within two hours of his arrest, he had confessed to his crimes. His lawyer appealed the case on the grounds that Miranda had not been advised of his constitutional rights (for example, the protection against self-incrimination and the right to legal counsel). In *Miranda*, the Supreme Court decided that the police had deprived Miranda of his Fourteenth Amendment right to due process. Those rights have since come to be known as Miranda rights.

Protection from Unreasonable Search and Seizure

The **Fourth Amendment** limits the power of the government to search for evidence of criminal activity. When the police want to search private property, in most circumstances they must first go before a judge and justify the search. If the judge is convinced that the search is likely to uncover evidence of illegality—called **probable cause**—the judge issues a **search warrant**, which limits where the police may search and what they may take as evidence. Evidence found by police who disregard this procedure may not be admitted as evidence in trial. This is called the **exclusionary rule**. The Supreme Court applied the exclusionary rule to federal trials in 1911.

As with all constitutional rights, however, there are exceptions to this rule. In 1984, the Supreme Court established the **objective good faith** exception, which allows for convictions in cases in which a search was not technically legal (either because it violated the warrant or because the warrant itself was faulty) but was conducted under the assumption that it was legal. The court has also determined that illegally seized evidence that would eventually have been found legally is also admissible in court. This principle is known as the **inevitable discovery rule**.

There are also circumstances under which the police may conduct a search without a warrant. Police may conduct an immediate search following a legal arrest, for example. Police may also conduct an immediate search of private property if the owner consents to that search. Evidence found in plain view may be seized immediately; if, for example, a person is growing marijuana on his or her front lawn, the police may seize that evidence without first acquiring a search warrant. Finally, police may conduct an immediate search if they have probable cause

Mapp v. Ohio
In the 1961 case *Mapp v. Ohio*, the court incorporated the exclusionary rule, thus making it applicable to state trials as well.

to believe they will find evidence of criminal activity, especially when there are **exigent circumstances**, or reason to believe evidence would disappear by the time they received a warrant and returned. The police would later have to demonstrate that they had probable cause in court.

Rights to an Attorney and a Speedy Trial

The **Sixth Amendment** guarantees criminal defendants the **right to an attorney in federal cases**. In 1932, the Supreme Court used the Fourteenth Amendment to incorporate this right in capital cases ("the Scottsboro boys" case). In the 1963 case *Gideon v. Wainwright*, the court ruled that all criminal defendants in state courts were entitled to legal counsel. In both cases, the court ruled that the state must provide a lawyer to defendants too poor to hire a lawyer. The court has since extended this protection to misdemeanor cases, provided those cases could result in jail time for the defendant. However, the court has held that states are not required to provide a lawyer to litigants in civil cases.

The Sixth Amendment also guarantees defendants **the right to a speedy trial**. The courts have become so overburdened with cases that the Supreme Court recently imposed a 100-day limit between the time of arrest and the start of a trial. The limit has had little practical effect, however, because both prosecutors and defense attorneys can request an extension to prepare their cases. Courts have generally granted such extensions. As a result, it is not unusual for a defendant to wait a year or more between his or her arrest date and a trial.

Protection from Excessive Bail and "Cruel and Unusual Punishment"

The **Eighth Amendment** states that "excessive bail shall not be required, nor excessive fines imposed, nor cruel and unusual punishments inflicted." The government is not required, however, to offer bail to all defendants. In 1984, Congress passed the Bail Reform Act to allow federal judges to deny bail to defendants considered either dangerous or likely to flee the country. The protection from excessive bail has *not* been incorporated, and states are therefore free to set bail as high as state law permits.

The **cruel and unusual punishment** clause of the Constitution lies at the heart of the debate over the death penalty. The court has placed limits on when the death penalty can be applied; however, it has upheld the constitutionality of the death penalty when properly applied. Critics point to statistics that those convicted of killing African Americans are far less likely to receive the death penalty than those convicted of killing Caucasians. The court has rejected this argument. In recent years, the court has moved to make it easier for states to carry out the death penalty by limiting the number and nature of appeals allowed by convicted murderers on death row. Recently too, however, some states have enacted moratoriums on the death penalty for reasons including methodology problems, flawed trial processes, and ethical objections.

Important Cases

Furman v. Georgia (1972). Here, the court looked at the patchwork quilt of
nationwide capital punishment decisions and found that its imposition was often racist and arbitrary. In *Furman*, the Court ordered a
halt to all death penalty punishments in the nation until a less arbitrary method of sentencing was found.

Woodson v. North Carolina (1976). North Carolina tried to satisfy the Court's
requirement that the imposition of the death penalty not be arbitrary—so they made it a mandatory punishment for certain crimes.
The Court rejected this approach and ruled mandatory death penalty
sentences as unconstitutional.

Gregg v. Georgia (1976). Georgia was finally able to convince the Court that it
had come up with a careful and fair system for trying capital offenses.
As a result, the Court ruled that under adequate guidelines the death
penalty did not, in fact, constitute cruel and unusual punishment.
Thus *Gregg* allowed the resumption of the death penalty in America.

Atkins v. Virginia (2002). Here, the United States lined up with most other nations in the world by forbidding the execution of defendants who are
mentally handicapped.

Roper v. Simmons (2005). Building on *Atkins*, the Court declared the death
penalty unconstitutional for defendants whose crimes were committed as minors, even if they were charged as adults.

THE RIGHT OF ALL AMERICANS TO PRIVACY

The right to privacy is not specifically mentioned in the Constitution. However,
in the 1965 Supreme Court case of *Griswold v. Connecticut,* the Court ruled that
the Bill of Rights contained an **implied right to privacy.** The Court ruled that the
combination of the First, Third, Fourth, Fifth, Ninth, and Fourteenth Amendments added up to a guarantee of privacy. The *Griswold* case concerned a state law
banning the use of contraception; the Supreme Court decision overturned that
law. *Griswold* also laid the foundation for the landmark *Roe v. Wade* case of 1973,
which legalized abortion.

Important Cases

Griswold v. Connecticut (1965). The Constitution never explicitly grants
Americans a right to privacy, but the court discovers one in this
landmark and controversial case. Writing for the majority, Justice
William O. Douglas noted that amendments like the Third, Fourth,
and Ninth all cast "penumbras and emanations" which showed that
the Founders really had intended for a right to privacy all along.

Roe v. Wade (1973). Though *Roe* is one of the most famous court cases in American history, legally it is really a subset of the *Griswold* decision. The court had already done the heavy lifting of discovering the right to privacy in the Constitution. As a result, in *Roe* they established national abortion guidelines by extending the inferred right of privacy from *Griswold*.

Webster v. Reproductive Health Services (1989). This case did not overturn *Roe v. Wade*, but it did give states more power to regulate abortion.

Planned Parenthood v. Casey (1992). A Pennsylvania law that would have required a woman to notify her husband before getting an abortion was thrown out, but laws calling for parental consent and the imposition of a 24-hour waiting period were upheld. All in all, the message was that states *can* regulate abortion but not with regulations that impose an "undue burden" upon women.

Lawrence v. Texas (2003). With this ruling, the Supreme Court struck down a sodomy law that had criminalized homosexual sex in Texas. The court had previously addressed the same issue in *Bowers v. Hardwick* (1986), where it did not find constitutional protection of sexual privacy. *Lawrence* explicitly overruled *Bowers* saying that consensual sexual conduct was part of the liberty protected under the Fourteenth Amendment.

CIVIL RIGHTS

The AP U.S. Government and Politics Exam occasionally tests your knowledge of key civil rights legislation. Below is what you need to know about civil rights for the test.

Civil Rights and African Americans

Prior to the Civil War, most of the African American population in the United States consisted of slaves who were denied virtually any legal rights whatsoever. Free blacks were also denied basic civil rights such as the right to vote and the right to equal protection under the law. Because the Supreme Court had ruled in 1833 that the Bill of Rights applied to the federal government only, states were free to enact discriminatory and segregationist laws. Many did so to ensure the oppression of African Americans.

The Civil War began the long, slow development toward equality of the races before the law. Here is a list of key events in that process.

- **The Civil War (1861–1865).** The Civil War began, at least in part, over the issue of slavery (the debate over the relative powers of the federal and state governments was also a major cause of the war). The war was more clearly defined as a war about slavery in 1863, when President Lincoln issued the **Emancipation Proclamation,** which declared the liberation of slaves in the rebel states. The Civil War also influenced the civil rights process in a less direct and less immediate way, as it resulted in an increase in the power of the federal government. One hundred years later, the increased power vested in the federal government would be the means of imposing and enforcing equal rights laws in the states.

- **Thirteenth Amendment (1865).** The Thirteenth Amendment, ratified after the Civil War, made slavery illegal.

- **Fourteenth Amendment (1868).** The Fourteenth Amendment, ratified during Reconstruction, was designed to prevent states in the South from depriving newly freed blacks of their rights. Its clauses guaranteeing **due process** and **equal protection** were later used by the Supreme Court to apply most of the Bill of Rights to state law. However, in the 1880s the Supreme Court interpreted the amendment narrowly, allowing the states to enact segregationist laws. The Fourteenth Amendment also made African Americans citizens of the nation and of their home states, overruling the **Dred Scott case** (1857), which had ruled that slaves and their descendants were not citizens.

- **Fifteenth Amendment (1870).** The Fifteenth Amendment banned laws that would prevent African Americans from voting on the basis of their race or the fact that they previously were slaves.

- **Civil Rights Act of 1875.** The Civil Rights Act of 1875 banned discrimination in hotels, restaurants, and railroad cars, as well as banned discrimination in selection for jury duty. The Supreme Court declared the Act unconstitutional in 1883.

- **Jim Crow laws and voting restrictions.** As the federal government exerted less influence over the South, states, towns, and cities passed numerous discriminatory and segregationist laws. The Supreme Court supported the states by ruling that the Fourteenth Amendment did not protect blacks from discriminatory state laws, and that blacks would have to seek equal protection from the states, not from the federal government. In 1883, the court also reversed the Civil Rights Act of 1875, thus opening the door to legal segregation. These segregationist laws are known collectively as **Jim Crow laws.** The states also moved to deprive blacks of their voting rights by imposing **poll taxes** (a tax that must be paid in order to vote) and literacy tests. To allow poor, illiterate whites to vote, some states passed **grandfather clauses** that exempted from these restrictions anyone whose grandfather had voted. Grandfather clauses effectively excluded blacks whose grandparents had been slaves and therefore could not have voted.

- **Equal Pay Act of 1963.** This federal law made it illegal to base an employee's pay on race, gender, religion, or national origin. The Equal Pay Act was also important to the women's movement and to the civil rights struggles of other minorities.

- **Twenty-Fourth Amendment (1964).** This outlawed poll taxes, which had been used to prevent blacks and poor whites from voting.

- **Civil Rights Act of 1964.** The Civil Rights Act of 1964 was a landmark piece of legislation. It not only increased the rights of blacks and other minorities, but also gave the federal government greater means of enforcing the law. The law banned discrimination in public accommodations (public transportation, offices, and so on) and in all federally funded programs. It also prohibited discrimination in hiring based on color and gender. Finally, it required the government to cut off funding from any program that did not comply with the law, and it gave the federal government the power to initiate lawsuits in cases of school segregation. States that had previously ignored federal civil rights mandates now faced serious consequences for doing so.
- **Voting Rights Act of 1965.** The Voting Rights Act was designed to counteract voting discrimination in the South. It allowed the federal government to step into any state or county in which less than 50 percent of the population was registered to vote, or in areas that used literacy tests to prevent voting. In those areas, the federal government could register voters (which is normally a function of the states).
- **Civil Rights Act, Title VIII (1968).** This banned racial discrimination in housing.
- **Civil Rights Act of 1991.** This law was designed to address a number of problems that had arisen in civil rights law during the previous decade. Several Supreme Court decisions had limited the abilities of job applicants and employees to bring suit against employers with discriminatory hiring practices; the 1991 act eased those restrictions.

Important Cases

Plessy v. Ferguson (1896). This case famously allowed southern states to twist the Equal Protection Clause of the Fourteenth Amendment by allowing "separate but equal" facilities based on race.

Brown v. Board of Education of Topeka (1954). In this landmark case, a unanimous court led by newly appointed Chief Justice Earl Warren ruled the doctrine of "separate but equal" to be unconstitutional.

Brown v. Board II (1955). One year later, the Warren Court saw that segregation was still ubiquitous. So in Brown II, they ordered schools to desegregate "with all due and deliberate speed."

Heart of Atlanta Motel, Inc. v. United States (1964). Did the Federal Civil Rights Act of 1964 mandate that places of public accommodation are prohibited from discrimination against African Americans? Yes, said the court.

Katzenbach v. McClung (1964). The Civil Rights Act of 1964 prohibited discrimination in public places, but what about in private businesses? The Katzenbach case established that the power of Congress to regulate interstate commerce extends to state discrimination statutes. This ruling made the Civil Rights Act of 1964 apply to virtually all businesses.

Regents of the University of California v. Bakke (1978). Alan Bakke was a
   white applicant who was rejected from medical school because of an
   affirmative action plan to boost the number of black students. The
   court ruled that Bakke had been unfairly excluded and that quotas
   requiring a certain percentage of minorities violated the Fourteenth
   Amendment. But the court also held that race-based affirmative
   action *was* permissible so long as it was in the service of creating
   greater diversity.

Grutter v. Bollinger (2003) and *Gratz v. Bollinger* (2003). These cases involved
   the University of Michigan Law School and the University of Michigan
   undergraduate school. Both used affirmative action, but the
   undergraduate school did so by giving minority applicants a large boost
   in the score used by officers deciding on admission. The court threw
   out the undergraduate system of selection, but generally upheld *Bakke*.

Although the number of major new civil rights laws has
decreased in the past decades, the fight for civil rights
for African Americans and other minority groups is
far from over. Although legally enforced segregation
of public facilities no longer exists, racial segregation remains a national concern. Most public school
systems remain essentially segregated because the
neighborhoods that feed them are segregated. The impact of this *de facto* **segregation** (as opposed to *de jure*
segregation, which is segregation by law) is increased
by the disparity in average incomes among whites and
blacks: Because many local school systems are supported
by property taxes, lower-income neighborhoods end up
with poorly funded, overcrowded schools.

> ### Attempts at Integration
> In the 1970s, the Supreme Court ruled that
> the government could bus children to different
> school districts to achieve the goal of integra-
> tion, provided the affected districts had been
> intentionally segregated. Busing plans failed,
> however, due to public protest and the aban-
> donment of cities by whites.

Furthermore, discrimination continues in employment, housing, and higher education. Because such discrimination is subtler—few employers tell job applicants,
"I won't hire you because you're black"—it is more difficult to enforce antidiscrimination laws and punish offenders in these areas. **Affirmative action** programs,
which seek to create special employment opportunities for minorities, women,
and other victims of discrimination, address these questions but have become increasingly controversial and politically unpopular in recent years. In *Regents of the
University of California v. Bakke* (1978), the Supreme Court ruled that affirmative
action programs could not use quotas to meet civil rights goals; however, it did
say that gender and race could be considered among other factors by schools and
businesses practicing affirmative action. Opponents of affirmative action programs
argue that such programs penalize whites and thus constitute **reverse discrimination,** which is illegal under the Civil Rights Act of 1964.

Civil Rights and Women

The granting of equal rights for women in the United States is a relatively recent
phenomenon. Women were not given the right to vote in all 50 states until 1920.
Employment discrimination based on gender was not outlawed until 1964.

As recently as the early 1990s, women were not guaranteed 12 weeks of unpaid leave from work after giving birth (this finally changed with the **Family and Medical Leave Act of 1993,** which gives this right to both mothers and fathers). Those who fought for the failed **Equal Rights Amendment** to the Constitution (1972–1982) continue to argue that women do not yet have a full guarantee of equality under the law from the federal government.

Here is a list of events of the women's rights movement that the AP U.S. Government and Politics Exam sometimes tests.

- **Nineteenth Amendment (1920).** Granted women the right to vote.
- **Equal Pay Act of 1963.** This federal law made it illegal to base an employee's pay on race, gender, religion, or national origin. Prior to this bill, many businesses and organizations maintained different pay and raise schedules for their male and female employees. In fact, many continued to do so after the bill passed. Federal enforcement of the law, however, has helped narrow the gap between the salaries and wages of the genders.
- **Civil Rights Act of 1964.** The provision pertaining to gender discrimination was included in the Civil Rights Act of 1964 by an opponent of the bill. Representative Howard Smith of Virginia believed his proposal was ridiculous and would therefore weaken support for the bill. Much to his surprise, the bill passed with the gender provision—prohibiting employment discrimination based on gender—included. The Ledbetter Fair Pay Act of 2009 enhanced those protections.
- **Title IX, Higher Education Act (1972).** This law prohibits gender discrimination by institutions of higher education that receive federal funds. Title IX has been used to force increased funding of women-only programs, such as women's sports. The **Civil Rights Restoration Act of 1988** increased its potency by allowing the government to cut off all funding to schools that violate the law (and not just to the specific program or office found in violation). As a result of these laws mandating equity in college athletics spending, colleges have eliminated many less popular men's sports, resulting in a backlash against Title IX and the Civil Rights Restoration Act.
- **Lilly Ledbetter Fair Pay Act of 2009.** This law closed a loophole that limited suits on discriminatory pay based on the timing of the issuance of the first discriminatory paycheck. The Ledbetter Act expanded those limits to allow suits based on any discriminatory paycheck, an important adjustment for employees who learn of inequities in wages or salary only after they have persisted for some time.

As women have entered the workplace in greater numbers, the issue of sexual harassment at work has gained prominence. **Sexual harassment** is defined as any sexist or sexual behavior—physical or verbal—that creates a hostile work environment. It can range from suggestive remarks to attempts to coerce sex from a subordinate. Like other forms of discrimination, it is difficult to prove legally.

Efforts to combat it range from public-awareness programs to sensitivity training to increased legal penalties for harassers.

Abortion has remained a controversial and prominent political issue since the Supreme Court affirmed a woman's right to an abortion in *Roe v. Wade* (1973). In that case, the court ruled that a woman's right to an abortion could not be limited during the first three months of pregnancy (increased limits are allowed as the development of the fetus progresses). Opponents of abortion, who call themselves *pro-life*, argue that the procedure is murder and should be criminalized. Those who support women's right to abortions (dubbed the *pro-choice* movement) argue that women should ultimately decide the ambiguous moral issues for themselves. Because of the very personal, life-and-death issues involved in the abortion debate, advocates on both sides of the issue feel very strongly, and as a result abortion is a major political issue. The decision in *Roe v. Wade* has influenced every election and Supreme Court nomination since; as a result of this case, candidates' opinions about the abortion issue are often the first thing the public learns about them. In most European countries, abortion rights were established legislatively (by laws). Many legal scholars believe that the judicial solution (left up to the courts) applied by the United States has opened the door to ideologues.

Other Major Civil Rights Advances

- **Age Discrimination Act of 1967.** As its name states, this law prohibits employment discrimination on the basis of age. The law makes an exception for jobs in which age is essential to job performance. An amendment to this law banned some mandatory retirement ages and increased others to 70.
- **Twenty-Sixth Amendment (1971).** Extended the right to vote to 18-year-olds.
- **Voting Rights Act of 1982.** This law requires states to create congressional districts with minority majorities in order to increase minority representation in the House of Representatives. The law has resulted in the creation of numerous strangely shaped districts, such as one in North Carolina that was 160 miles long and, at points, only several hundred yards wide. The Supreme Court nullified the district just described, leaving it unclear how the government may both achieve the goals of the Voting Rights Act and maintain the regional integrity of congressional districts.
- **Americans with Disabilities Act of 1990.** This law requires businesses with more than twenty-four employees to make their offices accessible to the disabled. It also requires public transportation, new offices, hotels, and restaurants to be wheelchair-accessible whenever feasible. Finally, it mandated the development of wider telephone services for the hearing-impaired.

Other Important Cases

Federalism

Marbury v. Madison (1803). This most important of all decisions established **judicial review**—the Supreme Court's power to strike down acts of United States Congress which conflict with the Constitution.

McCulloch v. Maryland (1819). This case is important because it established a precedent of federal courts using judicial review to strike down congressional legislation.

Gitlow v. New York (1925). *Gitlow* began the process of selective incorporation—the practice of transferring protections that Americans had from the federal government and applying them to state governments.

South Dakota v. Dole (1987). The federal government mandated the 21-year-old drinking age by threatening to withhold federal highway funds from all states that did not comply. In this case, such withholding was held to be constitutional.

United States v. Lopez (1995). Congress had used the commerce clause to aggressively create legislation governing what seemed to be purely local matters. Here, the court blocks them a bit by holding that the commerce clause of the Constitution does not give Congress the power to regulate guns near state-operated schools.

Executive Power

Korematsu v. United States (1944). This case was not the Supreme Court's finest hour, as it ruled that American citizens of Japanese descent could be interned and deprived of basic constitutional rights due to executive order.

United States v. Nixon (1974). In this case, Congress claimed that there was no such thing as **executive privilege** as it went after tapes that President Nixon had made of all his conversations in the Oval Office. The court disagreed and allowed for executive privilege. But they forbid its usage in criminal cases, which meant that Nixon ultimately did have to turn over the tapes.

Clinton v. New York (1998). This case banned the presidential use of a line-item veto as a violation of legislative powers.

KEY TERMS

- civil liberties
- civil rights
- selective incorporation
- indictment
- First Amendment
- freedom of speech
- clear and present danger test
- slander
- libel
- obscenity
- preferred position doctrine
- *Schenck v. United States*
- freedom of the press
- prior restraint
- shield laws
- three-part obscenity test
- freedom of assembly
- freedom of association
- freedom of religion
- Lemon test
- rights of the accused
- Warren Court
- *Gideon v. Wainwright*
- self-incrimination
- *Miranda v. Arizona*
- Fourth Amendment
- probable cause
- search warrant
- exclusionary rule
- objective good faith
- inevitable discovery rule
- Sixth Amendment
- Eighth Amendment
- cruel and unusual punishment
- implied right to privacy
- *Griswold v. Connecticut*
- *Roe v. Wade*
- Thirteenth Amendment
- Fourteenth Amendment
- due process
- equal protection
- Fifteenth Amendment
- Jim Crow laws
- poll tax
- grandfather clause
- Twenty-Fourth Amendment
- Civil Rights Act of 1964
- Voting Rights Act of 1965
- *Plessy v. Ferguson*
- *Brown v. Board of Education*
- *de facto* segregation
- *de jure* segregation
- affirmative action
- reverse discrimination
- Family and Medical Leave Act of 1993
- Equal Rights Amendment
- Nineteenth Amendment
- Lilly Ledbetter Fair Pay Act of 2009
- sexual harassment
- abortion
- Twenty-Sixth Amendment
- executive privilege

Summary

o It is very important to remember that the Bill of Rights protects Americans only from the federal government. It wasn't until the passage of the Fourteenth Amendment and the advocacy of the twentieth-century Supreme Court that these freedoms were selectively incorporated to the states.

o Know about freedom of speech, clear and present danger, and the preferred position doctrine.

o Freedom of the press is protected by the ban on prior restraint, but has limits (as in the case of slander or libel).

o The rights of the people to assemble generally can't be limited, though there are some exceptions to this rule.

o The Constitution forbids the creation of an official religion through the establishment clause, but also prevents the government from infringing on religious freedom through the free exercise clause.

o We have seen a steady expansion of the rights of the accused, particularly since the decisions of the Warren Court.

o Rising from the disgrace of slavery and Jim Crow laws, the court has acted in the latter half of the twentieth century to protect racial minorities from discrimination. Today, most controversy swirls around the issue of affirmative action and whether it constitutes a form of reverse racism and thus constitutes a violation of the Fourteenth Amendment.

Chapter 10 Drill

See Chapter 11 for answers and explanations.

1. The *Gratz* and *Grutter* cases served primarily to

   (A) reinforce primacy of "diversity" as established in *Bakke*
   (B) remove "diversity" as the focus of affirmative action
   (C) abolish affirmative action
   (D) justify affirmative action by noting that it "righted past wrongs"
   (E) establish a quota system

2. Prior restraint (for non-student newspapers) was prohibited by

   (A) *Brown v. Board of Education*
   (B) *Betts v. Brady*
   (C) *Near v. Minnesota*
   (D) *Sheppard v. Maxwell*
   (E) President Johnson in 1967

3. The right to always have counsel present in court cases was established by

   (A) *Powell v. Alabama*
   (B) *Betts v. Brady*
   (C) *Gideon v. Wainwright*
   (D) *Escobedo v. Illinois*
   (E) *Miranda v. Arizona*

4. The Supreme Court case that allowed the resumption of the death penalty was

   (A) *Furman v. Georgia*
   (B) *Woodson v. North Carolina*
   (C) *Bunn v. North Carolina*
   (D) *Oregon v. Smith*
   (E) *Gregg v. Georgia*

5. The Supreme Court uses the Lemon test to determine statutory violations associated with

   (A) freedom of speech
   (B) freedom of the press
   (C) freedom of assembly
   (D) freedom of association
   (E) freedom of religion

6. The *Shelby v. Holder* Supreme Court case dealt most directly with which of the following?

   (A) The Nineteenth Amendment
   (B) The Twenty-Sixth Amendment
   (C) The Age Discrimination Act of 1967
   (D) The Voting Rights Act of 1965
   (E) The Equal Pay Act of 1963

REFLECT

Respond to the following questions:

- For which content topics discussed in this chapter do you feel you have achieved sufficient mastery to answer multiple-choice questions correctly?

- For which content topics discussed in this chapter do you feel you have achieved sufficient mastery to discuss effectively in an essay?

- For which content topics discussed in this chapter do you feel you need more work before you can answer multiple-choice questions correctly?

- For which content topics discussed in this chapter do you feel you need more work before you can discuss effectively in an essay?

- What parts of this chapter are you going to re-review?

- Will you seek further help, outside of this book (such as a teacher, tutor, or AP Students), on any of the content in this chapter—and, if so, on what content?

Chapter 11
Chapter Drills:
Answers and
Explanations

CHAPTER 4 DRILL

1. **B** After feeling the pressure of the strong British central government, the founders of the new nation wanted something looser and less binding: the Articles of Confederation. But the Articles had no provision for the creation of a central army, and Shays' Rebellion—an uprising of Massachusetts farmers—scared many people and led to the desire for a stronger form of government.

2. **E** This is a NOT question, so be careful to note that it is asking which of the answer choices is NOT a problem with the Articles. Because the Articles had no strong army, were almost impossible to amend, did have states taxing trade with other states, and did have states establishing ties with foreign powers, the answer is (E); after all, the states had so much freedom that many thought the United States was in danger of dissolution.

3. **A** The southern states wanted to count slaves for the purpose of representation, but not taxation. The North held the opposite point of view. Ultimately they compromised, counting slaves as three-fifths of a person for both taxation and representation. Thus (A) is correct.

4. **C** No nation had ever had powers divided between a central government and strong regional governments before the United States—this was federalism, which makes (C) correct. Separation of powers, limited government, checks and balances, and judicial review are all important principles but have nothing to do with the division of powers between the federal government and the states.

5. **B** One of the main sticking points at the Constitutional Convention was how to balance the interest of the large states against those of the small. The large states endorsed the Virginia Plan, which would have created a bicameral legislature in which the large states were dominant. So (B) is the correct response.

6. **E** The Northwest Ordinance is considered one of the few successes of the U.S. government under the Articles of Confederation. It was reaffirmed with only small changes by Congress and President Washington in 1789, after the passing of the Constitution. By establishing a method of admitting new states into the Union it laid the groundwork for Indiana, Illinois, Michigan, Ohio, and Wisconsin to gain statehood early in the nineteenth century.

7. **D** The Fifth Amendment is closely associated with protecting individuals' "due process" rights during criminal trial proceedings. Rights protected by the Fifth Amendment include protection against self-incrimination, a grand jury for "capital, or otherwise infamous crime[s]," and against being tried twice for the same offense. This last instance is known as protection from double jeopardy.

CHAPTER 5 DRILL

1. **A**   Small groups can often wield disproportionate power over public policy, and often this comes down to the strength, or intensity, of their feelings. So (A) is correct. Saliency, (B), is the degree to which an issue is important to a particular group, while stability, (C), is how much public opinion changes over time. Choices (D) and (E) are not terms that are generally used to describe public opinion.

2. **D**   This is a NOT question, so we are looking for the one answer choice which is NOT a source of political socialization. Family, school, life experiences, and religion are all major sources of political socialization due to the influence they have on people's world views. Neither party really engages in large-scale indoctrination, making (D) the best choice.

3. **C**   Liberals tend to want the government to use redistributionist policies to help the poor, making (C) correct. Choices (A), (B), (D), and (E) are all examples of ideas that appeal more to conservatives.

4. **B**   Conservatives are traditionally skeptical of any government attempts to control business and industry, and thus (B) is the answer here. Choices (A), (C), (D), and (E) are all examples of ideas that appeal more to liberals.

5. **E**   In this NOT question, we are asked to decide which factor does NOT determine ideological behavior. Race and ethnicity, religion, gender, and region are all major factors in determining whether someone will be liberal or conservative. So (E) is the answer, as birth order has never been proven to have any relevance in this area.

6. **C**   Politicians who want to garner favorable media coverage perform activities that are popular with most Americans or appeal to media outlets by giving them access. However, politicians who switch positions on controversial topics often face intense scrutiny. Famously, John Kerry generated such negative coverage and was labeled a "flip-flopper" during the 2004 presidential campaign after he explained contrary votes on funding military operations in Iraq: "I actually did vote for the $87 billion before I voted against it."

7. **A**   As highly visible figures who often make controversial decisions that affect large numbers of people, the stability of presidential approval ratings is low and fluctuates numerous times during each four-year term. The lifetime tenure of Supreme Court Justices and the lower visibility of most rulings leads to more stability in public opinion. An incumbent running for reelection unopposed will not be highly pressured into making controversial decisions. People may switch party identifications 0, 1, or 2 times in their lifetimes, but don't generally drift between parties multiple times in a four-year period. Social Security benefits have been popular with the American public for decades, especially those who benefit most directly, like the senior population.

CHAPTER 6 DRILL

1. **D** Oftentimes, voters will become dissatisfied with the two parties in power and splinter off to a new, third party. Ross Perot's Reform Party is a classic example of a "splinter" party, making (D) correct. Choices (A), (B), (C), and (E) are all examples of ideological parties and are thus incorrect.

2. **B** In this NOT question, we are looking for the one example of a function that parties are NOT expected to do. Because the United States is a stable democracy, political parties are not expected to foment revolution, making (B) the answer. Choices (A), (C), (D), and (E) are all examples of legitimate political party functions, making them the wrong choices.

3. **D** Cuban Americans, evangelicals, white Southerners, and pro-lifers all represent groups that are generally part of the Republican coalition. Mexicans and other non-Cuban Hispanics are far more likely to vote Democratic, making (D) correct.

4. **A** While many Americans may be skeptical of interest groups and the power that they wield, comparatively few resort to breaking the law and engaging in outright bribery, making (A) the answer here. Choices (B), (C), (D), and (E) are all examples of tactics commonly used by interest groups to accomplish their goals.

5. **B** Unions and corporations have clear policy goals and want to elect candidates that will accomplish those goals. But federal law prohibits them from donating directly to candidates—thus the PAC was born. Because PACs are allowed to accept and give out only set amounts of money, (C) is incorrect and (B) is right. Choices (A), (D), and (E) do not come close to defining the role and purpose of PACs.

6. **B** During the past three decades Republicans have been less likely than Democrats to support environmentalists' positions, from combating climate change, to drilling on federal land, to the Keystone XL pipeline. Environmentalists are not considered a part of the Republican coalition.

7. **D** When party coalitions fall apart and come together to the advantage of one of the two parties, it is called party realignment. The last time an American realignment occurred was in the 1930s, when New Deal policies helped establish an era of Democratic governance. For example, between 1928 and 1932, Democrats went from holding 38% to 72% of seats in the House of Representatives. Democratic presidential candidates went on to win seven of the next nine elections.

CHAPTER 7 DRILL

1. **E** States that use open primaries allow voters of any party to vote in one party primary of their choice, making (E) correct. Choices (A), (B), (C), and (D) do not meet the definition of an open primary and are thus incorrect.

2. **D** Rules about campaign finance have changed since 2002, but one rule that has remained constant is that PACs can give candidates $5,000 and no more than $5,000 per election cycle. So (D) should be your choice.

3. A   Choices (B), (C), (D), and (E) are all examples of groups that assemble at nominating conventions, but the position of a party is known as its platform, and this is formed by (A) the Platform Committee.

4. A   The president of the United States is the person who receives a majority of votes in the electoral college, making (A) correct. If a candidate has only a plurality of votes in the electoral college, (C), then the House decides the president. Unanimity is nice, but not necessary for victory, making (E) wrong. The popular vote plays no role in who becomes president, making (B) and (D) wrong.

5. B   Though there are exceptions, studies have overwhelmingly shown that the older and more educated a person is, the more likely he or she is to vote. The 65-year-old college professor is the oldest and best educated member of the group of choices, so (B) is correct.

6. B   Caucuses usually have lower turnout than primaries because they are meetings that require more time-intensive commitments than primaries. Often, caucuses also have complex rules for voting. Primaries work like voting in the general election—there may be a line, but once in, voters can check the necessary boxes and leave.

7. C   In a presidential election, the popular vote does not determine the winner. Each state awards electoral votes to the winner, mostly in a winner-take-all-system (Maine and Nebraska are the exceptions). The candidate who wins the majority of electoral votes is the winner.

CHAPTER 8 DRILL

1. B   Though he is mostly limited to ceremonial duties and to breaking the occasional tie, the vice president of the United States is officially the president of the Senate, making (B) correct. The majority leader, (D), is the actual leader of the body, while the president *pro tempore,* (C), also ceremonial, is outranked by the vice president. Neither the president, (A), nor the chief whip, (E), has leadership roles in the Senate.

2. E   The power to choose a president, the power to propose amendments to the Constitution, treaty ratification, and confirmations are all examples of non-legislative powers of Congress. To legislate means to make laws, and only (E) meets this definition.

3. D   Controversial as it may be, the process of redistricting has always been controlled by state legislatures in the United States—making (D) correct. Though many experts have called for nonpartisan commissions, currently only Iowa uses one to draw its district lines. The Senate and the president have no influence over districting. And while the Supreme Court is empowered to rule on matters of redistricting, it rarely does so.

4. A   The Constitution doesn't make any mention of the cabinet, but all presidents have had them, and as high-ranking members of the executive branch, they must be chosen by the president and confirmed by the Senate, making (A) correct. The House does not confirm presidential appointments, so (B) is false. Neither the House, (C), nor the Supreme Court, (D), chooses cabinet officials. And as seen from (A), presidential choices for the cabinet do necessitate Senate approval, making (E) false.

5. **A** Because it is so informal and because its members need to give frank and unvarnished advice to the president, the EOP is exempt from congressional oversight and is a favored tool of the presidency, making (A) correct. The fact that the EOP is unmentioned in the Constitution, (B), does not detract from its power. It is not located in the Department of Defense, (C), nor is it a dumping ground, (D). And the vice president does not run it, making (E) false.

6. **C** The NSC is a key part of the EOP, and presidents have relied on it for many years, as NSC advisors like Henry Kissinger and Condoleezza Rice have used their positions to influence presidents. Its main function is to advise the president and to coordinate foreign policy, and to do so away from the prying eyes of Congress. None of the other answer choices correctly defines the NSC.

7. **D** Though the president gets to select all the judges who sit on the federal bench, all district court judges operate out of a specific state. By tradition, the senators from that state must approve of the president's selections to fill vacancies—this is known as senatorial courtesy, making (D) correct. Judicial appointments are not approved in the House, (A), and Supreme Court justices, (B), are not subject to senatorial courtesy. Senators cannot appoint judges, (C), and senators are not immune to prosecution, (E).

8. **B** *Marbury v. Madison* is one of the most important of all Supreme Court decisions as it established judicial review, which is the Supreme Court's ability to strike down federal and state laws that are in conflict with the Constitution, making (B) correct. Choice (A) is incorrect because *certiorari* is a legal document used by the Supreme Court to obtain records from lower courts, and it was not established by any case. Choice (C) is incorrect because it refers to *Gideon v. Wainwright*. Choice (D) is incorrect because it refers to *Katz v. United States*, and (E) is incorrect because it is a false statement; a quota system was never established by the court.

9. **E** From the presidency of Thomas Jefferson, but especially since that of Andrew Jackson, government jobs were given to political supporters—an arrangement known as the spoils system. The Pendleton Act, passed in 1883, limited this, so (E) is the answer. Choice (A) refers to the Hatch Act, and (B), (C), and (D) are simply untrue.

10. **E** Also known as a subgovernment, the alliance of congressional committees, interest groups, and bureaucracies is so strong that it is often called an iron triangle, so (E) is correct. Choices (A), (B), and (D) are all things that come in three, but none are known as iron triangles. Choice (C) is false because iron triangles are fairly common in the United States.

CHAPTER 9 DRILL

1. **C** The Office of Management and Budget (OMB) evolved out of the Bureau of the Budget—used by FDR to help guide the nation through the Great Depression. Its primary function is to plan the budget for the president, making (C) the correct response. The OMB exists to serve the president, not Congress, so (B) is incorrect. Assessing the nation's economic health (A) is more the job of the

National Economic Council (NEC), and the NEC would also be in charge of (D). Protecting the environment, (E), is the job of the EPA.

2. B   Policy formulation, (A); policy implementation, (C); policy evaluation, (D); and agenda setting, (E), are all part of the policy-making process. But abandoning the government means abandoning policy making, so (B) is the correct answer.

3. D   A supporter of laissez-faire economic policy would be in favor of "letting things be" in the free market, less regulation, and fewer taxes. For these reasons, Choices (E), (A), and (B) are wrong. While free-marketers are traditionally skeptical of labor unions for controlling the labor supply, another way to cross out (C) and keep (D) would be to recognize that "letting things be" would mean applying the same treatment to everyone rather than manipulating the law based on individual circumstances—a flat tax does exactly that.

4. E   Retired workers, survivors of retirees, the handicapped, and the short-term unemployed all receive benefits from Social Security. Though a family that is chronically poor may receive money from the government, they wouldn't get it from Social Security, so (E) is correct.

5. A   When a nation imports more than it exports, it is running a trade deficit, so (A) is right. A surplus, (B), occurs when exports exceed imports. Choices (C), (D), and (E) are all factually incorrect.

6. A   The outline of the Keynesian school of fiscal policy is that economies are cyclical. During prosperous times, governments should save some tax revenue. During economic downturns, governments should keep the economy as prosperous as possible by spending the money saved during better times. Even if the money hasn't been saved, Keynesians endorse deficit spending on domestic programs during downturns, making (A) the correct answer.

7. E   The Budget Enforcement Act of 1990 categorizes government spending as either mandatory or discretionary. Education spending is the only answer choice categorized as discretionary spending; the other choices are mandatory spending.

CHAPTER 10 DRILL

1. A   The cases of *Gratz* and *Grutter* in 2002 involved lawsuits against the University of Michigan by white students who did not get accepted as a result of affirmative action. Though many observers of the court speculated that affirmative action might be overturned, ultimately the justices upheld it and reinforced the *Bakke* case. So (A) is correct. Diversity remains the goal of affirmative action, so (B) is wrong. As seen above, (C) did not occur. Though many support affirmative action to right past wrongs, its legal foundation still rests on diversity, making (D) incorrect. Quotas have been illegal since *Bakke*, so (E) is incorrect as well.

2. **C** The state cannot engage in prior restraint, the prevention of publication of articles it might find offensive, and this was affirmed in the *Near* case, making (C) correct. *Brown* ended segregation, *Betts* provided lawyers for defendants who were mentally deficient, *Sheppard* established rules about protecting defendants from being tried in the media, and President Johnson was never involved in prior restraint issues.

3. **C** Later recounted in the book *Gideon's Trumpet*, the case of *Gideon v. Wainwright* established that all defendants have the right to counsel, so (C) is correct. *Gideon* overruled *Betts*, so (B) is wrong, and *Powell*, (A), was overruled by *Brady* and is also wrong. *Escobedo*, (D), said that the accused cannot be denied a lawyer after they ask for one, and *Miranda*, (E), held that the arrested need to be informed of their rights.

4. **E** In the early 1970s, the Supreme Court ruled that the death penalty was being unfairly applied and banned it in the case of *Furman v. Georgia*, so (A) is incorrect. North Carolina tried to get capital punishment restored by making the death penalty mandatory in some cases, but in *Woodson v. North Carolina*, the court struck down this approach, making (B) wrong. Finally, in *Gregg v. Georgia*, the court allowed the death penalty to resume, making (E) correct. Both *Bunn* and *Smith* are cases that deal with religious freedom and are incorrect.

5. **E** In 1971, the Supreme Court established the Lemon test in the case *Lemon v. Kurtzman*. The test is used to determine whether a statute violates the establishment clause (against establishing a state religion). The three-pronged test asks the following questions: (1) Does the statute have a legitimate secular purpose?, (2) Does the statute have the primary effect of either advancing or inhibiting religion?, and (3) Does the statute result in an excessive entanglement of government and religion? If the court answers "Yes" to any of the three questions, the statute is in violation of the Establishment Clause and unconstitutional.

6. **D** *Shelby v. Holder* invalidated part of the Voting Rights Act of 1965, which had been designed to counteract voting discrimination in the South. Section 4(b) of the Act required certain jurisdictions (states and local governments) to preclear any changes to their voting practices with the federal government. (In other words, the federal government had the power to stop voting practices it deemed discriminatory in states and local governments found to have a history of racially discriminatory voting practices.) The Supreme Court found this section unconstitutional because it found the 40-year old formula used to determine which states and counties are subject to preclearance outdated. Following this ruling, more states passed voter ID laws.

Glossary

adversarial system   A system of law in which the court is seen as a neutral area where disputants can argue the merits of their cases.

affirmative action   Government-mandated programs that seek to create special employment opportunities for African Americans, women, and other victims of past discrimination.

amendment   Addition to the Constitution. Amendments require approval by two-thirds of both houses of Congress and three-quarters of the states. The first ten amendments make up the Bill of Rights.

amicus curiae **briefs**   "Friend of the court" briefs that qualified individuals or organizations file in lawsuits to which they are not a party, so the judge may consider their advice in respect to matters of law that directly affect the cases in question.

appellate jurisdiction   Term used to describe courts whose role is to hear appeals from lower courts.

Articles of Confederation   The United States' first constitution. The government formed by the Articles of Confederation lasted from 1781 (the year before the end of the Revolutionary War) to 1789. The government under the Articles proved inadequate because it did not have the power to collect taxes from the states, nor could it regulate foreign trade to generate revenue from import and export tariffs.

bicameral legislature   Consisting of two legislative houses. The United States has a bicameral legislature; its two houses are the House of Representatives and the Senate.

Bill of Rights   First ten amendments to the U.S. Constitution. The Bill of Rights guarantees personal liberties and limits the powers of the government.

blanket primary   Primary election in which voters may select a candidate from any party for each office. Blanket primaries use the same procedure as general elections.

block grants   Federal money given to states with only general guidelines for its use. The states have the authority to decide how the money will be spent.

bread-and-butter issues   Those political issues that are specifically directed at the daily concerns of most working-class Americans, such as job security, tax rates, wages, and employee benefits.

broad constructionism   Belief that the Constitution should be interpreted loosely when concerning the restrictions it places on federal power. Broad constructionists emphasize the importance of the elastic clause, which allows Congress to pass laws "necessary and proper" to the performance of its duties.

Brown v. Board of Education   The 1954 case in which the Supreme Court overturned the "separate but equal" standard as it applied to education. In a 9-to-0 decision, the court ruled that "separate educational facilities are inherently unequal." "Separate but equal" had been the law of the land since the court had approved it in *Plessy v. Ferguson* (1896).

budget deficit   Condition that arises when federal expenditures exceed revenues; in other words, when the government spends more money than it takes in.

budget resolution   Set of budget guidelines that must pass both houses of Congress in identical form by April 15. The budget resolution guides government spending for the following fiscal year.

categorical grants   Federal aid given to states with strings attached. To receive the money, the states must agree to adhere to federally mandated guidelines for spending it.

caucus   Meeting of local party members for the purpose of choosing delegates to a national party convention. The term also refers to a meeting of the Democratic members of the House of Representatives.

census   The process, mandated by the Constitution, by which the population of the United States is officially counted every ten years. Census data is then used to help distribute federal money and to reapportion congressional districts.

checks and balances The system that prevents any branch of government from becoming too powerful by requiring the approval of more than one branch for all important acts.

civil court Court in which lawsuits are heard. In contrast, criminal cases are heard in criminal court.

civil disobedience Nonviolent civil disobedience requires activists to protest peacefully against laws they believe unjust and to be willing to accept arrest as a means of demonstrating the justice of their cause. The notion was popularized by nineteenth-century American writer Henry David Thoreau and was practiced by Martin Luther King, Jr.

civil liberties Those protections against government power embodied in the Bill of Rights and similar legislation. Civil liberties include the right to free speech, free exercise of religion, and right to a fair trial.

civil rights Those protections against discrimination by the government and individuals. Civil rights are intended to prevent discrimination based on race, religion, gender, ethnicity, physical handicap, or sexual orientation.

Civil Rights Act of 1964 Federal law that made segregation illegal in most public places, increased penalties and sentences for those convicted of discrimination in employment, and withheld federal aid from schools that discriminated on the basis of race or gender.

civil service system Method of hiring federal employees based on merit rather than on political beliefs or allegiances. This system replaced the spoils system in the United States.

class action suit A lawsuit filed on behalf of a group of people, and whose result affects that group of people as a whole. Interest groups such as the NAACP often use these as a means of asserting their influence over policy decisions.

clear and present danger test Interpretation by Justice Oliver Wendell Holmes regarding limits on free speech if it presents clear and present danger to the public or leads to illegal actions; for example, one cannot shout "Fire!" in a crowded theater.

closed primary Primary election in which voting is restricted to registered members of a political party.

cloture A motion in the Senate to end debate, often used in the event of a filibuster. A cloture vote requires a three-fifths majority of the Senate.

coalition A combination of groups of people who work together to achieve a political goal. The coalition on which the Democratic Party rests, for example, is made up of Northern urban dwellers, Jews, African Americans, and labor unions. Coalitions also form among legislators who work together to advance or defeat a particular bill.

commander in chief The president's role as leader of all United States military forces. This is one of the executive powers authorized in the Constitution.

concurrent powers Constitutional powers shared by the federal and state governments.

conference committee Congressional committee that includes representatives of both houses of Congress. Their purpose is to settle differences between the House and Senate versions of bills that have been passed by their respective legislatures.

Congressional Budget Office Congressional agency of budget experts who assess the feasibility of the president's plan and who help create Congress's version of the federal budget.

congressional district The geographically defined group of people on whose behalf a representative acts in the House of Representatives. Each state is divided into congressional districts of equal population, with larger states having more districts and representatives than small states. Congressional districts are reapportioned every ten years according to new census data.

conservative A political ideology that tends to favor defense spending and school prayer and to disapprove of social programs, abortion, affirmative action, and a large, active government. Conservatives are generally affiliated with the Republican party.

constitutional convention An as-of-yet untried method by which the Constitution may be amended. To call a constitutional convention, two-thirds of all state legislatures must petition the federal government; not to be confused with the Constitutional Convention when the Constitution was written.

cooperative federalism Preeminent form of U.S. federalism since the passage of the Fourteenth Amendment. The Fourteenth Amendment initiated the long demise of dual federalism by providing the national government the means to enforce the rights of citizens against state infringement. The Progressive Era, the New Deal, and the Great Society all increased federal involvement in state government. The result is a system called cooperative federalism in which the national and state governments share many powers.

criminal court Court in which criminal trials are heard. In contrast, lawsuits are heard in **civil court**.

dealignment A recent trend in which voters act increasingly independent of a party affiliation. This is partially the result of television because candidates can appeal directly to the electorate without relying on their party. One consequence is split-ticket voting, which leads to a divided government in which neither party controls both the executive and the legislative branch.

delegated powers Constitutional powers granted solely to the federal government.

direct democracy Form of government in which all enfranchised citizens vote on all matters of government. In contrast, in a representative democracy, voters choose representatives to vote for them on most government issues.

divided government A government in which the presidency is controlled by one party and Congress is controlled by the other. This has become a common occurrence in recent decades as voters have begun to act more independent of parties and increasingly vote split tickets.

double jeopardy The act of trying an individual a second time after he has been acquitted on the same charges. Double jeopardy is prohibited by the Constitution.

dual federalism Form of U.S. federalism during the nation's early history. During this period, the federal and state governments remained separate and independent. What little contact most Americans had with government occurred on the state level, as the national government concerned itself primarily with international trade, construction of roads, harbors, and railways, and the distribution of public land in the West.

due process Established legal procedures for the arrest and trial of an accused criminal.

earmark A provision within legislation that appropriates money to a specific project, usually to benefit a small number of individuals or a region.

elastic clause The section of the Constitution that allows Congress to pass laws "necessary and proper" to the performance of its duties. It is called the elastic clause because it allows Congress to stretch its powers beyond those that are specifically granted to it (enumerated) by the Constitution.

electoral college Constitutionally established body created for the sole purpose of choosing the president and vice president. During general elections, voters choose a presidential ticket. The winner in each state usually receives all of that state's electoral votes in the electoral college. A majority of electoral votes is required for victory in the electoral college; if such a majority cannot be reached, the election result is determined by the House of Representatives.

eminent domain The power of the government to take away property for public use as long as there is just compensation for property taken.

entitlement programs Social insurance programs that allocate federal funds to all people who meet the conditions of the program. Social Security is the largest and most expensive entitlement program. Because they are a form of mandatory spending, it is incredibly difficult to cut funds to entitlement programs during the budgetary process.

Equal Rights Amendment Failed constitutional amendment that would have guaranteed equal protection under the law for women (1970s).

establishment clause Section of the Constitution that prohibits the government from designating one faith as the official religion of the United States.

ex post facto laws If allowed, these laws would punish people for actions that occurred before such actions were made criminal.

exclusionary rule Rule that prohibits the use of illegally obtained evidence at trial. The Supreme Court has created several exceptions to the exclusionary rule, notably the objective good faith rule and the inevitable discovery rule.

executive agreements Presidential agreements made with foreign nations. Executive agreements have the same legal force as treaties but do not require the approval of the Senate.

executive privilege The right of the president to withhold information when doing so would compromise national security (for example, in the case of diplomatic files and military secrets). Executive privilege is not mentioned in the Constitution. It is, rather, part of the unwritten Constitution.

extradition Process by which governments return fugitives to the jurisdiction from which they have fled.

Federal Reserve Board Executive agency that is largely responsible for the formulation and implementation of monetary policy. By controlling the monetary supply, the Fed helps maintain a stable economy.

federalism Term describing a system under which the national government and local governments (state governments, in the case of the United States) share powers. Other federal governments include Canada, Switzerland, and Australia.

The Federalist Papers A series of essays written by James Madison, Alexander Hamilton, and John Jay to defend the Constitution and persuade Americans that it should be ratified. These documents presented the concerns and issues the Framers faced as they created a blueprint for the new government.

Fifteenth Amendment (1870) Prohibited states from denying voting rights to African Americans. Southern states circumvented the Fifteenth Amendment through literacy tests and poll taxes.

filibuster A lengthy speech that halts all legislative action in the Senate. Filibusters are not possible in the House of Representatives because strict time limits govern all debates there.

First Amendment Protects the rights of individuals against the government by guaranteeing the freedom of speech, the press, religion, and assembly.

fiscal year Twelve-month period starting on October 1. Government budgets go into effect at the beginning of the fiscal year. Congress and the president agree on a budget resolution in April to guide government spending for the coming fiscal year.

Fourteenth Amendment (1868) Prevented the states from denying "due process of law" and "equal protection under the law" to citizens. The amendment was specifically aimed at protecting the rights of newly freed slaves. In the twentieth century, the Supreme Court used the amendment to strike down state laws that violate the Bill of Rights.

Freedom of Information Act (1974) Act that declassified government documents for public use.

front-loading Because early primaries have grown increasingly important in recent years, many states have pushed forward the date of their primary elections. Political analysts refer to this strategy as front-loading.

full faith and credit clause Section of the Constitution that requires states to honor one another's licenses, marriages, and other acts of state courts.

general election Election held on the Tuesday after the first Monday of November, during which voters elect officials.

gerrymandering The practice of drawing congressional district lines to benefit one party over the other.

Gideon v. Wainwright (1963) Supreme Court case in which the court ruled that a defendant in a felony trial must be provided a lawyer free of charge if the defendant cannot afford one.

Gramm-Rudman-Holings Bill (1985) Set budget reduction targets to balance budget but failed to eliminate loopholes.

Great Compromise Settlement reached at the Constitutional Convention between large states and small states. The Great Compromise called for two legislative houses: one in which states were represented by their populations (favoring the large states) and one in which states received equal representation (favoring the small states).

Great Society President Lyndon B. Johnson's social/economic program, aimed at raising the standard of living for America's poorest residents. Among the Great Society programs are Medicare, Medicaid, Project Head Start, Job Corps, and Volunteers in Service to America (VISTA).

Griswold v. Connecticut (1965) Supreme Court decision in which the court ruled that the Constitution implicitly guarantees citizens' right to privacy.

Hatch Act (1939) A congressional law that forbade government officials from participating in partisan politics and protected government employees from being fired on partisan grounds; it was revised in 1993 to be less restrictive.

House of Representatives Lower house of U.S. Congress, in which representation is allocated to states in direct proportion to their population. The House of Representatives has sole power to initiate appropriations legislation.

House Rules Committee Determines the rules for debate of each bill, including whether the bill may be amended. This is the most powerful committee in the House. The Senate, which is smaller, has no rules for debate.

impeachment Process by which a president, judge, or other government official can be tried for high crimes and misdemeanors. Andrew Johnson was impeached but was found not guilty and was not removed from office.

indictment A written statement of criminal charges brought against a defendant. Indictments guarantee that defendants know the charges against them so they can plan a defense.

inevitable discovery Exception to the exclusionary rule that allows the use of illegally obtained evidence at trial if the court determines that the evidence would eventually have been found by legal means.

initiative Process through which voters may propose new laws. One of several Progressive Era reforms that increased voters' power over government.

interest group Political group organized around a particular political goal or philosophy. Interest groups attempt to influence public policy through political action and donations to sympathetic candidates.

iron triangle Also called subgovernment. Iron triangles are formed by the close working relationship among various interest groups, congressional committees, and executive agencies that enforce federal regulations. Working together, these groups can collectively exert a powerful influence over legislation and law enforcement.

Jim Crow laws State and local laws passed in the post–Reconstruction Era South to enforce racial segregation and otherwise restrict the rights of African Americans.

joint committee Congressional committee composed of members of both houses of Congress, usually to investigate and research specific subjects.

judicial activism Term referring to the actions of a court that frequently strikes down or alters the acts of the executive and/or legislative branches.

judicial restraint Term referring to the actions of a court that demonstrates an unwillingness to break with precedent or to overturn legislative and executive acts.

judicial review The power of the Supreme Court to declare laws and executive actions unconstitutional.

Ku Klux Klan Nativist hate group founded during the Reconstruction Era. The Klan terrorized African Americans throughout the south, especially those who attempted to assert their civil rights. The Klan also preaches hatred of Catholics and Jews.

legislative oversight One of Congress's most important tasks. In order to check the power of the executive branch, congressional committees investigate and evaluate the performance of corresponding executive agencies and departments.

liberal Descriptive of an ideology that tends to favor government spending on social programs, affirmative action, a woman's right to an abortion, and an active government, and to disfavor defense spending and school prayer. Liberals are generally affiliated with the Democratic Party.

Lilly Ledbetter Fair Pay Act (2009) Law that closed the loophole that limited suits on discriminatory pay.

limited government Principle of government that states that government powers must be confined to those allowed it by the nation's Constitution.

line-item veto Power held by some chief executives (such as governors) to excise some portions of a spending bill without rejecting the entire bill. The purpose of this power is to allow executives to eliminate frivolous appropriations. The president's claim to the line-item veto was denied by the Supreme Court.

mandate Level of support for an elected official as perceived through election results.

Marbury v. Madison (1803) Supreme Court decision that established the principle of **judicial review**.

Marshall, John Third Chief Justice of the Supreme Court (he served from 1800 to 1835). A Federalist who worked to increase the powers of the federal government over the states. Marshall established the principle of judicial review.

Miranda v. Arizona (1966) Supreme Court case in which the court ruled that, upon arrest, a suspect must be advised of the right to remain silent and the right to consult with a lawyer.

national convention Occasion at which a political party officially announces its presidential nominee and reveals its party platform for the next four years. Today's national conventions are merely media events; nominees have already been determined by primary election results.

National Organization for Women (NOW) Feminist political group formed in 1967 to promote legislative change. NOW lobbied for the failed Equal Rights Amendment to the Constitution.

National Security Council Presidential advisory board established in 1947. The NSC consults with the president on matters of defense and foreign policy.

Nineteenth Amendment (1920) Granted voting rights to women.

nomination Endorsement to run for office by a political party.

objective good faith Exception to the exclusionary rule that allows the use of illegally obtained evidence at trial if the court determines that police believed they were acting within the limits of their search warrant when they seized the evidence.

Office of Management and Budget Executive branch office responsible for drawing up the president's proposals for the federal budget.

open primary Primary election in which voters may vote in whichever party primary they choose, though they must select that party before entering the voting booth.

original jurisdiction Term used to describe a court's power to initially try a case. Courts in which cases are first heard are those with original jurisdiction in the case. By contrast, appellate courts hear challenges to earlier court decisions.

override The Constitutional power of Congress to supersede a president's veto by a two-thirds majority in both houses. Such a vote is difficult to achieve, however, so overrides are fairly rare.

pardon Cancellation of criminal punishment. Presidents and governors have the power to grant pardons to those awaiting trial and to those convicted of crimes.

Patriot Act (2001) Act passed in response to the terrorist attacks of September 11, 2001, granting broad police authority to the federal, state, and local governments to interdict, prosecute, and convict suspected terrorists.

platform Statement of purpose and policy objectives drafted and approved by political parties at their national conventions. Party platforms rarely exert much influence on day-to-day politics.

Plessy v. Ferguson (1896) Supreme Court ruling that "separate but equal" facilities for different races are not unconstitutional. This ruling opened the door to 75 years of state-sanctioned segregation in the South.

pocket veto If the president fails to approve a bill passed during the last ten days of a congressional session, the bill does not become law. This process is called a pocket veto.

poison-pill amendment Amendment to a bill proposed by its opponents for the specific purpose of decreasing the bill's chance of passage. Also known as a killer amendment.

policy implementation The process by which executive departments and agencies put legislation into practice. Agencies are often allowed a degree of freedom to interpret legislation as they write guidelines to enact and enforce the law.

political action committee (PAC) The fundraising apparatus of interest groups. Donations to and contributions from PACs are regulated by federal law. PACs contribute heavily to the reelection campaigns of representatives and senators sympathetic to the PAC's political agenda.

political party Group of people with common political goals which hopes to influence policy through the election process. Parties run candidates for office who represent the political agenda of party members. They therefore serve as an institutional link between the electorate and politicians.

Populists Political party of the late 1800s. The Populists primarily represented farmers and working-class Americans. They sought inflationary economic policies to increase farm income. They also lobbied for a number of Democratic reforms that would later be adopted by the Progressives, such as direct election of senators.

pork barrel Budget items proposed by legislators to benefit constituents in their home state or district. Such expenditures are sometimes unnecessary but are passed anyway because they are politically beneficial.

president *pro tempore* Individual chosen to preside over the Senate whenever the vice president is unavailable to do so. The president *pro tempore* is chosen by the Senate from among its members.

primary elections Form of election held by the majority of states, during which voters select the nominees for political parties. Winners of primary elections appear on the ballot during the general election.

prior restraint Censorship of news material before it is made public.

privileges and immunities clause Section of the Constitution stating that a state may not refuse police protection or access to its courts to U.S. citizens because they live in a different state.

progressive income tax A progressive tax increases tax rates for people with higher incomes. Those citizens at the poverty level, for example, may pay few or no taxes. Middle-class citizens may be taxed at a 15% rate, while the wealthy are taxed at two or three times that rate. The goal of a progressive tax is to allow those with greater need to keep more of what they earn while taking more from those who can best afford it.

quorum The minimum number of people required for the legislature to act.

realignment Occurs when a party undergoes a major shift in its electoral base and political agenda. The groups of people composing the party coalition may split up, resulting in a vastly different party. Realignments are rare and tend to be signaled by a critical election. The last realignment occurred during the New Deal, when many working-class and ethnic groups joined together under the Democratic party.

recall election Process through which voters can shorten an office holder's term. One of several Progressive Era reforms that increased voters' power over government.

redistricting Process by which congressional districts are redrawn to reflect population changes reported by census data. Each district must have an equal number of residents. Redistricting typically occurs with reapportionment, a process in which seats are redistributed among states in the House. States may lose or gain seats during reapportionment, but the total House membership remains 435.

referendum Process through which voters may vote on new laws. One of several Progressive Era reforms that increased voters' power over government.

regulatory agency Executive agency responsible for enforcing laws pertaining to a certain industry. The agency writes guidelines for the industry, such as safety codes, and enforces them through methods such as inspection.

representative democracy Form of government under which citizens vote for delegates who in turn represent citizens' interests within the government. In contrast, a direct democracy requires all citizens to vote on all government issues. The United States is a representative democracy.

reserved powers Constitutional powers that belong solely to the states. According to the Tenth Amendment, these powers include any that the Constitution does not either specifically grant the national government or deny the state governments.

Roe v. Wade (1973) Supreme Court case that decriminalized abortion.

runoff primary Election held between top two vote-getters in a primary election, when neither received a legally required minimum percentage of the vote. Many states require a runoff when no candidate receives at least 40% of the primary vote for his or her party.

sampling error Margin of error in public opinion poll. Most polls are accurate within a margin of ±4%.

saving amendment Amendment to a bill proposed in hopes of softening opposition by weakening objectionable elements of the bill.

Schenck v. United States Supreme Court case involving limits on free speech rights. The *Schenck* case established the "clear and present danger" principle in determining what type of speech could be restricted.

search warrant Document issued by the courts to allow the police to search private property. To obtain a warrant, the police must go before a judge and explain (1) where they want to search and (2) what they are looking for. A search warrant also limits where the police may search and what they may take as evidence (Fourth Amendment).

select committee Temporary committee of Congress, usually created to investigate specific issues.

selective incorporation Process by which the Supreme Court has selectively applied the Fourteenth Amendment to state law.

Senate Upper house of Congress, in which each state has two representatives. The Senate has the sole power to approve cabinet, ambassadorial, and federal judicial appointments. International treaties must receive two-thirds approval from the Senate.

senatorial courtesy A tradition whereby candidates for the federal bureaucracy are appointed by the president and selected from a list of nominees submitted by senators.

separation of powers The system that prevents any branch of government from becoming too powerful by dividing important tasks among the three branches. Also called the system of checks and balances.

shield law Law guaranteeing news reporters the right to protect the anonymity of their sources. Many states have passed shield laws, but there is no federal shield law.

Sixteenth Amendment (1913) Authorized Congress to impose and collect federal income taxes.

soft money Political donations made to parties for the purpose of general party maintenance and support, such as get-out-the-vote campaigns, issue advocacy, and advertisements that promote the party (but not individual candidates). Soft money contributions to political parties were banned in 2002 by the Bipartisan Campaign Reform Act (BCRA) (also known as the McCain-Feingold Bill).

Speaker of the House Individual chosen by members of the House of Representatives to preside over its sessions.

split-ticket voting Choosing candidates from different parties for offices listed on the same ballot. Voters have been more inclined to vote a split ticket in recent decades. This trend has led to divided government.

spoils system The political practice of trading government jobs and preferences for political and financial support. President Andrew Jackson was the first to be widely accused of using the spoils system to reward political friends and supporters.

standing committee A permanent congressional committee.

strict constructionism Belief that the Constitution should be read in such a way as to limit the powers of the federal government as much as possible. Strict constructionists emphasize the importance of the Tenth Amendment, which reserves to the states all powers not explicitly granted to the federal government.

Super PAC A type of political action committee that does not have donation limits, but cannot donate directly to a specific candidate.

supremacy clause Section of the Constitution that requires conflicts between federal and state law to be resolved in favor of federal law. State constitutions and laws that violate the U.S. Constitution, federal laws, or international treaties can be invalidated through the supremacy clause.

Supreme Court Highest court in the United States. The only federal court specifically mentioned in the U.S. Constitution.

Thirteenth Amendment (1865) Abolished slavery.

Three-Fifths Compromise Agreement reached at the Constitutional Convention between Southern and Northern states. The South wanted slaves counted among the population for voting purposes but not for tax purposes; the North wanted the exact opposite. Both sides agreed that three-fifths of a state's slave population would be counted toward both congressional apportionment and taxation.

Twenty-Fourth Amendment (1964) Outlawed poll taxes, which had been used to prevent the poor from voting.

Twenty-Second Amendment (1951) Limited the number of years an individual may serve as president. According to the Twenty-Second Amendment, a president may be elected no more than twice.

Twenty-Sixth Amendment (1971) Lowered the voting age from 21 to 18.

unanimous consent decree Agreement passed by the Senate that establishes the rules under which a bill will be debated, amended, and voted upon.

United Nations International organization established following World War II. The United Nations aims to preserve international peace and foster international cooperation.

unwritten Constitution Certain deeply ingrained aspects of our government that are not mentioned in the Constitution, such as political parties, political conventions, and cabinet meetings.

veto The power held by chief executives (such as the president or governors) to reject acts of the legislature. A presidential veto can be overridden by a two-thirds majority vote of both houses of Congress.

Voting Rights Act of 1965 Federal law that increased government supervision of local election practices, suspended the use of literacy tests to prevent people (usually African Americans) from voting, and expanded government efforts to register voters. The Voting Rights Act of 1970 permanently banned literacy tests.

War on Poverty Those programs of President Lyndon Johnson's Great Society that were specifically aimed at assisting the poor. Among these programs was Volunteers in Service to America (VISTA), Medicaid, and the creation of the Office of Economic Opportunity.

War Powers Act Law requiring the president to seek periodic approval from Congress for any substantial troop commitment. Passed in 1973 in response to national dissatisfaction over the Vietnam War.

Warren Court (1953–1969) The Supreme Court during the era in which Earl Warren served as Chief Justice. The Warren Court is best remembered for expanding the rights of minorities and the rights of the accused.

Watergate The name of the hotel in which spies working for President Richard Nixon's 1972 reelection campaign were caught breaking into Democratic National Headquarters. The name Watergate soon became synonymous with a number of illegal activities undertaken by the Nixon White House. The resulting scandal forced Nixon to resign the presidency in 1974.

writ of *certiorari* A legal document issued by the Supreme Court to request the court transcripts of a case. A writ of *certiorari* indicates that the court will review a lower court's decision.

writ of *habeas corpus* A court order requiring an explanation as to why a prisoner is being held in custody.

The Constitution of the United States of America

Note: Text in *italics* indicates that a section of the Constitution is no longer in effect.

Preamble

We the people of the United States, in order to form a more perfect union, establish justice, insure domestic tranquillity, provide for the common defense, promote the general welfare, and secure the blessings of liberty to ourselves and our posterity, do ordain and establish this Constitution for the United States of America.

Article I

Section 1. All legislative powers herein granted shall be vested in a Congress of the United States, which shall consist of a Senate and House of Representatives.

Section 2. The House of Representatives shall be composed of members chosen every second year by the people of the several states, and the electors in each state shall have the qualifications requisite for electors of the most numerous branch of the state legislature.

No person shall be a Representative who shall not have attained to the age of twenty-five years, and been seven years a citizen of the United States, and who shall not, when elected, be an inhabitant of that state in which he shall be chosen.

Representatives *and direct taxes*[1] shall be apportioned among the several states which may be included within this union, according to their respective numbers, *which shall be determined by adding to the whole number of free persons, including those bound to service for a term of years, and excluding Indians not taxed, three-fifths of all other Persons.*[2] The actual Enumeration shall be made within three years after the first meeting of the Congress of the United States, and within every subsequent term of ten years[3], in such manner as they shall by law direct. The number of Representatives shall not exceed one for every thirty thousand, but each state shall have at least one Representative; and until such enumeration shall be made, the state of New Hampshire shall be entitled to choose three, Massachusetts eight, Rhode Island and Providence Plantations one, Connecticut five, New York six, New Jersey four, Pennsylvania eight, Delaware one, Maryland six, Virginia ten, North Carolina five, South Carolina five, and Georgia three.

When vacancies happen in the Representation from any state, the executive authority[4] thereof shall issue writs of election to fill such vacancies. The House of Representatives shall choose their speaker and other officers; and shall have the sole power of impeachment.

Section 3. The Senate of the United States shall be composed of two Senators from each state, *chosen by the legislature thereof*[5], for six years; and each Senator shall have one vote.

Immediately after they shall be assembled in consequence of the first election, they shall be divided as equally as may be into three classes. The seats of the Senators of the first class shall be vacated at the expiration of the second year, of the second class at the expiration of the fourth year, and the third class at the expiration of the sixth year,[6] so that one third may be chosen every second year; *and if vacancies happen by resignation, or otherwise, during the recess of the legislature of any state, the executive thereof may make temporary appointments until the next meeting of the legislature, which shall then fill such vacancies.*[7]

No person shall be a Senator who shall not have attained to the age of thirty years, and been nine years a citizen of the United States and who shall not, when elected, be an inhabitant of that state for which he shall be chosen. The vice president of the United States shall be President of the Senate, but shall have no vote, unless they be equally divided. The Senate shall choose their other officers, and also a President *pro tempore*[8], in the absence of the vice president, or when he shall exercise the office of President of the United States. The Senate shall have the sole power to try all impeachments. When sitting for that purpose, they shall be on oath or affirmation. When the President of the United States is tried, the Chief Justice shall preside: And no person shall be convicted without the concurrence of two thirds of the members present.

Judgment in cases of impeachment shall not extend further than to removal from office, and disqualification to hold and enjoy any office of honor, trust or profit under the United States: but the party convicted shall nevertheless be liable and subject to indictment, trial, judgment and punishment, according to law.

Section 4. The times, places and manner of holding elections for Senators and Representatives, shall be prescribed in each state by the legislature thereof; but the Congress may at any time by law make or alter such regulations, except as to the places of choosing Senators.

The Congress shall assemble at least once in every year, *and such meeting shall be on the first Monday in December*[9], unless they shall by law appoint a different day.

Section 5. Each House shall be the judge of the elections, returns and qualifications of its own members, and a majority of each shall constitute a quorum[10] to do business; but a smaller number may adjourn from day to day, and may be authorized to compel the attendance of absent members, in such manner, and under such penalties as each House may provide.

Each House may determine the rules of its proceedings, punish its members for disorderly behavior, and, with the concurrence of two thirds, expel a member.

Each House shall keep a journal of its proceedings, and from time to time publish the same, excepting such parts as may in their judgment require secrecy; and the yeas and nays of the members of either House on any question shall, at the desire of one fifth of those present, be entered on the journal.

Neither House, during the session of Congress, shall, without the consent of the other, adjourn for more than three days, nor to any other place than that in which the two Houses shall be sitting.

Section 6. The Senators and Representatives shall receive a compensation for their services, to be ascertained by law, and paid out of the treasury of the United States. They shall in all cases, except treason, felony and breach of the peace, be privileged from arrest during their attendance at the session of their respective Houses, and in going to and returning from the same; and for any speech or debate in either House, they shall not be questioned in any other place.

No Senator or Representative shall, during the time for which he was elected, be appointed to any civil office under the authority of the United States, which shall have been created, or the emoluments[11] whereof shall have been increased during such time: and no person holding any office under the United States, shall be a member of either House during his continuance in office.[12]

Section 7. All bills for raising revenue shall originate in the House of Representatives; but the Senate may propose or concur with amendments as on other Bills.

Every bill which shall have passed the House of Representatives and the Senate, shall, before it become a law, be presented to the President of the United States; if he approve he shall sign it, but if not he shall return it[13], with his objections to that House in which it shall have originated, who shall enter the objections at large on their journal, and proceed to reconsider it. If after such reconsideration two thirds of that House shall agree to pass the bill, it shall be sent, together with the objections, to the other House, by which it shall likewise be reconsidered, and if approved by two thirds of that House, it shall become a law[14]. But in all such cases the votes of both Houses shall be determined by yeas and nays, and the names of the persons voting for and against the bill shall be entered on the journal of each House respectively. If any bill shall not be returned by the President within ten days (Sundays excepted) after it shall have been presented to him, the same shall be a law, in like manner as if he had signed it, unless the Congress by their adjournment prevent its return[15], in which case it shall not be a law.

Every order, resolution, or vote to which the concurrence of the Senate and House of Representatives may be necessary (except on a question of adjournment) shall be presented to the President of the United States; and before the same shall take effect, shall be approved by him, or being disapproved by him, shall be repassed by two thirds of the Senate and House of Representatives, according to the rules and limitations prescribed in the case of a bill.

Section 8. The Congress shall have power to lay and collect taxes, duties, imposts and excises, to pay the debts and provide for the common defense and general welfare of the United States; but all duties, imposts and excises shall be uniform throughout the United States;

- To borrow money on the credit of the United States;
- To regulate commerce with foreign nations, and among the several states, and with the Indian tribes;
- To establish a uniform rule of naturalization, and uniform laws on the subject of bankruptcies throughout the United States;
- To coin money, regulate the value thereof, and of foreign coin, and fix the standard of weights and measures;
- To provide for the punishment of counterfeiting the securities and current coin of the United States;
- To establish post offices and post roads;
- To promote the progress of science and useful arts, by securing for limited times to authors and inventors the exclusive right to their respective writings and discoveries;
- To constitute tribunals inferior to the Supreme Court;
- To define and punish piracies and felonies committed on the high seas, and offenses against the law of nations;
- To declare war, grant letters of marque and reprisal[16], and make rules concerning captures on land and water;
- To raise and support armies, but no appropriation of money to that use shall be for a longer term than two years;
- To provide and maintain a navy;
- To make rules for the government and regulation of the land and naval forces;
- To provide for calling forth the militia to execute the laws of the union, suppress insurrections and repel invasions;

- To provide for organizing, arming, and disciplining the militia, and for governing such part of them as may be employed in the service of the United States, reserving to the states respectively, the appointment of the officers, and the authority of training the militia according to the discipline prescribed by Congress;
- To exercise exclusive legislation in all cases whatsoever, over such District (not exceeding ten miles square) as may, by cession of particular states, and the acceptance of Congress, become the seat of the government of the United States[17], and to exercise like authority over all places purchased by the consent of the legislature of the state in which the same shall be, for the erection of forts, magazines, arsenals, dockyards, and other needful buildings; and
- To make all laws which shall be necessary and proper for carrying into execution the foregoing powers, and all other powers vested by this Constitution in the government of the United States, or in any department or officer thereof.[18]

Section 9. *The migration or importation of such persons as any of the states now existing shall think proper to admit, shall not be prohibited by the Congress prior to the year one thousand eight hundred and eight, but a tax or duty may be imposed on such importation, not exceeding ten dollars for each person.*[19]

The privilege of the writ of habeas corpus[20] *shall not be suspended, unless when in cases of rebellion or invasion the public safety may require it.*

- No bill of attainder[21] or *ex post facto* law[22] shall be passed.
- *No capitation, or other direct, tax shall be laid, unless in proportion to the census or enumeration herein before directed to be taken.*[23]
- No tax or duty shall be laid on articles exported from any state.
- No preference shall be given by any regulation of commerce or revenue to the ports of one state over those of another: nor shall vessels bound to, or from, one state, be obliged to enter, clear or pay duties in another.
- No money shall be drawn from the treasury, but in consequence of appropriations made by law; and a regular statement and account of receipts and expenditures of all public money shall be published from time to time.
- No title of nobility shall be granted by the United States: and no person holding any office of profit or trust under them, shall, without the consent of the Congress, accept of any present, emolument, office, or title, of any kind whatever, from any king, prince, or foreign state.

Section 10. No state shall enter into any treaty, alliance, or confederation; grant letters of marque and reprisal; coin money; emit bills of credit; make anything but gold and silver coin a tender in payment of debts; pass any bill of attainder, *ex post facto* law, or law impairing the obligation of contracts, or grant any title of nobility.

No state shall, without the consent of the Congress, lay any imposts or duties on imports or exports, except what may be absolutely necessary for executing its inspection laws; and the net produce of all duties and imposts, laid by any state on imports or exports, shall be for the use of the treasury of the United States; and all such laws shall be subject to the revision and control of the Congress.

No state shall, without the consent of Congress, lay any duty of tonnage, keep troops, or ships of war in time of peace, enter into any agreement or compact with another state, or with a foreign power, or engage in war, unless actually invaded, or in such imminent danger as will not admit of delay.

Article II

Section 1. The executive power shall be vested in a President of the United States of America. He shall hold his office during the term of four years, and, together with the vice president, chosen for the same term, be elected, as follows:

Each state shall appoint, in such manner as the Legislature thereof may direct, a number of electors, equal to the whole number of Senators and Representatives to which the State may be entitled in the Congress: but no Senator or Representative, or person holding an office of trust or profit under the United States, shall be appointed an elector.

The electors shall meet in their respective states, and vote by ballot for two persons, of whom one at least shall not be an inhabitant of the same state with themselves. And they shall make a list of all the persons voted for, and of the number of votes for each; which list they shall sign and certify, and transmit sealed to the seat of the government of the United States, directed to the President of the Senate. The President of the Senate shall, in the presence of the Senate and House of Representatives, open all the certificates, and the votes shall then be counted. The person having the greatest number of votes shall be the President, if such number be a majority of the whole number of electors appointed; and if there be more than one who have such majority, and have an equal number of votes, then the House of Representatives shall immediately choose by ballot one of them for President; and if no person have a majority, then from the five highest on the list the said House shall in like manner choose the President. But in choosing the President, the votes shall be taken by States, the representation from each state having one vote; a quorum for this purpose shall consist of a member or members from two thirds of the states, and a majority of all the states shall be necessary to a choice. In every case, after the choice of the President, the person having the greatest number of votes of the electors shall be the vice president. But if there should remain two or more who have equal votes, the Senate shall choose from them by ballot the vice president.[24]

The Congress may determine the time of choosing the electors, and the day on which they shall give their votes; which day shall be the same throughout the United States.

No person except a natural born citizen, or a citizen of the United States at the time of the adoption of this Constitution[25], shall be eligible to the office of President; neither shall any person be eligible to that office who shall not have attained to the age of thirty five years, and been fourteen years a resident within the United States.

In case of the removal of the President from office, or of his death, resignation, or inability to discharge the powers and duties of the said office, the same shall devolve on the vice president, and the Congress may by law provide for the case of removal, death, resignation or inability, both of the President and vice president, declaring what officer shall then act as President, and such officer shall act accordingly, until the disability be removed, or a President shall be elected.[26]

The President shall, at stated times, receive for his services, a compensation, which shall neither be increased nor diminished during the period for which he shall have been elected, and he shall not receive within that period any other emolument[27] from the United States, or any of them.

Before he enter on the execution of his office, he shall take the following oath or affirmation: "I do solemnly swear (or affirm) that I will faithfully execute the office of President of the United States, and will to the best of my ability, preserve, protect and defend the Constitution of the United States."

Section 2. The President shall be commander in chief of the Army and Navy of the United States, and of the militia of the several states, when called into the actual service of the United States; he may require the opinion, in writing, of the principal officer in each of the executive departments, upon any subject relating to the duties of their respective offices, and he shall have power to grant reprieves and pardons for offenses against the United States, except in cases of impeachment.

He shall have power, by and with the advice and consent of the Senate[28], to make treaties, provided two thirds of the Senators present concur; and he shall nominate, and by and with the advice and consent of the Senate, shall appoint ambassadors, other public ministers and consuls, judges of the Supreme Court, and all other officers of the United States, whose appointments are not herein otherwise provided for, and which shall be established by law: but the Congress may by law vest the appointment of such inferior officers, as they think proper, in the President alone, in the courts of law, or in the heads of departments.

The President shall have power to fill up all vacancies that may happen during the recess of the Senate, by granting commissions which shall expire at the end of their next session.

Section 3. He shall from time to time give to the Congress information of the state of the union, and recommend to their consideration such measures as he shall judge necessary and expedient; he may, on extraordinary occasions, convene both Houses, or either of them, and in case of disagreement between them, with respect to the time of adjournment, he may adjourn them to such time as he shall think proper; he shall receive ambassadors and other public ministers; he shall take care that the laws be faithfully executed, and shall commission all the officers of the United States.

Section 4. The President, vice president and all civil officers of the United States, shall be removed from office on impeachment for, and conviction of, treason, bribery, or other high crimes and misdemeanors.

Article III

Section 1. The judicial power of the United States, shall be vested in one Supreme Court, and in such inferior courts as the Congress may from time to time ordain and establish. The judges, both of the supreme and inferior courts, shall hold their offices during good behavior, and shall, at stated times, receive for their services, a compensation, which shall not be diminished during their continuance in office.

Section 2. The judicial power shall extend to all cases, in law and equity, arising under this Constitution, the laws of the United States, and treaties made, or which shall be made, under their authority; to all cases affecting ambassadors, other public ministers and consuls; to all cases of admiralty and maritime jurisdiction; to controversies to which the United States shall be a party; to controversies between two or more states; between a state and citizens of another state[29]; between citizens of different states; between citizens of the same state claiming lands under grants of different states, and between a state, or the citizens thereof, and foreign states, citizens or subjects.

In all cases affecting ambassadors, other public ministers and consuls, and those in which a state shall be party, the Supreme Court shall have original jurisdiction. In all the other cases before mentioned, the Supreme Court shall have appellate jurisdiction, both as to law and fact, with such exceptions, and under such regulations as the Congress shall make.

The trial of all crimes, except in cases of impeachment, shall be by jury; and such trial shall be held in the state where the said crimes shall have been committed; but when not committed within any state, the trial shall be at such place or places as the Congress may by law have directed.

Section 3. Treason against the United States, shall consist only in levying war against them, or in adhering to their enemies, giving them aid and comfort. No person shall be convicted of treason unless on the testimony of two witnesses to the same overt act, or on confession in open court.

The Congress shall have power to declare the punishment of treason, but no attainder of treason shall work corruption of blood, or forfeiture except during the life of the person attainted.[30]

Article IV

Section 1. Full faith and credit shall be given in each state to the public acts, records, and judicial proceedings of every other state.[31] And the Congress may by general laws prescribe the manner in which such acts, records, and proceedings shall be proved, and the effect thereof.

Section 2. The citizens of each state shall be entitled to all privileges and immunities of citizens in the several states.

A person charged in any state with treason, felony, or other crime, who shall flee from justice, and be found in another state, shall on demand of the executive authority of the state from which he fled, be delivered up, to be removed to the state having jurisdiction of the crime.[32]

No person held to service or labor in one state, under the laws thereof, escaping into another, shall, in consequence of any law or regulation therein, be discharged from such service or labor, but shall be delivered up on claim of the party to whom such service or labor may be due.[33]

Section 3. New states may be admitted by the Congress into this union; but no new states shall be formed or erected within the jurisdiction of any other state; nor any state be formed by the junction of two or more states, or parts of states, without the consent of the legislatures of the states concerned as well as of the Congress.

The Congress shall have power to dispose of and make all needful rules and regulations respecting the territory or other property belonging to the United States; and nothing in this Constitution shall be so construed as to prejudice any claims of the United States, or of any particular state.

Section 4. The United States shall guarantee to every state in this union a Republican form of government, and shall protect each of them against invasion; and on application of the legislature, or of the executive (when the legislature cannot be convened) against domestic violence.

Article V

The Congress, whenever two thirds of both houses shall deem it necessary, shall propose amendments to this Constitution, or, on the application of the legislatures of two thirds of the several states, shall call a convention for proposing amendments, which, in either case, shall be valid to all intents and purposes, as part of this Constitution, when ratified by the legislatures of three fourths of the several states, or by conventions in three-fourths thereof, as the one or the other mode of ratification may be proposed by the Congress; provided that no amendment which may be made prior to the year one thousand eight hundred and eight shall in any manner affect the first and fourth clauses in the ninth section of the first article; and that no state, without its consent, shall be deprived of its equal suffrage in the Senate.

Article VI

All debts contracted and engagements entered into, before the adoption of this Constitution, shall be as valid against the United States under this Constitution, as under the Confederation.

This Constitution, and the laws of the United States which shall be made in pursuance thereof; and all treaties made, or which shall be made, under the authority of the United States, shall be the supreme law of the land[34]; and the judges in every state shall be bound thereby, anything in the Constitution or laws of any State to the contrary notwithstanding.

The Senators and Representatives before mentioned, and the members of the several state legislatures, and all executive and judicial officers, both of the United States and of the several states, shall be bound by oath or affirmation, to support this Constitution; but no religious test shall ever be required as a qualification to any office or public trust under the United States.

Article VII

The ratification of the conventions of nine states, shall be sufficient for the establishment of this Constitution between the states so ratifying the same.

Done in convention by the unanimous consent of the states present the seventeenth day of September in the year of our Lord one thousand seven hundred and eighty seven and of the independence of the United States of America the twelfth. In witness whereof We have hereunto subscribed our Names,

Signed:

G. Washington—President, and 38 representatives of the states

Amendments to the Constitution
[Note: Amendments I through X are collectively known as the "Bill of Rights."]

Amendment I (1791)
Congress shall make no law respecting an establishment of religion, or prohibiting the free exercise thereof[35]; or abridging the freedom of speech, or of the press; or the right of the people peaceably to assemble, and to petition the government for a redress of grievances.

Amendment II (1791)

A well regulated militia, being necessary to the security of a free state, the right of the people to keep and bear arms, shall not be infringed.

Amendment III (1791)

No soldier shall, in time of peace be quartered in any house, without the consent of the owner, nor in time of war, but in a manner to be prescribed by law.

Amendment IV (1791)

The right of the people to be secure in their persons, houses, papers, and effects, against unreasonable searches and seizures, shall not be violated, and no warrants shall issue, but upon probable cause, supported by oath or affirmation, and particularly describing the place to be searched, and the persons or things to be seized.

Amendment V (1791)

No person shall be held to answer for a capital[36], or otherwise infamous crime[37], unless on a presentment or indictment of a grand jury, except in cases arising in the land or naval forces, or in the militia, when in actual service in time of war or public danger; nor shall any person be subject for the same offense to be twice put in jeopardy of life or limb[38]; nor shall be compelled in any criminal case to be a witness against himself, nor be deprived of life, liberty, or property, without due process of law; nor shall private property be taken for public use, without just compensation.

Amendment VI (1791)

In all criminal prosecutions, the accused shall enjoy the right to a speedy and public trial, by an impartial jury of the state and district wherein the crime shall have been committed, which district shall have been previously ascertained by law, and to be informed of the nature and cause of the accusation; to be confronted with the witnesses against him; to have compulsory process for obtaining witnesses in his favor, and to have the assistance of counsel for his defense.

Amendment VII (1791)

In suits at common law, where the value in controversy shall exceed twenty dollars, the right of trial by jury shall be preserved, and no fact tried by a jury, shall be otherwise reexamined in any court of the United States, than according to the rules of the common law.

Amendment VIII (1791)

Excessive bail shall not be required, nor excessive fines imposed, nor cruel and unusual punishments inflicted.

Amendment IX (1791)

The enumeration in the Constitution, of certain rights, shall not be construed to deny or disparage others retained by the people.

Amendment X (1791)

The powers not delegated to the United States by the Constitution, nor prohibited by it to the states, are reserved to the states respectively, or to the people.

Amendment XI (1795)

The judicial power of the United States shall not be construed to extend to any suit in law or equity, commenced or prosecuted against one of the United States by citizens of another state, or by citizens or subjects of any foreign state.

Amendment XII (1804)

The electors shall meet in their respective states and vote by ballot for President and vice president, one of whom, at least, shall not be an inhabitant of the same state with themselves; they shall name in their ballots the person voted for as President, and in distinct ballots the person voted for as vice president, and they shall make distinct lists of all persons voted for as President, and of all persons voted for as vice president, and of the number of votes for each, which lists they shall sign and certify, and transmit sealed to the seat of the government of the United States, directed to the President of the Senate.

The President of the Senate shall, in the presence of the Senate and House of Representatives, open all the certificates and the votes shall then be counted; the person having the greatest number of votes for President, shall be the President, if such number be a majority of the whole number of electors appointed; and if no person have such majority, then from the persons having the highest numbers not exceeding three on the list of those voted for as President, the House of Representatives shall choose immediately, by ballot, the President. But in choosing the President, the votes shall be taken by states, the representation from each state having one vote; a quorum for this purpose shall consist of a member or members from two-thirds of the states, and a majority of all the states shall be necessary to a choice. And if the House of Representatives shall not choose a President whenever the right of choice shall devolve upon them, *before the fourth day of March next following*[39], then the vice president shall act as President, as in the case of the death or other constitutional disability of the President.

The person having the greatest number of votes as vice president, shall be the vice president, if such number be a majority of the whole number of electors appointed, and if no person have a majority, then from the two highest numbers on the list, the Senate shall choose the vice president; a quorum for the purpose shall consist of two-thirds of the whole number of Senators, and a majority of the whole number shall be necessary to a choice. But no person constitutionally ineligible to the office of President shall be eligible to that of vice president of the United States.

Amendment XIII (1865)

Section 1. Neither slavery nor involuntary servitude, except as a punishment for crime whereof the party shall have been duly convicted, shall exist within the United States, or any place subject to their jurisdiction.

Section 2. Congress shall have power to enforce this article by appropriate legislation.

Amendment XIV (1868)

Section 1. All persons born or naturalized in the United States, and subject to the jurisdiction thereof, are citizens of the United States and of the state wherein they reside.[40] No state shall make or enforce any law which shall abridge the privileges or immunities of citizens of the United States; nor shall any state deprive any person of life, liberty, or property, without due process of law; nor deny to any person within its jurisdiction the equal protection of the laws.

Section 2. Representatives shall be apportioned among the several states according to their respective numbers, counting the whole number of persons in each state[41], excluding Indians not taxed. But when the right to vote at any election for the choice of electors for President and vice president of the United States, Representatives in Congress, the executive and judicial officers of a state, or the members of the legislature thereof, is denied to any of the *male* inhabitants of such state, being *twenty-one* years of age, and citizens of the United States, or in any way abridged, except for participation in rebellion, or other crime, the basis of representation therein shall be reduced in the proportion which the number of such *male* citizens shall bear to the whole number of male citizens *twenty-one* years of age in such state.[42]

Section 3. No person shall be a Senator or Representative in Congress, or elector of President and vice president, or hold any office, civil or military, under the United States, or under any state, who, having previously taken an oath, as a member of Congress, or as an officer of the United States, or as a member of any state legislature, or as an executive or judicial officer of any state, to support the Constitution of the United States, shall have engaged in insurrection or rebellion against the same, or given aid or comfort to the enemies thereof. But Congress may by a vote of two-thirds of each House, remove such disability.

Section 4. The validity of the public debt of the United States, authorized by law, including debts incurred for payment of pensions and bounties for services in suppressing insurrection or rebellion, shall not be questioned. But neither the United States nor any state shall assume or pay any debt or obligation incurred in aid of insurrection or rebellion against the United States, or any claim for the loss or emancipation of any slave; but all such debts, obligations and claims shall be held illegal and void.

Section 5. The Congress shall have power to enforce, by appropriate legislation, the provisions of this article.

Amendment XV (1870)

Section 1. The right of citizens of the United States to vote shall not be denied or abridged by the United States or by any state on account of race, color, or previous condition of servitude.

Section 2. The Congress shall have power to enforce this article by appropriate legislation.

Amendment XVI (1913)

The Congress shall have power to lay and collect taxes on incomes, from whatever source derived, without apportionment among the several states, and without regard to any census of enumeration.

Amendment XVII (1913)

The Senate of the United States shall be composed of two Senators from each state, elected by the people thereof, for six years; and each Senator shall have one vote. The electors in each state shall have the qualifications requisite for electors of the most numerous branch of the state legislatures.

When vacancies happen in the representation of any state in the Senate, the executive authority of such state shall issue writs of election to fill such vacancies: Provided, that the legislature of any state may empower the executive thereof to make temporary appointments until the people fill the vacancies by election as the legislature may direct.

This amendment shall not be so construed as to affect the election or term of any Senator chosen before it becomes valid as part of the Constitution.

Amendment XVIII (1919)

Section 1. After one year from the ratification of this article the manufacture, sale, or transportation of intoxicating liquors within, the importation thereof into, or the exportation thereof from the United States and all territory subject to the jurisdiction thereof for beverage purposes is hereby prohibited.

Section 2. The Congress and the several states shall have concurrent power to enforce this article by appropriate legislation.

Section 3. This article shall be inoperative unless it shall have been ratified as an amendment to the Constitution by the legislatures of the several states, as provided in the Constitution, within seven years from the date of the submission hereof to the states by the Congress.[43]

Amendment XIX (1920)

Section 1. The right of citizens of the United States to vote shall not be denied or abridged by the United States or by any state on account of sex.

Section 2. The Congress shall have power to enforce this article by appropriate legislation.

Amendment XX (1933)

Section 1. The terms of the President and vice president shall end at noon on the twentieth day of January, and the terms of Senators and Representatives at noon on the third day of January, of the years in which such terms would have ended if this article had not been ratified; and the terms of their successors shall then begin.[44]

Section 2. The Congress shall assemble at least once in every year, and such meeting shall begin at noon on the third day of January, unless they shall by law appoint a different day.

Section 3. If, at the time fixed for the beginning of the term of the President, the President elect shall have died, the vice president elect[45] shall become President. If a President shall not have been chosen before the time fixed for the beginning of his term, or if the President elect shall have failed to qualify, then the vice president elect shall act as President until a President shall have qualified; and the Congress may by law provide for the case wherein neither a President elect nor a vice president elect shall have qualified, declaring who shall then act as President, or the manner in which one who is to act shall be selected, and such person shall act accordingly until a President or vice president shall have qualified.

Section 4. The Congress may by law provide for the case of the death of any of the persons from whom the House of Representatives may choose a President whenever the right of choice shall have devolved upon them, and for the case of the death of any of the persons from whom the Senate may choose a vice president whenever the right of choice shall have devolved upon them.

Section 5. Sections 1 and 2 shall take effect on the fifteenth day of October following the ratification of this article.

Section 6. This article shall be inoperative unless it shall have been ratified as an amendment to the Constitution by the legislatures of three-fourths of the several states within seven years from the date of its submission.

Amendment XXI (1933)

Section 1. The eighteenth article of amendment to the Constitution of the United States is hereby repealed.

Section 2. The transportation or importation into any state, territory, or possession of the United States for delivery or use therein of intoxicating liquors, in violation of the laws thereof, is hereby prohibited.[46]

Section 3. This article shall be inoperative unless it shall have been ratified as an amendment to the Constitution by conventions in the several states, as provided in the Constitution, within seven years from the date of the submission hereof to the states by the Congress.

Amendment XXII (1951)

Section 1. No person shall be elected to the office of the President more than twice, and no person who has held the office of President, or acted as President, for more than two years of a term to which some other person was elected President shall be elected to the office of the President more than once. But this article shall not apply to any person holding the office of President when this article was proposed by the Congress, and shall not prevent any person who may be holding the office of President, or acting as President, during the term within which this article becomes operative from holding the office of President or acting as President during the remainder of such term.

Section 2. This article shall be inoperative unless it shall have been ratified as an amendment to the Constitution by the legislatures of three-fourths of the several states within seven years from the date of its submission to the states by the Congress.

Amendment XXIII (1961)[47]

Section 1. The District constituting the seat of government of the United States shall appoint in such manner as the Congress may direct:

A number of electors of President and vice president equal to the whole number of Senators and Representatives in Congress to which the District would be entitled if it were a state, but in no event more than the least populous state; they shall be in addition to those appointed by the states, but they shall be considered, for the purposes of the election of President and vice president, to be electors appointed by a state; and they shall meet in the District and perform such duties as provided by the twelfth article of amendment.

Section 2. The Congress shall have power to enforce this article by appropriate legislation.

Amendment XXIV (1964)

Section 1. The right of citizens of the United States to vote in any primary or other election for President or vice president, for electors for President or vice president, or for Senator or Representative in Congress, shall not be denied or abridged by the United States or any state by reason of failure to pay any poll tax or other tax.

Section 2. The Congress shall have power to enforce this article by appropriate legislation.

Amendment XXV (1967)

Section 1. In case of the removal of the President from office or of his death or resignation, the vice president shall become President.

Section 2. Whenever there is a vacancy in the office of the vice president, the President shall nominate a vice president who shall take office upon confirmation by a majority vote of both Houses of Congress.

Section 3. Whenever the President transmits to the President pro tempore of the Senate and the Speaker of the House of Representatives his written declaration that he is unable to discharge the powers and duties of his office, and until he transmits to them a written declaration to the contrary, such powers and duties shall be discharged by the vice president as Acting President.

Section 4. Whenever the vice president and a majority of either the principal officers of the executive departments or of such other body as Congress may by law provide, transmit to the President pro tempore of the Senate and the Speaker of the House of Representatives their written declaration that the President is unable to discharge the powers and duties of his office, the vice president shall immediately assume the powers and duties of the office as Acting President.

Thereafter, when the President transmits to the President pro tempore of the Senate and the Speaker of the House of Representatives his written declaration that no inability exists, he shall resume the powers and duties of his office unless the vice president and a majority of either the principal officers of the executive department or of such other body as Congress may by law provide, transmit within four days to the President pro tempore of the Senate and the Speaker of the House of Representatives their written declaration that the President is unable to discharge the powers and duties of his office. Thereupon Congress shall decide the issue, assembling within forty-eight hours for that purpose if not in session. If the Congress, within twenty-one days after receipt of the latter written declaration, or, if Congress is not in session, within twenty-one days after Congress is required to assemble, determines by two-thirds vote of both Houses that the President is unable to discharge the powers and duties of his office, the vice president shall continue to discharge the same as Acting President; otherwise, the President shall resume the powers and duties of his office.

Amendment XXVI (1971)

Section 1. The right of citizens of the United States, who are 18 years of age or older, to vote, shall not be denied or abridged by the United States or any state on account of age.

Section 2. The Congress shall have the power to enforce this article by appropriate legislation.

Amendment XXVII (1992)

No law, varying the compensation for the services of the Senators and Representatives, shall take effect, until an election of Representatives shall have intervened.

Notes

[1] This clause says that the government may only assess taxes on the states on the basis of population. Amendment XVI changed this by allowing the government to tax individuals' incomes.

[2] *Other persons* meant slaves. Amendment XIII abolished slavery, and Amendment XIV nullified the *three-fifths* clause.

[3] This is the clause that requires a national census every 10 years. The census is taken to apportion congressional representation; it is also used by Congress to decide how to distribute federal funding.

[4] The *executive authority* of a state is the governor.

[5] Amendment XVII changed this; senators are now elected by state voters, not by the state legislature.

[6] This section applied only to the first two Senates to guarantee senatorial elections every two years from the beginning of the Republic.

[7] Amendment XVII changed this by allowing the governor to make such temporary appointments.

[8] The president *pro tempore* presides over Senate when the vice president is not present.

[9] Amendment XX changed this date to January 3.

[10] *Quorum* means the minimum number of people required for the legislature to act. In other words, the Senate cannot begin a session unless at least 51 members are in attendance. Once a session has begun, however, the senators may leave the floor.

[11] *Emoluments* means payments.

[12] A congressperson cannot hold a second government job. This is a central component of the *separation of powers* within the U.S. government.

[13] The president's veto power.

[14] Congress can override a presidential veto with a two-thirds vote in both houses.

[15] This is called a *pocket veto* by the president. He does not return the bill to Congress, but because Congress has adjourned, the bill does not become law. Congress must then re-pass the law in its next session to force the president to consider it again.

[16] *Letters of marque and reprisal* allow private citizens to arm their boats so that they can attack enemy ships. In other words, Congress has the power to license private navies (called *privateers*). Given the circumstances of modern warfare, the chances that Congress will ever again exercise this power are pretty small.

[17] This section refers to the District of Columbia (Washington, D.C.).

[18] This is the elastic clause.

[19] This section prohibited Congress from outlawing the importation of slaves until the year 1808. In 1808, Congress did in fact outlaw the import of slaves.

[20] A *writ of habeas corpus* is used by a defendant to appear before a judge, who determines whether the government has the right to hold the defendant as a prisoner. A defendant's right to a writ of habeas corpus is what prevents the government from arresting and imprisoning people without just cause.

[21] A *bill of attainder* is a law that finds an individual guilty of a capital offense (usually treason). Because it denies an individual's right to a fair trial, it is prohibited by the Constitution.

[22] An *ex post facto* law is one that declares an action a crime retroactively.

[23] Amendment XVI negated this section by altering Congress' power to impose taxes.

[24] Amendment XII overrides this section of the Constitution.

[25] This clause was inserted to provide for the first presidents, who as colonists had been born British subjects.

[26] This entire paragraph was modified by Amendments XX and XXV.

[27] *Emolument* means payment.

[28] This paragraph enumerates several key features of the system of *checks and balances*.

[29] Amendment XI prohibits an individual from using the federal courts to sue a state other than her state of residence.

[30] This paragraph says that if Congress finds a person guilty of treason, it may punish that person but not his heirs.

[31] States must accept the actions of one anothers' governments. Every state must accept every other state's driver's licenses, marriage licenses, legal decisions, and so on.

[32] The process described in this section is called *extradition*.

[33] This section refers to escaped slaves. It was nullified by Amendment XIII.

[34] This means that federal law takes priority when federal law and state law conflict. In *McCulloch v. Maryland*, Chief Justice Marshall interpreted this to mean that the federal government could nullify laws that contradicted federal law.

[35] *Free exercise* means the freedom to practice whatever religion you choose.

[36] A *capital* crime is one punishable by death.

[37] An *otherwise infamous crime* is one that is considered serious enough to be punishable by imprisonment.

[38] This is the *double jeopardy* clause. A person cannot be tried again if a court finds him not guilty in a prior trial.

[39] Amendment XX changed this date to January 20th.

[40] This sentence grants citizenship to the former slaves.

[41] This sentence overrides the *three-fifths* clause in the body of the Constitution.

[42] This section grants voting rights only to males over the age of 21. Amendment XIX extended voting rights to women; Amendment XXVI lowered the voting age to 18.

[43] Amendment XVIII was repealed by Amendment XXI.

[44] This amendment shortened the amount of time that a president serves after he has been voted out of office.

[45] *President elect* refers to someone who has been elected president but has not yet taken the oath of office. Whenever the presidency changes hands by election, there is a president elect between Election Day and Inaugural Day.

[46] Amendment XXI repealed prohibition but it did not prohibit state and local governments from imposing prohibition. This section makes it a federal crime to transport liquor to a dry county (area in which alcoholic beverages are prohibited).

[47] This amendment gave residents of the District of Columbia the right to vote for president.

Part VI
Practice Test 2

Practice Test 2

Completely darken bubbles with a No. 2 pencil. If you make a mistake, be sure to erase mark completely. Erase all stray marks.

1. YOUR NAME:
(Print)
Last   First   M.I.

SIGNATURE: _____ DATE: ___/___/___

HOME ADDRESS: _____
(Print)
Number and Street

City   State   Zip Code

PHONE NO. : _____
(Print)

IMPORTANT: Please fill in these boxes exactly as shown on the back cover of your test book.

2. TEST FORM
_____

3. TEST CODE

4. REGISTRATION NUMBER

⓪	Ⓐ
①	Ⓑ
②	Ⓒ
③	Ⓓ
④	Ⓔ
⑤	Ⓕ
⑥	Ⓖ
⑦	
⑧	
⑨	

6. DATE OF BIRTH

Month	Day		Year	
◯ JAN				
◯ FEB				
◯ MAR	⓪	⓪	⓪	⓪
◯ APR	①	①	①	①
◯ MAY	②	②	②	②
◯ JUN	③	③	③	③
◯ JUL		④	④	④
◯ AUG		⑤	⑤	⑤
◯ SEP		⑥	⑥	⑥
◯ OCT		⑦	⑦	⑦
◯ NOV		⑧	⑧	⑧
◯ DEC		⑨	⑨	⑨

7. SEX
◯ MALE
◯ FEMALE

The Princeton Review®
© The Princeton Review, Inc.
FORM NO. 00001-PR

5. YOUR NAME

First 4 letters of last name				FIRST INIT	MID INIT
Ⓐ	Ⓐ	Ⓐ	Ⓐ	Ⓐ	Ⓐ
Ⓑ	Ⓑ	Ⓑ	Ⓑ	Ⓑ	Ⓑ
Ⓒ	Ⓒ	Ⓒ	Ⓒ	Ⓒ	Ⓒ
Ⓓ	Ⓓ	Ⓓ	Ⓓ	Ⓓ	Ⓓ
Ⓔ	Ⓔ	Ⓔ	Ⓔ	Ⓔ	Ⓔ
Ⓕ	Ⓕ	Ⓕ	Ⓕ	Ⓕ	Ⓕ
Ⓖ	Ⓖ	Ⓖ	Ⓖ	Ⓖ	Ⓖ
Ⓗ	Ⓗ	Ⓗ	Ⓗ	Ⓗ	Ⓗ
Ⓘ	Ⓘ	Ⓘ	Ⓘ	Ⓘ	Ⓘ
Ⓙ	Ⓙ	Ⓙ	Ⓙ	Ⓙ	Ⓙ
Ⓚ	Ⓚ	Ⓚ	Ⓚ	Ⓚ	Ⓚ
Ⓛ	Ⓛ	Ⓛ	Ⓛ	Ⓛ	Ⓛ
Ⓜ	Ⓜ	Ⓜ	Ⓜ	Ⓜ	Ⓜ
Ⓝ	Ⓝ	Ⓝ	Ⓝ	Ⓝ	Ⓝ
Ⓞ	Ⓞ	Ⓞ	Ⓞ	Ⓞ	Ⓞ
Ⓟ	Ⓟ	Ⓟ	Ⓟ	Ⓟ	Ⓟ
Ⓠ	Ⓠ	Ⓠ	Ⓠ	Ⓠ	Ⓠ
Ⓡ	Ⓡ	Ⓡ	Ⓡ	Ⓡ	Ⓡ
Ⓢ	Ⓢ	Ⓢ	Ⓢ	Ⓢ	Ⓢ
Ⓣ	Ⓣ	Ⓣ	Ⓣ	Ⓣ	Ⓣ
Ⓤ	Ⓤ	Ⓤ	Ⓤ	Ⓤ	Ⓤ
Ⓥ	Ⓥ	Ⓥ	Ⓥ	Ⓥ	Ⓥ
Ⓦ	Ⓦ	Ⓦ	Ⓦ	Ⓦ	Ⓦ
Ⓧ	Ⓧ	Ⓧ	Ⓧ	Ⓧ	Ⓧ
Ⓨ	Ⓨ	Ⓨ	Ⓨ	Ⓨ	Ⓨ
Ⓩ	Ⓩ	Ⓩ	Ⓩ	Ⓩ	Ⓩ

Section I
Start with number 1 for each new section.
If a section has fewer questions than answer spaces, leave the extra answer spaces blank.

1. Ⓐ Ⓑ Ⓒ Ⓓ Ⓔ
2. Ⓐ Ⓑ Ⓒ Ⓓ Ⓔ
3. Ⓐ Ⓑ Ⓒ Ⓓ Ⓔ
4. Ⓐ Ⓑ Ⓒ Ⓓ Ⓔ
5. Ⓐ Ⓑ Ⓒ Ⓓ Ⓔ
6. Ⓐ Ⓑ Ⓒ Ⓓ Ⓔ
7. Ⓐ Ⓑ Ⓒ Ⓓ Ⓔ
8. Ⓐ Ⓑ Ⓒ Ⓓ Ⓔ
9. Ⓐ Ⓑ Ⓒ Ⓓ Ⓔ
10. Ⓐ Ⓑ Ⓒ Ⓓ Ⓔ
11. Ⓐ Ⓑ Ⓒ Ⓓ Ⓔ
12. Ⓐ Ⓑ Ⓒ Ⓓ Ⓔ
13. Ⓐ Ⓑ Ⓒ Ⓓ Ⓔ
14. Ⓐ Ⓑ Ⓒ Ⓓ Ⓔ
15. Ⓐ Ⓑ Ⓒ Ⓓ Ⓔ

16. Ⓐ Ⓑ Ⓒ Ⓓ Ⓔ
17. Ⓐ Ⓑ Ⓒ Ⓓ Ⓔ
18. Ⓐ Ⓑ Ⓒ Ⓓ Ⓔ
19. Ⓐ Ⓑ Ⓒ Ⓓ Ⓔ
20. Ⓐ Ⓑ Ⓒ Ⓓ Ⓔ
21. Ⓐ Ⓑ Ⓒ Ⓓ Ⓔ
22. Ⓐ Ⓑ Ⓒ Ⓓ Ⓔ
23. Ⓐ Ⓑ Ⓒ Ⓓ Ⓔ
24. Ⓐ Ⓑ Ⓒ Ⓓ Ⓔ
25. Ⓐ Ⓑ Ⓒ Ⓓ Ⓔ
26. Ⓐ Ⓑ Ⓒ Ⓓ Ⓔ
27. Ⓐ Ⓑ Ⓒ Ⓓ Ⓔ
28. Ⓐ Ⓑ Ⓒ Ⓓ Ⓔ
29. Ⓐ Ⓑ Ⓒ Ⓓ Ⓔ
30. Ⓐ Ⓑ Ⓒ Ⓓ Ⓔ

31. Ⓐ Ⓑ Ⓒ Ⓓ Ⓔ
32. Ⓐ Ⓑ Ⓒ Ⓓ Ⓔ
33. Ⓐ Ⓑ Ⓒ Ⓓ Ⓔ
34. Ⓐ Ⓑ Ⓒ Ⓓ Ⓔ
35. Ⓐ Ⓑ Ⓒ Ⓓ Ⓔ
36. Ⓐ Ⓑ Ⓒ Ⓓ Ⓔ
37. Ⓐ Ⓑ Ⓒ Ⓓ Ⓔ
38. Ⓐ Ⓑ Ⓒ Ⓓ Ⓔ
39. Ⓐ Ⓑ Ⓒ Ⓓ Ⓔ
40. Ⓐ Ⓑ Ⓒ Ⓓ Ⓔ
41. Ⓐ Ⓑ Ⓒ Ⓓ Ⓔ
42. Ⓐ Ⓑ Ⓒ Ⓓ Ⓔ
43. Ⓐ Ⓑ Ⓒ Ⓓ Ⓔ
44. Ⓐ Ⓑ Ⓒ Ⓓ Ⓔ
45. Ⓐ Ⓑ Ⓒ Ⓓ Ⓔ

46. Ⓐ Ⓑ Ⓒ Ⓓ Ⓔ
47. Ⓐ Ⓑ Ⓒ Ⓓ Ⓔ
48. Ⓐ Ⓑ Ⓒ Ⓓ Ⓔ
49. Ⓐ Ⓑ Ⓒ Ⓓ Ⓔ
50. Ⓐ Ⓑ Ⓒ Ⓓ Ⓔ
51. Ⓐ Ⓑ Ⓒ Ⓓ Ⓔ
52. Ⓐ Ⓑ Ⓒ Ⓓ Ⓔ
53. Ⓐ Ⓑ Ⓒ Ⓓ Ⓔ
54. Ⓐ Ⓑ Ⓒ Ⓓ Ⓔ
55. Ⓐ Ⓑ Ⓒ Ⓓ Ⓔ
56. Ⓐ Ⓑ Ⓒ Ⓓ Ⓔ
57. Ⓐ Ⓑ Ⓒ Ⓓ Ⓔ
58. Ⓐ Ⓑ Ⓒ Ⓓ Ⓔ
59. Ⓐ Ⓑ Ⓒ Ⓓ Ⓔ
60. Ⓐ Ⓑ Ⓒ Ⓓ Ⓔ

The Exam

AP® U.S. Government and Politics Exam

SECTION I: Multiple-Choice Questions

DO NOT OPEN THIS BOOKLET UNTIL YOU ARE TOLD TO DO SO.

At a Glance

Total Time
45 minutes
Number of Questions
60
Percent of Total Grade
50%
Writing Instrument
Pencil required

Instructions

Section I of this examination contains 60 multiple-choice questions. Fill in only the ovals for numbers 1 through 60 on your answer sheet.

Indicate all of your answers to the multiple-choice questions on the answer sheet. No credit will be given for anything written in this exam booklet, but you may use the booklet for notes or scratch work. After you have decided which of the suggested answers is best, completely fill in the corresponding oval on the answer sheet. Give only one answer to each question. If you change an answer, be sure that the previous mark is erased completely. Here is a sample question and answer.

Sample Question

Sample Answer

Ⓐ ● Ⓒ Ⓓ Ⓔ

Chicago is a
(A) state
(B) city
(C) country
(D) continent
(E) village

Use your time effectively, working as quickly as you can without losing accuracy. Do not spend too much time on any one question. Go on to other questions and come back to the ones you have not answered if you have time. It is not expected that everyone will know the answers to all the multiple-choice questions.

About Guessing

Many candidates wonder whether or not to guess the answers to questions about which they are not certain. Multiple-choice scores are based on the number of questions answered correctly. Points are not deducted for incorrect answers, and no points are awarded for unanswered questions. Because points are not deducted for incorrect answers, you are encouraged to answer all multiple-choice questions. On any questions you do not know the answer to, you should eliminate as many choices as you can, and then select the best answer among the remaining choices.

GO ON TO THE NEXT PAGE.

UNITED STATES GOVERNMENT AND POLITICS

Section I

Time—45 minutes

60 Questions

Directions: Each of the questions or incomplete statements below is followed by five suggested answers or completions. Select the one that is best in each case and then fill in the corresponding oval on the answer sheet.

1. To which characteristic of American government does the term "federalism" refer?

   (A) The system of checks and balances within the national government
   (B) The power of the Supreme Court to review the constitutionality of laws
   (C) The Bill of Rights' protection of the rights of the accused
   (D) The process by which the size of each state's delegation to the House of Representatives is determined
   (E) The division and sharing of power between the national and state governments

2. The swift adoption of the Bill of Rights in the years following ratification of the Constitution demonstrates the

   (A) Framers' unqualified commitment to individual rights
   (B) small states' determination to receive equal representation in the legislature
   (C) Northern states' support for abolitionism
   (D) states' fears of an overpowerful national government
   (E) Federalists' concerns that the system of checks and balances would weaken the national government

3. Which of the following is true of court cases in which one private party is suing another?

   (A) They are tried in civil court.
   (B) The federal court system has exclusive jurisdiction over them.
   (C) They are tried in criminal court.
   (D) The state court system has exclusive jurisdiction over them.
   (E) They are tried before a grand jury.

4. The term "budget deficit" refers to the

   (A) annual increase in federal spending on the military
   (B) amount of interest on the national debt
   (C) difference between the initial budget proposals made by the president and Congress
   (D) period after the fiscal year ends during which the government operates without an official budget
   (E) amount the government spends in excess of its revenues

5. The legislative successes of the National Rifle Association, antiabortion activists, and other powerful interest groups demonstrate that

   (A) United States domestic policy grew more conservative in the 1990s
   (B) the influence of political action committees has weakened in recent years
   (C) the power of interest groups depends on the degree of support for their positions in the White House
   (D) majority opinion on an issue can sometimes be overridden by the intensity of a minority's commitment to activism
   (E) the most powerful interest groups in the United States are generally those that support uncontroversial positions

GO ON TO THE NEXT PAGE.

6. During the second half of the twentieth century, the Supreme Court's position on free speech was that

   (A) free speech is essential to liberty and therefore may be abridged only under extreme circumstances

   (B) the government may never limit speech because free speech is protected by the First Amendment

   (C) state governments may place limits on free speech, but the national government may not because of the First Amendment

   (D) the government may limit speech that the majority of Americans finds offensive

   (E) the government may place limits on free speech in print and broadcast media but may not limit the spoken word

7. The national and state governments share all of the following powers EXCEPT the power to

   (A) administer elections
   (B) impose taxes
   (C) establish courts
   (D) borrow money
   (E) enact laws

8. Which group most frequently benefits from political action committee (PAC) donations?

   (A) Charitable organizations
   (B) Federal judges
   (C) Political interest groups
   (D) Research institutes
   (E) Incumbents running for reelection

9. The president executes a "pocket veto" by doing which of the following?

   (A) Publicly expressing rejection of a bill
   (B) Issuing an executive order invalidating a recently passed bill
   (C) Failing to sign a bill after Congress has adjourned
   (D) Recalling ambassadors from a peace negotiation
   (E) Refusing to seat a federal judge whom the Senate has confirmed

Composition of State Legislatures, by Party Affiliation, 1990 to 1996

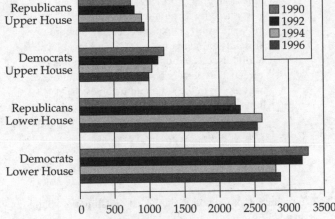

10. The graph above supports which of the following conclusions?

   (A) If the trend shown on the chart continues, the Republican party will soon control most state legislatures.

   (B) In most states, registered Democrats outnumber registered Republicans.

   (C) Democrats had more seats than Republicans in state legislatures throughout the early 1990s.

   (D) The number of Republican governors increased between 1990 and 1996.

   (E) The Democrats and Republicans controlled an equal number of state legislatures in 1996.

GO ON TO THE NEXT PAGE.

11. Which of the following is an accurate statement about the leadership of the two major political parties?

    (A) The national party organization controls all facets of party activity throughout the country.
    (B) Party leadership is dispersed among numerous officials at the national, state, and local levels.
    (C) The highest elected official in each national party directs that party's activities and operations all the way down to the state and local levels.
    (D) All major decisions concerning party activities are made during each party's presidential nomination conventions.
    (E) Prominent former officeholders, such as ex-presidents, lead their respective political parties.

12. The media play a major role in establishing the public agenda by

    (A) deciding how prominently to cover issue-related news stories
    (B) refusing to publicize the opinions of any pundit deemed "too political"
    (C) reviewing the accuracy of candidates' campaign advertisements
    (D) reporting political news from foreign nations
    (E) making available the complete text of presidential addresses and press releases

13. All of the following can be considered true about the impact of a higher level of education on voting habits EXCEPT

    (A) voters are more likely to support government-enforced affirmative action programs
    (B) voters are more likely to support environmental protection efforts
    (C) voters are more likely to support public prayer in schools
    (D) voters are less likely to support restrictions on abortion rights
    (E) voters are more likely to support laws that promote civil liberties

14. In *Gideon v. Wainwright*, the Supreme Court ruled that criminal defendants in state cases have the right

    (A) to representation by an attorney
    (B) not to incriminate themselves
    (C) to a speedy trial
    (D) not to be punished excessively
    (E) to a jury trial

15. All of the following are consequences of low voter turnout in the United States EXCEPT

    (A) a perception of the government as illegitimate
    (B) a lack of true democracy
    (C) a lack of minority representation
    (D) a sense of divide among elected officials and their constituents
    (E) an imposition of a fine on non-voters

Questions 16–17 refer to the following amendment to the Constitution.

Amendment X

The powers not delegated to the United States by the Constitution, nor prohibited to the states, are reserved to the states respectively, or to the people.

16. The Tenth Amendment most often comes into conflict with which section of the Constitution?

    (A) The "full faith and credit" clause
    (B) The "necessary and proper" clause
    (C) The provisions for the impeachment of a president
    (D) The clause prohibiting states from coining money and entering into treaties
    (E) The provisions for constitutional amendment

17. People who interpret the Tenth Amendment as greatly restricting the powers of the national government are often referred to as

    (A) Federalists
    (B) isolationists
    (C) laissez-faire capitalists
    (D) loose constructionists
    (E) states' righters

18. Which committee in the House of Representatives determines the procedure by which bills are debated and amended?

    (A) Ways and Means
    (B) Judiciary
    (C) Ethics
    (D) Rules
    (E) Government Reform

GO ON TO THE NEXT PAGE.

19. The government often finds it difficult to make substantive changes to entitlement programs for which of the following reasons?

    (A) Most such programs were established by constitutional amendment.
    (B) These programs are extremely popular among their numerous beneficiaries.
    (C) Such programs are vital to national defense.
    (D) Most such programs primarily benefit the wealthy, a powerful political bloc.
    (E) These programs' budgets are determined by nonelected bureaucrats, not by Congress.

20. The relative stability of American public policy is achieved largely through

    (A) cooperation between the two major political parties
    (B) judicial activism
    (C) the constitutional fragmentation of power
    (D) affirmative action programs
    (E) the delegation of unique reserved powers to each house of Congress

21. Uncertainty over the limits to presidential power is caused primarily by the fact that

    (A) the constitutional definition of those powers is broad and unspecific
    (B) most people agree that the Constitution places too many limits on presidential power
    (C) the Supreme Court consistently refuses to rule on cases concerning presidential powers
    (D) constitutional amendments have greatly increased presidential powers
    (E) some states cede more power to their governors than the national government cedes to the president

22. The responsibilities of the secretary of state are most likely to overlap with those of

    (A) the secretary of the interior
    (B) the secretary of the treasury
    (C) the speaker of the house
    (D) the president's chief of staff
    (E) the chief national security advisor to the president

23. In the past decade many states have moved forward the date of their presidential primary elections in an effort to

    (A) minimize the cost of running the election
    (B) convince the national government to move forward the date of the general election
    (C) restrict the number of entrants in the presidential race
    (D) focus greater national attention on their state primary races
    (E) increase the significance of their election results

24. Incumbent members of the House of Representatives win reelection more often than incumbent senators for all of the following reasons EXCEPT

    (A) representatives' constituents more often belong largely to the representative's party
    (B) senators have more political power than representatives, and Senate races are accordingly contested more aggressively
    (C) representatives may use federal funds to publicize their achievements via direct mail to constituents
    (D) representatives more often run uncontested
    (E) the fact that Senate races are held statewide generates more media coverage and thus more public awareness

25. A member of the president's cabinet is said to have "gone native" when that cabinet member

    (A) resigns to take a position as a consultant to lobbying groups
    (B) cedes control of his or her department to lifelong bureaucrats within the department
    (C) places his or her department's priorities above the president's
    (D) accepts bribes or expensive favors from businesses regulated by his or her department
    (E) suggests merging his or her department into another executive department

GO ON TO THE NEXT PAGE.

26. Congress would be required to use the "elastic clause" of the Constitution to

   (A) change citizenship requirements
   (B) impose workplace safety standards
   (C) increase tax rates
   (D) authorize the treasury to print money
   (E) declare war

27. Which of the following is true of the Supreme Court?

   (A) Every case appealed to the Supreme Court is ruled upon by the court.
   (B) The court helps set the public agenda by deciding which appeals to hear.
   (C) The court hears all cases when two or more justices agree that the case has merit.
   (D) In deciding cases, the chief justice's vote counts as two votes.
   (E) The court does not rule on cases in which five justices refuse to sign a single opinion.

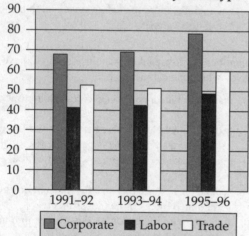

PAC Contributions to Candidates, in millions of dollars, by PAC Type

Corporate   Labor   Trade

28. Which of the following conclusions is supported by the graph?

   (A) Corporations have more political influence than do labor unions.
   (B) Trade PACs are the fastest-growing sector of political activism in the United States.
   (C) Corporate PACs are more likely to donate to Republican candidates than to Democratic candidates.
   (D) In the first half of the 1990s, PACs consistently contributed more than $150 million to different candidates.
   (E) American workers had more disposable income in 1995–1996 than they had in 1993–1994.

29. Which of the following statements best describes the central constitutional issue concerning the death penalty?

   (A) The death penalty violates the prohibition of double jeopardy.
   (B) Different states use different means of executing convicts in capital cases.
   (C) The death penalty arguably constitutes cruel and unusual punishment.
   (D) Federal law and state law differ in their definitions of what constitutes a capital crime.
   (E) Capital trials fail to meet the standard set by the "speedy and public trial" clause.

30. The Supreme Court has used the Fourteenth Amendment to apply portions of the Bill of Rights to state law by citing the amendment's

   (A) prohibition on unreasonable search and seizures
   (B) due process clause
   (C) guarantee of privacy rights
   (D) abolition of slavery
   (E) "reserved powers" provision

31. The Framers of the Constitution sought to insulate the Senate from public opinion by

   (A) restricting Senate membership to those who previously served in the House of Representatives
   (B) delegating the responsibility for electing senators to the state legislatures
   (C) requiring all spending bills to originate in the House of Representatives
   (D) empowering the Senate to provide advice and consent to the executive branch
   (E) assigning exactly two senators to each state's congressional delegation

32. Under the Articles of Confederation, the national government had the power to

   (A) negotiate treaties
   (B) collect taxes
   (C) establish a federal judiciary
   (D) enforce its laws
   (E) regulate interstate commerce

GO ON TO THE NEXT PAGE.

33. Congress has attempted to protect independent regulatory agencies from political influence by requiring that each agency

    (A) be led by a group of commissioners representing both major political parties
    (B) plan policy cooperatively with the appropriate congressional committees
    (C) reapply for funding at the end of each fiscal year
    (D) submit all planned policy changes to the president for approval
    (E) seek the advice and cooperation of the industries they regulate

34. Which of the following most accurately states the impact of the Civil Rights Act of 1964 on school desegregation in the South?

    (A) Because it included no enforcement provisions, the Civil Rights Act of 1964 had no appreciable effect on school desegregation.
    (B) By overturning the "separate but equal" principle, the Civil Rights Act of 1964 ended segregation in public schools.
    (C) The Civil Rights Act of 1964 hastened school desegregation by cutting off federal funds to discriminatory school systems.
    (D) The Civil Rights Act of 1964 sent federal troops to every segregated public school in the South to force school desegregation.
    (E) The Civil Rights Act of 1964 required all southern public schools to mirror the racial demographics of their home states.

35. The rules governing the electoral college make it especially important for presidential candidates to

    (A) win as many states as possible, regardless of the size of the states
    (B) spend most of their time campaigning in the South
    (C) campaign most aggressively among those who will be chosen as electors
    (D) concentrate their campaign efforts on "battleground" states
    (E) concentrate on the states in which they are farthest behind, to reduce the margin of their eventual losses in those states

36. The opinions of congressional committees often fail to accurately mirror public opinion because

    (A) the membership of committees often overrepresents constituencies with the greatest stake in the committee's business
    (B) most committees are too small to include representatives of all popular opinions
    (C) the minority party controls nearly half of all committees
    (D) committee members often lose track of their constituents' priorities because of their frequent contact with special-interest lobbyists
    (E) committee members rely primarily on their legislative aides to develop their positions on committee business

37. The absence of a political party solely dedicated to labor and working class issues in the United States

    (A) proves U.S. politicians are not concerned about serving working-class constituencies
    (B) is the result of government restrictions placed on the political activities of labor unions
    (C) reflects the difficulty of unifying a party around a single issue in a "winner-take-all" format
    (D) demonstrates that, in the United States, most political issues regarding workers have been decided in the workers' favor
    (E) illustrates that race, not class, is the primary political division in the United States

38. In the majority of cases, federal programs are implemented by

    (A) private businesses working as subcontractors to the government
    (B) state and local governments, by means of federal funding
    (C) Congress, through the local offices of its elected representatives
    (D) the federal courts, by means of criminal prosecutions
    (E) federal agencies, through their many local offices in cities and towns

GO ON TO THE NEXT PAGE.

39. Which of the following is an accurate statement about the federal court system?

   (A) The creation of new federal courts requires a constitutional amendment.
   (B) The creation of new federal courts requires the unanimous consent of all 50 states.
   (C) The Supreme Court has the sole power to create new federal courts.
   (D) Congress has the power to create new federal courts.
   (E) The number of federal courts is fixed by the Constitution and cannot be changed.

40. Both the War Powers Act of 1974 and the Budget and Impoundment Control Act of 1974 represent efforts by Congress to limit the powers of the

   (A) Joint Chiefs of Staff
   (B) House Ways and Means Committee
   (C) Central Intelligence Agency
   (D) secretary of defense
   (E) president

41. An open primary is a primary election in which

   (A) voters registered as "independents" may not vote
   (B) candidates do not specify the office for which they are running
   (C) voters may register at their polling place on election day
   (D) candidates need not announce their candidacy until the day of the primary
   (E) voters may vote in the election of a party other than the one to which they are registered

42. Which of the following describes an unintended result of the Federal Election Campaign Act of 1974?

   (A) Limits were placed on the amount of money individuals could donate to a federal election campaign.
   (B) Federal funding became available to presidential candidates who agree to abide by spending limits.
   (C) Candidates drastically decreased the amount of money spent on television advertising.
   (D) Thousands of political action committees were created to raise funds for candidates.
   (E) The number of third-party campaigns for the presidency decreased dramatically.

43. Politicians and political reporters are natural adversaries; the adversarial nature of their relationship, however, is tempered by the fact that

   (A) younger politicians who are more comfortable with the media are gradually displacing older politicians
   (B) government regulations on interaction between the two groups are very strict
   (C) each group is dependent on the other to perform its job effectively
   (D) very few media outlets will cover a story that is embarrassing to a political leader
   (E) most government activity is classified and therefore inaccessible to the media

44. All of the following contribute to lower voting rates among Americans in the 18-to-25 age bracket EXCEPT

   (A) college attendance in a state other than one's home state
   (B) frequent relocation of one's primary residence
   (C) the remoteness of most political issues to the daily lives of young people
   (D) the fact that the minimum voting age in some states is 21
   (E) military service

45. Which of the following defines the salience of a political issue?

   (A) The amount of coverage the issue receives in the major news media
   (B) The degree to which public opinion on the issue is likely to shift quickly
   (C) The number of people affected by the issue
   (D) The degree to which the issue can be addressed through government action
   (E) The importance of the issue to a particular individual or group

46. When the Democratic Party pursues liberal social policies, it is most likely to alienate which of its traditional bases?

   (A) People holding advanced academic degrees
   (B) Northeastern city dwellers
   (C) Southerners
   (D) Jewish Americans
   (E) Urban African Americans

GO ON TO THE NEXT PAGE.

47. When the Supreme Court decides to take a case on appeal it

   (A) issues a writ of *habeas corpus*
   (B) issues a writ of *certiorari*
   (C) issues *amicus curiae* briefs
   (D) engages in judicial review
   (E) engages in judicial activism

48. The Supreme Court case *Regents of University of California v. Bakke* concerned which of the following issues?

   (A) The rights of students to protest on a publicly funded campus
   (B) In-class prayer at a publicly funded school
   (C) The rights of students to carry concealed weapons on campus
   (D) Accommodations for disabled students at publicly funded schools
   (E) The use of racial quotas in public university admissions

49. The principles of freedom—"we hold these truths to be self-evident, that all men are created equal"— stated in the Declaration of Independence were influenced by the beliefs of political philosopher

   (A) Thomas Hobbes
   (B) Niccolo Macchiavelli
   (C) Jonathan Edwards
   (D) John Locke
   (E) John Calvin

50. In "Federalist No. 10," James Madison argues that a federal system of government reduces the danger of political factions by

   (A) creating insurmountable obstacles to the founding of factions
   (B) making it difficult for one faction to gain the power necessary to govern
   (C) requiring equal representation of all factions within the government
   (D) restricting factional political activity to the state level only
   (E) allowing federal agencies to strictly regulate the activities of factions

51. Under which of the following circumstances does a president usually experience a reduction in political power?

   I. The president is in the final two years of his or her second term
   II. The number and severity of international crises is increasing
   III. Different parties control Congress and the White House
   IV. The economy is strong and the president's approval ratings are high

   (A) I only
   (B) I and II only
   (C) I and III only
   (D) II and III only
   (E) II, III, and IV only

52. House members are more concerned about their committee assignments than are senators because

   (A) House members may serve on only one committee at a time
   (B) Senate committees have relatively little power to alter legislation
   (C) bills in the Senate must pass through all committees before reaching the floor
   (D) senators may change their committee assignments whenever they wish
   (E) the rules make it extremely difficult for representatives to influence legislation on the House floor

53. Which of the following is true of most third parties in U.S. history?

   (A) They arose and succeeded during times of prosperity.
   (B) They were created to protest wars.
   (C) At some point they won a majority of seats in Congress.
   (D) They flourished during periods of widespread dissatisfaction.
   (E) They arose in response to increased government regulation.

GO ON TO THE NEXT PAGE.

54. Failed felony prosecutions at the state level are sometimes retried at the federal level

    (A) on appeal by state prosecutors
    (B) under the "double jeopardy" provision of the Constitution
    (C) because new evidence has voided the state-level verdict
    (D) as a result of a gubernatorial veto
    (E) as civil liberties violations

55. Which of the following is true of Congress's power of oversight?

    (A) Congressional oversight activities most often take place at the committee and subcommittee levels.
    (B) State challenges to congressional oversight have severely weakened Congress's oversight powers.
    (C) Congressional oversight is primarily directed at the judicial branch.
    (D) Constituent input does not influence congressional oversight.
    (E) Congressional oversight primarily concerns Congress's power to discipline its own members.

56. Which of the following statements about voting patterns is NOT true?

    (A) Non-whites are more likely to vote Democratic than are whites.
    (B) Women are more likely to vote Democratic than are men.
    (C) Low-income Americans are more likely to vote Democratic than are upper-income Americans.
    (D) Evangelical Christians are more likely to vote Democratic than are non-religious Americans.
    (E) Homosexuals are more likely to vote Democratic than are heterosexuals.

57. Considered as a single group, the Small Business Administration, the Small Business committees in the House and Senate, and small business advocacy groups are an example of

    (A) an iron triangle
    (B) a conference committee
    (C) a regulatory agency
    (D) dual federalism
    (E) a third party

58. Which of the following is true of federal judges?

    (A) They serve four-year terms that coincide with the presidential term.
    (B) They are appointed for life and can only be removed by impeachment.
    (C) They are elected by Congress and serve ten-year terms.
    (D) They are appointed for life and cannot be removed from office.
    (E) They are appointed by the Supreme Court to life terms.

59. Filibusters are less likely to occur in the House of Representatives than in the Senate because

    (A) Senate decorum forbids one senator from attempting to stop another's speech
    (B) the House meets for substantially fewer hours per day than does the Senate
    (C) Senate sessions, unlike House sessions, are open to the public
    (D) debate in the House is in most instances strictly regulated by the rules
    (E) all speeches in the House are delivered by the House Speaker

60. Which of the following is true of congressional redistricting?

    (A) The responsibility for redrawing congressional districts belongs to congressional committees.
    (B) It is a noncontroversial process because it has few political ramifications.
    (C) It occurs every 10 years to reflect changes in population according to the census.
    (D) The Supreme Court has ruled that legislators may not consider racial demographics when redrawing districts.
    (E) When redrawing districts, the chief concern of legislators is to maintain the integrity of neighborhoods.

STOP
END OF SECTION I
IF YOU FINISH BEFORE TIME IS CALLED, YOU MAY CHECK YOUR WORK ON THIS SECTION.
DO NOT GO ON TO SECTION II UNTIL YOU ARE TOLD TO DO SO.

UNITED STATES GOVERNMENT AND POLITICS

SECTION II

Time—1 hour and 40 minutes

<u>Directions:</u> You have 100 minutes to answer all four of the following questions. Unless the directions indicate otherwise, respond to all parts of all four questions. It is suggested that you take a few minutes to plan and outline each answer. <u>Spend approximately one-fourth of your time (25 minutes) on each question</u>. In your response, use substantive examples where appropriate. Make certain to number each of your answers as the question is numbered below.

1. Since the 1960s, Congress has addressed the problem of gender bias on numerous occasions.

    (a)   Choose one of the laws listed below. Describe how it has attempted to address the problem of gender bias in American society.

- the Equal Pay Act of 1963
- the Civil Rights Act of 1964
- the Lilly Ledbetter Fair Pay Act of 2009

    (b)   Describe this law and evaluate its effectiveness.

    (c)   Choose one of the legislative actions listed below. Describe how it has attempted to address the problem of gender bias in American society.

- Title IX of the Higher Education Act of 1973
- the Equal Rights Amendment to the Constitution

    (d)   Describe this action and evaluate its effectiveness.

GO ON TO THE NEXT PAGE.

2. The debate over federalism was one of the most important features of American politics in the years following the Revolutionary War and continued to be an important issue in later years.

    (a)   Define "federalism."

    (b)   Describe the opposing points of view expressed about federalism in the early years of the United States (1776–1862).

    (c)   Describe the opposing points of view expressed about federalism in later years of the United States (1862–present).

GO ON TO THE NEXT PAGE.

3. The media have a large influence on American politics.

    (a)   Describe why the media are so important and why they have such influence.

    (b)   Identify and describe THREE examples of media coverage that have influenced American politics in the past twenty years.

    (c)   Explain the argument that in politics, the media tend to overemphasize stories that are easy to tell at the expense of those that are more complicated.

GO ON TO THE NEXT PAGE.

"The prosecution of [impeachments] will seldom fail to agitate the passions of the whole community, and to divide it into parties more or less friendly or inimical to the accused. In many cases it will connect itself with pre-existing factions, and will enlist all their animosities, partialities, influence, and interest on one side or the other, and in such cases there will always be the greatest danger that the decision will be regulated more by the comparative strength of parties, than by the real demonstrations of innocence or guilt."

—Alexander Hamilton, *Federalist 65*

4. The House of Representatives has twice impeached sitting presidents, both of whom avoided removal from office by the Senate.

    (a)   Define impeachment and removal, and describe the process of impeachment and removal as listed in the Constitution.

    (b)   Assess the accuracy of Hamilton's observations as applied to both cases of presidential impeachment.

    (c)   Identify one strength and one weaknesses of checks and balances in dealing with Hamilton's concerns.

END OF EXAMINATION

Practice Test 2:
Answers and
Explanations

PRACTICE TEST 2 SCORING WORKSHEET

Section I: Multiple-Choice

_____ × 1.0000 = _____
Number of Correct   Weighted
(out of 60)   Section I Score
                           (Do not round)

Section II: Free Response

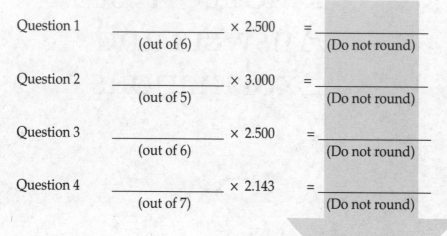

Question 1   _____ × 2.500 = _____
                  (out of 6)   (Do not round)

Question 2   _____ × 3.000 = _____
                  (out of 5)   (Do not round)

Question 3   _____ × 2.500 = _____
                  (out of 6)   (Do not round)

Question 4   _____ × 2.143 = _____
                  (out of 7)   (Do not round)

AP Score Conversion Chart U.S. Government and Politics

Composite Score Range	AP Score
93–120	5
82–92	4
66–81	3
48–65	2
0–47	1

Sum = _____
        Weighted Section II
        Score (Do not round)

Composite Score

_____ + _____ = _____
   Weighted   Weighted   Composite Score
Section I Score   Section II Score   (Round to nearest
                                          whole number)

ANSWER KEY

1.	E	21.	A	41.	E
2.	D	22.	E	42.	D
3.	A	23.	E	43.	C
4.	E	24.	C	44.	D
5.	D	25.	C	45.	E
6.	A	26.	B	46.	C
7.	A	27.	B	47.	B
8.	E	28.	D	48.	E
9.	C	29.	C	49.	D
10.	C	30.	B	50.	B
11.	B	31.	B	51.	C
12.	A	32.	A	52.	E
13.	C	33.	A	53.	D
14.	A	34.	C	54.	E
15.	E	35.	D	55.	A
16.	B	36.	A	56.	D
17.	E	37.	C	57.	A
18.	D	38.	B	58.	B
19.	B	39.	D	59.	D
20.	C	40.	E	60.	C

MULTIPLE-CHOICE SECTION: ANSWERS AND EXPLANATIONS

1. **E** *Federalism* is a government system under which the national government shares power with subnational governments. Under federalism, both the national and state governments are granted *exclusive* powers. They share many other *concurrent* powers, such as the powers to tax and write laws.

    Incorrect Answers:

    (A) The term *system of checks and balances* refers to the manner in which government power at the national level is divided to prevent any single office or faction from gaining control of the government. It applies specifically to the national government; *federalism* refers to the relationship between the national and state governments.

    (B) The power of the Supreme Court to review the constitutionality of laws is called *judicial review*.

    (C) The Bill of Rights' protection of the rights of the accused occasionally has an impact on federalism, as when the Supreme Court requires the state laws to conform to provisions in the Bill of Rights. However, this answer does not provide the definition of the term *federalism*.

    (D) The size of state delegations to the House of Representatives is determined by the national census, which is taken every 10 years.

2. **D** During the ratification debate, the Constitution received its strongest opposition from those objecting to its lack of a Bill of Rights, which raised fears that the new government may grow too powerful and suppress individual rights. Had supporters of the Constitution not conceded the speedy addition of a Bill of Rights after ratification, the Constitution may never have received the necessary support.

    Incorrect Answers:

    (A) Had the Framers been wholeheartedly committed to individual rights, the Constitution would originally have included a Bill of Rights. Its later addition reveals that the Framers did not consider a Bill of Rights necessary.

    (B) The Bill of Rights enumerates the rights of individuals and thus provides protection against an overpowerful national government. Choice (B) refers to a concession the small states received during the framing of the body of the Constitution. That concession resulted in the creation of the Senate, where all states receive equal representation.

    (C) The Bill of Rights is silent on the issue of slavery, so it cannot be cited as evidence of abolitionism in the North.

    (E) The system of checks and balances is laid out in the body of the Constitution, not in the Bill of Rights.

3. **A** *Civil court* is the venue for lawsuits. It is where disputes between two private parties, such as individuals or corporations, are settled (as opposed to *criminal court*, where the state tries accused criminals).

Incorrect Answers:

(B) Suits may be filed in either state or federal court, depending on the nature of the case.

(C) *Criminal court* is where the state tries accused criminals.

(D) Suits may be filed in either state or federal court, depending on the nature of the case.

(E) A *grand jury* hears preliminary evidence in a criminal case. Its job is to decide whether prosecutors have enough evidence to bring an indictment against the accused. When a grand jury indicts, the case moves on to the criminal courts.

4. **E** A *budget deficit* is the difference between government income and government spending, when spending is greater than income. When income is greater, this difference is called a *budget surplus*.

Incorrect Answers:

(A) See the explanation for (E).

(B) Interest on the national debt may contribute to the deficit, but it is not synonymous with the term *budget deficit*.

(C) See the explanation for (E).

(D) Occasionally the federal fiscal year ends before Congress and the president can agree on a new budget. When this happens, Congress usually passes emergency spending bills to cover government expenses. This can contribute to *budget deficits*, because it is more expensive to run the government on this *ad hoc* basis, but the situation described is not synonymous with the term *budget deficit*.

5. **D** Many successful interest groups—such as those cited in the question—at times represent minority positions. Their power derives from the fact that the minorities they represent base their votes almost exclusively on a candidate's position on that issue. The intensity of their commitment overrides their numerical disadvantage, because their opposition more often considers other issues when voting.

Incorrect Answers:

(A) In fact, domestic policy grew more liberal during the period described. Such a policy shift is common under Democratic administrations.

(B) Political action committees have remained powerful in recent years and will continue to do so as long as current campaign-finance laws and practices remain in place.

(C) No, both the NRA and antiabortion rights activists were opposed by the Clinton White House, yet both remained influential in Washington, D.C.

(E) The groups described are powerful AND they support extremely controversial positions.

6. **A** This answer choice encapsulates the *preferred position doctrine*, framed by the Supreme Court in the 1940s.

Incorrect Answers:

(B) The Supreme Court has accepted limits on free speech, most notably in *Schenck v. United States*, in which the court established the "clear and present danger" limit on speech.

(C) This was, in fact, true between 1830 and 1925. In 1830, the court ruled in *Barron v. Baltimore* that the Bill of Rights applied only to the national government, not to state governments. In 1925, however, the court ruled in *Gitlow v. New York* that free speech was protected from state infringement by the "due process" clause of the Fourteenth Amendment. Since the 1940s, the court's position on free speech has been the *preferred position doctrine* (see above).

(D) The First Amendment protects offensive speech. A classic example of protected offensive speech is graphic pornography; most Americans find it offensive, yet it proliferates nonetheless.

(E) The exact same First Amendment rights that protect print and broadcast media protect individuals as well.

7. **A** The power to administer elections is reserved to the states. All powers described in the other answer choices are concurrent powers, granted to both the national and the state governments.

Incorrect Answers:

(B) Both state and national governments have the constitutional power to impose taxes. See the explanation for (A).

(C) There are both state and national level courts established by state and national governments, respectively. See the explanation for (A).

(D) Both state and national governments can borrow money. See the explanation for (A).

(E) A government that cannot enact laws is an odd and questionable form of government, and it is necessary that both national and state governments have the ability to do so.

8. **E** PACs contribute primarily to incumbents because (1) incumbents usually win their elections, and (2) the PACs hope to gain influence with the candidates by donating to their campaigns. The key is that PAC money usually goes toward influencing elections.

Incorrect Answers:

(A) Political action committees usually donate to influence elections, which are only indirectly related to charitable organizations.

(B) Federal judges are nominated by the president, so PACs affect the judges only indirectly.

(C) Political interest groups perform a similar function to PACs in that they both give money to influence elections. However, political interest groups are not usually the target of PAC expenditures.

(D) Research institutes may support the ideological positions of some PACs, but they are not directly involved in elections.

9. **C** A *pocket veto* can be used only on bills passed in the final days of a congressional session. The Constitution requires the president to sign a bill within 10 days of its reaching his desk. If the president fails to sign a bill while Congress is in session, the bill is returned to Congress, whereupon it becomes law. (Presidents who wish to express disapproval of a law, but not veto it, occasionally use this constitutional process.) However, if Congress is not in session, the bill cannot be returned to Congress, so it simply dies. This process is called a pocket veto.

Incorrect Answers:

(A) While using the pocket veto, the president may or may not express disapproval of the bill. A public rejection of the bill, however, is not a necessary element of a pocket veto.

(B) See the explanation for (C).

(D) See the explanation for (C).

(E) The situation described in this answer choice does not describe a pocket veto. Furthermore, it describes an extremely unlikely scenario because the president must first nominate federal judges before the Senate can confirm them.

10. **C** Compare each of the four "Democratic Upper House" bars with the corresponding "Republican Upper House" bars on the bar graph. In each case, the Democratic bar is larger. The same holds true for the lower houses. If you did *not* choose this answer, perhaps the wording of the answer choice confused you. The answer choice does *not* say that Democrats held majorities in the majority of legislative chambers, an assertion that the bar graph does not support. Rather, it simply says that Democrats had more seats in all the legislatures. That is precisely what this graph shows.

Remember that graph questions on the AP U.S. Government and Politics Exam ask only that you identify indisputable conclusions. Do not try to "read between the lines" and interpret the data—you will only get into trouble that way.

Incorrect Answers:

(A) While the chart does demonstrate an increase in Republican representation in state legislatures, this answer choice goes too far in drawing its conclusion. The trend shown is simply not dramatic enough to support this assertion.

(B) This chart does not include information about registered voters and therefore cannot support the conclusion drawn in this answer choice.

(D) This chart does not include information about governors and therefore cannot support the conclusion drawn in this answer choice.

(E) This chart does not include information about party representation in individual state legislatures and therefore cannot support the conclusion drawn in this answer choice.

11. **B** As in U.S. government, power in political parties is spread out among various national, state, and local officials. National party organizations exert little influence over local party officials and elected officers. In contrast, the national party organizations in parliamentary democracies (such as Britain) tightly control the activities and votes of party members in government.

Incorrect Answers:

(A) This statement is true of national parties within parliamentary governments, but not of those within the United States federal government.

(C) The president and his counterpart in the opposition party are too busy running the government to direct party activities. Both serve as important fundraisers and ideological leaders of their parties, but neither typically spends much time on day-to-day party operations.

(D) If the parties waited for their nominating conventions (which occur once every four years) to make important decisions, they would never get anything done. In fact, important decisions of any kind are rarely made at conventions, which are instead carefully choreographed pageants designed to sell the party's candidates to voters.

(E) Gerald Ford, Jimmy Carter, and George H. W. Bush all played minimal roles in their political parties.

12. **A** By covering some events heavily and downplaying others, the media help set the public agenda. The amount of exposure given to an issue by the media directly affects whether the public perceives that issue as important. Furthermore, because the public relies on the media for information, the way in which the media present news (and the frequency with which they report certain stories) naturally influences the public's viewpoint.

Incorrect Answers:

(B) Pundits who are "overly political" are in high demand during elections.

(C) News media play an important role in elections by dissecting campaign advertisements. However, this highly specified task does not "play a major role in establishing the public agenda."

(D) Except in times of crisis, most Americans pay little attention to news from overseas. Consequently, political reporting from overseas usually has little impact on the public agenda.

(E) Again, this answer describes a media service of interest to only a small portion of the voting public.

13. **C** Support for prayer in schools is weakest among those with higher levels of education. The less education a person has, the more likely that person is to support school prayer (Gallup poll, 1992).

Incorrect Answers:

(A) Government-enforced racial affirmative action programs are more likely to be supported as the level of education increases.

(B) The more educated, the more likely voters are to hold progressive or liberal views about the environment.

(D) The more educated, the more likely voters are to hold progressive or liberal views about abortion.

(E) The more educated, the more likely voters are to hold progressive or liberal views about civil liberties.

14. **A** In 1963, Clarence Earl Gideon won an appeal of his criminal conviction. His appeal argued that the state of Florida had denied him a fair trial because its court had refused to provide him with a defense attorney. The Supreme Court agreed, ruling that Florida had violated Gideon's right to due process under the Fourteenth Amendment. Because of *Gideon v. Wainwright*, poor defendants are now entitled to court-appointed attorneys in felony cases.

Incorrect Answers:

(B) The right against self-incrimination, commonly referred to as "pleading the Fifth," was a central concept of *Miranda v. Arizona*, but not *Gideon*.

(C) The right to a speedy trial is guaranteed by the Sixth Amendment, but was not at issue in *Gideon*.

(D) The Eighth Amendment guarantees against "cruel and unusual punishment," which was not an issue in *Gideon*.

(E) The Sixth Amendment gives U.S. citizens the right to an "impartial jury" in criminal prosecutions, but this was not a part of *Gideon's* holding.

15. **E** Political scientists and pundits lament low voter turnout for a variety of reasons. Some countries, like Australia, impose a fine on people who fail to vote, but there is no such fine in the United States, so (E) is correct.

Incorrect Answers:

(A) Other countries, or even United States citizens, can view the government as illegitimate, since it wasn't truly elected by the citizens when voter turnout is low, so eliminate this choice.

(B) The United States government is intended to operate with the consent of the governed, but when people don't vote, they aren't consenting to anything and they aren't being represented accurately.

(C) Minorities have more barriers to voting, such as identification requirements or difficulty getting to polling places, so low voter turnout generally means fewer minority voters than would be expected.

(D) See reasoning for eliminating Choice (B) above.

16. **B** The "necessary and proper" clause, often referred to as the elastic clause, allows Congress to pass laws "necessary and proper" to the performance of its duties. Congress can use this clause to expand its authority, often by citing its power to regulate interstate commerce. The "necessary and proper" clause comes into conflict with the Tenth Amendment because Congress uses this clause to gain control in areas previously under state supervision. Avid states' rights advocates argue that these congressional actions usurp the states' reserved powers.

Incorrect Answers:

(A) The "full faith and credit" clause requires states to honor one another's laws, licenses, and so on. Because it does not involve infringements on state governments by the national government, it does not pertain to the Tenth Amendment.

(C) The provisions for the impeachment of a president pertain only to the national government and so cannot come into conflict with the Tenth Amendment.

(D) The clause prohibiting states from coining money and entering into treaties appears in the body of the Constitution. These powers are "delegated to the United States by the Constitution," as acknowledged in the Tenth Amendment, and so do not conflict with the amendment.

(E) The provisions for constitutional amendment lay out a process for amending the Constitution that does not infringe on states' rights and therefore do not conflict with the Tenth Amendment.

17. **E** *States' Rightists* believe that the Constitution limits the national government to its specifically enumerated powers. They also believe that the vast majority of governance should be left entirely to the states.

Incorrect Answers:

(A) The term *Federalist* refers either to those who support the federal system or to members of the Federalist Party, which existed from the late 1700s until the late 1810s. Either way, it describes a person who supports a strong central government.

(B) The term *isolationist* refers to a person who believes that the government should avoid involvement with foreign governments and nations.

(C) The term *laissez-faire capitalist* refers to a person who believes the government should regulate the economy as little as possible.

(D) The term *loose constructionist* refers to a person who believes the national government should use the elastic clause to expand its powers. Loose constructionists argue that the national government may do anything not expressly forbidden by the Constitution. They do not see the Tenth Amendment as a significant limitation of federal power.

18. **D** Because the membership of the House is so large, the process by which the House debates and amends bills must be regulated. The task of setting these limits falls to the House Rules Committee. Because the Rules Committee controls crucial aspects of the legislative process, it is the most powerful committee in the House. The Speaker of the House nearly always chairs this committee.

Incorrect Answers:

(A) The Ways and Means Committee has jurisdiction over tax and trade legislation. It is an extremely powerful committee.

(B) The Judiciary Committee is a powerful committee with a wide range of responsibilities. It has jurisdiction over matters concerning the judiciary, immigration, and constitutional amendments. This committee heard the evidence in the impeachment proceedings against Bill Clinton and reported to the full membership of the House, recommending impeachment.

(C) The Ethics Committee determines the rules of proper behavior for representatives. It punishes those who violate the rules.

(D) The Committee on Government Reform performs oversight on executive agencies.

19. **B** Entitlement programs include Social Security and Medicare. Many people, especially among the elderly, rely on these programs to cover living and medical expenses. Recipients of entitlements form a large and powerful voting bloc. Consequently, it is considered political suicide even to suggest substantial reductions in entitlement benefits.

Incorrect Answers:

(A) Entitlement programs are created by acts of Congress. Social Security was established during the New Deal; Medicare was created as part of Lyndon Johnson's Great Society program.

(C) Entitlement programs are not defense-related. See the explanation for (B).

(D) Entitlement recipients do indeed constitute a powerful political bloc, but the vast majority of entitlement recipients are not wealthy. In fact, most are extremely protective of their entitlements precisely because they have very little money.

(E) Congress can alter entitlement budgets, although in theory these budgets are supposed to be separately funded (through payroll withholding taxes) and thus "untouchable." If Congress and the president were unable to alter entitlement budgets, these budgets would not be the hot political issue that they are.

20. **C** The fact that power is divided among so many different government branches and agencies guarantees slow, conservative government action. Only during times of extreme crisis—such as during the Great Depression—can the government move quickly AND effect substantial change. Otherwise, the conflicting interests of the many parties involved slow both the process and the rate of change, resulting in relatively stable policy.

Incorrect Answers:

(A) The two major parties rarely cooperate. The lack of cooperation between them, in fact, slows the political process, increasing political stability.

(B) Judicial activism—the process by which courts change policy by reinterpreting the law—decreases stability by effecting rapid change to the legal system. The Warren Court's alterations of criminal rights, for example, quickly changed policing and trial procedures in the United States.

(D) Affirmative action programs, which attempt to redress previous racial and gender inequality, are a recent phenomenon. Because American public policy has always been relatively stable, this cannot be the correct answer.

(E) The delegation of specific powers to the House and Senate plays an important role in the functioning of the legislature, but it does not have a major influence on the stability of public policy.

21. **A**   The Constitution provides a broad outline of the president's duties but does not define them specifically. Nor does the Constitution enumerate the limits on those powers, except in the broadest of terms. Consequently, presidents are often left to define for themselves the limits of their powers under such mandates as "Commander in Chief" and "Head of State." Presidential power is accordingly fluid, dependent on the popularity and skills of the office holder. Franklin D. Roosevelt was able to establish an extremely strong presidency; Presidents Ford and Carter, conversely, found their presidencies limited by post-Watergate mistrust of the executive branch.

Incorrect Answers:

(B)   Whether the Constitution places too many or too few limits on presidential power is a subject of endless debate. "Most people" do not agree that the presidency is too weak.

(C)   The Supreme Court is not unwilling to rule on such cases. In the 1930s, the court frequently struck down Roosevelt's New Deal programs on constitutional grounds. In the 1970s, the court decided against the Nixon administration several times, in each instance ruling that Nixon had overstepped his authority as president.

(D)   No constitutional amendments have increased presidential power. One amendment limits the number of terms a president may serve. This amendment arguably decreases presidential power by creating a "lame duck" period for second-term presidents, during which presidents' ability to influence Congress invariably declines.

(E)   This is simply not an issue in the debate over presidential power.

22. **E**   The secretary of state is responsible for international relations. The chief national security advisor consults with the president on foreign policy matters. Consequently, the responsibilities of the two officials overlap. This was most evident in the late 1960s and early 1970s, when President Nixon clearly favored the advice of National Security Advisor Henry Kissinger over that of Secretary of State William Rogers.

Incorrect Answers:

(A)   The secretary of the interior is responsible for administering public lands, such as national parks and wildlife refuges, within the United States.

(B)   The secretary of the treasury oversees the Treasury Department.

(C)   The speaker of the House leads the House of Representatives. The speaker is always a member of the majority party in the House.

(D)   The president's chief of staff manages the president's schedule and controls access to the president.

23.   **E**   In primary elections, momentum translates into donations, the lifeblood of the campaign. Accordingly, early victories are extremely important. Because of this emphasis placed on early primaries, many states have pushed their primary dates forward. By enhancing the prominence of their primaries, states hope to influence the direction of the campaign, perhaps even gaining promises of increased federal support from candidates hopeful of winning in their states.

Incorrect Answers:

(A) State expenses in elections are not a major concern to the states. While candidates spend many millions, the states' expenses are confined to maintaining voting machines, hiring poll workers, and so on. Changing the primary date would do little to alter these costs, which are nominal at any rate.

(B) General elections are always held on the Tuesday after the first Monday of November. There is no public interest in changing that date.

(C) Other factors—primarily the ability to raise money—restrict the number of entrants in the presidential race. While moving primary dates forward may have exacerbated this situation, this was not the states' intent in changing their primary dates.

(D) *State-level* primary races rarely generate national attention. The exception to this rule is the rare controversial primary, such as when David Duke, an ex-member of the Ku Klux Klan, ran in—and won—Louisiana's Republican primary for governor in 1990.

24.   **C**   Neither senators nor representatives are allowed to use federal funding to finance their campaigns.

Incorrect Answers:

(A) Senators represent entire states, in which party identification is rarely lopsided. A representative from an inner-city district, however, may have a constituency that is 95% Democratic.

(B) In terms of political currency, a Senate seat is simply more valuable than a seat in the House. The length of term in office, the limited number of seats in the chamber, and the special powers of the body all confer extra status on senators. Accordingly, Senate races are usually hotly contested. House incumbents, conversely, frequently run uncontested.

(D) See the explanation for (B).

(E) House races rarely generate much media attention. Senate races always do, at least within the state (and often nationally as well). This increased public interest makes it more difficult for Senate incumbents to win reelection.

25. **C** Cabinet members head executive departments. As they work with the bureaucrats within their departments, many come to see themselves as their department's chief advocate within the administration. As such, they grow more concerned with their department's priorities and less concerned with the president's, a process referred to as "going native." This is why presidents more often turn to their personal advisors than to cabinet members for advice.

Incorrect Answers:

(A) While cabinet members may take consultant positions in lobbying groups following their government service, this doesn't mean they've "gone native."

(B) "Gone native" refers to supporting a department's priorities above the president's, not ceding control to bureaucrats within the department.

(D) Accepting bribes is an illegal activity for a cabinet member, but this doesn't mean they've "gone native."

(E) Since "gone native" refers to an attempt to strengthen a department, (E) is an opposite choice, as it would most likely dilute that department's power.

26. **B** The Constitution does not specifically grant Congress the authority to impose workplace safety standards. Congress does so by citing its power to regulate interstate commerce and exercising the elastic clause, which allows Congress to pass laws "necessary and proper" to the execution of its enumerated powers.

Incorrect Answers:

NOTE: All of the incorrect answers appear in Article I, Section 8 of the Constitution.

(A) The Constitution specifically empowers Congress to "establish a uniform rule of naturalization."

(C) The Constitution specifically empowers Congress to "collect taxes, duties, imposts, and excises."

(D) The Constitution specifically empowers Congress to "coin money [and] regulate the value thereof."

(E) The Constitution specifically empowers Congress to declare war.

27. **B** The Supreme Court hears less than 5% of all appeals. It chooses its cases carefully, fully aware that each court decision could have a major impact on society. In choosing its cases, the court helps set the public agenda. Whenever the court agrees to hear an abortion case, for example, abortion immediately leaps to the top of the public agenda, with activists on all sides of the issue stepping up activities.

Incorrect Answers:

(A) The court hears less than 5% of all appeals.

(C) Four or more justices must agree to hear a case. When four justices reach this agreement, the court issues a writ of *certiorari* requesting all transcripts for the case.

(D) The vote of the chief justice counts as one vote, as do the votes of all nine members of the court.

(E) The court will rule in favor of one side or another even if the justices cannot reach a majority agreement on a single opinion. For example, five justices may vote in favor of one party. They may not agree, however, on why the party has won the case. All five justices may then write separate opinions, or (more often) several will sign on to one justice's opinion, while another justice will offer a separate *concurring opinion* on the case.

28. **D** Add the totals of all PAC contributions in each of the listed elections from the early 1990s. In each election, the sum is greater than $150 million. Remember that this is only the tip of the iceberg: Candidates raise money from private donors and many other sources as well.

Remember that graph questions on the AP U.S. Government and Politics Exam ask only that you identify indisputable conclusions. Do not try to "read between the lines" and interpret the data—you will only get into trouble that way.

Incorrect Answers:

(A) The graph measures money, not political influence.

(B) This false answer choice asks about political activism, which is different than monetary contributions measured by the graph.

(C) While this may be true in real life, don't choose this answer, because the graph does not measure the amount given to parties to which PACs contribute.

(E) American workers are not synonymous with "Corporate," "Labor," or "Trade" and so the graph does not measure their disposable income.

29. **C** Former Supreme Court justices William Brennan and Thurgood Marshall were among the numerous legal experts who have argued that the death penalty constitutes "cruel and unusual punishment." While theirs is the minority opinion, it is one that is widely held among opponents of the death penalty.

Incorrect Answers:

(A) The double jeopardy clause protects individuals from a second prosecution once a court has found them "not guilty."

(B) The Constitution addresses this issue only in its "cruel and unusual punishment" clause, and then only if the states impose the death penalty in a cruel manner. While hanging and the electric chair were arguably "cruel and unusual," the most common form of execution today—lethal injection—is less so.

(D) Federal and state laws vary on most issues. This is a fundamental feature of federalism and is not particularly controversial.

(E) This may be an issue in some death penalty cases, but it is not the central constitutional issue concerning the death penalty.

30. **B** The process described in this question is called *selective incorporation*. You should have been able to use process of elimination to answer this question, because none of the incorrect answers appears in the Fourteenth Amendment.

Incorrect Answers:

(A) The Fourth Amendment guarantees this right.

(C) The Constitution does not explicitly guarantee this right. The Supreme Court has found an implied right to privacy, however, in the combined effect of the Bill of Rights and the Fourteenth Amendment.

(D) The Thirteenth Amendment abolished slavery.

(E) The "reserved powers" provision appears in the Tenth Amendment.

31. **B** Under the provisions of the Constitution as ratified in 1789, state legislatures selected senators. The Framers considered the House of Representatives to be the "people's house," as evidenced by the provision for direct election of representatives. The Seventeenth Amendment (1913) provided for the direct election of senators.

Incorrect Answers:

(A) No such restriction appears in the Constitution.

(C) While the Constitution does in fact require all spending bills to originate in the House, the purpose of this provision was not to insulate the Senate from public opinion. Rather, the purpose was to increase the accountability of those who spent the people's money.

(D) While the Constitution does in fact give this power to the Senate, the purpose of this provision was not to insulate the Senate from public opinion. Rather, the purpose was to reinforce the system of checks and balances.

(E) The purpose of this provision was to create one legislative body in which each state received equal representation, not to insulate the Senate from public opinion.

32. **A** Under the Articles of Confederation, the states remained nearly autonomous, united in a loose confederation empowered to perform only those few tasks necessary to the maintenance of a single nation. Of the powers listed in the answer choices, only the power to negotiate treaties belonged to the national government.

Incorrect Answers:

(B) The Framers of the Articles left the national government dependent on the states to collect taxes and enforce its laws, tasks that the states could not be compelled to perform and which therefore were performed erratically, if at all.

(C) The Articles did not empower the national government to create a judiciary.

(D) The Articles were notoriously weak and left the government unable to enforce its laws. This weakness became especially apparent during Shays' Rebellion when the federal government and the state of Massachusetts were unable to quash a rebellion of farmers for more than six months.

(E) The Articles did not empower the national government to regulate interstate commerce.

33. **A** Federal law requires that a panel of commissioners drawn from both parties lead independent regulatory agencies. Commissioners serve long terms that do not usually coincide with the changes of presidential administrations. All of these provisions are intended to protect regulatory agencies from the political pressures of electoral politics. In reality, of course, political pressures cannot be avoided, given the weighty impact of regulatory agencies' decisions. Politicians, businesses, and public-interest groups all work hard to influence regulatory policy.

Incorrect Answers:

(B) Regulatory agencies must often defend their decisions before congressional committees, but they are not required to plan policy cooperatively with them. Furthermore, interactions with Congress increase the political pressure on regulators.

(C) This process increases political pressure on regulatory agencies by leaving them dependent on Congress.

(D) Interactions between the president and regulatory agencies increase the political pressure on those agencies.

(E) Regulatory agencies are not required to seek the advice of the industries they regulate, although almost all do as a matter of course. Such interactions, however, increase political pressure on regulatory agencies.

34. **C** The government could not immediately enforce the 1954 Supreme Court decision *Brown v. Board of Education* because it had little enforcement power. Short of sending troops to force integration, the government had few powers over uncooperative states. The Civil Rights Act of 1964 changed that by allowing the government to cut off funding to discriminatory school systems. The loss of federal funding would have crippled many school systems and so persuaded many to comply with *Brown*.

Incorrect Answers:

(A) See the explanation for (C).

(B) *Brown v. Board of Education* overturned the "separate but equal" principle. See the explanation for (C).

(D) See the explanation for (C).

(E) The process described in this answer choice would have been impossible, given residential segregation. To make each public school population mirror state residential demographics would require transporting some students many, many miles. The impracticality of this answer choice should have helped you eliminate it.

35. **D** The winner-take-all arrangement in the electoral college places a high premium on victory in battleground states, which are determined by used polling data. Presidential candidates spend relatively little time in strongly ideological states such as New York (Democratic) or Texas (Republican), preferring states like Florida and Pennsylvania where the vote is up for grabs.

Incorrect Answers:

(A) It is possible for a candidate to win more than half the states in the electoral college and still lose the election. California alone has as many electoral votes as the 15 least populous states combined!

(B) Though the South has swung from being solidly Democratic to being solidly Republican, its importance is not absolute and can vary from election to election.

(C) Because the votes of electors always reflect their home state's election results, candidates need not campaign among electors at all.

(E) The winner-take-all arrangement of the electoral college encourages candidates to give up on states in which they are farthest behind and to concentrate instead on those in which they have a chance of winning.

36. **A** A good example is the Agriculture Committee, which is invariably populated almost entirely by congresspersons from agricultural states. Accordingly, agricultural consumers and other constituencies with an interest in agriculture are underrepresented on this committee. This pattern holds true throughout the many special-interest committees in Congress.

Incorrect Answers:

(B) Membership in congressional committees is reasonably large, certainly large enough to include representation of all popular opinions. Congress simply chooses not to populate its committees in that manner.

(C) The majority party controls every committee. The chairperson is a member of the majority party, and more than half the seats on every committee go to majority party members. The fact that the minority party controls some committee seats tends to make committee members more broadly representative of public opinion, not less.

(D) This is a pretty good distractor answer. However, most members of Congress keep constant tabs on their constituents' priorities through regular polling.

(E) Even if this were so, it would not explain why the opinions of committee members do not accurately reflect public opinion.

37. **C** Winning an election in a two-party system requires coalition building, which is not possible when one of the parties clings to one issue or ideological position. But it is possible in electoral systems (based on proportional representation) that allow for single-cause parties, such as the German Green party, to win a share of the seats in parliaments.

Incorrect Answers:

(A) U.S. politicians must serve all classes in their constituency to win in a two-party system.

(B) During the early and middle parts of the last century there was an expansion of the power of labor and unions in the economy, society, and politics.

(D) The struggle between different interests within the two-party system has not led to the domination of labor, or any other interest in the political representation of party.

(E) Race, although represented as a political cleavage within the parties, does not rank as high as class standing and political affiliation.

38.　**B**　The majority of federal programs are administered through *grants-in-aid* to the states. The federal government provides the states with a set of guidelines and the money to carry them out, but leaves administration of the programs to the states.

Incorrect Answers:

(A)　Since the majority of federal programs are run through state and local governments, private businesses are less prominent, making this choice worse than (B).

(C)　Congress legislates but does not implement laws and federal programs.

(D)　Criminal prosecutions do not apply to most federal programs.

(E)　The principle of federalism is strongly at work in the implementation of federal programs— while federal programs originate at the national level, they are implemented at the state and local levels.

39.　**D**　The Constitution empowers Congress to create new federal courts (see Article III, Section 1).

Incorrect Answers:

(A)　Since Article III, Section I of the Constitution directly addresses the creation of new federal courts, constitutional amendments are not needed.

(B)　Congress has the power to create new courts during legislative sessions, so the "unanimous consent of all 50 states" is not necessary.

(C)　Congress has the power to create new courts, so it isn't a power of the Supreme Court.

(E)　This statement is factually incorrect—Congress can create new federal courts.

40.　**E**　The War Powers Act requires the president to seek periodic approval from Congress for any substantial troop commitment. The bill was passed in response to the Vietnam War. The Budget and Impoundment Control Act requires congressional approval of presidential impoundments of federal funds. The bill was passed in response to impoundments made by President Nixon, who tried to cut federal spending by impounding, or refusing to allocate, funds Congress had appropriated. Both bills sought to limit the president's powers by requiring the president to seek congressional approval for specific actions.

Incorrect Answers:

(A)　These acts were attempts to specifically target presidential powers, not those of the Joint Chiefs of Staff in the Department of Defense, who were only affected indirectly.

(B)　This answer choice is an opposite, since the House Ways and Means Committee is a part of Congress, which was trying to increase, not decrease, its own power in relation to the Executive Branch.

(C) The Central Intelligence Agency was not directly affected by the 1974 acts.

(D) The secretary of defense is a member of the president's cabinet and would only have been affected by the 1974 acts through the president, making (E) a better choice.

41. **E** In an *open primary*, voters enter the voting booth and then decide in which party's primary they wish to vote. They may vote in only one party's primary, however; they may not hopscotch across the ballot, for example, by voting in the Democratic primary for president and then the Republican primary for governor. Voting in such a manner is permitted only in a *blanket primary*.

Incorrect Answers:

(A) Independents may vote in open and blanket primaries. They may not vote in closed primaries, which are limited only to members of the respective parties. (Democrats may vote only in the Democratic primary and Republicans may vote only in the Republican primary).

(B) There is no such primary election as the one described in this answer choice. See the explanation for (E).

(C) See the explanation for (E).

(D) There is no such primary election as the one described in this answer choice. See the explanation for (E).

42. **D** The FECA was intended to reduce the influence of money on election campaigns by limiting donations from individuals, corporations, and interest groups. To achieve this goal, the FECA allowed interest groups to form political action committees to advance their political goals. These PACs are subject to donation limits. As a result, thousands of new PACs arose to solicit funds for various causes. Consequently, money became an even more important factor in elections.

Incorrect Answers:

(A) This answer describes an intended result of the FECA.

(B) This answer describes an intended result of the FECA.

(C) The amount of money spent on televised campaign advertising continues to increase from election to election.

(E) Since the passage of the FECA, there have been several credible third-party candidates, for example, John Anderson in 1980 and Ross Perot in 1992. The FECA does not appear to have dampened third-party presidential efforts.

43. C Politicians need to reach the public for a number of reasons: to rally support and to publicize their reelection efforts, to name two. Political reporters need politicians as well: Without quotes to put in their news stories and confidential information from political insiders, the media would not be able to report the news. Each group needs the other, a fact that softens the antagonistic nature of their relationship.

Incorrect Answers:

(A) There is no real distinction between younger and older politicians' comfort level with the media. Some of the most savvy handlers of the press are older politicians, whose experiences have taught them how to manipulate the press.

(B) The First Amendment prevents the government from regulating press activity in nearly all situations.

(D) Most media outlets will gladly cover a story embarrassing to a politician if they believe their audiences are interested. For one obvious example, consider the coverage of Bill Clinton's affair with Monica Lewinsky.

(E) Most government activity is accessible to the public. When information is classified, it tends to exacerbate the antagonistic relationship between the media and politicians. The media try to uncover the classified information (to find out whether it is newsworthy), much to the annoyance of the government.

44. D The Twenty-Sixth Amendment to the Constitution established a uniform voting age of 18 for the entire nation. This answer states the facts incorrectly.

Incorrect Answers:

(A) Many people in this age bracket attend college out of state. This requires them to either register in the new state (some states will not allow such students to register, requiring them to vote in their old home states instead) or vote in their former state of residence by absentee ballot. Both of these procedures are complicated enough to discourage some from voting.

(B) Many people in this age bracket move frequently, requiring them to register at their new place of residence. Some do not, preferring instead not to vote.

(C) Many people in this age bracket simply do not see the pertinence of most political issues to their daily lives. This results in a lower voting rate.

(E) People in this age bracket serving in the military must vote by absentee ballot. This discourages some from voting.

45.   **E**   A political issue's salience is defined as the degree to which it is important to a particular individual or group. For a discussion of the different aspects of public opinion on issues, see Chapter 5.

Incorrect Answers:

(A)   While the media can influence an issue's saliency, the amount of media coverage does not define it.

(B)   Choice (B) presents the definition of a political issue's stability.

(C)   The number of people affected by a political issue doesn't define its salience. Sometimes political issues have a direct affect on people's lives, but they are unaware of the issue and its degree of importance.

(D)   The degree to which an issue can be addressed by government action speaks to central concepts of the scope of government power, but it is not an accurate definition of salience.

46.   **C**   Among its traditional constituencies, the Democratic Party has the weakest hold on the south, where the party's progressive social policies are often at odds with the general conservatism of the region. For decades, the Democratic Party could count on solid support from the south merely because the Republican Party was "the party of Lincoln" and was thus "responsible" for the Civil War. In recent years, however, the Republican Party has made major inroads in the region.

Incorrect Answers:

(A)   People holding advanced academic degrees generally support the liberal social policies advanced by traditional Democrats.

(B)   Northeastern city dwellers generally support the liberal social policies advanced by traditional Democrats.

(D)   Jewish Americans generally support the liberal social policies advanced by traditional Democrats.

(E)   Urban African Americans generally support the liberal social policies advanced by traditional Democrats.

47.   **B**   If you have studied Latin, that will come in handy with this question. The U.S. Supreme Court only reviews cases on appeal if four of the nine justices agree to review it. If so, the court issues a writ of *certiorari*, which functions as a request for lower court transcripts of a case.

Incorrect Answers:

(A)   *Habeas corpus* is incorrect because it is a legal term used to describe the principle that an accused person must be brought before a judge in criminal court.

(C)   *Amicus curiae* briefs are legal documents filed by third parties in the hope of swaying the court toward one decision or the other.

(D) Judicial review is a power that permits the U.S. Supreme Court to repeal congressional legislation that it finds unconstitutional—definitely not the correct answer here.

(E) Judicial activism describes judges who often use judicial review to repeal congressional legislation, so this choice can be eliminated also.

48. **E** This 1978 case concerned a white male who had been denied admission to the University of California at Davis medical school. The student, Alan Bakke, discovered that Davis had reserved 16 of the 100 slots in the class specifically for minority students. Bakke discovered further that some of the students admitted in those slots had lower MCAT scores and college GPAs than him. Bakke argued reverse discrimination, pointing out that minority students could compete for all 100 slots in the class but that he could compete for only 84, resulting in an unfair reduction of his chances of admission. The court agreed with Bakke, but its decision was a complicated one that still allowed colleges to use affirmative action, so long as they did so in the name of diversity and avoided setting quotas.

Incorrect Answers:

(A) 1961's *Tinker v. Des Moines* upheld students' constitutional rights within schools, specifically the right to protest.

(B) 1962's *Engel v. Vitale* case prohibited the state-sponsored recitation of prayer in public schools.

(C) 1995's *United States v. Lopez* held that Congress does not have the power to regulate guns near state-operated schools.

(D) *Regents of University of California v. Bakke* did not address the rights of disabled students.

49. **D** Thomas Jefferson's Declaration of Independence reflects John Locke's philosophy regarding natural rights and the participation of the individual in politics.

Incorrect Answers:

(A) Thomas Hobbes held a pessimistic view of humanity and favored a strong monarchy with limitations on individual liberty.

(B) Niccolo Macchiavelli wrote *The Prince*, which advocates a strong, centralized leader, and an "ends justify the means" school of political thought.

(C) Jonathan Edwards, an early colonial theologian, felt that rights were granted to people by God, not by government.

(E) John Calvin, a protestant reformer, advocated a theocractic type of government.

50. **B** In the most famous of *The Federalist Papers*, James Madison bemoaned the evils of political factions and explained how a federal republic, by dividing power among many parties, minimizes the damage that factions can cause. AP U.S. Government and Politics questions referring to *The Federalist Papers* almost invariably center on this essay and, more particularly, on this point. Make sure you know it.

Incorrect Answers:

(A) In addition to not being what Madison wrote, this wouldn't reduce the danger of a faction so much as make it impossible for new ones to form.

(C) Madison did not stipulate that all factions had to be equally represented.

(D) Madison argued that political factions were dangerous at any level, not just the federal one.

(E) This is a form of regulation that is a danger in of itself.

51. **C** As a president enters the final two years of his second term, his political influence diminishes. Through the second midterm election of his tenure, the president carries considerable influence with the electorate and therefore can persuade Congress to cooperate through threats (such as "I will campaign against you, and you will lose"). Once that threat has passed, the president, no longer able to run for reelection, loses political capital. Congress accordingly defers to him less frequently. A president saddled with a Congress led by the opposing party will also experience a diminution in power because his ability to implement his programs will meet a challenge from the legislature. Bill Clinton proved adept at accomplishing some goals despite opposition from a Republican Congress; nonetheless, divided control of the legislative and executive branches unquestionably weakens a president.

Incorrect Answers:

(A) As noted in the discussion of (C), this is true, but it's not the only reason.

(B) International crises often do exactly the opposite, which is to strengthen the president's position. Congress is often reluctant to challenge a president when the United States is challenged abroad, preferring instead to present a unified front to the world.

(D) See the explanation for (B).

(E) Presidents always thrive when the economy is strong and approval ratings are high. Because the United States is a republican democracy, popularity confers substantial political power because popularity translates into votes.

52. **E** Senators have much greater leeway to alter legislation on the Senate floor than representatives have on the House floor. The size of the House prohibits lengthy debate and a prolonged amendment process. To complete its work on legislation, the House imposes strict rules on floor debates and amendments. All such work in the House is done in committee, making a representative's committee assignments a critical aspect of his or her ability to accomplish political goals.

Incorrect Answers:

(A) Like senators, House members may serve on several committees simultaneously.

(B) Senate committee members enjoy all the same powers as House committee members.

(C) The committee system works in roughly the same manner in both legislative chambers. A Senate bill does not have to pass through every committee. Were this procedure in place, it would certainly grind the legislative process to a halt.

(D) A special committee assigns committee membership in the Senate. The House uses the same procedure.

53. **D** Third parties arise primarily out of discontent with the two major parties. The Republicans, for example, arose to represent Northern abolitionists, who could not find a voice in either of the two major parties of the 1840s and 1850s. The Populists gave farmers a political outlet in the 1890s; the Socialists represented disaffected workers in the early 1900s.

Incorrect Answers:

(A) During times of prosperity, most Americans pay little attention to politics. The interest level of most Americans is too low during such periods to support a third party.

(B) While some third parties fit this description, most do not.

(C) Unless you count the Republicans as a third party, no third party has ever won a majority of seats in Congress. By the time a party accomplishes this feat, it has become one of the two major parties.

(E) While some third parties fit this description, most do not.

54. **E** The dual judicial system of the United States encompasses state and federal courts. Usually the two domains remain distinct, but some crimes are prosecutable in both systems. Recently, the federal government has sought to correct perceived injustices in state courts—primarily in high-profile acquittals—by prosecuting the accused in federal court. Some such defendants include the police officers who were captured on videotape beating Rodney King in Los Angeles, and a young African American who stabbed a rabbinical student in Brooklyn during a racially charged riot. In these and other similar cases, the government charges the accused with violating the civil rights of their victims, thereby bringing the case within the jurisdiction of the federal courts.

Incorrect Answers:

(A) The constitutional prohibition of double jeopardy prevents state prosecutors from appealing a case in which the defendant is found not guilty.

(B) The double jeopardy clause would seem to prevent such double prosecutions but does not for the reasons given in the explanation for (E).

(C) New evidence alone cannot provide grounds for a new trial unless it can be proven that the accused in some way participated in hiding the evidence. If this were not the case, the government could theoretically withhold evidence from a trial. If the government did not get the "guilty" verdict it desired, it could then introduce the new evidence and try the defendant again.

(D) Governors may pardon convicts, but they may not veto "not guilty" verdicts.

55. **A** Both houses of Congress have standing committees that handle government oversight. Other committees provide oversight in the course of their business as they review the actions of regulatory agencies and other executive departments whose work coincides with the committee's area of concern. Oversight by the full body of either house would simply be too time-consuming, which is why oversight is performed in committee.

Incorrect Answers:

(B) Congress oversees the workings of the federal government, particularly the executive branch. The states have not challenged this power of oversight.

(C) Congressional oversight focuses primarily on the executive branch.

(D) Constituent input influences nearly everything that Congress does, including performing its oversight duties.

(E) Congressional oversight focuses primarily on the executive branch. Both houses maintain committees on ethics to regulate and discipline errant legislators.

56. **D** The fundamentalist vote is largely Republican, in large part because of Ronald Reagan's and George W. Bush's efforts to win these voters with their conservative social agendas.

Incorrect Answers:

(A) The Democratic commitment to poverty relief programs attracts minority voters, many of whom are disproportionately represented in lower-income groups.

(B) Women support Democratic candidates more frequently than do men. The Democratic Party's commitment to gender issues such as equal pay and maternity leave has helped the party in this area.

(C) The Democratic commitment to poverty relief programs, along with Republican antagonism toward such programs, persuades many poor Americans to vote Democratic.

(E) The conservative social agenda of the Republican Party, combined with the Democratic commitment to government-enforced equal rights, persuades many homosexuals to vote Democratic.

57. **A** Iron triangles—also called *subgovernments*—result from the workings of particular federal agencies, congressional committees that provide oversight for those agencies, and related public interest groups. Members of these groups forge relationships through constant interaction and form a strong bond because they are often pursuing the same goals. Consider the example cited by the question. Advocacy groups for small businesses pursue legislation beneficial to their constituents. The Small Business Administration champions these goals, both for the benefit of small businesses and because new small business initiatives strengthen the agency (by providing it with new tasks to perform). Congressional committees dealing with small business issues support the goals as a means of serving an important constituency: those who own or work at small businesses. This type of alliance can grow extremely powerful, dominating a particular area of policy.

Incorrect Answers:

(B) A *conference committee* is a committee composed of members of the House and Senate. Conference committees meet when the House and Senate have passed differing versions of the same bill. Their goal is to work out a compromise bill that both houses can pass.

(C) A *regulatory agency* regulates a particular area of policy. The Environmental Protection Agency, the Nuclear Regulatory Commission, and the Federal Communications Commission are some examples of regulatory agencies. Regulatory agencies are part of the executive branch of government.

(D) The term *dual federalism* refers to a federal system in which the national and local governments have separate and distinct responsibilities.

(E) A third party is a political party other than the Democratic or Republican parties.

58. **B** To protect federal judges from political influence, the Framers of the Constitution gave judges tenure for life. Judges serve "during good behavior" and can be removed from office only by impeachment.

Incorrect Answers:

(A) A federal judge serves a life-long term.

(C) A federal judge is nominated by the president and then confirmed by Congress; there is no electoral process.

(D) As noted in the explanation for (B), a judge can, under certain extreme situations, be removed from office.

(E) See the explanation for (C).

59. D Guidelines issued by the Rules Committee strictly limit debate in the House; in most cases, representatives may speak on a bill for no more than five minutes. A *filibuster* is a speech of indefinite length, given by a senator in an effort to derail a particular Senate action, or to force a concession on that action. A three-fifths majority vote is required to end debate (such a vote is called a vote of *cloture*). A cloture vote is one of only two means to end a filibuster. The other is a unanimous consent agreement.

Incorrect Answers:

(A) The Senate prides itself on having greater civility than the House, but this decorousness does not extend to suffering interminable speeches without protest.

(B) House sessions are roughly the same length as Senate sessions.

(C) Sessions of both chambers are open to the public.

(E) All members of the House, not just the speaker, may speak on the floor of the chamber.

60. C The Constitution requires that a census be taken every 10 years for the express purpose of apportioning seats in the House of Representatives. See Article I, Section 2, paragraph 3 of the Constitution.

Incorrect Answers:

(A) State legislatures are responsible for redrawing congressional districts.

(B) Redistricting has huge political ramifications. Seats in Congress are won and lost depending on where the lines are drawn, and whichever party is in power attempts to redraw the districts to its political advantage. This occasionally results in oddly shaped districts whose constituents have little in common other than their political party.

(D) The Supreme Court has interpreted the Voting Rights Act to mean that states must consider racial demographics when redrawing districts, to remedy previous practices used to artificially reduce minority representation in the House. The result of this ruling has been to dramatically increase minority representation in the House.

(E) Legislators' chief concern in redistricting is political outcomes, not allowing neighbors to be in the same district. Opposite sides of a street may fall into different districts.

FREE-RESPONSE SECTION: ANSWERS AND EXPLANATIONS

Question 1

You receive full credit for this free response if you correctly identify two of the four congressional actions mentioned in the question and accurately assess the effectiveness of each of those legislative actions.

The Equal Pay Act of 1963

The Equal Pay Act outlaws wage discrimination based on gender. The law also outlaws wage discrimination based on skin color, religion, or nationality (you need not mention the latter fact in your response to receive full credit, but it is useful information).

Here are several assessments of the effectiveness of the Equal Pay Act of 1963. Your essay needs to include only one accurate assessment to receive full credit.

- The law increased awareness of the problem of unequal pay for equal work. It persuaded some employers to end wage discrimination in their businesses.
- The law was initially difficult to enforce. It requires women to file a complaint against their employer, an action many workers hesitate to take for fear of reprisal (firing, workplace harassment, and so on).
- Because the law did not prohibit employment discrimination, it allowed employers to favor men in hiring for prestigious, higher-paying jobs. Thus, the law did little to remedy the fundamental problem of workplace discrimination. Even after the Equal Pay Act became law, women remained "ghettoized" in low-paying clerical, teaching, and nursing jobs.
- As the government passed more civil liberties laws and as the public grew more aware and supportive of gender rights issues, the Equal Pay Act became a useful tool for those fighting for women's rights.

The Civil Rights Act of 1964

The Civil Rights Act prohibits employment discrimination based on gender. The difference between the Equal Pay Act and the Civil Rights Act is that the Equal Pay Act did not prevent employers from awarding better jobs to men based on gender. Instead, it merely required them to pay the same wages to men and women performing the same jobs. The Civil Rights Act corrected this problem. The law also outlaws employment discrimination based on skin color, religion, or nationality (again, you need not mention this in your essay to receive credit, but it is good to know). The following are several assessments of the Civil Rights Act.

- The law increased awareness of the problem of gender discrimination in hiring. It persuaded some employers to end gender discrimination in their businesses.
- The law did not immediately end gender discrimination. Enforcement required legal action, which in turn required women to complain when they believed they had been victims of gender discrimination. Because of the time, effort, expense, and risk involved in lodging such a complaint, many women were unwilling to do so.

- Although the Civil Rights Act changed the law, it did not change the deeply ingrained attitudes of employers, judges, government officials, and so on. This proved another obstacle to enforcement. At least in its early years, enforcement of the gender discrimination provisions of the Civil Rights Act of 1964 met with considerable institutional resistance.
- Eventually, as societal attitudes toward gender issues changed, the Civil Rights Act of 1964 became a powerful tool in forcing businesses to change their hiring practices. The law, in combination with the Equal Pay Act, proved a powerful tool for those willing to sue businesses over discrimination.
- The United States has not achieved gender equality in the workplace; therefore, the Civil Rights Act of 1964 has not been entirely effective.

The Lilly Ledbetter Fair Pay Act of 2009

The Ledbetter Act strengthened protections under the Civil Rights Act of 1964 after the Supreme Court ruled Lilly Ledbetter was not entitled to sue for discriminatory pay under the 1964 law as written. Here are some assessments of the Ledbetter Act.

- The Ledbetter Act was a much needed enhancement to the Civil Rights Act of 1964 and helps provide women with more protection under the law.
- The Ledbetter Act was another half-measure that, while expanding existing protections for women, still falls short of offering the ironclad promise of equality that the failed Equal Rights Amendment would have.
- The Ledbetter Act represents an unnecessary intrusion of government into the world of business because existing rules under the Civil Rights Act of 1964 already offered women an avenue for redress in issues of discriminatory pay. Women who didn't file suit within the set time limit under the 1964 law have rightly forfeited their chance to complain.

Title IX of the Higher Education Act of 1972

Title IX prohibits gender discrimination at colleges and universities that receive federal aid. Here are some assessments of Title IX.

- Title IX employed the federal government's most powerful enforcement tool: the cessation of federal aid. Because noncompliant schools risk losing essential funding, Title IX has been easier to enforce than either the Equal Pay Act or the Civil Rights Act. The threat of lost funding is a powerful one.
- Title IX ended public funding for all-male schools, increased financial aid to female students, and encouraged the development of women's studies and other gender-related academic disciplines. It has had a tremendous impact on college athletics. On some campuses it has dramatically increased funding to women's sports programs. On others, it has resulted in a reduction of men's programs (to erase the difference between spending on men's and women's programs).
- Congress strengthened Title IX in 1988 by passing a law stating that all programs at a school are subject to Title IX even if only one or two programs at the school receive federal funding. This action, taken in response to a Supreme Court ruling, increased the effectiveness of Title IX in eliminating gender bias on publicly funded campuses.

The Equal Rights Amendment to the Constitution

The ERA would have inserted into the Constitution a prohibition against all gender discrimination. Although it received the necessary support in Congress, it did not receive the required approval from three-fourths of the states. Here are some assessments of the ERA.

- The Equal Rights Amendment generated a tremendous amount of public interest in the gender rights issue. By placing the issue at the forefront of the public agenda, the ERA made it easier for women's rights activists to publicize their message.
- The Equal Rights Amendment also generated considerable opposition to the women's rights movement. This may have reinforced gender bias in some quarters.
- The Equal Rights Amendment failed to gain the necessary support of three-quarters of the states. In this regard, the ERA was a failure.
- The struggle for the ERA (and the public outcry in the aftermath of its failure) resulted in the passage of numerous state-level anti-gender–bias laws. Sixteen states now have equal rights amendments in their constitutions. Considered in this light, the ERA was effective in advancing the cause of gender equality.

Here's How to Crack It

1. Since the 1960s, Congress has addressed the problem of gender bias on numerous occasions.
   (a) Choose one of the laws listed below. Describe how it has attempted to address the problem of gender bias in American society.
      - the Equal Pay Act of 1963
      - the Civil Rights Act of 1964
   (b) Describe this law and evaluate its effectiveness.
   (c) Choose one of the legislative actions listed below. Describe how it has attempted to address the problem of gender bias in American society.
      - Title IX of the Higher Education Act of 1973
      - the Equal Rights Amendment to the Constitution
   (d) Describe this action and evaluate its effectiveness.

Describe two of the four congressional actions accurately and then state one reason why they were or were not effective in addressing the problem of gender bias.

Sample Excellent Free Response

While most of the major civil rights advancements of the 20th century were spearheaded by the Supreme Court, Congress also played a prominent role. More specifically, it has addressed the issue of gender rights on many occasions. Among the most prominent examples of its efforts are the Equal Pay Act of 1963 and Title IX of the Higher Education Act.

The Equal Pay Act of 1963 outlaws wage discrimination based on sex. Before the Equal Pay Act, it was legal to pay women and men different amounts for doing the same jobs. The feminist movement in the United States did not become very strong until the 1970s, but there was still support in Congress for the act—even if most justified its passage due to economic considerations. Interestingly enough, one of the major reasons for the bill's passage was to prevent employers from using women as a source of cheap labor that would depress the prevailing wage.

How effective was the Equal Pay Act? At first, it was not very good at preventing the payment disparities it was designed to eliminate. It was difficult to enforce and forced injured parties to engage in time-consuming litigation against their employers. It also failed to get at the deeper problem of sex discrimination, because employers were still allowed to discriminate when it came to hiring. So rather than pay a man more than a woman for doing the same job, the employer could just promote the man and then pay him the appropriate (male) wage for the new job. As the women's movement became more powerful with the passage of the Civil Rights Act of 1964, the Equal Pay Act became increasingly effective. Still, in 2009, Congress had to pass the Lilly Ledbetter Fair Pay Act to combat continuing discrimination.

Title IX of the Higher Education Act is one of the most controversial laws passed in recent time. The law itself called for an end to sex discrimination in schools and threatened to cut off federal funding to any school, college or university that engaged in discriminatory practices. Because many schools, public and private, are very reliant on federal funds, they complied quite readily.

The question of effectiveness needs to be broadened to the issue of athletics. In 1979, the Department of Health defined Title IX as requiring schools to spend equal amounts of money on male and female athletics. Because far fewer women have joined sports teams, this has forced many schools to kill male sports that are less popular (like wrestling or track) in order to keep the proportion of spending the same. Critics claim that this quota system is devastating male sports for no good reason, while defenders say that Title IX has led to increased spending that resulted in a generation of empowered athletic American women.

Question 2

No doubt your AP teacher put a big emphasis on federalism at the beginning of the year. Remember the Federalists and the Anti-Federalists? Simply put, federalism is the power that the federal government has in relation to state governments. Over time, more and more power has tended to gravitate away from the states and toward Washington, DC.

After you define federalism for part (a), your paragraph for part (b) should include some of the following:

- **Articles of Confederation**—The Articles of Confederation gave very little power to the federal government. For instance, it could not levy taxes. Bonus points if you mentioned **Shay's Rebellion (1786)**, a Massachusetts farmers' rebellion that pointed out the weakness of the Articles and bolstered the **Federalist** cause to create a stronger federal government.
- **Revolutionary war debt**—Since the early federal government could not levy taxes, it proved incapable of paying off war debts. This weakened the economy in early America and hindered the progress of the new Republic.
- **Bill of Rights (1787)**—The first ten Amendments to the Constitution were demanded by Anti-Federalists to serve as a bulwark against excessive federal power. The Tenth Amendment specifically grants all powers not delegated to the federal government to revert back to the sovereignty of individual states.

- **James Madison**—Fourth president and "Father of the Constitution," he co-authored the **Federalist Papers** (along with **Alexander Hamilton** and **John Jay**). Interestingly, Madison started out as a Federalist, favoring a strong central government, then converted to Anti-Federalism in 1791, joining **Thomas Jefferson** in the newly formed (**Anti-Federalist**) **Democratic-Republican** Party.

- **Geographical and cultural influences**—Generally speaking, Federalists tended to be wealthy, Northern, and engaged in trade with Europe. They favored a strong central government in order to ensure a steady economic relationship with foreign powers, a strong military in order to protect national interests, and a national bank. Anti-Federalists, such as Jefferson, were oriented to more local economic interests, such as farming, real estate, and small business. They viewed federal power as a potential threat to or in conflict with local interests and preferred to put power in the hands of states and local municipalities. Power, they maintained, once given to the federal government, could not easily be wrested from it.

- **Loose Constructionism**—Putting more power in the hands of the federal government requires a flexible interpretation of the Constitution, since the Constitution does not explicitly grant many powers to Washington, DC (though it does not forbid them, either). The creation of the **First National Bank** by **Alexander Hamilton**, for instance, was opposed by Anti-Federalists who tend toward **strict constructionism** (limitation of federal power to only powers enumerated in Article I).

- **Alien and Sedition Acts**—Now perceived as a federal overreach, these Acts criminalized certain forms of speech deemed critical of the federal government. Federalists defended the Acts on the basis of national security. Anti-Federalists asserted that the Sedition Act was designed to suppress them. Jefferson and Madison wrote the **Virginia and Kentucky Resolutions** asserting the states' rights to nullify laws if they were tyrannical or unconstitutional.

- **Louisiana Purchase (1803)**—No doubt a positive manifestation of Federalism, the Louisiana Purchase doubled the size of the United States. Such a vast tract of land could not have been acquired without federal money and influence. Napolean ceded the Louisiana Territory in exchange for cash and debt forgiveness.

- **War of 1812**—If you're feeling ambitious, the War of 1812 is an interesting study in federalism. On the one hand, Federalists opposed the War, since they desired to maintain good trade relationships with England and France. Ironically, though, their opposition to the War weakened public opinion of Federalists, culminating in the fateful Hartford Convention, where Federalists protested the War. Meanwhile, General Andrew Jackson "won" the Battle of New Orleans, England surrendered, and the Federalists were perceived as short-sighted and weak. As a side note, the War of 1812 was difficult to wage, since the federal government still lacked the cash and military might to wage a large-scale war against a major European power.

- **Taxation/Debt**—Increased federal power inevitably leads to national taxation and debt. Anti-Federalists argued that it is oppressive to tax working people to pay off wealthy bankers. Federalists argued that a strong central government benefits everyone, including the working poor.

- *McCulloch v. Maryland* (1819)—Under Supreme Court Chief Justice John Marshall, this case allowed the Federal government to pass laws not explicitly mentioned in the Constitution. It grants to Congress **implied powers** in order to create a functioning national government. The case stopped the state of Maryland's tax on the Second Bank of the United States. The court ruled that this was a form of nullification that impeded the functioning of the federal government.

- **Chief Justice Roger B. Taney (1836–1864)**—Chief Justice Taney, a Jacksonian Democrat and advocate of states' rights, was the successor to Marshall, who tended toward the promotion of federal power. Taney's decisions largely prevented use of federal power that would restrict individual rights, although he is well known for the infamous *Dred Scott* decision, which ruled that slaves were not citizens. Taney was opposed to a national bank.

Your paragraph for part (c) should include some of the following:

- **Land-grant colleges**—This is an interesting example of federalism, since both the federal and state governments worked together to create colleges devoted to agricultural education, most of which today are thriving state universities. Federal land paired with state administration and funding encouraged land-grant colleges to prosper. Other primary schools, too, have occasionally been recipients of federal land.
- **National Banking Acts of 1863–1866**—After the expiration of the Second Bank of the United States, this series of acts permanently established a nationally regulated banking system and a national currency.
- **Sixteenth Amendment (1913)**—This amendment arguably expanded federal power more than any other law had done up to this point, since it allowed Congress to levy a broad-based tax on personal and business income. For the first time, all Americans with income could be required to participate in the financial maintenance of government bureaucracy. The federal budget has expanded rapidly since the passage of a national income tax.
- **Seventeenth Amendment (1913)**—This amendment ended the practice of the election of senators by state legislatures and provided for the direct election of senators by citizens at the ballot box. Although the amendment certainly gave more power to the populous, it took power away from state legislatures, thus radically altering the balance of federalism up to that point. Those who favored the amendment argued that it diminished the influence of corruption and cronyism at the state level. Opponents argued that direct election of senators would allow senators to disregard the concerns of their home states.
- **New Deal (1993–1938)**—A tremendous assertion of federal power, the New Deal enacted various federally funded programs to help rebuild the American economy after the Great Depression. President Franklin D. Roosevelt's national government needed state and local government cooperation in order to implement its policies. The New Deal was highly controversial both because it required a significant outlay of federal dollars in order to succeed and because it bypassed state legislatures. President Lyndon Johnson's **Great Society** welfare programs of the 1960s were controversial for the same reasons.
- **Block grants (1980s)**—President Ronald Reagan attempted to turn some power back to the states by distributing federal money in the form of block grants. Unlike previous grants which greatly restricted the way federal money could be spent, block grants allowed states to spend money the way they see fit.
- **Decriminalization/Legalization of marijuana (1990s to present)**—Various states' attempts to legalize marijuana for either medicinal or recreational use have tested the boundaries of federalism in a power struggle that is not yet resolved. Several states currently have laws which allow for the medicinal cultivation, possession, and use of marijuana, while Colorado has legalized its use for recreational purposes. Federal law, however, does not officially acknowledge these state laws. Federal agents are still legally allowed to raid growers and users, though enforcement has been inconsistent. As more states follow Colorado's lead, this will no doubt continue to be an important test of the balance of state and federal power.
- **Gun control**—Gun control is an interesting example of the see-saw of federalism. The Second Amendment of the Constitution guarantees the individual right to keep and bear arms, while states and cities have broad latitude to limit ownership in certain locales, set requirements for ownership of guns, and need not recognize the gun laws of other states. The federal government, on the other hand, asserts its authority upon states by requiring background checks, forbidding the ownership of guns by felons, and banning the possession of guns on school property.

Sample Excellent Free Response

Federalism in the United States refers to the balance of power between Washington, D.C., and the state and local governments which regulate issues of local importance. In the early days of the Republic, the federal government had virtually no control over the states. States coined their own money, levied taxes, and functioned virtually as independent republics. The Articles of Confederation were the first attempt to unify the states, but gave little authority to the federal government. In 1787, the Constitutional Convention convened in Philadelphia and drafted the Constitution, a substitute for the weak Articles of Confederation. Federalists such as James Madison and Alexander Hamilton argued that a strong federal government was necessary to ensure a strong defense, while Anti-Federalists such as Thomas Jefferson feared the possible ramifications of federal power. The Bill of Rights is recognized as a victory for Anti-Federalists and was a necessary compromise for the passage of the newly drafted Constitution. Since the writing of the Constitution, federalism has continued to provoke controversy.

In the years before the Civil War, the controversy over federal power often divided along geographical lines. Federalists were often wealthy Northerners from established English families who sought to wield power in Washington, D.C. John Adams was elected president under the Federalist Party platform and even George Washington was not opposed to Federalist principles. Federalists saw centralized power has crucial to maintaining positive trade relationships with Europe and ensuring the stability of the national economy. Alexander Hamilton advocated for the establishment of a national bank and uniform currencies. These endeavors did not require violating the Constitution, but did require going beyond its explicit mandates. Chief Justice John Marshall reinforced the principles of federalism by expanding the federal regulation of industry, commerce, and banking. He also established the principle of "judicial review" which allowed the Supreme Court to override state legislation.

Anti-Federalists tended to be Southern and/or oriented toward agricultural interests. President Thomas Jefferson dramatically cut the size of the federal government during his tenure. As slavery became more controversial, Anti-Federalists relied on the principle of states' rights to defend their local economic interests. One could argue that the Civil War was the ultimate conflict over federalism. Abraham Lincoln and other Republicans wanted to keep the South under the umbrella of federal power, while Anti-Federalist Democrats wanted the freedom to decide their own affairs. As we all know, the South lost the war, and federal power continued to advance.

Although there are few people in the modern era who call themselves "federalists" or "anti-federalists," the balance of power continues to play an important role in American politics. An important example from the 20th Century is President Franklin D. Roosevelt's New Deal. The New Deal sought to restore the health of the American economy prior to the stock market crash of 1929. New Deal programs, such as Social Security, work programs, and unemployment compensation, were passed without the involvement of the states, yet required state cooperation in order to succeed. As with all federal programs, they required tax revenue to sustain themselves. Republicans of that era (unlike the Republicans of Lincoln's time) were suspicious of federal programs and spending and opposed Roosevelt's policies. Some of his plans were overturned by the Supreme Court, but some survive to this day. The passage of a national income tax, along with the New Deal, may well be the greatest examples of federal expansion in American history.

Federal power has no doubt expanded greatly in American history, although we are by no means a federal monolith. There are still fifty states with their own distinct constitutions, tax policies, and legislative agendas. American government thrives on a variety of approaches to problem-solving. Time will tell how citizens and states respond to federal power in the future.

Question 3

The prompt starts out by stating a fact: "The media have a large influence on American politics." This is a given, and so there's no point arguing with it. All you have to do here is describe *why* the media are important, give three *specific* examples of their importance over the last twenty years, and determine whether the media excessively cover trivial events at the expense of more substantial news.

The first thing you'll want to do is come up with a list of reasons why the media have so much power in the world of American politics as well as the different forms that media take:

- Most Americans do not have the time, energy, or motivation to watch live coverage of Congress in action, or to dig through the public pronouncements of government agencies. Therefore, the media do these things and present the information to the public.
- Indeed, the word "media" is related to the words *medium* and *middle*. And the role of the media is to stand between the universe of things happening in the world and the people who consume some section of those events, presented in the form of news.
- There are a broad variety of sources for news about politics. Traditionally, news in the United States was purveyed by newspapers and other printed publications. Today, many people still get their news from papers like *The New York Times*, *The Wall Street Journal*, and *USA Today*. Additionally, news-magazines like *Time*, *Newsweek*, and *The Economist* also shape how many Americans get their news. The advent of newer technologies has led to news being delivered via radio, television, and now the Internet.
- Currently, the traditional model of news reporting seems as if it may be in jeopardy. Many of the largest print publications in the United States are losing money at a dramatic rate, television audiences are dwindling as more people watch niche cable channels, and Internet news still generally fails to turn a profit.
- Nevertheless, the media are still often called "the fourth branch of government" for good reason. Whether it is answering the question of who should run for president, evaluating whether a government program is being mismanaged, or determining if a section of the economy is crying out for increased regulation, it is the media that control the agenda.

Next, you'll need to think of three examples of media coverage that have shaped American politics over the past 30 years. There are thousands of examples. Below are some that might work for this response.

- The story of the rise of Barack Obama
- The dissemination of a secretly recorded tape of Mitt Romney remarking that 47% of Americans are "dependent upon government" during the 2012 presidential campaign
- The collapse of the American economy in 2008
- The bungling of the Iraq War and discovery of abuse photos from the American-run prison Abu Ghraib
- The attacks of September 11, 2001
- The controversial 2000 election and the Florida recount
- President Clinton's infidelities and impeachment
- The 1994 Republican Revolution
- Saddam Hussein's invasion of Kuwait
- The Iran-Contra Affair
- Reagan and supply-side economics
- John Edward's infidelities and campaign finance violation charges

The third part of the prompt asks for an evaluation of whether the media covers news that is really significant. This judgment call can be easily added to the end of the response.

Here's How to Crack It

3. The media have a large influence on American politics.

   (a) Describe why the media are so important and why they have such influence.
   (b) Identify and describe THREE examples of media coverage that have influenced American politics in the past twenty-five years.
   (c) Explain the argument that in politics, the media tend to overemphasize stories that are easy to tell at the expense of those that are more complicated.

Choose your position. Brainstorm a list of examples that support your position. Choose three that you would like to write about. Make sure to clearly identify your examples. Remember that the question specifies that your examples must be drawn from the previous two decades. Do not provide examples that are more than ten years old. Do not write about more than three examples. Graders can give you credit only for three, no matter how many more you come up with.

Write an introductory paragraph explaining your position. Follow with one paragraph for each of your three examples. Write a conclusion if you have time.

Sample Excellent Free Response

There is no question that the media has an inordinate influence in American political life, and this influence happens for very good reason. First, it is important to remember that most Americans work full-time jobs and don't think about politics all that often. As a result, there is a need for those who can digest the massive amount of information that exists about government, curate it, and present it in an easy-to-digest form. This is the role of the media. There is simply no way that Americans could get a handle on what is happening in their government if the media was not there to point the way.

Media coverage has dramatically shaped American political life in a number of ways over the last thirty years, and perhaps nowhere as dramatically as our involvement in Iraq. Things got started when stories appeared in all the major news publications and broadcast outlets about Saddam Hussein's invasion of the small kingdom of Kuwait on August 2, 1990. "This aggression will not stand," declared President George H. W. Bush. He proceeded to create a multinational coalition of armies led by the United States, a coalition that easily defeated Hussein's forces in a matter of months—protecting the freedom of the Kuwaitis as well as the world oil supply. Nevertheless, Bush was criticized roundly for failing to depose Hussein as well as allowing Shi'a rebels who opposed the Hussein regime in southern Iraq to be brutally crushed.

Eleven years later, nineteen hijackers successfully attacked the United States, bringing about the destruction of the World Trade Center in New York as well as thousands of fatalities. After an initial attack on Afghanistan, the media quickly focused on the danger that Iraq presented, particularly if it had weapons of mass destruction (WMDs). After all, if 19 men and some airplanes could kill so many, what damage might a nuclear-armed Saddam Hussein wreak? Reporters like Judith Miller of the *New York Times* repeatedly insinuated that WMDs were present and that they were a major threat to the United States. In no small part, these stories helped to create strong public support for an American invasion of Iraq to topple the Hussein regime.

If the media helped to whip up a firestorm for invasion, they also showed how badly things can go. By 2004–2005, the seemingly quick and easy victory in Iraq had turned into a bloody slog against an increasingly bold rag-tag army of insurgents. A steady drumbeat of bad news from Iraq acted to diminish public support for the war, lowering President Bush's popularity numbers as the months progressed—and making a mockery of the infamous time that he posed in a flight suit on an aircraft carrier with a "Mission Accomplished" banner hanging in the background. The culmination of this bad news was the May 2004 story "Torture at Abu Ghraib," in the *New Yorker*, in which Seymour Hersh uncovered shocking treatment of humiliation and torture photographs of Iraqis by American guards at the Abu Ghraib prison in Baghdad. The accompanying photographs were deeply shocking to many Americans and led to a further reduction in support for the war. The result of all this bad news was the destruction of the Republican majority in Congress in 2006, and the election of Barack Obama in 2008—the most anti-war of the conventional Democratic candidates.

Does the media cover excessively trivial news? This is a difficult question to answer. Inaccurate reporting got us into the Iraq War, but courageous accounts also showed the many difficulties that were wrought by invasion and occupation. In the end, Americans consume news that is most interesting to them, which means some news stories are highly substantial while others are not.

Question 4

You receive full credit if you correctly identify Andrew Johnson and Bill Clinton, state clearly whether Hamilton's quotation applies to each case, and correctly describe and analyze the various roles of the House, Senate, and Supreme Court as effective checks in the impeachment process.

Identification

Clearly identify Andrew Johnson and Bill Clinton as the two impeached presidents in question. Even though the question does not specifically ask you to do so, you will not receive full credit if you fail to cite them both by name.

In Each Case, Is Hamilton's Quotation Accurate?

- Congress impeached Andrew Johnson for violation of the Tenure of Office Act, a law that forbade Johnson to fire certain federal appointees to the executive branch. Johnson fired Secretary of War Stanton, a radical Republican who opposed Johnson's plans for Reconstruction. Hamilton's assessment of the impeachment process accurately describes Johnson's situation. Johnson's impeachment certainly "agitated the passions of the whole community" and "divided it into parties more or less friendly or inimical to the accused." These "pre-existing factions," divided over the nature of Reconstruction, were similarly divided over Johnson's impeachment. Republicans, who held the majority in Congress, lined up against Johnson. Democrats, arguing that the Tenure of Office Act violated the system of checks and balances (by giving Congress undue power over the executive branch), lined up behind Johnson. The outcome was regulated by "the comparative strength of the parties," as the vast Republican majority in the post–Civil War Congress assured Johnson's impeachment and very nearly his conviction by the Senate. Seven senators crossed party lines to vote for Johnson's acquittal, allowing Johnson to escape removal from office by a single vote. The Supreme Court later found the Tenure of Office Act unconstitutional, a fact that further underscores the political nature of Johnson's impeachment.

- Congress impeached Bill Clinton for crimes arising from the cover-up of an extramarital affair. Clinton was accused of having lied about the affair in a deposition in a civil suit and then again before a federal grand jury. He was also accused of encouraging others to lie, thereby obstructing justice, and of using the powers of his office to impede investigations into his wrongdoings. Do Hamilton's statements apply to Clinton's impeachment? Regardless of your personal feelings about Clinton's culpability, you should be ready to acknowledge the accuracy of Hamilton's warnings as they apply to the Clinton impeachment. The congressional vote for Clinton's impeachment fell almost exclusively along party lines, fulfilling Hamilton's warning of "pre-existing factions... [enlisting] all their animosities, partialities, influence, and interest in on one side or the other." You may also point out that Congress rushed its impeachment vote to maintain the Republican party-line advantage. Midterm elections had reduced the Republican majority in the upcoming session, and Republican leaders feared that defections in the next Congress could deny them a majority for impeachment. You may also make the argument that the charges against Clinton, while embarrassing, did not rise to the level of "high crimes and misdemeanors" and were only so defined because of "the comparative strength of parties."

The Effectiveness of the System of Checks and Balances

Simply put, Hamilton's primary concern was that factions, or parties, would taint the impeachment process by infusing it with partisan agenda. The Constitution addresses the problem of factions through the system of checks and balances, which divides power to make it difficult for a faction to gain control of the government.

The Constitution allows for impeachment as a check on the power of the president. But it also places a series of checks in the impeachment process as a protection against hasty or imprudent congressional action. Chief among these checks is the division of trial responsibilities between the two houses of Congress. The House of Representatives is empowered to bring impeachment charges (not only against the president, but also against the vice president and other civilian government officials, including federal judges). Impeachment by the House requires only a majority vote. Impeachment trials occur in the Senate, where a two-thirds majority vote is required for conviction. Thus the system works to make impeachment possible (requiring merely a simple majority vote) but conviction difficult. It also places the ultimate responsibility for determining the fate of the accused in the hands of the Senate, which the Framers regarded as the more cautious and deliberative of the legislative bodies. The chief justice of the Supreme Court presides over impeachment trials. This stipulation serves several purposes. First, it prevents an obvious conflict of interest; if not for this provision, the vice president would preside over the trial as president of the Senate. Additionally, it involves a second branch of government—the judicial branch—in this important process. As a representative of a separate, ostensibly less political branch of government, the chief justice provides a check on Senate power and injects an element of impartiality into a very partisan process.

The system of checks and balances works to prevent the excesses of political factions in the impeachment process. History provides the evidence: Congress has impeached only two presidents, neither of whom was removed from office. In one other instance—that of Richard Nixon—the House would surely have impeached and the Senate may well have convicted the president, had Nixon not resigned first. The charges against Nixon, however, more clearly fit the definition of "high crimes and misdemeanors" than did the charges in either of the two presidential impeachments to reach the Senate.

"The prosecution of [impeachments] will seldom fail to agitate the passions of the whole community, and to divide it into parties more or less friendly or inimical to the accused. In many cases it will connect itself with pre-existing factions, and will enlist all their animosities, partialities, influence, and interest on one side or the other, and in such cases there will always be the greatest danger that the decision will be regulated more by the comparative strength of parties, than by the real demonstrations of innocence or guilt."

—Alexander Hamilton, *Federalist 65*

4. The House of Representatives has twice impeached sitting presidents, both of whom avoided removal from office by the Senate.

   (a) Define impeachment and removal, and describe the process of impeachment and removal as listed in the Constitution.

   (b) Assess the accuracy of Hamilton's observations as applied to both cases of presidential impeachment.

   (c) Explain one strength and one weakness of checks and balances in dealing with Hamilton's concerns.

Correctly identify the two presidents who have been impeached. Do not write about Richard Nixon, as he resigned before the House could impeach him. Recall the basic details of both impeachment trials, being careful to apply Hamilton's quotation to your recollection. Was Hamilton correct or not? Your narratives must address this question. Then discuss the roles of the House of Representatives, Senate, and Supreme Court in the impeachment process. Answer the question: Do they provide sufficient checks and balances against the abuse of power?

Sample Excellent Free Response

In *Federalist 65*, Alexander Hamilton warned that presidential impeachments could be politically motivated. Pointing out that impeachments "will seldom fail to agitate the passions of the whole community," Hamilton observed that pre-existing factions, such as political parties, could use impeachment to advance their political goals, regardless of the validity of their charges. Hamilton's words proved prophetic, accurately foretelling the impeachments of Andrew Johnson and Bill Clinton.

Andrew Johnson was impeached for violating the Tenure of Office Act, which forbade the president to fire certain federal appointees, among them the secretary of war. Johnson ignored the law and fired the secretary of war, who was a holdover from the Lincoln Administration and a political enemy of the president. As Hamilton predicted, Johnson's impeachment "agitated the passions of the whole community" and "divided it into parties more or less friendly or inimical to the accused." Republicans, especially the radical faction of the party, lined up against Johnson, while Democrats supported him. Again, as Hamilton predicted, the outcome of the impeachment was regulated by "the comparative strength of the parties." The vast Republican majority in the post–Civil War Congress assured Johnson's impeachment and very nearly brought about his conviction by the Senate. Johnson won acquittal by a single vote.

Bill Clinton was impeached for crimes arising from the cover-up of an extramarital affair. As did Johnson, Clinton faced accusation by a Congress controlled by his political opposition. The House vote on Clinton's impeachment fell almost entirely along party lines, showing how the process could be influenced by "pre-existing factions...[enlisting] all their animosities, partialities, influence, and interest on one side or the other." Did President Clinton's actions rise to the level of "high crimes and misdemeanors"? Almost every House Republican voted "yes," and almost every House Democrat voted "no." This mirrors Hamilton's observation that such matters could be decided by "the comparative strength of parties [rather] than by real demonstrations of innocence or guilt."

Fortunately, the Framers of the Constitution installed a system of checks and balances to make politically motivated impeachment extremely difficult. In impeachment, the most important check is the division of trial responsibilities between the two houses of Congress. The House of Representatives brings impeachment charges through a majority vote. Impeachment trials occur in the Senate, where a two-thirds majority vote is required for conviction. This system makes impeachment feasible but removal difficult. The Framers intentionally gave the Senate the power to remove the president from office, regarding that legislative body as the more cautious of the two. Another check on the system requires the chief justice of the Supreme Court to preside over impeachment trials. The chief justice lends an air of impartiality to the proceedings. As a non-elected official, the chief justice is uniquely situated to defend the Constitution. Unlike House and Senate members, the chief justice can do his job unaffected by the latest poll results.